Which Contract?

Which Contract?

Choosing the appropriate building contract

Fifth Edition

Hugh Clamp, Stanley Cox, Sarah Lupton
and Koko Udom

RIBA **Publishing**

First Edition (1989) by Stanley Cox and Hugh Clamp
Second Edition (1999) by Stanley Cox and Hugh Clamp
Third Edition (2003) by Stanley Cox and Hugh Clamp
Fourth Edition (2007) by Sarah Lupton
Fifth Edition (2012) Koko Udom

Published by RIBA Publishing
15 Bonhill Street
London EC2P 2EA

ISBN–13 978 1 85946 461 8

Stock Code 77974

British Library Cataloguing in Publications Data
A catalogue record for this book is available from the British Library.

Commissioning Editor: James Thompson
Project Editor: Neil O'Regan
Design and typesetting by Ben Millbank
Printed and bound by MPG Books, Cornwall

Forms of building contract referred to are those believed to be current at the time of writing.

While every effort has been made to check the accuracy of the information given in this book, readers should always make their own checks. Neither the Authors nor the Publisher accept any responsibility for misstatements made in it or misunderstandings arising from it.

RIBA Publishing is part of RIBA Enterprises Ltd. www.ribaenterprises.com

Contents

Contents continued

Foreword

This fifth edition is an update of the fourth edition of this popular text. There have been significant changes in the construction industry since the publication of the previous edition, the most prominent being the commencement of Part 8 of the Local Democracy, Economic Development and Construction Act 2009 on 1 October 2011 for England and Wales, 1 November 2011 for Scotland and proposed to come into effect sometime in 2012 for Northern Ireland. The legislation amends Part II of the Housing Grants, Construction and Regeneration Act 1996. The change in law has necessitated the publication of new editions of some standard forms of construction contracts, like the JCT suite, and the issuance of amendments to terms of others, like the NEC3 documents. Also some new forms of construction contracts have been added to the pool of industry standard forms, prominent among which is the Infrastructure Conditions of Contract published by the Association of Consultancy and Engineering and the Civil Engineering Contractors Association, which is based on the ICE conditions.

The period has also seen the Institution of Civil Engineers (ICE) withdraw ICE conditions of contracts from publication and sale, ending a rich history that started in 1945.

This fifth edition accounts for all these changes and also provides insight into new government initiatives on construction and new forms being proposed, such as the Chartered Institute of Builders (CIOB) Complex Projects Contract, a review edition of which has been released. The book retains much of the sound advice included in the fourth edition, edited by Sarah Lupton, and the first three editions edited by Stanley Cox and Hugh Clamp.

Koko Udom

Introduction

The last twenty-five years have seen an exponential growth in the range of standard forms of contract available for use in the procurement of building projects. The wide range of forms currently available in the UK is the result of a long history of invention, development and refinement, which began in 1870 when the first 'Heads of Conditions of Builder's Contract' appeared, published by the RIBA with the London Builders Society. Subsequently the RIBA published its own Conditions of Contract in 1895, intended for traditional procurement, and for almost fifty years, there was effectively only one standard form of building contract in use. This document has been revised, expanded and re-published under numerous new editions, its current manifestation being the 2011 edition of the JCT Standard Building Contract, available in three variants, depending on whether quantities are specified or not.

In 1945 the Institution of Civil Engineers (ICE) published a standard form, the first available for use on a project let on a measurement basis. The first edition of *Keating on Construction Contracts* made reference to both the ICE and the JCT Conditions of Contract and, together with the earlier *Hudson's Building and Civil Engineering Contracts*, provided authoritative legal commentary on the interpretation of these forms. The ICE has now withdrawn this form to give full support to the NEC forms that were first introduced in 1993.

During the decades following the Second World War there were extensive changes in the construction industry, resulting from an increased volume of construction, new construction technology, and new methods of working. From the 1960s alternative methods of procurement and standard forms began to appear. The JCT published the Prime Cost Contract in 1967 and the Agreement for Minor Building works in 1968, followed by four new forms in the 1980s; the Standard Form 'with contractor's design' for design and build procurement, the Intermediate Form of Building Contract, the Standard Form of Management Contract, and the Measured Term Contract.

This upward curve is reflected in the activity of other publishing organisations. Following the publication of its first edition of the Conditions of Contract in 1945, the ICE went on to publish a further three forms, including the New Engineering Contract in 1993. FIDIC published its first form in the 1950s, the Government published GC/Works/1 in 1973, and the ACA first published its form in 1982. The first edition of *Which Contract?* in 1989 covered around 15 forms of contract.

The Latham Report (*Constructing the Team*, by Sir Michael Latham, HMSO (1994)) has had a considerable effect on contract forms and procedures. This was a wide-ranging look at the industry as it then existed. It recommended better project strategy, more integrated ways of working, fairer tendering, improved payment procedures, and the rapid resolving of disputes by adjudication. It stressed the place of clients as the driving force, the importance of a full brief, design quality to be considered alongside the lowest price to determine best value, fair dealing for all parties in an atmosphere of mutual cooperation, and the outlawing of unfair conditions. It laid the foundations for new thinking about procurement, the place of partnering, and the benefits of long-term relationships.

The Egan Report (*Rethinking Construction*, the report of a Construction Task Force chaired by Sir John Egan, HMSO (1998)), built on many of the points raised by the Latham Report, and took further the call for greater efficiency. In particular, it stressed the need for improvements in construction costs, construction time, predictability concerning delivery, and a reduction in the number of building defects. It called for the elimination of wastage through lean thinking, and a reduction in the number of site accidents. The idea of targets, performance measurement indicators and benchmarking as aids to achieving planned and consistent improvement, reflected a changing climate of opinion on procurement.

These two reports, together with Part II of the Housing Grants, Construction and Regeneration Act 1996 (HGCRA), which followed as a direct result of the Latham Report, have significantly affected procurement methods, and the text of current contract forms. In 2009, after a series of industry consultations, the Local Democracy, Economic Development and Construction Act 2009 (LDEDCA) was passed to amend the HGCRA. Part 8 of the LDEDCA, on construction contracts, did not come into force until summer 2011.

The initiatives, organisations and publications that followed the Latham and Egan Reports are listed in the following chronology, and discussed further in Chapter 3, along with recent government policies intended to improve the way the construction industry operates – in particular the Government Construction Strategy 2011.

The 1990s and early 2000s was an important period in the development of construction contracts in the industry. The JCT became a distinct legal entity, its focus continuing to be on the consolidation and improvement of its suite of contracts. The period 1998–2005 saw the JCT publish various updates of the JCT suite and new contracts like the Home Owner/Occupier forms, which are analysed later in this book, were added to the suite.

Other institutions were also active, and continuing the collaboration theme of the Latham Report and the subsequent enactment of the Housing Grants, Construction and Regeneration Act 1996, the ICE published the third edition of its NEC suite of documents and started the process of expanding the contracts on offer with this suite. The ACA also published PPC2000 and subsequently SPC2005 and TPC 2005. Not to be left out, the JCT collaborated with Be (now part of Constructing Excellence) to publish the JCT Constructing Excellence – its version of a collaborative contract.

Introduction

There are currently over 40 standard forms of building contract used in the UK, emanating from nine publishing sources. The JCT now publish 18 forms of main contract, including variants and the two framework agreements, plus numerous sub- contracts, warranties and guides, most of which have been updated in the JCT 2011 suite. The Property Advisors to the Civil Estate publish around 15 forms, including variants. The ICE publish the NEC suite of 23 documents, the ACE and CECA publish the Infrastructure Conditions of Contract (ICC) and the ACA publish four key forms, including PPC2005.

Figure 1·1

Chronology of development of standard forms:

Dates show:

first publication of forms (including some new editions)
first publication of books and reports
foundation of institutes and organisations

1818	Institution of Civil Engineers
1834	Royal Institute of British Architects
1870	Heads of Conditions of Builders' Contract *RIBA with the London Builders' Society*
1891	Hudson's Building and Civil Engineering Contracts
1895	RIBA / LBA Form of Contract
1902	RIBA / LBA Form of Contract *alternatives for contracts with and without quantities included*
1909	RIBA Conditions of Contract
1931	Joint Contracts Tribunal
1931	RIBA Standard Form of Contract
1939	RIBA Standard Form of Contract
1945	ICE Conditions of Contract
1955	Keating on Building Contracts
1963	JCT Standard Form of Building Contract 1963 edition *Two versions, private and local authority, each with alternative editions for use with or without bills of quantities*
1967	JCT Prime Cost Contract
1968	JCT Agreement for Minor Building Works
1973	GC/Works/1 *The first government sponsored standard form of building contract*
1973	Association of Consultant Architects (ACA)
1979	JCT SFBC With Approximate Quantities
1980	JCT Standard Form of Building Contract 1980 edition *Six variants, private and local authority*
1981	JCT Intermediate Form of Building Contract

1981	JCT Standard Form of Contract with Contractor's Design
1982	ACA Form of Building Agreement
1987	JCT Standard Form of Management Contract
1988	Construction Industry Council (CIC) *Pan-industry forum representing all aspects of the built environment*
1989	Which Contract?
1989	JCT Measured Term Contract
1989	Association of Consultant Architects *Amalgamation of the Faculty of Architects and Surveyors and the Construction Surveyors Institute*
1990	GC/Works/2
1991	Reading Construction Forum
1992	Private Finance Initiative introduced *Emphasis on reducing the public sector borrowing requirement*
1992	ICE Design and Construct Conditions of Contract *(Government decision to use design and build for road schemes)*
1993	GC/Works/1 design and build
1993	NEC first edition
1994	Constructing the Team *Sir Michael Latham*
1995	Trusting the Team *Reading Construction Forum – a best practice guide to partnering*
1995	Construction Industry Board (CIB) *Set up by the Government, mainly concerned with the implementation of the recommendations in the Latham Report and the Egan Report, ceased to exist in June 2001, its initiatives now mostly run by the Government through the CIC*
1995	NEC second edition
1996	Housing Grants, Construction and Regeneration Act
1996	Partnering in the Team *CIB*
1997	*PFI emphasis shifted to 'value for money'*
1997	Lean Construction Institute
1998	The Seven Pillars of Partnering *Reading Construction Forum*
1998	JCT Ltd formed
1998	JCT standard forms *Revised to comply with HGCR Act and Latham recommendations*
1998	Rethinking Construction *Government sponsored review of industry, chaired by Sir John Egan, identified five drivers for change, and four process improvements, one of which was partnering the supply chain*

1998	Movement for Innovation (M4i) *Established to oversee implementation of the Rethinking Construction recommendations*
1998	Construction Best Practice Programme *Working alongside M4I, CPBB disseminates the innovations and lessons learnt from demonstration projects*
1999	JCT Building Contract for a Home Owner/Occupier
1999	Achieving Excellence launched *Government response to Egan, focuses on improving the public sector as a client, and on improving the efficiency of the construction industry*
1999	A Guide to Project Team Partnering *CIC, contained suggested heads of terms for a partnering contract. Second edition 2002*
1999	Model Project Pact *CIB*
1999	Building Down Barriers: Prime Contractor Handbook of Supply Chain Management *Recommends long-term strategic supply chain alliances*
1999	M4i publishes KPI *(revised April 2000; comprised 11 key performance indicators)*
2000	Sold on Health *Sets out a range of initiatives to improve the NHS's planning, procurement, and operation of its estate*
2000	NHS ProCure21 *Introduces a partnering framework for the Department of Health and the NHS*
2000	PPC2000 *New partnering contract published by Association of Consultant Architects, developed by the CIC partnering task force*
2000	GC/Works amendment *Supplemental clauses: risk assignment, value engineering*
2000	Confederation of Construction Clients (CCC) *Formerly the Construction Clients Forum, aims to encourage clients 'to achieve value for money through best practice'*
2001	JCT Practice Note 4 (second series): Partnering
2001	Construction Clients Charter launched *Construction Clients Forum*
2001	Strategic Forum Replaces CIB
2002	JCT Building Contract for Home Owner/Occupier with consultants agreement
2002	Accelerating change *Strategic Forum. Sets out measurable targets for improving performance in construction, including client involvement, integrating the team and people issues*

2002	JCT Contract for Home Repairs and Maintenance
2002	JCT Construction Management documents
2002	Architects and the Changing Construction Industry *RIBA*
2003	Be (Collaborating for the Built Environment) formed *Reading Construction Forum merges with Design-Build Foundation*
2003	Be Collaborative contract Reading Construction Forum; Working Group 2
2003	JCT Major Projects Form
2004	Constructing Excellence *Includes: RCF, Design Build Foundation, Construction Best Practice Programme, M4i, the Housing Forum, Rethinking Construction, Be, LGTF Construction Clients' Forum*
2005	NEC3 *Office of Government Commerce recommends the use of NEC3 by public sector construction procurers on their construction projects*
2005	JCT standard forms *New suite of forms published*
2005	JCT Framework agreements
2006	KPIs *New KPIs launched by Constructing Excellence*
2007	JCT Construction Excellence Contract (forthcoming)
2009	Local Democracy, Economic Development and Construction Act becomes law
2011	Government Construction Strategy published, which indicates a push towards a paradigm change with proposals for the introduction of Building Information Modelling (BIM) and new methods of procurement
2011	ACE and CECA publish the Infrastructure Conditions of Contract (ICC) based on the ICE Conditions of Contract
2011	JCT standard forms – new suite of forms published
2011	Amendments to NEC3 contracts published
2011	Local Democracy, Economic Development and Construction Act becomes effective in England, Wales and Scotland, amending the HGCRA

Thinking about contracts 1

Context

The term 'procurement method' is used to describe the often complex network of relationships which are formed between clients, consultants and construction companies, to enable a building project to be realised. Frequently these relationships are formalised by entering into legal contracts. These are usually bilateral (ie with two parties), but are occasionally multilateral, ie with many parties. Often 'chains' of contracts develop, for example client-service provider, service-provider-main contractor, main contractor-specialist-contractor, specialist-sub-contractor, sub-contractor-supplier. The term 'supply chain' has been coined to describe this relationship, but in reality the pattern is often more accurately described as a network. In any given project procurement there will usually be a network of bilateral contracts, with each individual entering into several.

It is important to distinguish the contractual relationships from managerial links, and in complex modern procurement systems this is sometimes far from easy. A contract is usually formed when an unconditional offer is unconditionally accepted (for a full explanation see a relevant legal text such as *Focus on Contract Formation*). A legally binding contract does not have to be evidenced in writing – oral contracts are now covered under the Construction Act, but it is good practice to ensure that construction contracts are in writing to prevent argument over the terms of the agreement. It has been common practice in the construction industry to use standard forms of contract, although specially written documents are equally binding, and are often used on larger projects (see below).

Architects and other professional consultants will be primarily concerned with two categories of contract: those under which professional services are provided and those under which construction work is carried out.

Although different in purpose, the two categories are essentially complementary. The authority and obligations of the professional acting for the client during the construction period might be significantly conditioned by the wording of the building contract. Likewise, the part played by the professional during the pre-contract stages, although determined largely by the contract for services, will be influenced by the type of procurement to be adopted and the role to be played by other professionals and by the contractor. To this extent at least, the choice of the one contract might be influenced by the content of the other.

Contracts for professional services

Many architects offer a wide range of skills not always directly building specific, it is for these skills that most are commissioned. Nowadays, architects increasingly find themselves asked to provide initially only a partial service, or a service which is not 'traditional' in the sense that they might not be the lead consultant. Sometimes they start out as the client's agent before eventually becoming part of the contractor's professional team. Some architects may gladly rise to the challenge of an entrepreneurial role as developer, others may be suited to a construction management role. But whatever format they take, architects' services need to be covered by an appropriate contract.

Some forms of appointment may require bespoke drafting because of the nature of the services to be provided, and it is increasingly common to find clients who insist on their own forms or who will require amendments to standard forms. However, in this book it is assumed that any contract for an architect's services is likely to be on one of the RIBA standard appointing documents with its Memorandum of Agreement or Letter of Appointment, Conditions of Engagement, Schedule of Services, and Schedule of Fees etc. It is important that the appointing document clearly identifies whether the commission relates to a role either as lead consultant, contract administrator, or design leader, and is compatible with the procurement method.

It might be that the appointment can initially only be up to a defined Plan of Work stage, and will need to be extended if the project proceeds. It might be that the agreement will require amending if the role of the Architect changes, or if there are shifts in the procurement procedures. The RIBA standard appointing documents are flexible and can be adapted for use in most situations. An alternative form may be the CIC Consultant's Appointment, which is appropriate for large development projects where the Architect can reasonably expect that the client's initial brief is deliverable within its time and cost parameters and the risks allocated accordingly.

Where the appointment is for services as a sub-consultant, it is vital to check that the Agreement is a back-to-back form as far as terms are concerned, and that the conditions are preferably compatible with those of standard RIBA forms of appointment. Equally if additional forms are proposed, whether these relate to partnering charters or collateral warranties, then a careful check is essential to ensure that the obligations are no more onerous than those which arise from the main appointing document.

Contracts for building

Building construction today often entails complex and intensive site operations, with huge sums of money locked into development programmes. Contractors may have partial or total design responsibilities, and in addition may undertake demanding management and coordinating roles; patterns of working have never been so diverse.

As outlined in the introduction, this change of emphasis, together with the increasing range and scale of work, has inevitably led to a proliferation of alternative forms of building contract, both standard and purpose drafted.

Standard forms

There are many advantages to using a standard form of building contract. It will normally be less expensive and generally more convenient to use a standard form than to arrange for one to be specially drafted. Many have detailed and comprehensive relevant guidance, which is in turn based on authoritative legal opinion, often having been tested in the courts.

For the majority of building contracts under which architects have a stated role, standard printed forms and in some instances online versions are readily available. JCT forms in particular are widely used, and have the unique distinction that they are produced by a tribunal on which there is representation of the professions, the industry, and client bodies. As a consequence these documents are generally held to be fair and balanced in the interests of the parties. A whole range of documents is now available to cover a variety of situations from jobbing or maintenance and repair work on the one hand to management contracting and partnering arrangements on the other. Many of the forms published by other bodies have also increased in popularity over recent years. A leading example in this regard is the NEC3 suite of documents.

Using standard forms

The Latham Report recommended that 'All parties in the construction process should be encouraged to use those Standard Forms without amendment' and this is undoubtedly sound advice. Bespoke amendments can easily impair the balance of the forms and the precise meaning of the contract conditions could be a matter for endless argument between lawyers. There is also the practical point that if a contractor is asked to tender knowing that it is proposed to use a special or amended form of contract, the contractor's first action will be to pass it to its legal advisers for checking. The cost of this will then be reflected in the tender. It is sound advice to resist alterations and amendments wherever possible.

Non-standard agreements

However, there may be instances where a non-standard form of building contract fits the client's requirements and a specially drafted agreement is needed. There is an increasing trend towards non-standard agreements on commercial or larger contracts. Any such drafting should be entrusted to a lawyer with the appropriate specialist knowledge, and he or she should always be engaged directly by the client. Architects without legal training and experience in such matters are strongly advised not to attempt even seemingly minor changes to standard wording or drafting of additional clauses which might make published documents non-standard.

1 Thinking about contracts

Standard forms of contract are drafted taking into account a legal backdrop of common law and statutory rules. It is generally useful to understand these rules, and they give insight into why many aspects of a form have been drafted in a particular way, and aid the interpretation of these forms.

The Sale of Goods Act 1979

Implies terms into contracts for the sale of goods regarding title, correspondence with description, quality and fitness for purpose, and sale by sample. For example Section 14 implies a term that where the seller sells goods in the course of business and the buyer, expressly or by implication, makes known to the seller any particular purpose for which the goods are being bought, there is an implied condition that the goods supplied under the contract will be reasonably fit for that purpose. The circumstances in which these rights can be excluded are limited by statute.

The Supply of Goods and Services Act 1982

Applies to contracts for work and materials, contracts for the hire of goods, and contracts for services. Implies terms into contracts for 'work and materials' equivalent to the SOG terms listed above with respect to any goods in which the property has been transferred under the contract. For services, the Act implies terms regarding care and skill, time of performance and consideration.

The Defective Premises Act 1972

Applies where work is carried out in connection with a dwelling, including design work, and states that 'a person taking on work in connection with the provision of a dwelling owes a duty to see that the work which he takes on is done in a workmanlike or, as the case may be, professional manner, with proper materials and so that as regards that work the dwelling will be fit for habitation when completed'.

Unfair Contract Terms Act 1977

This has the effect of rendering various exclusion clauses void including: any clauses excluding liability for death or personal injury resulting from negligence; any clauses attempting to exclude liability for Sale of Goods Act 1979 Section 12 obligations (and the equivalent under the Supply of Goods and Services Act); any clauses attempting to exclude liability for Sale of Goods Act 1979 Sections 13, 14 or 15 obligations (and the equivalent under the Supply of Goods and Services Act) where they are operating against any person dealing as a consumer. It also renders certain other exclusion clauses void in so far as they fail to satisfy a test of reasonableness, for example liability for negligence other than liability for death or personal injury, and liability for breach of Sections 13, 14 and 15 obligations in contracts which do not involve a consumer.

Unfair Terms in Consumer Contracts Regulations 1999

Applies to terms in contracts between a seller of goods or supplier of goods and services and a consumer, and where the terms have not been individually negotiated (this would generally include all standard forms). A consumer is defined as a person who, in making a contract, is acting 'for purposes which are outside his business' which would include a home owner. An 'unfair term' is any term that causes a significant imbalance in the parties' rights to the detriment of the consumer, and the regulations state that any such term will not be binding on the consumer.

The Cancellation of Contracts made in a Consumer's Home or Place of Work, etc. Regulations 2008

This regulation became effective on 1 October 2008 and extended the existing law on cooling-off periods and cancellation rights for consumers. Under the regulation a trader must include a cooling-off period of at least seven days, retain the consumers right to cancel for any payment above £35 and to be notified of this right.

Traders under the regulations would include construction companies involved in residential and non-commercial projects.

The Housing Grants, Construction and Regeneration Act 1996 (as amended by LDEDCA 2009)

Requires that all construction contracts falling within the definition in the Act contain certain provisions including the right to stage payments, the right to notice of the amount to be paid, the right to suspend work for non-payment, and the right to take any dispute arising out of the contract to adjudication. If the parties fail to include these provisions in their contract, the Act will imply terms to provide these rights by means of the relevant Scheme of Construction Contracts, ie The Scheme for Construction Contracts (England and Wales) Regulations 1998 (Amendment) (England) Regulations 2011. The Act is of broad application but does not apply to a 'construction contract' with a residential occupier.

Late Payment of Commercial Debts Interest Act 1998 as amended

Provides for interest to be paid by purchasers on the late payment of debt in a commercial contract for the supply of goods or services. The rate of interest is set by Order of the Secretary of State, the current rate being 8 per cent per annum over the official dealing rate. It is not possible to exclude this right unless a contract contains a 'substantial' remedy for late payment (most JCT standard forms contain their own remedy).

The Contracts (Rights of Third Parties) Act 1999

Enables persons who are not parties to a contract (termed 'third parties') to be able to enforce its terms against a person who is a party to that contract. It is possible to give a third party rights if a contract expressly agrees that a third party may enforce specific terms then that third party or where the contract purports to confer a benefit on the third party. The third party who is being given the right to enforce the contract must be either identified in the contract as a member of a class or answering a particular description. The contract may expressly exclude or limit liability.

The Public Contracts Regulations 2006

Sets out new rules for public procurement of contracts for works, services and supplies. These Regulations implement the European Commission's Consolidated Directive, adopted in March 2004, into UK law, and cover the tendering and award of public contracts. Strict rules now apply to frameworks agreements, for example, they must not generally exceed a term of four years and the terms of any framework must be determined at the outset. At the time of writing there are ongoing proposals and negotiations about updating the overhauling of the public procurement regulations.

Advising the client

In some procurement contexts, the choice of contract may be determined by external factors, such as requirements of the funder. For example the World Bank now require the FIDIC forms of contract to be used on projects of over £6 million, and the NEC form was the preferred choice for the 2012 Olympic construction programme. In such cases the form to be used will have been selected before the Architect and other consultants are appointed.

However it is frequently the case that where the Architect provides full professional services, it may be his or her duty 'to consult with and advise the Employer as to the form of contract to be used' (*Hudson's Civil Engineering and Building Contracts* 10th Edition, 1970). These words might not find favour with the majority of architects today, and it has been said that the best course is to give the 'for and against' leaving the Employer to make the choice. Interestingly, the endorsement on many JCT forms of contract refers to the client engaging 'a professional consultant to advise on and to administer its terms'. The JCT has published a most helpful Practice Note on deciding on the appropriate JCT Form of contract – this can be downloaded from the JCT website.

There are very few cases recorded of an architect being successfully sued for recommending a contract which was later held not to have been appropriate. But the range of available forms is increasing, just keeping up to date with such changes is often a taxing business. Also, there is sometimes a disconcerting time lag between the publication of authorised amendments and instructions confirming their use, particularly by bodies in the public sector that have a strong influence upon such matters. Advising on the edition of a form to be used and whether particular amendments are to be incorporated extends the Architect's need for care in carrying out this duty and requires a thorough knowledge of the state of the art.

Advising on forms of contract is unlikely to be easy in the wider European context. Problems can arise in construing the meaning of provisions which may have been poorly translated, or which may be subject to interpretation under a different legal system than that which obtains in the courts of England and Wales. Problems can also arise when working on projects overseas, where the contractor or suppliers are based in another country, and perhaps the law of the contract has not been clearly established. Many standard forms can be adapted for use under the laws of Northern Ireland or Scotland but not all. Some specifically state that they are not for use in Scotland. The Scottish Building Contracts Committee has published its own range of forms specifically for use under Scots law.

Recommending a contract for a particular set of circumstances is not something to be undertaken lightly: it requires a knowledgeable and methodical approach. The contract in question should first be studied carefully both in respect of the content and conditions, and also for its appropriateness in the known circumstances.

There are still a few architects who minimise the significance of contract wording by referring to the importance of trust. They blandly talk of the best kind of contract as being the one which is put into the drawer and only taken out when things go wrong. An appropriate contract, fairly and firmly administered, is the best means of trying to ensure that things do not go wrong in the first place!

Despite the Egan Report's stated ambition to replace contracts with performance measurement and bring reliance on formal documents to an end, for most present situations the cautious advice must remain – never proceed on the basis of a 'handshake' agreement. Whilst it cannot be denied that an atmosphere of trust and confidence is desirable, it is total folly to rely on some 'understanding' that has not been properly documented. Different people can have genuine but quite different understandings of what was agreed.

As architect Ronald Green once pointed out in *The Architect's Guide to Running a Job*, Architectural Press (1986): 'The difficulty about a gentleman's agreement is that it depends on the continued existence of the gentlemen'!

Watchpoints

- Give thorough consideration to contract matters and choice at the earliest possible time.
- Remember that contracts for professional services and building contracts, although distinct, may have implications for each other. The method of procurement has repercussions on roles and documentation.
- Assuming that the procurement method has not been decided before the architect is appointed as lead consultant, it may be the architect's duty to advise on the appropriate contract. If so, do not allow this to be left to other consultants.
- Although oral contracts are now covered under the Construction Act, endeavour to ensure that contract agreements and conditions are set down in writing and the agreement executed before work starts.
- Recommend the use of standard forms of contract whenever possible.

- If particular circumstances require specially drafted or extensively amended contracts, it is essential that legal advice is taken.
- Before recommending a form of contract, study its contents and understand its implications. It is important to set up a control system which ensures that stipulated procedures are followed.

Establishing a contract profile 2

There may be clients who choose to misinterpret the Egan Report's message of increased efficiency and think that it is now possible to construct a quality building at breakneck speed for a knock-down price. Any such unfounded euphoria needs to be dispelled at the outset.

The reality is that although the three most important considerations for any client are usually cost, time and quality, the business of building procurement invariably calls for some compromise or conscious balancing of these priorities. This requires adequate thinking time and careful thought.

We live at a time when visual presentation for such management tools as benchmarking, performance indicators and the like has become part of life. With the push for the adoption of Building Information Modelling (BIM) these are bound to become even more common practice. For an increasing number of construction professionals so-called 'radar charts' are a useful reminder of key points to be considered and performances recorded. Therefore it might prove an interesting exercise to set up a kind of radar chart or similar diagrammatic analysis in advance of any proposed building contract. This could be simply a manual exercise to help focus the mind on the balance of priorities – for example what level of quality is required, how much time is available before construction and for operations on site, and to what extent and in what respects cost considerations are paramount.

The profile that emerges might also suggest where design responsibilities are to rest and their extent, and the most suitable procurement methods and construction procedures. This in turn will affect tendering arrangements and the amount and format of the information needed.

Figure 2·1 is a radar chart which presents the three elements of cost, time, and quality in terms of contract priorities. Even where they are not in conflict, these elements need to be reconciled and ideally balanced. Asking the right questions at the right time might result in a visual profile which allows quick comparisons, and help in arriving at the appropriate contract.

Figure 2·1 indicates the contract priorities for a project at the minimum capital cost to be built in the shortest possible time. There must be reasonable certainty over cost and timing, and all this combined with the desire for reasonable design quality from the client's consultants!

Taking these three elements in greater detail:

Figure 2·1: A contract profile

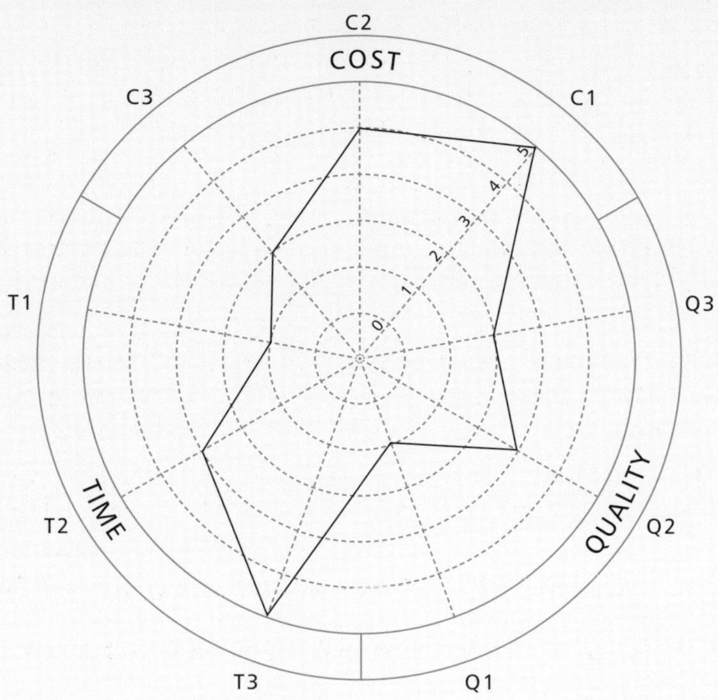

	Criteria		Priority (0 lowest–5 highest scale)				
			1	2	3	4	5
COST	C1	Lowest possible capital expenditure					✓
	C2	Certainty over contract price, no fluctuation				✓	
	C3	Best value for money overall		✓			
TIME	T1	Earliest possible start on site	✓				
	T2	Certainty over contract duration			✓		
	T3	Shortest possible contract period					✓
QUALITY	Q1	Top quality, minimum maintenance	✓				
	Q2	Sensitive design, control by employer			✓		
	Q3	Detailed design not critical, leave to contractor		✓			

Cost

In this country, at least until quite recently, cost has been the decisive factor in building contracts. The repercussions are well known. Design briefs have often been subject to unrealistic cost constraints from the outset, sometimes even failing to distinguish between initial capital outlay and long-term costs. The quantity surveyor's role has assumed greater importance because of the need for stringent financial control throughout the project. To many client bodies, lump sum contracts have seemed attractive because they promise, at least in theory, cost certainty. Design and build or management contracts have been let on the basis of a guaranteed maximum lump sum, although the design information is known to be incomplete at the time of tendering. Despite the considerable risks which sometimes attend keen competition, all too frequently the lowest price has been the determining factor.

Although there is a conscious attempt to shift emphasis from predominantly immediate costs of the project to criteria such as whole life costing, Most Economically Advantageous Tender (MEAT), as well as sustainability, cost is still an important criterion.

It is particularly important to clarify some of the cost considerations, by addressing such questions to the client at the outset. For example the lead consultant might wish to raise:

Q. ***Is there a set limit, which the Contract Sum must not under any circumstance exceed?***
Comment: the client might have limited funding and require the reassurance of a fixed price with no risk of fluctuation.

Q. ***Is it essential to know precisely the cost of the work before operations start on site?***
Comment: this suggests that the work needs to be measured and described in detail at tender stage – possibly by use of firm quantities.

Q. ***Once the contract is signed, in the event of variations is the client authorised to incur additional expenditure?***
Comment: it may be that the client has to rely heavily on some 'once and for all' external source of grant aid or other funding, and there may be conditions attached.

Q. ***Is the contract to be awarded to the lowest tenderer regardless of other considerations?***
Comment: value for money will not always be achieved by this process. Designing down to a figure might mean excessive running and maintenance costs later on, which the client should take into account. There might also be stipulations concerning quality, imposed by a grant aiding body where this is conservation work.

Q. Is the tenderer expected to allow for any increases in labour and materials etc. when pricing?
Comment: it may be in the interests of the client to forgo cost certainty and accept a price based on known factors, assuming that fair and controlled increases can be dealt with under fluctuations provisions. Much will depend on the state of the market at the time, on the anticipated duration of the job, and on the projected means of recovering the capital expenditure.

Q. Is total accountability an imperative? Must every penny be satisfactorily accounted for?
Comment: public bodies in particular are subject to the scrutiny of the auditor, and are also understandably sensitive about any allegations of dubious practice.

Q. Does the client have rules or standing orders which require evidence of competition when sub-contractors or suppliers are invited to tender?
Comment: commercially minded clients often need it to be demonstrated that no opportunity for the best deal has been overlooked. Many public bodies have approved lists for selected items.

Q. What is understood by 'cost considerations'? Capital expenditure only, or are maintenance and life cycle costs also to be taken into account?
Comment: the lead consultant has a duty to advise the client of any long-term implications.

Quality

No one really expects to buy a Rolls Royce for the price of a family saloon, yet there are clients who conveniently overlook the fact that in this world you only get what you pay for. It is essential to agree what is meant by 'quality' both in respect of services and the finished project, and to define what measurable standards are to apply. For example the lead consultant might wish to raise questions such as:

Q. Are considerations of commercial prestige and public image likely to influence the degree of quality desirable?
Comment: some client bodies have a house style which expresses the efficiency or market-commanding confidence of the company, and which they would wish to see embodied in their buildings.

Q. Is it important to use high quality materials?
Comment: for example, the project might be located in an environmentally sensitive spot such as a conservation area, or perhaps subject to stringent planning permission conditions. On the other hand, the project might just be an envelope for some retailing or industrial process.

Q. *Is this a historic building or, for example, a Passiv Haus, where work will require higher than average standards of craftsmanship?*
Comment: in a historic building, it may not be possible to establish how much work is likely to be entailed, or to describe and measure it before opening up. Control by the client as work proceeds is essential, and anybody responsible for funding might impose conditions.

Q. *Is it essential that all matters of design and specification are firmly under the control of the design team, and that specialist sub-contractors or suppliers are named or otherwise selected by the client?*
Comment: where the architect is lead designer, in the absence of anything to the contrary, this is likely to bring at first instance design responsibility. Even where design work is to be undertaken by others, the responsibility for coordination and integration into the overall design will remain with the lead designer.

Q. *Is it safe to entrust certain design details to the contractor's own organisation (with agreement to sub-let) without the quality of the design concept overall being impaired?*
Comment: unless a contractor's design obligation is expressly referred to in the building contract, this is unlikely to be implied under standard forms of contract. Even where the contractor or sub-contractor is responsible for some design input, it might be essential to make a provision for designs to be submitted to the client before work is actually carried out.

Q. *Is the building intended to be relatively maintenance-free?*
Comment: this is not an attainable goal! The best that can be achieved is minimum maintenance. So what is the expected life span? When will major components be in need of upgrading or replacing? Is the overall appearance intended to last for a fashionable cycle only and due for a face-lift which will not involve structural change? Is there need for such eventualities to be programmed at the outset?

Q. *Does it make good commercial sense for the client to provide for a constant site presence to monitor the contractor's control of quality?*
Comment: should the contract allow for this, and if so by what means will it be achieved? What might be expected of the contractor in terms of quality management and perhaps evidence through relevant KPI information?

Q. *Can some or all of the work only be performed by a firm with specialist expertise?*
Comment: this might mean selecting a contractor after interview and negotiation rather than by competitive tendering. It might result in appointing the contractor at design stage in order to benefit from advice on construction methods and materials, and possibly to provide specialist design input. It would probably affect the production of information. It could result in appointing a specialist firm as the main contractor, leaving general builders' work to be sub-contracted.

Time

Quality and speed are not obviously happy bedfellows. Where fast construction relies on the use of numerous prefabricated major components and systems, much will depend on whether manufacture has taken place under monitored and controlled conditions, in order that specified performance can be guaranteed.

Good supply chain management can reduce both wastage and construction time. Savings can also be achieved through overlapping detailed design and construction stages, where the contractor controls the flow of necessary information, and where the contract allows the contractor freedom in the choice of sub-contractors and substitutions. Real savings in overall project time comes through effective management, and not by taking shortcuts like premature rushed starts.

Clients, who sometimes take a long time to make up their minds to proceed, are understandably disappointed when an immediate start on site is not advisable. Whatever method of procurement is adopted, it is important to allow sufficient time for all the relevant matters to be properly considered at the pre-contract stage. Design and build, for example, depends largely for its success on whether the client's requirements have been carefully worked out, and time should be allowed for this. The overall time of a project from inception to completion is of greater significance than the time taken for site operations alone. Having said all that, the construction industry has a poor record of excessive construction times, and failure to complete on time. Predictability is an important factor for most clients.

Time considerations can significantly affect the profile of the contract and must be explored thoroughly. For example, the lead consultant might raise with the client questions such as:

Q. Is there time for a full brief to be systematically developed, so that the client's detailed requirements can be properly reflected in the tender documents?
Comment: this will be essential for those tendering who need full information when submitting a lump sum price. Anything less could bring the uncertainty of remeasurement. However, in the event of rapid action being required, say in the case of restoring damaged premises, a hand-to-mouth approach might be unavoidable.

Q. Does the client have heavy rental or other financial commitments which mean that the earliest date for completion is likely to be an overriding objective?
Comment: as above this might be an overriding consideration which justifies the earliest possible start, and accepting the probability of some uneconomic working.

Q. *Are there any commercial or other external pressures which make it imperative to complete by a certain date?*
Comment: the need to catch seasonal trade for instance, or to be completed in time for a major event which is already programmed and immovable, such as the Olympic Games. In such a case a guaranteed completion date might be needed despite the contractor pricing for the risk.

Q. *Is phased or sectional completion necessary?*
Comment: for example, to allow some office units to be occupied, or parts of an industrial complex to be commissioned, ahead of completion of the whole contract. Not all contracts will allow for this, and to be effective it needs to be included in the contract conditions as a programmed requirement.

Q. *Is it desirable to phase possession by the contractor and limit it to successive parts of redevelopment of the Works, in order that business can continue during the building work?*
Comment: during redevelopment within a site, is it essential to control phasing and also to accommodate some decanting of occupants and processes during site work? Is it necessary to restrict operations to certain times of day or intermittent periods? Many standard building contracts appear to assume exclusive possession by the contractor, and with small domestic projects in particular this is not practical and some allowances may be needed.

Which procurement method? 3

In some instances the procurement method will have already been decided before an architect is appointed, either as the result of company or authority laid down policy, or because circumstances or constraints leave very limited options, or because the choice has already been made by the client advised by a lead consultant who is not the Architect.

It is generally accepted that there are three key methods of procurement currently practised in this country. The traditional or conventional approach, in which at least in theory design and construction are seen as separate elements; design and build, which implies a more integrated approach; and management, by which either the client or a contractor assumes the central management responsibility. There are in addition many variants, hybrids and compounds of these methods. Moreover there have been many recent developments, which, although possibly termed a 'procurement method' might more accurately be described as an approach to procurement. For example most partnering arrangements are an over-arching agreement, which encompass one or several contracts let under one of the three key methods. Similarly, within PFI projects it is frequently possible to identify contracts let on a design and build or management basis. It is therefore useful to start by clearly differentiating the three principal methods, before moving on to discuss some more recent developments.

Which procurement method is likely to prove the most appropriate in a given situation will depend upon the nature and scope of the work proposed, how the risks are to be apportioned, how and where responsibility for design is to be placed, how the work is to be coordinated, and on what price basis the contract is to be awarded.

An important point to remember is that the choice of form (or forms) of contract cannot usually be settled until the procurement method and the type of contract have been established. This will mean considering the following:

Design responsibility

Design has been defined as devising an arrangement, then specifying the components needed to realise that arrangement, and lastly detailing a method of joining or erecting those components. Design can mean the overall concept or form of the building, it can relate to the component parts including specialist installations, or can be the result of meeting specified criteria for durability, performance etc.

It is important to establish:

- how, if at all, design responsibilities are to be apportioned between the Architect as lead designer, other consultants, the contractor and specialist sub-contractors and suppliers;
- what contractual provisions will apply to the design of the Works.

Coordination responsibility

This might include responsibility for workmanship, goods and materials, working methods, programming, ordering, general coordination and supervision.

It is important to establish:

- what contractual arrangements will apply for the coordination of the work;
- whether the Works are to be carried out under a single contract, or under a combination of separate contracts, either in sequence or in parallel.

Price basis

A contract might be let on the basis of a lump sum price, or if this is not possible or desired, then measurement to some agreed basis might be the only practical option. Alternatively a cost plus approach might be appropriate, although there is the risk that the final figure could differ greatly from the first estimated cost. The questions of what tendering methods are most suitable, and what tender documents will be needed, will rest on the choice of procurement method.

Plan of Work

The procurement method to be adopted and type of contract will have implications for the 'Plan of Work'. This logical division of a project into stages was devised by the RIBA in the 1960s and has since become accepted throughout the building industry. The Outline Plan of Work 2008 amended 2009 moves from preparation stages (Appraisal and Design Brief) through design, pre-construction and construction to post-construction and use activities. It has been widely adopted as the basis for calculating consultants' fees, and gives a very useful description of work stages, particularly in traditional methods of procurement.

With Plan of Work the client and the appointed professionals are involved throughout the project, but the design and construction work stages are separated as is usual with traditional procurement. This results in a linear pattern (see Figure 3·1).

With design and build, although similar work stages are still present, they are not so compartmented. The contractor will normally be involved at design stage, to an extent depending on how much he is responsible for scheme design as opposed to developing a design already produced by the client's consultants and embodied in the client's requirements. Some of the work stages are arranged in a different sequence, permitting parallel working or fast tracking to save time overall. The contractor will normally continue detailed design during construction stages (see Figure 3·2).

Plan of Work is still relevant to management procurement, whether management contracting or construction management. Figure 3·3 shows an admittedly over-simplified picture of operations. On a large project there might, for example, be 50 or more works or trade packages and the operational pattern can become very complex. There needs to be considerable involvement and collaboration between the consultants and the managing contractor throughout, as parallel working continues and abortive work can easily occur.

Procurement using traditional methods

In the traditional approach, the client accepts that consultants are appointed for design, cost control, and contract administration, and that the contractor is responsible for carrying out the Works. The responsibility of the latter extends to all workmanship and materials, including work by sub-contractors and suppliers.

In some cases the client will select some of the sub-contractors to be engaged by the contractor (variously referred to as named, nominated, or pre-selected). In such cases the contractor may take full responsibility for their performance, or the contractor's responsibility may be limited in some way, in which case a collateral warranty between client and sub-contractor will be essential. The contractor is usually chosen after competitive tendering on documents giving complete information. However, the contractor can be appointed earlier, either through negotiation or on the basis of partial or notional information.

The traditional method, but using two stage tendering or negotiated tendering, is sometimes referred to as the 'Accelerated Traditional Method'. By this variant, design and construction can run in parallel to a limited extent. Whilst this allows an early start on site, it also entails less certainty about cost.

Watchpoints

- A traditional lump sum approach requires the production of a full set of documents before tenders are invited. Adequate time must be allowed for this.
- The traditional procurement method assumes that design will be by appointed consultants, and it does not generally imply that the contractor has any design obligations. If this is to be the case, for example with specialist sub-contract work or performance specified work, express terms should be included in the contract.
- Because the client appoints consultants to advise on all matters of design, and cost, he thereby retains control over the design and quality required.
- There is certainty of cost, to the extent that a lump sum is known before work begins, even if it has to be adjusted during the construction period as provided for in the contract.
- The contractor depends heavily upon the necessary information and instructions from the architect being issued on time. There is a risk of claims if they are delayed. Information release dates are sometimes agreed beforehand, but making these contractually binding can cause problems.
- The client may decide which specialist firms the contractor is to use if provided for in the contract, although the contractor will require certain safeguards relating to performance.

- All matters of valuation and payment are the responsibility of the client's consultants.
- If it is impossible to define precisely the quantity or nature of some of the work, it is still possible to adopt a traditional method on the basis of approximate quantities, provisional sums or cost reimbursement. However, this is a less than perfect solution: the fuller and more accurate the information, the nearer to the relative safety of the lump sum approach.
- There are widely accepted codes of procedure for single stage or two stage tendering, whether competitive or on the basis of a negotiated price. These should be used whenever possible.

Figure 3·1: Plan of Work stages: traditional procurement

Preparation	Design	Pre-construction	Construction	Use
1 AB	2 CD			
	3 E	4 F		
		5 G		
		6 H	7 J	
			8 K	9 L L2 L3
Consultants	Consultants	Consultants		Consultants
			Contractor	Contractor

Key

1 Appraisal and strategic briefing work by consultants
2 Outline and detailed proposals by consultants and application for required planning permission.
3 Preparation by the consultant of technical designs and specification sufficient to coordinate the various components and elements of the project and satisfy statutory standards and safety.
4. Preparation of production information in sufficient detail to enable tenders to be obtained and also sufficient to seek statutory approvals. It also presupposes the preparation of further information required for the building contract.
5 Tender documentation by consultants
6 Tender action – appointment of contractor
7 Mobilisation by contractor
8 Administration of construction to practical completion.
9 Administration of the contract after completion and assisting building user with initial occupation and review of project performance in use; this would be undertaken by both the contractor and the consultants

Procurement using design and build methods

The client may need to appoint consultants to advise on his design requirements and costs, if he does not have this expertise available in-house. The contractor is responsible to a greater or lesser extent for design, as well as for carrying out the work and may appoint its own consultants. The arrangement may be for total design and construction, or for design development and production information based on a scheme design supplied by the client's consultants. Figure 3·2 recalibrates the RIBA Plan of Work to show the movement and combination of work stages required to achieve this method of procurement.

Figure 3·2: Plan of Work stages: design and build procurement

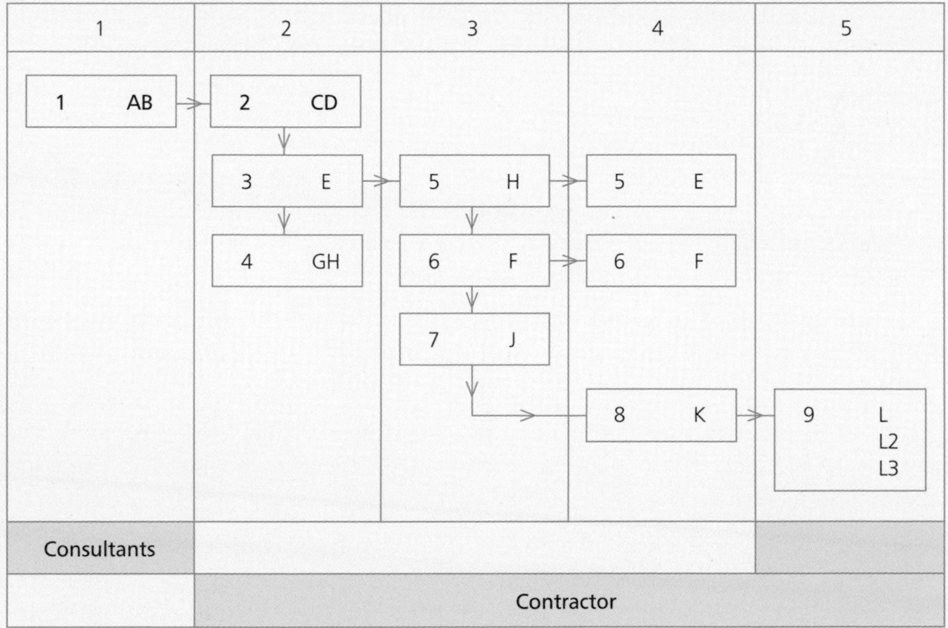

Key

1 Appraisal and strategic briefing work by consultants
2 Outline proposals/client's requirements
3 Detailed proposals by contractor
4 Tender action including contractor's proposals
5 Final proposals by contractor and specialists
6 Production information
7 Mobilisation by contractor
8 Construction to completion and after completion
9 Administration of the contract after completion and assisting building users with initial occupation and review of project performance in use.

The contractor may be appointed either by competitive tender or as the result of a negotiated agreement. Where a design and build agreement is negotiated with just one contractor, it is sometimes referred to as 'Single Direct Design and Build'. Where an approach is made to a number of contractors, even if this is a two stage operation with only the most promising proceeding to the second stage, the agreement is sometimes referred to as 'Competitive Design and Build'. It tends to take slightly longer, but it usually results in a more developed design and greater certainty of cost and timing.

Frequently, in design-build procurement the client wishes to require the contractor to appoint some or all of its consultants at the time the design and build contract is entered into. This process is usually referred to as novation or consultant switch. It requires a complex tripartite agreement to be entered into between client, consultant and contractor. In addition to the client-architect and contractor-architect terms of appointment published by the RIBA, the CIC publishes suitable forms for novation and collateral warranties.

Watchpoints

- In the most straightforward of design and build contracts, in theory there is usually a single point of responsibility. The client therefore has the advantage of only one firm to deal with – and one firm to blame if things go wrong. In practice, however, the client's requirements are often detailed to the extent that the contractor's design contribution, and therefore liability, is diminished.
- The client lacks control over detailed aspects of design; however, this might be acceptable where the broad lines of the scheme are satisfactory and the detail relatively less important.
- Construction work can be started early as a great deal of detailed design work can proceed in parallel. It is mainly the contractor, however, who benefits from the operational flexibility.
- Responsibility for completing on time rests wholly with the contractor. There should be little risk of claims because of allegations that information from the client is late. This obligation on the contractor to be responsible for the flow of his necessary information is one of the most attractive features of design and build.
- There is greater certainty of cost, even to the extent that, if required, responsibility for investigating site and sub-soil conditions can be made entirely the contractor's. Any significant changes in the client's requirements will affect the Contract Sum however, and are likely to prove costly.
- Often the client requires that the contractor appoints the client's consultants to develop the design under a consultant switch agreement or by novation. If this is not the case, it is always advisable to ask for information about who the contractor intends using as designer. Adequate professional indemnity insurance should always be a requirement.

- The client should appoint consultants to advise on the preparation of the requirements, and it is important that adequate time is allowed for these to be properly prepared.
- The requirements might include specific items, or even provisional sums, but generally it is prudent to prescribe performance criteria, so that a high degree of reliance is placed on the contractor.
- In the absence of any stipulations to the contrary, the contractor's design obligations are absolute. However, they are usually reduced in standard forms of contract to those of the professional's duty of using reasonable skill and care.
- Valuation of changes by the client is entirely the responsibility of the contractor, and the client has no quantity surveyor to intervene on his behalf.
- It is often difficult to evaluate design and build tenders objectively where both schemes and prices are submitted. Tenderers should be informed of the criteria to be used, and whether price is likely to be the prime consideration.
- Benefits can arise from designers and estimators having to work closely together. The contractor's awareness of current market conditions and delivery times can ensure that a contract runs smoothly, economically and expeditiously.
- The client's agent or representative should be selected with great care. He or she can be a key member of the Employer's organisation, a professional consultant, a project manager or, depending on the nature of the work, a clerk of works. The extent to which an agent is empowered to act for the client needs to be clearly established.

Procurement using management methods

There are several variants of management procurement practised in this country, but management contracts and construction management are the two most common. With management contracts the client usually starts by appointing consultants to prepare project drawings and a project specification. The management contractor is selected by a process of tender and interviews, and paid on the basis of the scheduled services, prime costs and management fee.

Its role is literally to manage the execution of the work, and he is not usually directly involved in carrying out any of the construction work, which will be done in 'packages' undertaken by works contractors usually appointed by the management contractor. In some procurement arrangements, the management contractor might also accept a design liability. In 'management contracting', works contractors are directly and contractually responsible to the management contractor. Its coordinated approach and potential for flexibility results in greater operational speed and efficiency.

Where the management contractor's obligation is total – where, that is, it accepts responsibility for both design and construction – the arrangement is sometimes referred to as 'Design, Manage, Construct'. It is usually featured as a contractor-led procurement method, but there is no real reason why it cannot equally well be architect-led. Indeed, where small works are sometimes carried out under direct trades contracts and coordinated by the Architect in the absence of a main contractor, this comes close to being such a procurement method. It does, however, demand a degree of highly specialised expertise and experience in setting up and managing operations which most architects are unlikely to possess.

With 'construction management' agreements, which will often be client drafted, there is usually a lead designer responsible for overall design, a construction manager responsible for the management and coordination of work, with the client responsible for directing the project and entering into all trades contracts. As the trades contractors are directly and contractually responsible to the client, the construction manager is in some ways less accountable for time and costs, whilst the client takes on the greater risk.

Watchpoints

- Management procurement methods are best suited to large, complex, fast-moving projects where early completion is desirable.
- This method of procurement depends upon a high degree of confidence and trust. There is unlikely to be a guarantee of firm contract price before the work actually starts on site, and the decision to go ahead usually has to be taken on the basis of an estimate on project information.
- The management contractor/construction manager acts for the client, and should therefore put the client's interests first throughout the job.
- It is essential to appoint the management contractor/construction manager at an early stage, so that his knowledge and expertise are available to the design team throughout the crucial pre-construction period.
- Much of the detailed design work can be left to proceed in parallel with the site operations for some work packages, thus reducing the time needed before the project starts on site. Indeed, a great deal of detailed design will need to be left to specialist sub-contractors or suppliers.
- The client has a considerable degree of flexibility on design matters. The design can be adjusted as construction proceeds, without sacrificing cost control. However, coordination of design work for components or elements can be difficult, with an attendant risk of costly abortive work.
- Specialist contractors can be selected and appointed and materials on long delivery ordered in good time without any of the uncertainties and complexities which attend traditional nomination procedures.
- Although the project proceeds on the basis of a contract cost plan only, effective cost control is still possible with the help of an independent quantity surveyor.

- A competitive tendering element is retained for all works or trades contracts, which usually account for most of the overall prime cost. Tenders for works packages will normally be on a lump sum basis.
- This method of procurement is most appropriate for large-scale, complex projects, so that only large construction firms with the relevant experience are likely to prove suitable. At present these are relatively few in number. Similarly, construction management is only likely to be of interest to experienced clients with in-house expertise to undertake the high degree of involvement needed.
- A management contractor's staff may lack the necessary experience and have difficulty in adjusting to the idea of abandoning a simple work-for-profit motive in favour of providing a service in the interests of the client. Before recommending the appointment of a management contractor it is essential to interview the key staff involved.
- Above all, a management contractor or construction manager should be appointed because of his or her assumed or preferably proven ability to manage. He or she will need to use and be familiar with a variety of sophisticated techniques to deal with the coordination of what is often a large number of works contracts. Figure 3·3 recalibrates the RIBA Plan of Work to show the movement and combination of work stages required to achieve this method of procurement.

Figure 3·3: Plan of Work stages: management procurement

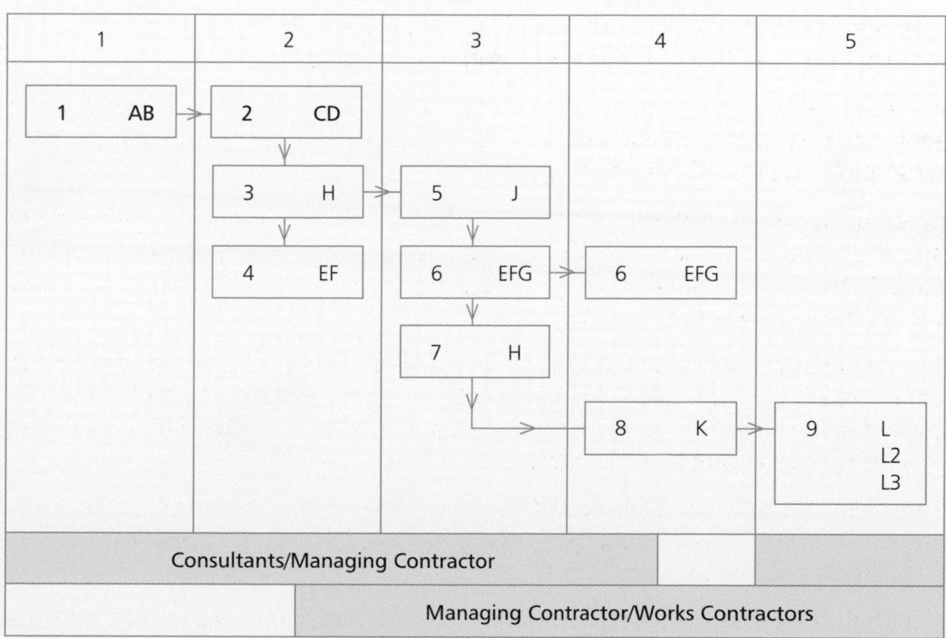

Key

1 Appraisal and strategic briefing by consultants and contractor
2 Outline and detailed proposals
3 Appointment of contractor and agreement on trade or works appointments
4 Final proposals and production information (continuing process)
5 Mobilisation
6 Production information and coordination of works packages
7 Tender action and adjustments (continuing process)
8 Construction to practical completion
9 Administration of the contract after completion and assisting building used with initial occupation and review of project performance in use

Contractual relationships

The pattern of contractual and functional relationships shifts or changes according to the procurement method adopted.

Figure 3·4: Contractual relationships: traditional procurement

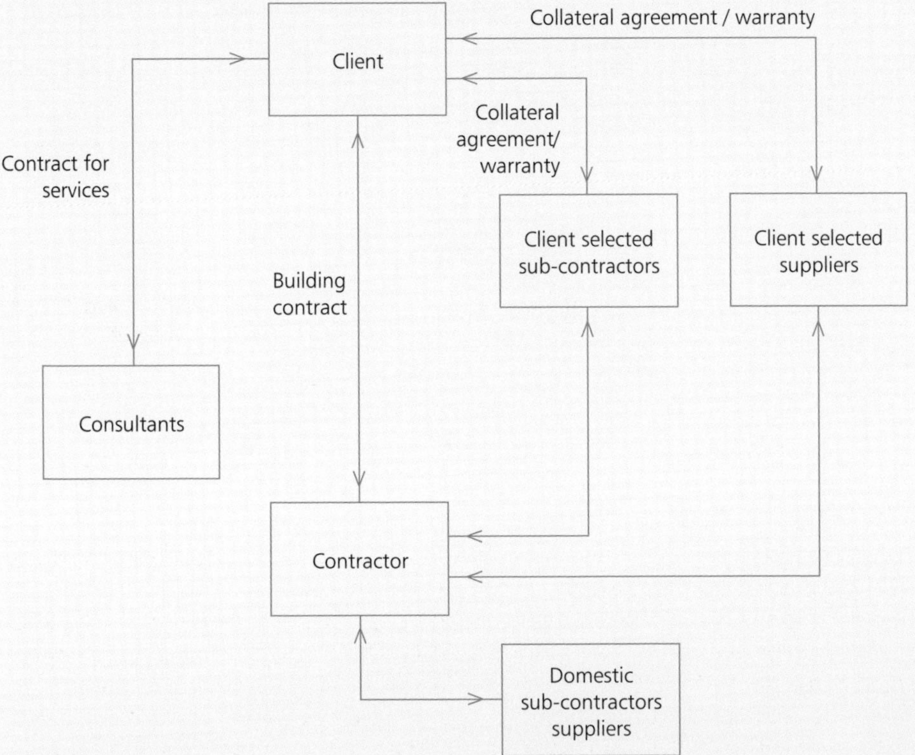

In the traditional approach, the client is in direct contractual relationship with the consultants on the one hand and the contractor on the other. Any contractual links for sub-contracts or sales contracts will be between the contractor and the firms in question. The consultants have no contractual link with the contractor, but the Architect or another consultant may be named in the building contract as the 'contract administrator'. Where the client selects any sub-contractor's or suppliers, it may be advisable to recommend collateral agreements to protect the client's interests, particularly in respect of matters which might lie outside the contractor's responsibilities.

Figure 3·5: Contractual relationships: design and build procurement

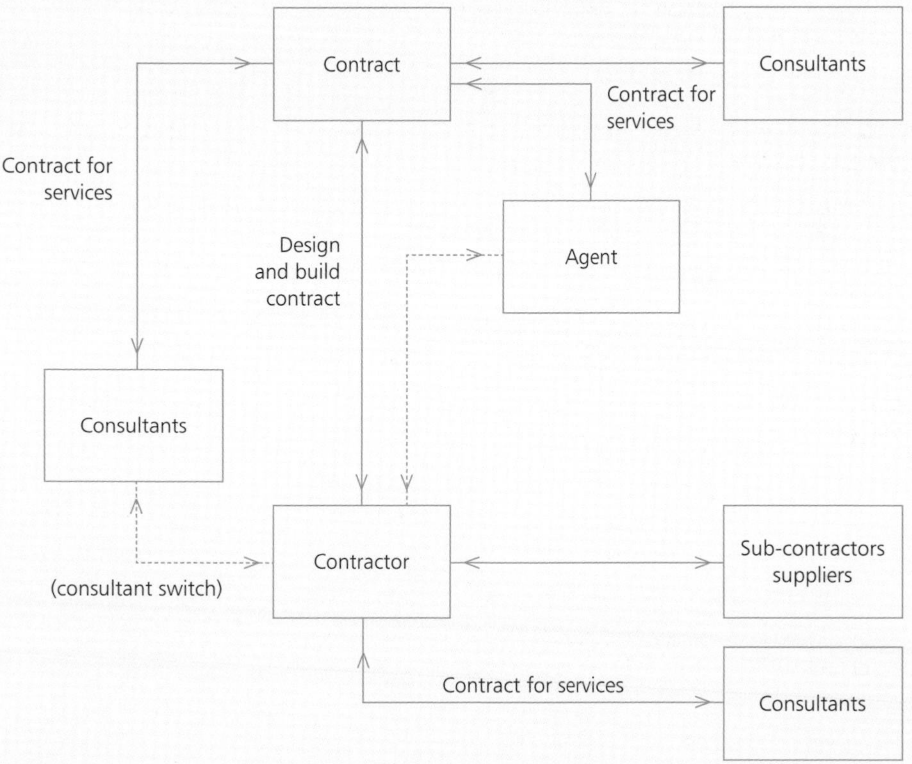

With design and build, it is likely that in the absence of in-house professional staff, the client will wish to engage outside consultants to advise on the preparation of requirements and to evaluate and select tenders, etc. Often one or more of these consultants will switch from being appointed by the client to being appointed by the contractor at the time the contractor is engaged. The main contractual link is between the client and the contractor and even the client's agent or representative has only a limited role. The contractor might also have a contractual link with his own design consultants, and with sub-contractors and suppliers. As the contractor is wholly responsible for their performance, both in terms of design and construction, there might be less need for collateral agreements between them and the client.

Figure 3·6: Contractual relationships: management procurement – management contracting

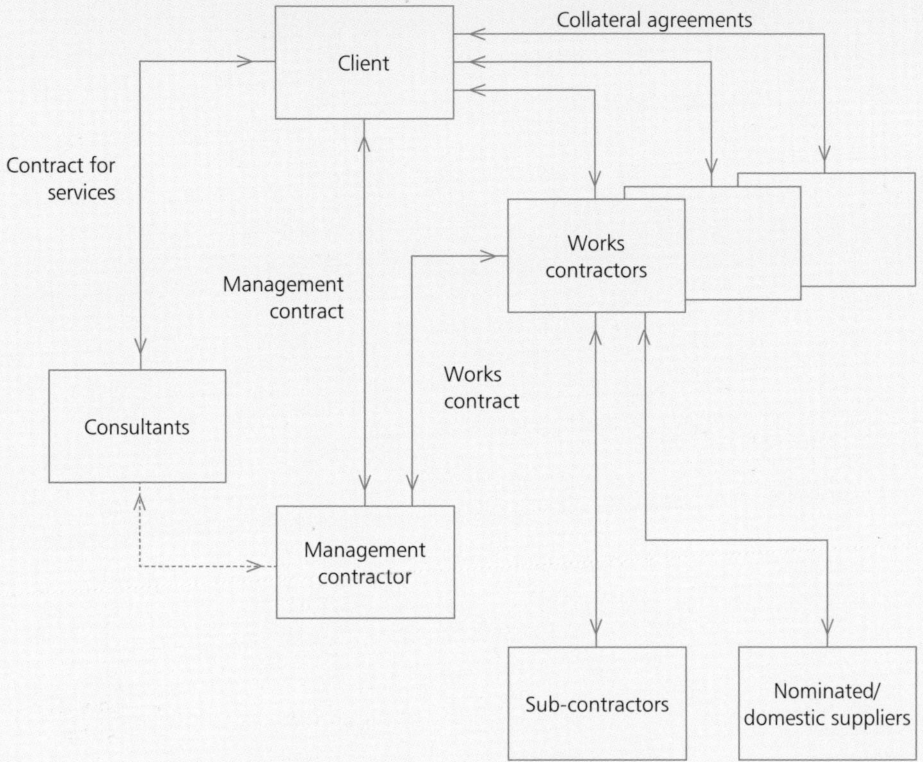

Figure 3·7: Contractual relationships: management procurement – construction management

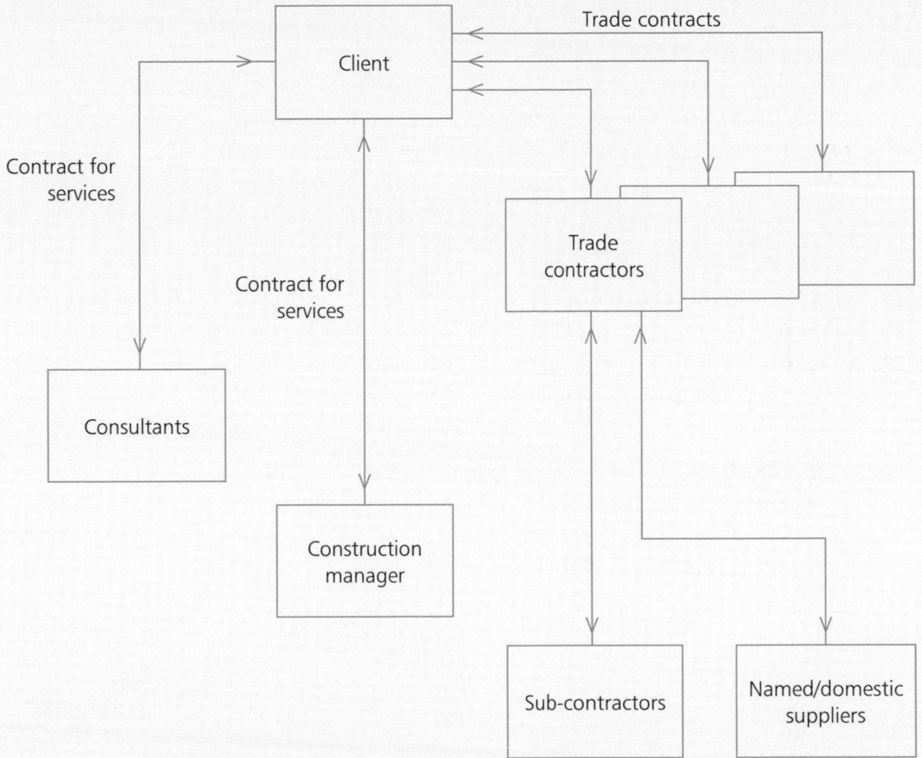

The contractual relationship in a management contract is between the client and the management contractor, with all works contractors in direct relationship with the latter. It may also be desirable to establish a contractual relationship between the client and each works contractor by means of a collateral agreement. In construction management the contractual relationship is between the client and the construction manager, with all trades contractors in direct relationship with the former.

Assessing the risks

In every building contract there is some degree of risk. People may be injured or property damaged. This category of risk, often referred to as pure and particular risk, is usually covered by the appropriate insurance. Contract conditions often make it a contractual obligation to take out the cover required against risks (for example, against injury to persons, or damage to property due to fire, storm, water, collapse, subsidence, vibration, or against terrorism, etc).

Another category of risk is fundamental risk. This will include damage due to war, nuclear pollution, supersonic bangs, etc. Such incidents are all the subject of statutory liability, and no insurance cover is normally available – or needed. The third category, often referred to as speculative risk, is something which can be apportioned in advance as decided by the parties to a contract. This may include losses in time or money which are the result of unexpected ground conditions, exceptionally adverse weather, unforeseeable shortages of labour or materials, and other similar matters wholly beyond the control of the contractor. It is essential to define at the outset who is to bear losses arising from such events.

With traditional lump sum contracts the intention is that there should usually be a fair balance of speculative risk between the parties. The balance can be adjusted as required, but obviously the greater the risk to be assumed by the contractor, the higher the tender figure is likely to be. The apportionment of risk accepted by the parties also varies considerably depending on the type of contract.

As can be seen from Figure 3·7, the balance of speculative risk will lie almost wholly with the contractor in the case of a design and build contract, where a complete package is supplied. Conversely, the balance is most onerous for the client where the management procurement path is adopted.

Figure 3·8: Speculative risk

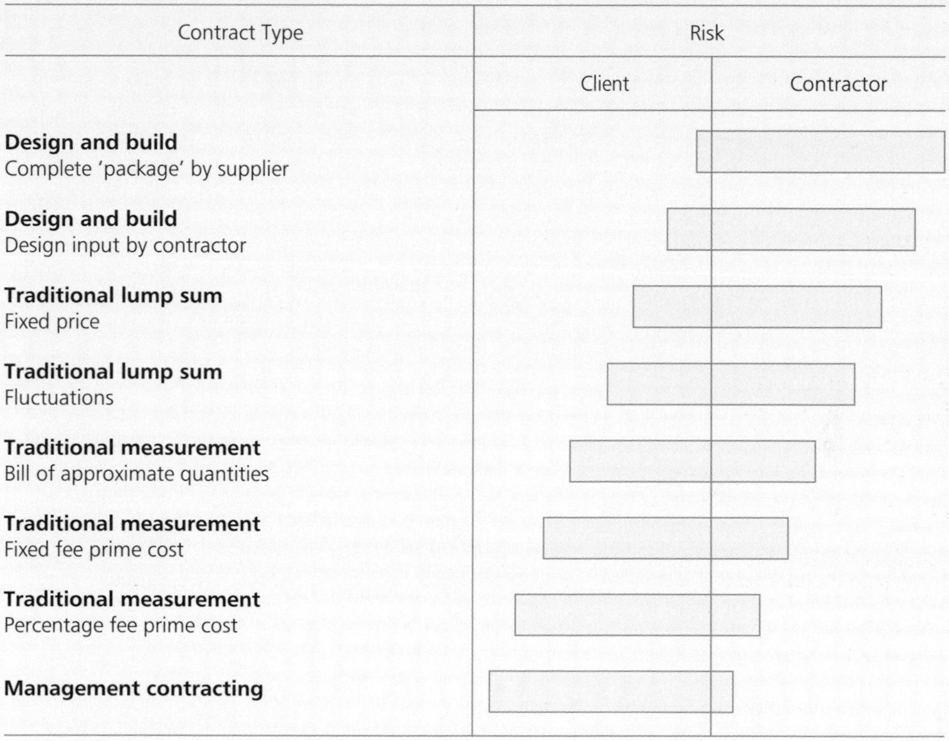

Contract Type	Risk	
	Client	Contractor
Design and build Complete 'package' by supplier		
Design and build Design input by contractor		
Traditional lump sum Fixed price		
Traditional lump sum Fluctuations		
Traditional measurement Bill of approximate quantities		
Traditional measurement Fixed fee prime cost		
Traditional measurement Percentage fee prime cost		
Management contracting		

Figure 3·9: Comparison of procurement method

	Speed	*Complexity*	*Quality*	*Flexibility*	
Traditional	Not the fastest of methods. Desirable to have all information at tender stage. Consider two stage or negotiated tendering.	Basically straightforward, but complications can arise if client requires that certain sub-contractors are used.	Client requires certain standards to be shown or described. Contractor is wholly responsible for achieving the stated quality on site.	Client controls design and variations to a large extent.	
Design and build	Relatively fast method. Pre-tender time largely depends on the amount of detail in the client's requirements. Construction time reduced because design and building proceed in parallel.	An efficient single contractual arrangement integrating design and construction expertise within one accountable organisation.	Client has no direct control over the contractor's performance. Contractor's design expertise may be limited. Client has little say in the choice of specialist sub-contractors.	Virtually none for the client once the contract is signed, without heavy cost penalties. Flexibility in developing details or making substitutions is to the contractor's advantage.	
Management	Early start on site is possible, long before tenders have even been invited for some of the Works packages.	Design and construction skills integrated at an early stage. Complex management operation requiring sophisticated techniques.	Client requires certain standards to be shown or described. Managing contractor responsible for quality of work and materials on site.	Client can modify or develop design requirements during construction. Managing contractor can adjust programme and costs.	

	Certainty	*Competition*	*Responsibility*	*Risk*	*Summary*
	Certainty in cost and time before commitment to build. Clear accountability and cost monitoring at all stages.	Competitive tenders are possible for all items. Negotiated tenders reduce competitive element.	Can be clear-cut division of design and construction. Confusion possible where there is some design input from contractor or specialist sub-contractors and suppliers.	Generally fair and balanced between the parties.	Benefits in cost and quality but at the expense of time.
	There is a guaranteed cost and completion date.	Difficult for the client to compare proposals which include for both price and design. Direct design and build very difficult to evaluate for competitiveness. No benefit passes to client if contractor seeks greater competitiveness for specialist work and materials.	Can be a clear division, but confused where the client's requirements are detailed as this reduces reliance on the contractor for design or performance. Limited role for the client's representative during construction.	Can lie almost wholly with the contractor.	Benefits in cost and time but at the expense of quality.
	Client is committed to start building on a cost plan, project drawings and specification only.	Management contractor is appointed because of management expertise rather than because his fee is competitive. However, competition can be retained for the Works packages.	Success depends on the management contractor's skills. An element of trust is essential. The professional team must be well coordinated through all the stages.	Lies mainly with the client – almost wholly in the case of construction management.	Benefits in time and quality but at the expense of cost.

Recent developments in procurement.

Some of the more recent developments in procurement are outlined below, roughly in order of their appearance. The outline is very brief, for further details readers should consult the references in the bibliography.

'Guaranteed maximum price' (GMP) contracts

GMP contracts have been around for some time, appearing first around the same time as the design build procurement method. There are no GMP standard forms of contract (the FIDIC Silver Book comes closest to ensuring a fixed price with limited areas for a review of price), so contracts are usually let on an amended standard lump sum form, or on the client's or contractor's own terms. There are a variety of possible arrangements, but normally the contractor is compensated for actual cost incurred plus a fixed fee, subject to an agreed ceiling. Therefore savings below a stipulated construction cost are passed on to the client (or in some cases shared) but the risk of any overrun is borne by the contractor. The exact extent of the risk assumed can only be determined by examining the terms of each contract. They frequently claim to pass all risks to the contractor, but in practice many, particularly those drafted by contracting companies, contain clauses which allow for additional payment in limited or exceptional circumstances.

PFI

The Private Finance Initiative (PFI) was introduced by the government in 1992 to enable major capital projects, to be funded without initially requiring the input of Government funds. The purpose of the PFI is to deliver all kinds of projects to the public sector, including the construction of buildings and the provision of associated operational services. The projects are funded and operated through a partnership of government and one or more private sector companies, sometimes referred to as PPP or P3.

There is a wide variety in the way PFI projects are organised, but they have some common features. Private consortia, usually involving large construction firms, are contracted to design, build, and in some cases manage new projects. The public sector authority first signs a contract with a private sector 'Operator'. Frequently the 'Operator' is a private sector consortium which forms a special company called a 'special purpose vehicle' (SPV) to build and maintain the asset. The consortium is usually made up of a building contractor, a maintenance company and a bank lender. As well as signing a contract with the government, the SPV will enter into contracts with other companies to design and/or build the facility and then maintain it. The PFI contract will typically last for 30 years, during which time the building is leased by a public authority.

In return for providing the service, the Operator is paid for the work over the course of the contract, linked to its performance in meeting agreed standards of provision.

This payment is frequently above the price that the public sector could have provided the service. If the Operator fails to meet any of the agreed standards it will normally lose an element of its payment until standards improve. If standards do not improve after an agreed period, the public sector authority is entitled to terminate the contract.

Constructing the Team

Sir Michael Latham's report *Constructing the Team* (HMSO, 1994) drew attention to the dissatisfaction among clients with the service and products provided by the construction industry. In particular, it noted that projects were not delivered on time, ran over budget, were not of the quality expected, and that too high a proportion of turnover was spent on disputes and claims. The report emphasised the importance of the client's role, the need for better briefing, new and less adversarial forms of procurement and contracts, improved methods of selecting the team, and more efficient ways of dealing with disputes.

Partnering

Partnering had already emerged prior to 1994, but was given greater impetus by the above report which stated *"We are confident that partnering can bring significant benefits by improving quality and timeliness of completion whilst reducing costs."* A series of reports followed including *Trusting the Team – the Best Practice Guide to Partnering in Construction* published by the Reading Construction Forum (RCF) in 1995; *Partnering in the Team* published by the Construction Industry Board in 1996, and in 1998 the RCF's follow-up report *The Seven Pillars of Partnering*.

Partnering in the Team defined partnering as follows:

"Partnering is a structured management approach to facilitate team working across contractual boundaries. Its fundamental components are formalised mutual objectives, agreed problem resolution methods, and an active search for continuous measurable improvements."

It is apparent from this definition that partnering was not intended as a particular type of contractual arrangement or procurement method, but an approach to procurement, aimed at improving performance over time, through team working, early identification and resolution of problems, and measurement of achievement against agreed objectives. Many organisations developed partnering charters or framework agreements, and some publishing bodies produced standard versions of these, such as the JCT non-binding partnering charter, all intended to be used alongside an underlying contract, which could be based on any of the three principal procurement methods. One standard form, PPC2000, was developed by the CIC Partnering Task Force, comprised both the partnering objectives and elements of design build procurement, and was uniquely a multilateral agreement.

The Construction Industry Board

The Latham recommendations were put into action through the work of the Construction Industry Board, set up in 1995, with its principal objective 'to implement, monitor and review' the recommendations of the Latham Report. Although no longer in existence, it has had a significant impact on the industry in securing 'a culture of co-operation, teamwork and continuous improvement in the industry's performance'.

Rethinking Construction

The work of the CIB was given further impetus by the report *Rethinking Construction* (DETR, 1998) prepared by the Construction Task Group chaired by Sir John Egan. This report echoed the Latham Report in its references to client dissatisfaction, and made comparisons with other industries, such as the car industry, whose processes were felt to be more efficient. It pointed out the urgent need for a reduction in accidents on site, and in the defects which frequently plague finished projects. It also called for a significant improvement in efficiency through more co-operative methods of procurement involving partnering and supply chain management identified five drivers for change, and four process improvements, one of which was partnering the supply chain.

M4I

The Movement for Innovation (M4I) was established in 1998 to coordinate the implementation of the '*Rethinking Construction*' recommendations through: the use of demonstration projects, working groups and knowledge exchange. Demonstration projects have an obligation to benchmark performance, be open and honest, share in the learning culture, set high standards in safety and respect for people and disseminate the results of their work to the rest of the industry through case histories, toolkits, etc. It had working groups covering: Key Performance Indicators and Benchmarking; the Knowledge Exchange; Partnering the Supply Chain; Culture Change; Education, Training and Research; Sustainability and Respect for People. M4I is now absorbed into Constructing Excellence, and information about demonstration projects, toolkits, etc. can be found on its website.

KPI's

The Egan Report set explicit and measurable targets for improvement. In 1999 M4I devised and published a set of Key Performance Indicators (KPIs), which were refined and re-published (April 2000). Eleven KPIs covered several aspects of the process of construction but did not cover the performance of the product. In April 2000 the M4I piloted a set of Sustainability Indicators, which went some way towards redressing the balance between process and product. A wide variety of organisations have now developed KPIs.

NHS ProCure21+

In its current form this is a National Framework Agreement with six supply chain teams that allows different NHS clients or joint ventures to select a supply chain for a capital investment construction scheme without the need to go through the public procurement process anew. The framework is across England and runs to 2016.

NHS LIFT

LIFT is an initiative of the NHS for the procurement of large bundles of major projects (at a larger scale than those under ProCure21). It combines PFI funding arrangements with principles of partnering. There is an equivalent initiative for the procurement of schools called 'LAPP'.

Government Construction Strategy 2011

The Government Construction Strategy, published on 30 May 2011, is aimed at making the government a more intelligent client, meeting the central government sustainability drive and reducing costs (the government aims to find 20% savings on construction projects from the various initiatives that are expected to follow the report).

The report identified poor procurement practices used at the time of its publication as leading to waste. As a result of this, a task group was set up to recommend new procurement methods that would serve the government and industry better.

The common features of the proposed new procurement methods are:

- Early Contractor Involvement
- Transparency
- Integration

The three methods require the following:

1. The client provides clear definition of the functional outcome desired from a series of similar forthcoming projects, including specific requirements where required, ie carbon reduction, use of apprentices, etc.
2. The client identifies typical costs to deliver such outcomes based on available data, benchmarking and cost planning work. This will enable the client to set a realistic yet challenging cost ceiling, with the expectation being that the cost ceiling would be achieved/bettered and costs would be further reduced over the series of projects.
3. Engagement with the supply chain embraces the principles of Early Contractor Involvement and high level of supply chain integration.
4. The completion of the capital phase occurs at the point that the specified output performance is achieved on the completion of the works.

Method 1 – Cost Led Procurement

In this method of procurement the client sets a challenging but realistic cost ceiling and engages one or more supply chain teams in a framework agreement. The team's selection is based primarily on ability to work collaboratively to deliver below the cost ceiling in the first project and to achieve further reductions in the subsequent projects forming part of the client's series of projects.

In the subsequent competitions (after the first one), the supply chain is expected to be engaged early with the client team to develop bids that drive further cost reduction based on their experience from the previous project and innovation.

The important criterion is that one of the teams in the framework must show capability to meet/better the cost ceiling. Where this is in place, selection is based on the relative attractiveness of the commercial and physical proposition offered by the team.

Where the cost ceiling (scheme price) cannot be matched or bettered by the teams in the framework, the project must be offered to suppliers outside the framework. Where the scheme price cannot be met, the project should not proceed; it is therefore important for the client to set a realistic cost ceiling.

Method 2 – Integrated Project Insurance

In this method of procurement the client holds a competition to appoint members of an integrated project team based on elements such as competence, track record, etc. The team that is chosen works together to present a preferred solution with cost savings against existing costs benchmarks. This 'solution' goes through a rigorous third party verification process to maintain good value in the project and to ensure that a balanced commercial position has been struck. The unique aspect of this method is that a single insurance policy will cover all the risks associated with the project. Thus, a single policy would cover all insurance policies that in other projects are held by the client, contractor and the supply chain. Also, the policy would cover the top slice of commercial risks covering any cost overruns in the project above and beyond the pain-share threshold set in the contract and apportioned between the client and the contractor and its supply chain. This would save about 2.5% on the costs of insurance to the different teams. Approximately 2.5 per cent is also estimated as the cost of insuring the top slice of commercial risk, thus this method of procurement is insurance cost neutral.

One of its major advantages is that it removes the need for adversarial and blame culture as excessive costs overrun is covered by insurance and all that is required for payment where such overruns occur is evidence of loss rather than the assignment of blame.

It is expected that to secure the insurance for a project, the team would have to produce a credible proposal validated by an independent expert assurer.

Method 3 – Two Stage Open Book

Under this model, the client invites suppliers on a framework agreement to bid for a project on the basis of an outline brief and costs benchmark. The bidders (contractor-consultant teams) are chosen at the first stage based on capacity, capability, stability, etc. The winning team then produces a proposal on the basis of open book cost that meets the client's stated outcomes and costs benchmark. The model also employs independent expert stage-gate reviews to ensure appropriate definition of scope, outcomes, risks, etc., with clear recommendations to the client and the contractor where improvements are required.

More information may be obtained from:

http://www.cabinetoffice.gov.uk/sites/default/files/resources/Procurement%20Lean%20Client%20Group%20Report%20Jan%202012_0.pdf

Which type of contract? 4

For traditional procurement

Under this method, with design separated from construction, most building contracts are strictly work and material contracts. The basic assumption is that the contractor is to carry out and complete the work as shown on or described in the documents supplied by the client, and is responsible for its own working methods. This might include the design of any temporary works necessary to enable the contractor to achieve the desired result. Apart from this, and in the absence of anything to the contrary expressly in the contract, it has no responsibility for design. The contract wording may of course be extended to expressly include for a limited design obligation by the contractor.

The contractor is responsible for workmanship and materials and this is in respect of complying with the standards of the contract as far as workmanship is concerned and of satisfying implied terms of merchantable quality etc concerning goods and material etc. This will normally extend to all sub-contractors of whatever description or status. The contractor will also be responsible for any defects, other than those which are directly attributable to faulty design or arise from misuse. The contractor is not normally responsible for maintaining the building: any such requirement would have to be expressly included in the contract.

Basically there are three types of contract available with the traditional procurement method:

- lump sum contracts: where the Contract Sum is determined before construction starts, and the amount is entered in the Agreement;
- measurement contracts: where the Contract Sum is accurately known only on completion, and after remeasurement to some agreed basis;
- cost reimbursement contracts: where the Contract Sum is arrived at on the basis of the actual costs of labour, plant and materials, to which is added a fee to cover the overheads and profit.

Lump sum contracts

The contractor undertakes to carry out a defined amount of work in return for an agreed sum. This can be a fixed amount not subject to recalculation, in which case there would be no opportunity for the client to make variations after work has started on site. The sum is more likely to be subject to limited fluctuations, usually to cover tax etc. changes not foreseeable at the time of tendering. The sum may be subject to fluctuations in the cost of labour, plant and materials – the so-called 'full fluctuations' provisions. Recovery may be by use of a formula, or by the tedious business of checking vouchers, invoices, etc.

Lump sum contracts 'with quantities' are priced on the basis of drawings and a firm bill of quantities. Items which cannot be accurately quantified can be covered by an approximate quantity or a provisional sum, but these should be kept to a minimum.

Lump sum contracts 'without quantities' are priced on the basis of drawings and another document. This may simply be a specification of a descriptive kind, in which case the lump sum will not be itemised, or one that is detailed to the extent that the Contract Sum is the total of the priceable items. The job might be more satisfactorily described by Schedules of Work, where the lump sum is the total of the priced items. In the latter cases, an itemised breakdown of the lump sum will be a useful basis for valuing any additional work. Where only a lump sum is tendered, then a supporting Schedule of Rates or a Contract Sum Analysis will be needed from the tenderer.

Tenders can be prepared on the basis of notional quantities, but they will need to be replaced by firm quantities if it is intended to enter into a 'with quantities' lump sum contract.

Measurement contracts

These are also sometimes referred to as 'remeasurement' contracts. This is where the work which the contractor undertakes to do cannot for some good reason be accurately measured before tendering. The presumption is that it has been substantially designed, and that a reasonably accurate picture of the amount and quality of what is required is given to the tenderer. Probably the most effective measurement contracts, involving least risk to the client, are those based on drawings and approximate quantities.

Measurement contracts can also be based on drawings and a Schedule of Rates or prices prepared by the client for the tenderer to complete. This type of contract might be appropriate where there is not enough time to prepare even approximate quantities, or where the quantity of work is very uncertain.

Obviously the client has to accept the risk involved in starting work with no accurate idea of the total cost, and generally this type of contract is best confined to small jobs.

A variant of this is the measured term contract under which rates can be established for categories of work, although instructions or orders will be required before any single job in the anticipated programme is carried out.

Cost reimbursement contracts

These are sometimes referred to as 'cost plus' contracts. The contractor undertakes to carry out an indeterminate amount of work on the basis that it is paid the prime or actual cost of labour, plant and materials. In addition the contractor receives an agreed fee to cover management, overheads and profit. Checking the prime costs which are directly related to the Works is relatively straightforward. The variable is the fee, which should be agreed beforehand, and establishing precisely what it covers. The basis of the fee can give rise to many variants of cost plus contracts. Which is likely to be the most appropriate will depend on the particular circumstances.

Cost plus percentage fee

The fee charged is directly related to the prime cost. It is usually a flat rate percentage, but it can also be on a sliding scale. However, the contractor has no real incentive to work at maximum efficiency, and this variant is only likely to be considered where requirements are particularly indeterminate pre-contract.

Cost plus fixed fee

The fee to be charged is tendered by the contractor. This is appropriate provided that the amount and type of work is largely foreseeable. The contractor has an incentive to work efficiently so as to remain profitable within the agreed fee.

Cost plus fluctuating fee

The fee varies in proportion to the difference between the estimated cost and the actual prime cost. The presumption is that if the latter cost increases due to the contractor's supposed inefficiency, then the fee will be reduced accordingly. This approach depends upon there being a realistic chance of ascertaining the amount and type of work at tender stage.

Cost reimbursement based on a target cost

This is a slight variant on the previous type. The fee is related to an agreed target. The actual prime cost above or below the target affects the fee earned.

It is of course always open to the client to pay direct for the cost of labour, materials, plant, hire charges etc, with the contractor receiving only an agreed fee for managing the execution of the Works.

For design and build procurement

This procurement method gained acceptance in the early 1980s with the introduction of a 'with contractor's design' variant of the standard JCT form. It was endorsed by the public sector as a preferred procurement option, and most publishers of standard forms now produce documents which allow for a contractor's design responsibility.

The contractor may have responsibility for some or all of the design of the project. The contract wording must expressly refer to this, and the extent of the design obligation needs to be set out as clearly as possible.

The requirements of the client can be stated briefly and simply, perhaps comprising little more than a site plan and schedule of accommodation. However, they are more likely to be stated in a document of several hundred pages with precise specifications, accompanied by a well worked out concept design. The design role of the contractor might even be restricted to developing design detail and preparing production information based on the design information supplied by the client.

Unless the contract states otherwise, it seems that the liability for design is an absolute liability under which the contractor warrants fitness for the purpose intended. However, usually standard design and build forms expressly limit the design liability of the contractor to the normal professional duty to exercise reasonable care and skill. Independent consultants engaged by the contractor are therefore under a liability no greater than normal. An indemnity or acceptance of liability is likely to be worthless unless backed by adequate indemnity insurance, and this is something that should be checked before a contractor is appointed. Where the contractor does not have in-house designers and intends to use outside consultants, their identity should be established before a tender is accepted.

Generally it is better to specify in terms of the performance requirement rather than to prescribe in detail, because this leaves the responsibility for design and selection firmly with the contractor. However, with some types of development (housing, for example) the more precise the requirements the less likely it is that a tenderer will start out with the fixed intention of utilising proprietary components or its own standard shell designs.

It is claimed that design and build contracts offer certainty on the Contract Sum and bring cost benefits. The close integration of design and working methods, and the relative freedom of the contractor to use its purchasing power and market knowledge most effectively, might suggest this. Unfortunately, it is often very difficult to find out just how competitive the figures are.

On the matter of speed, it should be possible to ensure a quicker start on site, and the close integration of design and construction should result in more effective programming. However, time is needed for the client's consultants to prepare an adequate set of requirements, and time is also needed to compare and evaluate offers and schemes from competing tenderers. The success or otherwise of a design and build operation depends to a large extent on the client properly setting out the requirements in the first place and then carefully evaluating the contractor's proposals. Once the contract is signed, any changes are likely to prove costly, and the client has little further opportunity to comment on how the requirements are to be met.

It may be possible to modify a traditional 'work and materials' agreement where it is desirable to make the contractor responsible for design of part of the Works. For example the Standard Form of Building Contract (SBC11) now incorporates provisions for a Contractor's Designed Portion. Work such as piling, roof trusses, etc. could well be made the subject of such an agreement, and even though the contractor might wish to sub-contract such work, it would nevertheless accept responsibility for its design. These provisions, however, should not be thought of as a way of introducing design obligations for a substantial part of the Works, thereby effectively changing the original contract into one of a design and build type.

For management procurement

Basically such contracts concentrate primarily on the management expertise of the contractor and are particularly suitable for fairly large projects with complex requirements. There are many variants, ranging from the procurement of a building designed by the client's professional team on the one hand, to in addition playing a major design role, to also accepting a wider facilities management obligation to fit out and maintain the operation of a building for some specific period, and even perhaps playing a substantial role in the immediate funding of the project. Clearly in the majority of such cases, developers will have to look to forms of contract specially drafted to suit their requirements.

There are some standard forms available for use with the main management procurement options, as follows.

Management contracts

The client appoints an independent professional team, and also a management contractor. The contractor's involvement at pre-construction stages will be as an adviser to the team, and during construction it will be responsible for executing the Works using direct works contractors.

With this type of contract it is possible to make an early start on site and achieve early completion. Because of its flexibility, it allows the client to develop the design during construction, because drawings and matters of detail can be adjusted and finalised as the work proceeds.

For a management contract to be successful there must be trust and good teamwork on the part of the client, the professionals and the management contractor. The latter should preferably be appointed no later than the outline design stage. The contractor can advise on the design programme, tender action, delivery of materials and goods, and construction programmes.

The management contractor will normally make a written submission which includes a proposed management fee, and will be appointed after interviews with the client and the professional team. The fee will include for the total management service, expressed as a percentage of the total project cost, and for a service to cover pre-construction stages should the project not proceed to site.

The management contractor undertakes the work on the basis of a contract cost plan prepared by the quantity surveyor, project drawings, and a project specification. The client accepts most of the risk because there is no certainty about costs or programme. Competitive tenders for the Works packages follow later, and they will usually, though not always, be lump sum contracts based on bills of quantities.

There is a Standard Form of Management Contract issued by the JCT, together with the Standard Works Contracts and an Agreement for use between the client and each works contractor.

Construction management

Again, the construction manager is appointed after a careful selection process and is paid a management fee.

One basic difference from a management contract is that the trades contracts, although arranged and administered by the construction manager, are direct between the client and the trade contractors. Although in a sense this gives the client a greater measure of control, it also means that he or she accepts virtually all of the risk. The construction manager is a coordinator, and usually cannot guarantee that the project will be finished to time or cost.

The client directs the project and the client is also likely to carry the greatest burden of the speculative risk. Obviously in-house expertise is essential.

Construction management seems to have increased in popularity over management contracts, but much work by this procurement method has been undertaken by experienced commercial clients using bespoke agreements. There are now also a few standard forms available for construction management.

Design, manage, construct and in some instances maintain

This variant is a more recent development of the management approach, offering a total integrated service from a single source. It can be led by the contractor, or by some other professional. The latter is only likely when the design aspects of the project are a high priority.

The FIDIC Gold Book is the only standard form that provides for this variant; in practice developers or contracting organisations mostly use specially drafted forms. Architects involved in this kind of work should engage a specialist lawyer to check forms, and advise on the terms. Maintenance is normally outside the scope of building contracts, and is the subject of facilities management or other special agreements.

Contracts where the Architect administers a series of separate trade contracts where there is no main or general contractor, may also fall into this category. As well as being the designer, the Architect assumes the managing and coordinating roles for the project. This arrangement sometimes occurs with fairly small projects and is a quite traditional way of working. Trades contracts will ordinarily be direct between the client and the firms concerned.

Choosing the type of contract

In trying to decide which type of contract to adopt, an architect will have to ask him or herself (or others) a number of questions:

Q. *What is the nature or category of the work?*
Comment: is it predominantly building or engineering work? Is it a completely new building or an addition to an existing one? Is it refurbishment work, maybe of a specialist nature such as restoration of a historic building? Is it concerned with new uses for an old building, involving major alterations? Is it small jobbing work, perhaps on a 'one-off' basis, or one of a series of jobs which form part of a term maintenance programme?

Q. *Who is to be responsible for design?*
Comment: is responsibility to rest entirely with the Architect as lead designer and the professional design team? Is the contractor to be directly involved in any important aspect of design? Is there to be significant design input from specialist sub-contractors or suppliers?

Q. *Will the nature of the work allow full and accurate tender documents to be prepared?*
Comment: it might be desirable to carry out exploratory work before going to tender, but this might not be possible in the event. With work to existing buildings, problems sometimes only become apparent after site operations have started.

Q. *Is there enough time to prepare full information at tender stage?*
Comment: does the urgent necessity for an early start on site mean that it will have to be made on the basis of notional or approximate information, to be replaced later with firm instructions?

Q. *What documents are needed for a particular type of contract?*
Comment: is this a project which can best be shown mainly in a drawn form? Are bills or schedules needed? Should the specification be a composite document which includes some descriptive sections, some scheduled and itemised, and some with quantities? What is then to be the status of the respective sections or documents in the event of conflict or discrepancies?

Q. *What is the method of selecting the contractor?*
Comment: is it to be by a direct negotiated approach, or by competition? Will competitive tendering be straightforward single stage, or is two stage tendering the only practical answer? This might affect the information to be prepared and will affect the time needed.

4 Which type of contract?

Q. Is the client able to state his requirements precisely before work starts?
Comment: is it desirable or necessary to allow for adjustments or design changes during the course of the work? What flexibility is needed and when are the critical times for final decisions?

Q. Does the client need to know a precise Contract Sum before work starts?
Comment: is construction cost of secondary importance to early completion (because, say, large sums of money are tied into property deals or the rental of existing premises, or because of dependence on economic returns)?

Q. Who is to be mainly responsible for coordinating the work on site?
Comment: is responsibility to rest primarily with the contractor, or does the client wish to reserve the right to nominate specialists, to arrange direct purchasing deals, or to have work carried out by others whilst the contractor is still in possession of the site?

Which contract form? 5

Decisions on the preferred procurement route will obviously have led to conclusions on the contract types which might be most suitable. Choice of the actual forms of contract to be used should depend on those circumstances surrounding the particular project, which need to be taken account of. The words and procedures described in the contract form need to adequately cover situations and foreseeable events which might arise during the carrying out of the work. The choice of form needs therefore to be based on an analysis of the intended work, and not be the result of prejudice, doctrinaire allegiance, or just lazily clinging to the familiar.

Some contract arrangements, particularly on major developments which might involve novel procurement or be projects of considerable complexity, could well require the use of specially drafted forms.

For most building operations in which the majority of architects are likely to be involved, one or more of the standard forms of contract should prove satisfactory. However, the tendency in recent years has been to introduce option clauses and supplements to make these forms more adaptable for use in a wider range of situations. The need to respond to recent legislation and changing practices in the construction industry, has also brought about a considerable increase in the number of forms which can be categorised as being standard. As a result there is now a considerable choice on offer, and the decision about which form, or even which combination of options is likely to be the most appropriate, becomes increasingly difficult to make.

Availability

Q. *Is there a published standard form which will satisfy the requirements, or will a specially drafted document be needed?*

If extensive amendment is needed, or if a specially drafted document seems advisable, then the matter should be referred to the client for appropriate legal advice. An exception might be a small job in very straightforward circumstances which could be adequately covered by an exchange of letters. Even so, such a task should never be undertaken lightly, and a standard form which uses widely understood terminology might well be preferable. The industry has addressed the need for agreements which can be used by consumers on domestic work where no consultants are involved during construction, and the JCT homeowners contracts, for example, are true consumer contracts. In all cases care is needed to ensure that contract provisions satisfy the requirements of relevant legislation.

5 Which contract form?

Q. What standard forms are published, and which is likely to be the most appropriate?
Chapters 6 to 13 below set out and compare, under a series of headings, the main features of the forms most commonly in use today.

Q. What if the contractor wants to use its own form of contract?
The client should be advised to pass any such document to his or her legal advisers for an opinion. Even simply worded and apparently clear documents can be heavily weighted in favour of the contractor's own interests, and the risks can rest largely with the client. A useful overview of the implications of various bespoke clauses is provided in Wevill, *Law in Practice: The RIBA Legal Handbook* (RIBA Publishing, 2012).

Q. What if the client wants alterations made to a standard form?
This might in effect make the contract non-standard and any ambiguous terms may be construed unfavourably. The basic rule is never to make amendments which might have unintended effects on other clauses and so upset the balance of the whole document. The Latham Report recommended that all parties in the construction process should be encouraged to use standard forms without amendment. Where there are exceptional reasons for such amendments, the Architect should make sure that the client is aware of and accepts the risks. Amendments should be dealt with by his or her legal advisers. Again, there is the practical point that ad hoc alterations often lead to inflated tender figures as the contractor prices the risks.

Sector

This can have a significant influence, and is sometimes a matter over which there is little choice. This can be as a result of the need to comply with the standing orders of an authority, or to follow some official guidance on procedural matters. Several standard forms of contract were published in alternative versions, for use by either the private or the public sector as applicable. The present trend is for forms in only one version which can be used regardless of sector, and the distinction between what is permissible for private sector and public sector use is now becoming more fluid.

Government contracts

In the past construction work for government departments was invariably carried out under one of the GC/Works contracts, then the responsibility of the Department of the Environment. Today the situation is less clear-cut.

For a start, the European Union now identifies three categories of authorities: central government departments (which seem to include NHS Trusts); sub-central government bodies (which include local authorities, police authorities, universities, etc.); private bodies subsidised by government (eg Arts Council or English Heritage grant funded projects). Secondly, the GC/Works contracts have not been updated to meet current regulatory requirements. Additionally, after the Latham Report's support for the New Engineering Contract, the NEC also received endorsement from the Office of

Government Commerce (this was the office dealing with procurement of works and services at the time), who recommended that NEC3 should be used for public projects. The JCT Constructing Excellence and the PPC2000 later received similar recommendations. It would appear that the government's future procurement plans lean in favour of JCT Constructing Excellence, NEC3 and PPC2000.

The GC/Works range of forms are still in use in some projects although it has not been updated to cater for changes in legislation.

Local authority requirements

The public sector (or, more accurately, local authorities) has for many years had its own version of the JCT Standard Form. However, now that the person administering the contract is referred to as 'the Architect/the Contract Administrator', and some provisions peculiar to local government have become redundant, the need for private and public versions has been removed. However, the JCT recently published a public sector supplement which introduced suggested amendments to its contracts suite to provide for changes in government policies.

In work for the public sector, there may also be need to take into account the published requirements of the particular department or client body. Some have firm views on the choice of forms, what amendments they insist are made and procedures which are to be followed concerning contract administration.

Familiarity

It is important, when considering an appropriate form of contract, to be thoroughly familiar with its provisions. Familiarity should never of course be the justification for choosing it. It takes time and effort to keep abreast of changes to published forms and any consequential effects on contract administration procedures.

Vigilance is also required to make sure that the editions of the contract forms and any addenda or supplements are the current issue and compatible. Checks are also advisable to make sure that the contract administration forms are current and compatible with the form of building contract being used. Pre-printed forms can quickly become out of date, and it is unreasonable to expect office staff to check these things when documents are issued. It is for the contract administrator to check such matters.

Personal preference

There is almost inevitably some subjective element in choosing a form of contract. An architect might feel a personal allegiance to one or other of the professional bodies. For example, ACA members might understandably incline towards an ACA form, while ASI members will feel a brand loyalty for their published forms. A majority of architects, mindful of the RIBA representation on the JCT and of its leading role historically, might instinctively turn to the JCT's range of standard forms.

Of course, equally it might be the client body which has strong preferences not only about the procurement method but also about the choice of form. Developers and members of organisations such as the British Property Federation might stipulate using forms which contain certain conditions. A project manager might advise the use of a form 'based upon' a well respected standard form (usually fairly loosely!), or a powerful funding body might require terms in a collateral agreement which necessitate considerable changes to those in the main contract.

Notwithstanding, the advantages of using a standard agreed form cannot be overstated. Modern forms drafted by experts and used without ad hoc alterations should result in fairer conditions and fairer tendering. Whatever the circumstances surrounding the choice of form, it should be the result of a thoughtful and logical analysis of the situation – an exercise in professional judgement.

Effect on contract for professional services

As discussed above, the choice of building contract form might also have implications for the contract for professional services. The Latham Report recognised this by its recommendation for a complete family of standard documents, including a total matrix of interlocking consultants' agreements and contracts. Publishers of some building contract forms also provide compatible sub-contracts, and ancillary documents including consultant agreements. However, the majority of consultants at present seem to prefer appointing documents published by their respective professional bodies.

The form of building contract chosen might have significance which should not be overlooked when calculating the fee for professional services relating to contract administration. For example, SBC11 demands fairly sophisticated procedures likely to be far more time-consuming than those needed under, say, MW11. The type of contract, and the actual contract form which it is proposed to use, needs to be taken into account when compiling a fee bid – always assuming that the contract choice is known in sufficient time.

Even with apparently straightforward traditional lump sum contracts, there could be special factors which need to be borne in mind. For example, it might be expedient to arrange for a preliminary or enabling contract to cover investigation work, demolition work, advanced site works, etc. ahead of the main contract, and this should not be overlooked when assessing fees; or again, it might be decided to have work carried out under a number of parallel trades contracts with the Architect assuming a management and coordinating role, and charging an additional fee for this additional service.

The services provided and the fee appropriate will always depend on the nature of the work. For example, work on the preservation or restoration of historic buildings might warrant a considerable departure from the Outline Plan of Work stages, with a great deal of investigation and reporting needed in the earlier stages followed by unusually frequent and detailed inspections both before and during construction.

Another matter which often brings close links between the building contract and contract for professional services is design liability. The Architect should only accept design liability to an extent agreed and intended and which is acceptable for professional indemnity insurance purposes. Care is needed not to acquire inadvertently any liability that is more onerous, for example, fitness for purpose as the result of incautiously entering into some collateral warranty with a tenant or purchaser, or when acting for a contractor involved in a package deal with strict liability.

Traditional procurement 6

Standard lump sum forms

The Joint Contracts Tribunal Ltd
Major Project Construction Contract 2011

The Joint Contracts Tribunal Ltd
Standard Building Contract 2011

The Joint Contracts Tribunal Ltd
Constructing Excellence Contract

The Stationery Office
GC/Works/1 With Quantities (1998)

The Institution of Civil Engineers
NEC Document
Engineering and Construction Contract Third Edition (with 2011 amendments)

Chartered Institute of Building
Major Projects Contract (Review Edition)

It should be noted that some of the forms listed above are also suitable for use with procurement other than traditional lump sum. They are listed under this heading for convenience, and in recognition of their seminal position as major forms of contracts.

JCT MP11

The Joint Contracts Tribunal Ltd

Major Project Construction Contract 2011 Edition

Background

The JCT Major Project Construction Contract was produced for employers who engage regularly in the construction of major projects and have extensive in-house contractual procedures. It is expected that the employer would provide the definition of his requirements, access to the site, review of design documents and payments while the contractor would proceed with the works without relying on the employer for further instructions or to administer the project.

The extended timescale of major projects has frequently necessitated proceeding in phases, in parallel working for both design and construction, in payments related to progress and performance, and with incentives for savings in time and cost. In the past this has often resulted in employers making extensive modifications to the conditions in otherwise standard forms of contract, or using bespoke forms. In 2003 JCT took the bold step of introducing an entirely new standard form to take account of the needs of this segment of the market. It is quite a significant departure from anything previously published by JCT, and in format, style and language, it breaks new ground. In some respects it might seem to be something of a hybrid, although direct comparisons with SBC11 or DB11 are not altogether helpful. However, it should certainly be regarded as a likely alternative to those well tried forms of contract, if used in the particular circumstances for which it is intended. In other circumstances the two long established forms might still offer an appropriate option.

As a document it is very open and flexible but demands such attributes of its users. The relative brevity, straightforward language, and clear procedures make it immediately attractive. However it is likely to be an appropriate choice only for parties who are already experienced in operations of a major scale, and who fully appreciate the nature of the conditions and procedures. They may be relatively brief and uncomplicated, but they depend on a high level of understanding and involvement by the parties.

Nature

MPF11 is much shorter than SBC11. This relative brevity is due in part to the use of enabling clauses which avoid the inclusion of that which might be irrelevant for the particular project, and allow the parties to include their own detailed project-specific requirements on matters such as insurance.

The 2011 edition of this contract replaces the 2005 edition, the major change between

JCT MP11

the two editions is the redrafting of the clauses on payment and payment notices to comply with the amendment of HGCRA 1996. There are also changes to the insurance section with regards to the terrorism cover, a new definition for insolvency, a redraft of the contractor's clause to limit the indemnity provisions and the extension of the contractor's duties to responsibilities under the Site Waste Management Plan (SWMP) Regulations.[1] MP11 is logically structured, but interestingly there are no conventional Articles or Recitals, and the document goes immediately into the 43 Contract Conditions which are set out under nine Section headings. The Conditions begin with an unusually full set of definitions including the meaning of practical completion.

Unlike most other JCT forms, in MP11 the Contract Particulars appear after the Conditions, at the back of the form. These require project-specific information to be entered, and the choice of option clauses to be indicated. Tables require entries relating to completion by Sections, and insurances. The particulars are followed by the Attestation. Understandably, this is a contract to be executed as a deed.

The document also includes three schedules: a Third Party Rights Schedule in respect of third party rights from the contractor in favour of the funder, and third party rights from the contractor in favour of a purchaser or tenant; and the Pricing Document. This includes the rules which govern the manner of payment to the Contractor, and pricing information. Details relating to an advance payment bond, Progress Payment schedule, and Contract Sum analysis must be attached where relevant. The Supplemental Schedule provides for collaborative working, health and safety, environment and sustainability clauses.

The form has a number of interesting key features including:

- the contractor is responsible for any additional design work required beyond that shown or described in the Employer's Requirements;
- the design submission procedure ensures that the Employer is invited to review and comment on all the contractor's design documents, however the contractor remains responsible for design despite such review;
- the Employer may name specialists and sub-contractors, and the contractor becomes responsible for their performance;
- the Employer may novate those consultants previously appointed and the contractor then becomes responsible for their services performed pursuant to the Requirements;
- the Employer gives the contractor access to the site, rather than possession;
- insurance arrangements are for the parties to agree upon;
- interim payments to the contractor will usually be made monthly, but may be to any terms the parties agree. There is no provision for retention, but bonds or security measures similar to retention could be created if required;

1 At the time of writing the government has indicated it intends to scrap SWMP Regulations.

JCT MP11

- there are provisions for acceleration, bonus for early completion, and sharing of benefits of savings or value improvements;
- the Employer must appoint a sole representative who has authority to act in all matters under the contract. Other consultants appointed by the Employer can expect cooperation from the Contractor, but will have no authority under the contract to act for the Employer.

For the purpose of comparisons, in this book the synopsis is in the same format as that employed for notes on the other forms of contract, although this will not directly reflect the structure used in the actual contract form. Clause numbers cited are those to be found in MP11.

Use

The form is published in one version only, and in theory is therefore available for use in both the private and public sectors. In practice it is likely to be used mainly with large commercial developments, but might also have relevance for PFI projects.

It is for a lump sum contract, and the Contract Sum is to be stated in the Contract Particulars. The Employer's Requirements could include bills of quantities, but there is no specific reference to these in the document. The Contractor's Proposals must be accompanied by a Contract Sum Analysis and pricing information. The Requirements and the Proposals are key documents on which the agreement is founded.

There is no provision for an independent and impartial contract administrator, and administrative functions required under the contract are to be taken direct by the Employer or the Contractor. The Employer's Representative may exercise all the powers and functions of the Employer.

Synopsis

1 Intentions

- The contractor is obliged to execute and complete the Project, that is for construction works and the completion of the design (7·1).
- The contractor warrants that it has the competence and resources to act as CDM Coordinator, Principal Contractor, and designer as required under the CDM Regulations (7·3).
- The Employer is responsible for the Requirements, and the contractor is not responsible for the contents of these, or for the adequacy of design contained in these (11·1).
- If a discrepancy within the Requirements is found, the contractor must notify the Employer which provision it intends to follow. If the Employer wishes the contractor to proceed otherwise, that instruction is treated as a Change (10·2).

JCT MP11

- If a discrepancy within the Proposals is found, the Employer will instruct the contractor which provision should be adopted and that instruction is not treated as a Change (10·3).
- Where the contractor takes over design, it warrants that it will perform to the standard of reasonable skill and care appropriate to a competent professional, and does not warrant fitness for purpose (11·3).
- Should it be thought necessary to stipulate a fitness for purpose obligation, then the JCT Major Project Construction Contract Guide suggests suitable wording, and also gives a reminder of some of the practical problems likely to arise with this kind of provision (footnote to 11·3).
- Materials and goods are to be of the kinds and standards described in the contract, and where not described are to be reasonably fit for the intended purpose (11·4).
- Where described goods and materials are not procurable the contractor must propose alternatives of an equivalent or better standard. Only if the alternative is of a lesser kind or standard, and acceptable to the Employer, will it be treated as a Change (11·4).
- Workmanship is to be of the standards described or otherwise is to be executed in a good and workmanlike manner (11·5).
- The contractor is responsible for the preparation of further design documents, and these are to be submitted to the Employer for review in the quantities and format all as identified in the Contract Particulars, and as shown on the design programme contained in the Requirements or Proposals (12·2).
- The Employer is to respond by returning design documents to the contractor marked either 'A Action', 'B Action' or 'C Action' (12·3).
- The contractor is to execute work marked 'A Action' and can expect to be paid accordingly (12·6·1).
- The contractor is to execute work marked 'B Action' provided that the Employer's comments are incorporated, and a further copy of the document is immediately submitted to the Employer. The contractor can expect to be paid accordingly (12·6·2).
- The contractor must not execute work marked 'C Action', but must resubmit a document which takes account of the Employer's comments (12·6·3).
- Regardless of comments made by the Employer and subsequently incorporated into the design, the contractor is still responsible for ensuring that any design document it prepares is in accordance with all the requirements of the contract (12·10).

2 Time

- The contractor must proceed regularly and diligently to achieve practical completion on or before completion date (15·1).

JCT MP11

- The contract allows for completion by Sections, and completion dates for each Section (together with rates of damages and bonus) are to be entered in the Contract Particulars.
- The contractor must use reasonable endeavours to prevent or reduce delay to progress or to completion (15·3).
- The contractor must notify the Employer when in its opinion Practical Completion has occurred and, if it agrees, the Employer will issue a certificate of Practical Completion (15·4).
- If the contractor fails to achieve practical completion by the completion date, it becomes liable for liquidated damages at the rate stated in the Contract Particulars (16·1).
- With the consent of the Contractor, the Employer may take over any part of the Project prior to practical completion, and must then issue a statement identifying the part, the date, and the value of the part (17·1).
- Unless there is anything to the contrary in the contract, the contractor will be entitled to an extension of time in respect of eight listed events. Of these four are for 'neutral causes', and the other four relate to any Change, interference by other persons on site, valid suspension of performance for non-payment, and acts of prevention by the Employer. Interestingly, adverse weather is not listed (18·1).
- Whenever the contractor becomes aware that progress of the Project is being or is likely to be delayed due to any cause, it must forthwith notify the Employer of the cause of the delay and likely effect upon completion of the Project (18·2).
- Where the contractor considers that delay is caused by one of these events, it must provide supporting evidence, and revise this as necessary (18·3).
- Within 42 days of receipt of such notification, the Employer must notify the contractor of such adjustment to the completion date as he or she then considers fair and reasonable, or give reasons why the completion date should not be adjusted (18·4).
- The Employer may review its decisions at any time in the light of further documentation (18·5).
- Within 42 days after practical completion of the Project, the contractor may provide further documentation to support any further adjustment to the completion date, and within 42 days of receiving that information the Employer must review decisions made previously, and either confirm or adjust the completion date (18·6).
- No adjustment to the completion date to bring an earlier completion date is possible except by agreement (18·8).

JCT MP11

- However, the Employer can investigate the possibility of acceleration by inviting proposals from the Contractor. The contractor must either make proposals or explain why it is impracticable to achieve an earlier date (19·1).
- If the date of practical completion is earlier than the completion date, then the Employer is liable to pay the contractor a bonus at the rate entered in the Appendix (20).

3 Control

- The contractor may not assign either the benefit or burden of the contract without the consent of the Employer, and this would apply both to construction work and to design work (35·1).
- However, the Employer may assign the benefit of the contract without consent (35·2) and furthermore the contractor consents to the Employer assigning both the benefit and burden of the contract to the Funder (named in the Contract Particulars) at any time (35·3).
- Rights of third parties in general are excluded, but a Third Party Rights Schedule forms part of the contract, in respect of the Funder, and a Purchaser or Tenant (4 and 36·1).
- The contract has no provision for a conventional contract administrator and the terms are to be administered direct by the Employer and contractor respectively. However, the Employer is required to appoint an Employer's Representative who will exercise the powers and functions of the Employer under the contract (21·1).
- The Employer may appoint other advisers who, although assured of cooperation from the Contractor, have no authority under the contract to act for the Employer (21·2).
- Instructions from the Employer must be in writing and must be empowered under the contract. The contractor must comply with such instructions (8·1).
- Where the contractor fails to comply, then subject to seven days' notice in writing, the Employer may engage others to give effect to the instruction and the contractor is liable for the extra cost (8·3).
- Where an instruction gives rise to a Change, this may entitle the contractor to additional payment and an extension of time. However, not all instructions will be treated as giving rise to a Change, and where the contract states this, the contractor will not receive additional payment or time. This will not relieve the contractor of any obligations under the contract (8·2).
- The Employer may instruct the contractor to open up and test work and materials. If the findings show all to be in accordance with the contract, this will constitute a Change. If the work, materials, or goods are not in accordance with the contract, it will not be a Change (22·1).

JCT MP11

- Where work, materials or goods are not in accordance with the contract then the Employer may instruct their removal, or may allow them to remain but with a price reduction. The contractor will not be entitled to loss and/or expense or extension of time. The Employer may also instruct additional work necessary as a consequence, and may also instruct further opening up and testing relating to similar work materials or goods elsewhere (22·2). No such instructions shall be treated as a Change (22·3).
- During the 12 months following Practical Completion (termed the Rectification Period), the Employer may instruct the contractor to remedy any defect.
- Where the contractor does not remedy defects as instructed, then the Employer may engage others to give effect to the instruction (23·1).
- After expiry of the Rectification Period, and with all defects rectified, the Employer shall issue a certificate to that effect (23·2).
- Consultants may be pre-appointed by the Employer with the intention that the appointment will be novated to the Contractor, and full details of their original appointment and the proposed Model Form of Novation should be included in the Requirements. This also requires an appropriate entry in the Contract Particulars (24·1).
- The Model Form of Novation must be executed immediately upon entering into MP11 (24·2).
- The Employer may also require the contractor to appoint named specialists (that is, subcontractors or consultants) by including a name, or list of names from which the contractor may chose, in the Requirements. Such appointments may be in respect of design or carrying out of works (24·3).
- The contractor becomes solely responsible under the contract for services provided by any pre-appointed consultant, and work undertaken by named specialists (24·4).
- Payment to the contractor by the Employer depends upon the novation of pre-appointed consultants and the appointment of specialists being carried out in the manner required under the relevant contract clauses (24·5).
- Contracts with pre-appointed consultants or specialists may not be amended or terminated by the contractor without the prior written consent of the Employer (24·6 and 24·7).
- Either before or immediately following termination of such contracts, the contractor must notify the Employer of the proposed replacement, and the Employer has seven days in which to raise reasonable objection (24·8).
- The contractor remains fully liable under the contract for replacement consultants or specialists, and entirely responsible for any delay and additional cost incurred (24·10).

JCT MP11

5 Money

- The Contract Sum, VAT exclusive, is entered in the Contract Particulars (31·1).
- The Pricing Document identified in the Contract Particulars is part of the contract, and should contain the rules which will determine the method of payment, the Contract Sum Analysis, and pricing information such as rates, preliminaries, and overheads which can be used in the valuation of Changes.
- Changes are alterations in the Requirements or Proposals which affect either the substance or manner of what the contractor is to provide under the contract. As the contractor is responsible for all further design information, then excepting discrepancies and statutory requirements, Changes will be mainly due to variations required by the Employer.
- Each party is to notify immediately the other if it is considered that an instruction gives rise to a Change, or any event occurs which should be treated as giving rise to a Change (26·1).
- Valuation of a Change and any adjustment of the completion date may be by agreement, or by the Employer on the basis of a quotation provided by the Contractor, or, if no quotation is received or agreed, on a fair valuation basis. The valuation is to be inclusive of any loss and/or expense (26·3 to 26·6).
- No later than 42 days after practical completion of the Project the contractor may provide particulars of any further valuation in respect of any Change, and within 42 days of receipt of the particulars the Employer must review relevant previous valuations (26·9).
- Other factors which may result in adjustments to the Contract Sum include amendments to the Requirements and Proposals as suggested by the contractor which will be cost savings and value improvements resulting in a financial benefit to the Employer (25), and a bonus payable for early completion (20). The former will be the proportion of any benefit calculated as stated in the Contract Particulars, and the latter will be at the daily rate entered in the table in the Contract Particulars.
- The contractor has only limited rights to reimbursement of loss and/or expense outside the inclusive valuation of Changes. If the contractor wishes to claim, it must give timely notification and provide an assessment of the loss and/or expense with information updated as necessary. Within 14 days of receipt of information, the Employer must ascertain the amount and notify the Contractor. Payment will be included in the next payment advice. Any claim for further ascertainment must be made by the contractor within 42 days after practical completion of the Project, and the Employer must review these particulars and notify the contractor of any additional payment appropriate within a further 42 days (27).

JCT MP11

- Relevant deletions in the Contract Particulars will indicate whether the contractor is to receive payments under Rule A (interim valuation), Rule B (stage payment), Rule C (Progress Payments), or Rule D (some other method). These Rules are described in the Pricing Document. If no Rule is selected then A will apply.
- Where a contractor considers that he is due a payment on the due date for interim payments stated in the Contract Particulars, the contractor should make a detailed application for payment to the Employer not later than seven days before the due date, stating the sums he considers should be included under items in the Employer's payment advice, the amount he considers due as interim payment on the due date and the basis for calculation (28·1).
- Where the contractor makes an application for payment or the Employer considers that a repayment is due him, he shall issue an interim payment advice to the contractor not later than five days after the due date of payment except that where an interim payment due date is on or immediately after practical completion there shall be no need to issue a payment advice if the amount due either party is below the minimum stated in the Contract Particulars (28·2).
- Each interim advice is to state the amount due to the contractor (determined in accordance with the Pricing Document), the value of any Changes, the amount of any reductions, any amount due either party because of any circumstance in the contract, and the total payments that have previously been made. It should be noted that there is no provision for payment of unfixed materials or cost fluctuations, although these could be incorporated if desired (28·3). There is no express provision for retention.
- The final date where payment is due the contractor is 14 days from the due date or if later, seven days from the date of the receipt of the VAT invoice from the contractor. Where payment is due the Employer the final date for payment will be 14 days from the due date for payment (28·5).
- Unless a Pay Less Notice is issued, the Employer (or contractor where repayment is due the Employer) shall pay the amount stated on the payment advice on the final payment date. Where a payment advice had not been issued in accordance with clause 28·3, the Employer shall pay the amount stated as due in the contractor's payment application (28·6).
- The Employer is to issue a final payment advice, after the statements required to be issued at the completion of the rectification period by the contract have been issued. The final payment advice should state the amount the contractor is entitled to, stating the Contract Sum, the final amounts with regards to interim payments and deductions and any deductions that may be necessary under the statement issued at the conclusion of the rectification period. The final payment advice should state who a final payment is due to – the contractor or the Employer (28·7).

JCT MP11

- The final payment advice shall be final, binding both parties on all issues relating to the amount owed the contractor by the Employer, unless 28 days after it is issued, the contractor disputes any aspect of it by commencing an adjudication or litigation.
- The Employer or the contractor may pay an amount less than the total stated in the payment advice or in the circumstance where it applies, the payment application, if it serves the other party with a Pay Less Notice seven days before the final date of payment, stating the amount it considers due and the basis of its calculation (29).
- Where a Pay Less Notice is issued, the amount stated therein must be paid on the final payment date (29·2).
- If payment is not made in accordance with the contract, interest of 5 per cent over base rate will become payable on outstanding amounts (30·1).

5 Statutory obligations

- Statutory requirements are defined as Acts of Parliament, local authority and statutory undertaker's regulations and byelaws, and any directive of the European Community having the force of law (1).
- The contractor is to comply with all statutory requirements and warrants that the design of the Project (except for that contained in the Requirements) complies with statutory requirements (9·1 and 11·2).
- The contractor is to make any applications and give any notices required by statute and will pass copies of relevant documents to the Employer (9·1).
- Unless the Requirements state that specific fees and charges are the responsibility of the Employer, the contractor will pay all fees or charges in connection with statutory requirements (9·2).
- Changes in statutory obligations that arise after the Base Date and were not previously announced must be taken into account and will be treated as giving rise to a Change (10·5).
- The contractor is appointed as both CDM Coordinator and Principal Contractor for the purposes of the CDM Regulations (1·2). The Contractor is also appointed the Principal Contractor for the purposes of the SWMP Regulations. The Contract Particulars also allow for the name of a CDM Coordinator previously appointed by the Employer to be entered, and if this person is to be retained then the contract would need amending (7·2).

6 Insurance

- The contractor indemnifies the Employer in respect of personal injury or death and damage to property other than the Project, always assuming that these arise in the course of carrying out the Project and are not due to some act or neglect for which the Employer has responsibility (32·1).

JCT MP11

- The Employer indemnifies the contractor against expense, liability, loss, claim or proceedings arising under statute or common law in respect of personal injury or death and damage to property other than the Project, always assuming that these arise in the course of carrying out the Project and are due to some act or neglect for which the Employer has responsibility (32·2).
- The contractor liabilities in 32·1 are limited to issues not included in the expected risks and he is not expected to provide an insurance for those matters, save for terrorism cover as required under 33.
- Most major projects are likely to need bespoke insurance arrangements and this contract requires the relevant documents to be attached with details identified in the Contract Particulars (33·1).
- Either party may be required to provide and maintain cover, and the other party may request documentary evidence (33·2). Failure to provide satisfactory evidence within seven days will allow the other party to take out insurance and recover the costs involved (33·3).
- Where compliance with the Joint Fire Code is a contract provision and the insurer requires remedial measures, the contractor must implement these and this is not treated as giving rise to a Change (33·1).
- Where the insurance for the site and materials excludes terrorism, the party responsible for maintaining such insurance shall take out and maintain terrorism cover. Where cover against terrorism is required but ceases to be available, the party responsible for that insurance must notify the other party (33·7). The risk then rests with the Employer (33·8).
- Where professional indemnity insurance is required, a relevant deletion is required in the Contract Particulars, and the limit of indemnity is to be entered. The contractor may be required to take out and maintain cover until 12 years from the date of practical completion of the Project, always assuming that cover remains available at commercially reasonable rates (34·2).

7 Termination

- The Employer may, by issuing a further notice, terminate the employment of the contractor if, after having given the contractor 14 days' notice of a material breach, the contractor has failed to remedy the breach (38·1 and 38·2). The contractor's employment may also be terminated in the event that the contractor becomes insolvent (38·3).
- Material breach by the contractor is defined, and includes failure to proceed regularly and diligently, failure to comply with an instruction, suspension of the Project, breach of the CDM Regulations, breach of provisions relating to named specialists or pre-appointed consultants (1).

JCT MP11

- Upon termination, the contractor must provide the Employer with all design documents, and must not remove any materials, plant or equipment from site without permission. The Employer may then make appropriate arrangements to complete the Project (38·4). Only when the Project has been completed or, if no other arrangements for completion have been made, within six months of termination, must the Employer issue a payment advice (38·5 and 38·7).
- The contractor may, by issuing a further notice, terminate its employment if, after having given the Employer 14 days notice of a material breach, the Employer has failed to remedy the breach (39·1 and 39·2). The contractor may also terminate its employment in the event that the Employer becomes insolvent (39·3).
- Material breach by the Employer is defined, and is confined to failure to issue a payment advice in accordance with the contract (1).
- Upon termination, the contractor must remove all his or her materials, plant or equipment from site without delay, and prepare an account of amounts due (39·4).
- Either party may terminate the contractor's employment if the Project is substantially suspended for the period stated in the Contract Particulars due to causes which include force majeure, specified peril, civil commotion, and terrorism (40·1).
- Upon termination the contractor must provide the Employer with all design documents, remove all materials, plant or equipment from site without delay, and prepare an account of amounts due (40·4).

8 Miscellaneous

- Definitions and meanings are fully tabled. Note in particular Design Documents, Model Form, practical completion, Requirements and Proposals (1).
- Rules for interpretation are set out, including a gender bias clause, and that a 'person' refers to an individual, firm, partnership, company, and any other body corporate (2).
- The contractor is given access (not exclusive possession) to the site or parts of the site, which leaves the Employer free to have work undertaken by others at the same time as the Project (15·1).
- Ground conditions or man-made obstructions encountered by the contractor will only give rise to a Change where they could not have been foreseen (14·2).
- Copyright in all design documents prepared by the contractor remains vested in the contractor and the Employer is given an irrevocable licence to use them for the purposes of the Project. Where the contractor does not own the copyright in any design document it shall procure a licence from the copyright holder (13·1 and 13·2).

JCT MP11

- The stated period in which acts are to be done will commence immediately after the specified date. Christmas Day, Good Friday and bank holidays are excepted (3).
- All communications between the parties relating to the contract are to be in writing, or may be made electronically by the procedures specified in the Contract Particulars (5·1). Any notice under the Third Party Rights Schedule or relating to termination must be given by actual delivery, registered post or recorded delivery (5·2).

9 Disputes

- Disputes or differences between the parties in relation to the Project (note not simply the customary 'arising under this contract') may be submitted to mediation if the parties agree, or referred to adjudication in accordance with the provisions of the relevant Scheme for Construction Contracts (41–43).
- Although the contract states that the objective of mediation should be to reach a binding agreement, the only final resolution of disputes would appear to be by legal proceedings. There is no provision for arbitration.
- The law of the contract is to be the law of England (6).

JCT MP11

This contract?

If considering using MP11 remember that:

It is intended for use where both the Employer and the Contractor, together with their respective teams of specialists and sub-contractors, are experienced in substantial commercial projects. The Employer is required to appoint a Representative who will exercise all the powers and functions of the Employer under the contract. Other advisers may be appointed but they will have no authority under the contract to act on behalf of the Employer.

The Requirements and the Proposals are at the heart of this contract, and it is important that both are full and explicit. There is no prescribed format but it should be remembered that this contract is very reliant on the Requirements stating clearly what is to be delivered, and the manner of delivery. Specific points which may be considered for inclusion are helpfully listed in the JCT Guide for this contract.

The contract provides for design by the Employer as shown and described in the Requirements, with further design by the Contractor. The Requirements may stipulate that the contractor engages consultants pre-appointed by the Employer under a novation agreement. The JCT Guide lists some of the matters which need to be covered in the novation agreement, which should become part of the Requirements (the parties may wish to consider using the CIC Novation Agreement). Normally design liability is that of reasonable care and skill, but the Requirements could include a fitness for purpose obligation although there might be practical difficulties. (This might be an important matter in the case of PFI projects.)

Completing the Contract Particulars requires entries on matters such as the Contract Sum, Requirements, Proposals, Pricing Document, names of Planning Supervisor, Funder, adjudicator, entries relating to the application of option clauses such as those for ground conditions, liquidated damages, bonus rates, pre-appointed consultants and named specialists, cost savings, payments, insurances, professional indemnity, and communications.

This is a form which is simpler and shorter than either SBC11 or DB11, and which can be tailored to the needs of the project. However, it should be approached carefully, because although the openness and apparent brevity of the Conditions is admirable, professional and sometimes legal advice might be advisable to produce a reasonably balanced set of documents. The contractor assumes more risks and responsibilities than under other JCT forms of contract, but provided that the risks can be fully identified and priced for at tender stage, this should not present a problem for experienced operators.

JCT MP11

Related matters

Documents

JCT Major Project Construction Contract 2011
JCT Major Project Sub-Contract 2011

References

JCT Major Project Construction Contract Guide

Commentaries

Note: these relate to the previous edition of the form.

Sarah Lupton
Guide to MPF03
RIBA Enterprises (2003)

Neil F. Jones
The JCT Major Project Form
Blackwell Publishing (2004)

JCT SBC11

The Joint Contracts Tribunal Ltd

Standard Building Contract 2011

Background

The original agreed Standard Form was published in 1909 and was known as the RIBA Form. In many respects the JCT Standard Building Contract 2011 edition (SBC11) is a direct descendant through a series of editions published in 1931, 1939, 1963, 1980, 1998 and 2005, although now the publication is the responsibility of The Joint Contracts Tribunal Ltd (JCT).

JCT80 was drafted to overcome various deficiencies which had appeared over time in the 1963 Edition, and in response to recommendations in the Banwell Report – in particular those relating to the treatment of sub-contractors. At the time it was felt that JCT80 had struck a fair balance between the interests of the contracting parties and others involved. Initially concern was expressed by some who saw the form as being much longer than its predecessor and more demanding to administer, yet it quickly gained acceptance as the form to be used for major building projects in the UK. Supplements were soon available to cater for contractor's design and, sectional completion, together with documentation for nominating sub-contractors and suppliers.

JCT80 was subject to 18 amendments, the last of which was an attempt to meet many of the recommendations in the Latham Report of 1994, and to ensure compliance with Part II of the Housing Grants, Construction and Regeneration Act 1996 in respect of adjudication and payment provisions. The 1998 Edition of the Standard Form was basically a consolidated version of JCT80 which subsequently received five amendments.

SBC05 constituted a radical overhaul of the form, in format, layout, language and content. The clauses have been re-grouped and re-numbered, and the language has been clarified throughout. The provisions of the Sectional Completion Supplement and the Contractor's Design Portion Supplement have been incorporated in the form, as have the fluctuations provisions. The nominated sub-contractor provisions and the performance specified work provisions have been omitted. The form contains a new design documents submission procedure, and provisions for Third Party Rights and warranties. For a full analysis of the changes see the references at the end of this section.

SBC11 primarily brings the contract up to date with the amendments of the HGCR Act 1996. The major changes relate to payment and payment notices and also changes in the insurance section to cover the provisions for terrorism insurance.

JCT SBC11

Nature

SBC11 runs to over 100 pages. The Articles of Agreement include Recitals, Articles, Contract Particulars (to be completed by the parties) and an Attestation. The numbering of Recitals and Articles may vary depending on the particular edition of SBC11, and if incorporating any separate amendments great care needs to be taken to achieve consistency.

The Conditions are set out in nine Sections. Section 1 deals with definitions and interpretation of the form. Section 2 sets out the contractor's general obligations, including its obligations with respect to programming, and the provisions for adjusting the completion date. Section 3 covers the control of the Works, including the giving of instructions. Sections 4 and 5 deal with valuation and payment, Section 6 with insurance, Section 7 with assignment and Third Party Rights, Section 8 with termination, and Section 9 with dispute resolution. Seven Schedules are included at the back of the form, which cover such matters as the design submission procedure, insurance options, bonds and fluctuations.

Obviously such a contract is not an 'easy read' and the number of options need to be considered with great care. For example, the Contract Particulars require very careful consideration of whether certain clauses come into the applies/does not apply category. Many of the clauses include not only legal conditions but also detailed procedures and rules. Some of these, especially those concerning extending time or payment, might appear to be arduous but they are intended to secure sound practice and should be followed meticulously.

Despite its length and complexity, SBC11 is basically simple in its overall structure, logical in its layout, with the grouping of some material under schedules, makes it easier to navigate.

Use

The form is published in three versions for use with quantities, without quantities, or with approximate quantities.

The With Quantities version should only be used where the Employer, through its professional consultants, has provided at the time of tender a full set of drawings and bills of quantities. An Information Release Schedule is part of the documentation in an attempt to identify responsibility for any further information which might be necessary to amplify the contract during the carrying out of the Works.

The Without Quantities version also requires preparation of a full set of drawings to be accompanied either by a Specification or Schedules of Work. In order to give valuation of variations and fluctuations a substantive basis the contractor is also required to submit a Schedule of Rates or a Contract Sum Analysis; this should be provided, and the measure of detail required of the contractor is often stipulated at tender stage by the Employer.

JCT SBC11

All three versions now incorporate sectional completion and a Contractor's Designed Portion, both optional provisions. The first allows for phased commencement and completion of the Works, and for setting separate rates for liquidated damages for each section. The second allows for the contractor to design an identified part or parts of the Works, and includes a new procedure for submitting its developing design information for comment. The parties should be careful to set out any requirements as to scope, format and timing of such submissions in the Contract Particulars.

In response to the Employer's Requirements the contractor is obliged to supply Contractor's Proposals and a CDP Analysis for that part of the Contract Sum which relates to the Contractor's Designed Portion. The latter will assist the valuation of variations.

SBC11 requires the appointment of a person to give effect to the various contract terms. The Employer will usually appoint an architect or a contract administrator to this role, and such a person will be regarded as independent and impartial. SBC11 also provides for the Employer to appoint an 'Employer's Representative' to act on behalf of the Employer. A footnote in the contract emphasises the fundamental difference in the roles.

Synopsis

1 Intentions

- The contractor is obliged to carry out and complete the Works in accordance with the Contract Documents, the Health and Safety Plan and Statutory Requirements (2·1).
- The contractor must complete the design of any Contractor's Designed Portion, and comply with all instructions of the Architect relating to the integration of the Portion with the rest of the Works (2·2). The contractor's liability for design is limited to the use of reasonable skill and care of an architect or other professional person.
- Materials, goods and workmanship are to be to the standard set out in the bills, Employer's Requirements or Contractor's Proposals as relevant. If stated to be to the Architect's satisfaction, they are to be to the Architect's reasonable satisfaction. Where no standard is set out, they are to be a standard appropriate to the Works (2·3).
- The Architect has power to issue directions to the contractor to make certain that the Designed Portion can be integrated into the design of the Works as a whole (2·2·2).
- The contractor's liability for design is limited to exercising reasonable care and skill (2·19·1). However, where the contract is for housing work which is subject to the terms of the Defective Premises Act 1972, then this limit of liability might not apply.
- Where the contractor is of the opinion that an instruction issued by the Architect/Contract Administrator will affect the efficacy of the Contractor's Designed Portion, the contractor is to notify the Architect/Contract Administrator within seven days of receipt of that instruction, specifying the injurious effect it might have. Such instruction by the Architect/Contract Administrator shall be of no effect unless confirmed by the Architect/Contract Administrator (3·10·3).

JCT SBC11

- The Contract Documents are to be read as a whole and the printed Articles, Conditions and Appendix have precedence (1·3).
- In the case of discrepancies in or divergences between documents corrective instructions must be given (2·15).
- The provision for dealing with a discrepancy or divergence include the Employer's Requirements, the Contractor's Proposals and the Analysis.
- Except where the contractor fails to notify a divergence of which it has become aware between the Contract Documents and statutory provisions as provided under clause 2·17, the contractor shall not be liable for the contents of the Employer's requirement or for verifying the adequacy of the design contained in them (2·13).
- The contractor must be provided with two copies of the information referred to in the Information Release Schedule by the stated times (2·11). The contractor must also be provided with such further drawings or details which are reasonably necessary (2·12). The contractor must keep on site two copies of all documents issued (2·8·3).
- The contractor is required to submit drawings and other documents it prepares in relation to the design (the 'Contractor's Design Documents'), as set out in the Contract Documents, or as reasonably necessary. The submission is to follow a procedure set out in Schedule 1 (2·9·4 and 2·9·5).
- The Employer is to respond by returning the design documents marked either 'A Action', 'B Action' or 'C Action' within 14 days of the receipt of the Contractor's Design Documents or (if later) within 14 days from either the date or expiry of the period for submission of such designs stated in the contract. The contractor is to execute work marked 'A Action' or 'B Action', in the case of the latter it must incorporate comments by the Employer. The contractor must revise drawings marked 'C Action and return for approval before executing any work' (Schedule 1).
- Where the Architect/Contract Administrator fails to respond in time it shall be regarded that the document has been marked A (Schedule 1:3). However neither compliance with the submission procedure nor carrying out the Architect/Contract Administrator's instructions relieves the contractor of his duty to ensure that the Contractor's Designed Portions comply with the Contract (Schedule 1- 8:3).
- The contractor is to supply copies of his master programme as soon as possible (2·9·1·2). (Many architects require a preliminary draft with the tenders.)
- The CDM Regulations oblige the Employer to nominate a CDM Coordinator and where relevant a Principal Contractor. This is also a contractual duty (3·23) and any need to appoint a replacement is also covered (3·24).

JCT SBC11

2 Time

- Dates for possession and completion should be entered in the Contract Particulars. There is provision for dividing the Works into Sections, and setting separate commencement and completion dates, and rates of liquidated damages for each section. All provisions relating to timing, for example extending the date for completion, apply separately to each section, except that there is only one Final Certificate.
- The contractor must proceed regularly and diligently and complete on or before completion date (2·4). Early completion is an option for the contractor and, if achieved, issue of the Practical Completion Certificate cannot be delayed. Conversely, the Employer is not obliged to assist the contractor in attempts to complete early.
- An option clause for deferment of possession not exceeding six weeks may apply, subject to an Appendix entry (2·5).
- Notice of delay must be given in writing by the Contractor, together with supporting information including its estimate of the likely effect on completion (2·27·1). The Architect is required to consider a new completion date, and to notify the contractor of his or her decision within 12 weeks (2·28·2). Thirteen 'relevant events' are listed which are grounds for an extension of time (2·29) the most recent of which relates to any impediment, prevention or default by the Employer. The interim decision is subject to review by the Architect no later than 12 weeks following practical completion. Whilst it is possible to reduce extensions already awarded, the original contract period cannot be reduced and there is no provision for accelerating progress, except by agreement. The procedures for dealing with delay and extensions of time are detailed and need to be followed with care.
- No extension of time is empowered because of delays arising out of design information to be provided by the contractor (2·20).
- Failure by the contractor to complete within the contract period is certified as a fact by the Architect (2·31) and liquidated damages may be deducted or otherwise recovered by the Employer (2·32). The Employer is obliged to give notice in writing beforehand.
- Practical completion is certified by the Architect (2·30).
- After this, the contractor is obliged to rectify defects (2·38) unless the Employer decides otherwise and agrees an appropriate deduction instead.
- There is provision for partial possession (2·33), and where the Employer wants to use part of the uncompleted works for storage, etc., this is possible subject to proper insurance arrangements (2·6·1).

3 Control

- The bar to assignment without written consent refers to 'the contract, or any rights thereunder' (7·1).

JCT SBC11

- The contract provides for Third Party Rights to be assigned to purchasers/tenants and funders. The requirement to grant third party rights to identified persons, together with information regarding limits to the contractor's liability, must be set out in the Contract Particulars. The rights are set out in Schedule 5.
- The contract provides for collateral warranties to be provided by the contractor to funders and purchasers/tenants, and by sub-contractors to the purchasers/tenants funders, and the Employer. The requirement to enter into warranties must be set out in the Contract Particulars, the relevant persons and sub-contractors identified, together with information regarding limits to the contractor's liability.
- The warranties to purchaser, funder and tenant are to be on the JCT standard forms CWa/P&T, CWa/F, SCWa/F and SCWa/P&T. The JCT also publish SCWa/E for use in relation to the Employer, although this is not referred to in the form.
- Sub-contracting any part of the work, including any design requires the Architect's written consent (3·7·1), and the contractor is responsible for the performance of all sub-contractors. It is a condition of any sub-letting that the sub-contract shall contain certain provisions (3·9).
- The contractor may sub-let to persons named in a list included in or annexed to the Contract Bills. There must be not less than three firms 'able and willing' to carry out the specified sub-contract work at the required time (3·8). Architects who use this might consider whether they require the contractor to indicate choice at the time of submitting its tender, in order to discourage so-called 'Dutch' auctioning.
- Visits, inspections, etc. by the Architect or clerk of works do not in any way diminish or affect the contractor's responsibility to carry out the Works in accordance with the Contract Documents (3·6).
- Architect's instructions must be in writing, although this can mean written confirmation of oral instructions (3·12). The contract clearly defines what instructions are empowered, and these may include variations (3·14), postponement of work (3·15) and expenditure of provisional sums (3·16).
- The contractor is required to have a competent person-in-charge on the site full time (3·2), and to permit the presence of the Employer's clerk of works. The clerk of works is solely an inspector, although he or she can issue directions which require confirmation by the Architect (3·4).
- Where work or materials do not comply with the contract, the Architect can order their removal from the site (3·18·1). Where, after consultation, it is agreed that non-conforming work should remain (3·18·2), then the Employer is entitled to an appropriate deduction. The Architect is empowered to order tests and inspection, and the likelihood of any non-compliance in similar work elsewhere is covered (13·18·4 and Schedule 4).

JCT SBC11

- The contract requires all work to be carried out in a proper and workmanlike manner, and in accordance with the Health and Safety Plan (2·1). In the event of failure to comply, and although this might under other circumstances be interference with the contractor's working methods, the Architect is empowered to issue instructions (3·19).
- The contract does allow for work under the direct control of the Employer to be carried out during the time that the contractor is in possession (2·7).

4 Money

- The Contract Sum is VAT exclusive (4·6) and may only be adjusted as provided for in the Conditions (4·2).
- The Conditions provide for the contractor to at least recover increases in taxes, including landfill tax, levies or contributions promulgated after the date of tender (Schedule 7, Option A). Increases in the cost of labour and materials may be recovered as net increases (Schedule 7, Option B) or in accordance with Formula Rules (Schedule 7, Option C), if either of these options is selected in the Contract Particulars.
- Where provisional sums have been included, instructions must be given to the contractor (3·16). The valuation of work carried out where an approximate quantity is included, or where provisional sums are included, or where a variation has been ordered, is to be by agreement or by the quantity surveyor's application of the valuation rules (5·2·1).
- In addition, the contractor may be invited to submit a 'Schedule 2 Quotation' for work which is the subject of an architect's instruction. Such a quotation, if accepted, would bind the contractor to the direct cost of work, the time implications and any loss and/or expense which might apply. The work would not be carried out on this basis unless a confirmed acceptance was issued. In the event that the quotation is not accepted, an instruction may still be issued to proceed with the work, but it will then be subject to the valuation rules and procedures (5·6·1).
- If the Architect issues a variation on work which is part of the Contractor's Designed Portion, then this is a modification of the Employer's Requirements and will be valued as such.
- The contractor must make written application for reimbursement of loss and/or expense. The grounds for any valid application are set out (4·24) and include only matters over which the contractor has no control and which occur because of action or failure by the Employer. The procedures should be followed precisely, and the contractor's proper written notice and supporting information is a requirement (4·23).
- SBC11 allows for advance payment of the contractor (4·8, an entry is required in the Contract Particulars) and this might be subject to an advance payment bond (Part 1, Schedule 6). The sum is to be reimbursed to the Employer in agreed amounts and at agreed times.

JCT SBC11

- Interim payments are made to the contractor following the issue of an Interim Certificate by the Architect. Up to practical completion the due dates for interim payment shall be at monthly dates stated in the Contract Particulars. After practical completion the due date shall be stated at an interval of two months (4·9).
- Interim valuations will be made by the quantity surveyor (4·11). However the contractor may, not less than seven days before the due date, make an interim application to the quantity surveyor, stating the sum it considers due him at the relevant due date and the basis on which the sum was calculated (4·11).
- Not later than five days after each due date the Architect/Contract Administrator shall issue an Interim Certificate stating the sum that he considers due to the contractor on the due date and the basis for its calculation (4·10).
- The Interim Certificate is to be prepared in accordance with clause 4·9·2 and should include any amount deducted as retention, cumulative total of any advance payments that have become due for reimbursement in accordance with the Contract Particulars, sums stated in previous Interim Certificates and any sums paid in respect of payment notices.
- The final date for payment is 14 days from its due date. The sum to be paid, subject to a Pay Less Notice, shall be the sums stated on the interim payment certificate (4·12).
- Where an interim payment certificate has not been issued in accordance with the contract, and if an application for payment had been made by the contractor in accordance with clause 4·11, the application of payment shall become an Interim Payment Notice, and the Employer unless it issues a valid Pay Less Notice, will be liable to pay the sums stated on such Interim Payment Notice (4·12·3).
- Where the Contractor had not made an interim payment application, it may at any time after the expiry of the five day period for the issuance of an interim payment certificate, give an Interim Payment Notice to the quantity surveyor, stating the sum the contractor believes is due on the relevant payment due date and the basis of the calculation (4·11·2·2). In such circumstances, the final date of payment shall be postponed by the same number of days as the number of days after the expiry of the five day period that the Payment Notice was issued.
- Where the Employer intends to pay less than the amount stated in the interim payment certificate or the Interim Payment Notice, it shall not later than five days before the final date of payment issue a Pay Less Notice, stating the amount it considers due and the basis of the calculation.
- Failure to pay by the final date for payment will attract a simple interest of 5 per cent over current base rate, and also gives the contractor a right to suspend some or all of the work (Section 1 – Definitions and 4·12·6).

JCT SBC11

- Where the traditional operating of retention is to apply, in preference to any form of bonding (4·19), then this will apply to all Interim Certificates (4·16). Half the retention amount will be released at practical completion.
- There are precise procedures to be followed in the preparation of the final account after practical completion (4·5). Issue of the Final Certificate is within two months of the last occurring of: the end of the Rectification Period, the date of issue of the Certificate of Making Good clause 2·39, or the date of sending the final statement of any ascertainment in accordance with clause 4·5·2. Similar rules apply to the Final Certificate with regard to notices, as those outlined above for Interim Certificates, except that the final date for payment is 28 days from the date of the certificate and the due date is the date of issue of the certificate.
- The Final Certificate of the Architect is only conclusive of certain matters as set out in clause 1·10, and is not conclusive that the Works have been carried out in accordance with the Contract (1·10·1·1).

5 Statutory obligations

- It is the contractor's duty to comply with all statutory obligations and give all required notices (2·1). The contractor is entitled to recover fees and charges not otherwise provided for (2·21).
- The contractor is to notify the Architect if it finds any conflict between statutory requirements and the Contract Documents (2·17·1). The Architect must issue an instruction and the contractor is thereafter not liable to the Employer under the contract for any non-compliance with statutory requirements resulting from the instruction (2·17·3).
- If divergences between statutory requirements and documents relating to the Contractor's Designed Portion are discovered, the contractor is to propose the necessary amendments, to be at its own cost unless one of the 2·17·2 exception applies.
- The contractor is empowered to carry out limited work for emergency compliance and this will be treated as a variation to be valued accordingly (2·18).
- The contractor is contractually obliged to comply with the CDM Regulations and particularly, where the project is notifiable, to comply with duties in relation to the Construction Phase Plan and the health and safety file (3·23).

6 Insurance

- What a particular contract includes will depend to a large extent on entries in the Contract Particulars (for example, whether option clauses are to apply, the minimum amount of cover required, etc·). The Architect may be obliged to issue instructions, call for documentary evidence, and pass to the Employer for checking.

JCT SBC11

- The contractor indemnifies the Employer in respect of personal injury or death (6·1), and injury or damage to property other than the actual works (6·2). This is to be backed by insurance (6·4) and the minimum amount of cover required is entered in the Contract Particulars.
- If instructed, the contractor is to take out joint names insurance for the Employer against the risk of claims arising due to legal nuisance. There is a list of exceptions, and damage must not be attributable to any negligence by the Contractor. An entry will indicate whether cover may be required (6·5), and the amount of cover to be provided.
- Insurance of 'the Works' is for all risks where new buildings are concerned and should be for full reinstatement value. It can be taken out either by the contractor (Schedule 3, Option A) or by the Employer (Schedule 3, Option B). Normally it is better to leave any risk with the contractor under Option A, since restoration under Option B is treated as variation work and will be valued accordingly.
- Insurance of existing structures and the contents is a matter for the Employer (Schedule 3, Option C) and is limited to specified perils. New work in existing buildings, although still a matter for the Employer, requires all risks cover.
- The contractor is required to carry professional indemnity insurance to cover its liability for design, details of which should be set out in the Contract Particulars.
- The contractor's liability for consequential loss arising due to design errors not covered by liquidated damages may be limited to a figure entered in the Contract Particulars.
- An entry in the Contract Particulars will show whether the Joint Code of Practice on the Protection from Fire of Construction Sites is to apply (6·13) and if so, both employer and contractor must comply with it. In the event of non-compliance, the insurers can specify remedial measures which must be undertaken. In the event that terrorism cover is withdrawn and is no longer available, the situation and options open to the Employer are dealt with in clause 6·10 as applicable.
- It is expected that where any act of terrorism has not been adequately covered under existing insurance policies, the party indicated as responsible for maintaining such policies, shall from time to time take out and maintain the appropriate insurance cover for terrorism. The contract points to the Pool Re Cover or such other successive schemes as appropriate avenues for such polices to be obtained.

7 Termination

- The Employer is allowed to terminate the employment of the contractor by reason of specified defaults (8·4). A warning notice may be issued by the Architect, but the notice of termination is a matter for the Employer. In the case of insolvency of the Contractor, depending on the circumstances, the Employer might enter into an agreement with the contractor for continuation or novation.

JCT SBC11

- If no such agreement is reached, and in all other cases, the Employer may have the Works completed by another contractor (8·7), or to decide not to have the Works carried out and completed at all after determination of the contractor's employment (8·8).
- The contractor is allowed to terminate its own employment for specified defaults by the Employer (8·9). Again, the procedures must be followed meticulously. In the event of insolvency of the Employer, the contractor may elect to terminate its own employment.
- Either party can terminate the employment of the contractor for listed neutral causes (8·11).
- The respective rights and duties of the parties concerning payment, removal and completion are set out (8·7 or 8·12).

8 Miscellaneous

- A list of definitions relevant to SBC11 is included (1·1). Rules for interpretation are set out, including a gender bias clause, and that a 'person' refers to an individual, firm, partnership, company, and any other body corporate (1·4).
- There is a contracting out of third party rights under the Contracts (Rights of Third Parties) Act 1999 (1·6).
- Access for the Architect is covered (3·1) but this might be subject to reasonable restrictions as far as workshops are concerned.
- The Architect has power to order the exclusion of persons from the Works (3·21).
- Where progress is disturbed because of the discovery of antiquities, the contractor is obliged to inform the Architect and to take all necessary action to preserve the status quo and avoid disturbance (3·22). The Architect must issue instructions, and the contractor is entitled to ascertained loss and/or expense (3·24).

9 Disputes

- Part II of the Housing Grants' Construction and Regeneration Act 1996 as amended gives either party a statutory right to refer any difference or dispute arising out of the contract to adjudication. Article 7 of SBC11 provides for this.
- The procedure for adjudication is as set out in the Scheme for Construction Contracts, subject to some limited provisions regarding the appointment of the adjudicator (9·2).
- The adjudicator's decision is binding on the parties at least until the dispute is finally determined at arbitration or by legal proceedings.

JCT SBC11

- Article 8 establishes arbitration as an agreed method of resolving disputes, provided the Contract Particulars indicate that Article 8 and clauses 9·3 to 9·8 are to apply.
- The appointment of the arbitrator is subject to an entry in the Contract Particulars, and his or her powers are defined (9·5).
- The parties agree that either may apply to the courts on a question of law (9·7).
- Arbitration is to be conducted in accordance with the JCT 2005 edition of the Construction Industry Model Arbitration Rules (9·3), and the provisions of the Arbitration Act 1996 shall apply (9·8).
- Where the Contract Particulars do not indicate that Article 8 is to apply, then any dispute or difference is to be determined by legal proceedings.

JCT SBC11

This contract?

If considering using SBC11 remember that:

It is intended for substantial lump sum contracts and is available for use with or without quantities. Work needs to be fully documented at tender stage, and is for completion within a stated period. The contractor may be required to design an identified part of the Works, in which case it must be provided with detailed Employer's Requirements at tender stage. Otherwise, the contractor is to be provided with fully detailed design information, ideally at tender stage, as any information provided later may give rise to claims. The Employer is required to appoint a contract administrator and a quantity surveyor.

If used for work in Northern Ireland an Adaptation Schedule should be incorporated, while for work in Scotland the Scottish Building Contract version of the form should be used.

Amendments are issued by the JCT from time to time. The form is available both in print and digitally. RIBA Enterprises publishes contract administration forms and contract administration software for SBC11.

It can include partial possession, and sectional completion. The completion date may be subject to adjustment if delays are caused by a range on 'neutral events', as well as by events which are the responsibility of the Employer.

It allows for sub-contractors to be chosen by the contractor from a list of not less than three names. The JCT has also published a Named Specialist update to be used with the contract.

When completing the form, entries are required relating to decisions on matters including deferment of possession; bonds (whether in lieu of retention, advance payment or 'listed items'); insurance of the Works; Joint Fire Code; liquidated damages; advance payment; fluctuations; and electronic communications.

If acting as contract administrator note that SBC11 requires a comprehensive understanding of its procedural rules, many of which are detailed and likely to prove time-consuming.

SBC11 places more risk on the Employer than some other standard forms, for example MP11 or GC/Works/1. The sometimes lengthy provisions are not always easy to grasp, although the latest edition has gone a long way towards improving its clarity and ease of use. The form is supported by a considerable body of case law, and many helpful commentaries and guides. It is still probably the most widely used form for major building work.

JCT SBC11

Related matters

References

Standard Building Contract With Quantities
Standard Building Contract Without Quantities
Standard Building Sub-contract Agreement
Standard Building Sub-contract Conditions
Standard Building Sub-contract with sub-contractor's design Agreement
Standard Building Sub-contract with sub-contractor's design Conditions
Contractor Collateral Warranty for a Funder
Contractor Collateral Warranty for a Purchaser or Tenant
Sub-contractor Collateral Warranty for a Funder
Sub-contractor Collateral Warranty for a Purchaser or Tenant
Sub-contractor Collateral Warranty for Employer

References

Standard Building Contract Guide
Standard Building Sub-contract Guide
JCT Practice Note: Deciding on the Appropriate JCT Form of Contract (2011) download from www.jctltd.co.uk

Commentaries

Sarah Lupton
Guide to SBC11
RIBA Publishing (2011)

David Chappell
SBC11 Contract Administration Guide
RIBA Publishing (2011)

JCT CE 2011

The Joint Contracts Tribunal Ltd

JCT Constructing Excellence Contract (CE 2011)

Background

With the emphasis being placed on collaborative working following the various industry reports highlighted in earlier chapters, JCT undertook a study of the partnering/ collaboration concept and in its Practice Note 4 (series 2) communicated its desire to develop an entirely new form of contract that would proactively encourage parties to collaborate.

The JCT Constructing Excellence Contract is JCT's response to the move towards collaborative contracts. The contract drafting process included the formation of a working group between JCT and Be (one of the industry groups formed as a result of the Latham and Egan Reports) and continued with the Constructing Excellence Group following Be's incorporation into that group. This contract is the result of these joint efforts. The guide to CE 2011 makes the point that in developing the terms of the contract, the interests of public sector clients were particularly considered.

This contract has been placed in this section to highlight the fact that it is intended to be a major contract, although it is sufficiently flexible to be an appropriate contract for engagement of the entire project team. The contract may be administered as a major lump sum contract using its Contract Sum provision.

The 2011 edition of CE builds on the 2006 edition and brings it up to date with current legislation. In particular it amends the payment and payment notices provisions, and modifies the professional indemnity insurance requirements, as well as offering a revised definition of insolvency.

Nature

The contract is one of the shorter contracts in the JCT suite numbering 64 pages. It has 12 sections. It commences with the Contract Particulars, Definitions and Interpretation through to Dispute Resolution and Supplementary Conditions. Its detailed Contract Particulars section requires more input from the parties than the usual JCT Standard Building Contract. The parties to the agreement are also referred to as Supplier and Purchaser.

The JCT Constructing Excellence Contract encourages collaborative behaviour by parties to the contract. It also includes an optional multi-party Project Team agreement which pushes the collective approach towards the entire Project Team. Arguably this

JCT CE 2011

contract's strongest provision is its Risks Allocation Schedule, which encourages the proactive management of risks. As should be expected for this type of contract, the attestation envisages that parties would be companies, however the footnotes provide guidance on alternative provisions if the parties are not corporate organisations or where parties are incorporated outside England and Wales.

Use

The unique feature of this contract is that it is intended to be used for the engagement of all members of a supply chain including consultants. Its flexibility means the same conditions may be used as a main construction contract, a sub-contract, or as conditions for the appointment of a consultant. It achieves this by means of optional clauses in the conditions and by using the Contract Particulars to determine the particular appointment being made. This is facilitated by the use of the term Purchaser (as a replacement for an Employer) and Supplier (replacing Contractor in more traditional contracts). The contract provides for two options in managing payments under it – Target Sum and Contract Sum. There is no provision for matters to be referred to arbitration; all disputes are to be settled by adjudication and failing that by litigation under the jurisdiction of English courts. If the intention is to use the contract outside England and Wales some amendments are required.

Synopsis

Intention

- The Purchaser and the Supplier are to operate the contract in collaboration, working together in good faith and in the spirit of trust and respect. In particular, the open sharing of information and feedback on performance, drawing attention to difficulties, will be pursued. This is to serve as the overriding principle of the contract (2·1). This overriding principle is to be given legal effect in any forum for dispute resolution of matters arising from the contract (2·9).
- In section 1 Contract Particulars the parties are expected to set out the general description of the services (a more detailed description is to be provided in section 3) and also an indication of whether the Supplier is retained as Professional Consultant (in which case certain listed clauses in the contract would not apply).
- Part 3 of the Contract Particulars is to be used to describe the service to be provided by the Supplier under the contract. Parties are allowed to refer to documents describing the service. This is an important field in the Contract Particulars and should include comprehensively all that is required of the Supplier in clear terms. This is the appropriate place to indicate any part of the works to be designed by the Supplier.
- Part 4 is for the Supplier to set out the key members of his team and supply chain along with their roles in the project and their area of expertise.

JCT CE 2011

- Two options are provided for duty of care for services provided by the supplier. One is reasonable skill and care, which is the usual standard of care for a professional, and the other option raises the bar to that of a competent designer that is appropriately qualified – this would raise the standard of care to that of a specialist professional (4·4, 4·5).
- Part of the Contract Particulars is devoted to defining the duties and responsibilities of the Supplier, thus the parties determine the role of the Supplier as Principal Contractor for CDM and SWMP Regulations, the Supplier's obligation with relation to the Project Programme, Supplier's obligation in relation to progress meeting, and the Supplier's obligation in relation to the perpetration and update of the Risk Register. Also the parties determine whether the Risk Allocation Schedule would apply.
- The contract is to be read as a whole; however, save for supplementary conditions set out or referred to in Part 9, in the case of any inconsistency, the conditions shall override other documents forming the contract (1·5).
- Either party is expected to notify the other on the occurrence of any risks included in the Risk Allocation Schedule and to work together to find the best way of mitigating the occurrence irrespective of whether the risks constitute a Relief Event or not.

Time

- The Supplier is to notify the Purchaser of any ambiguities or discrepancies in information provided by the Purchaser or any other member of the project team and agree on how to resolve such ambiguities. If not resolved amicably, the Purchaser shall issue an instruction. Specific time periods are to be specified for the provision of further information by both parties and for giving approvals and decisions. The default position is seven days if none is stated (3·1, 3·2 and 4·1).
- The Purchaser is to provide the Supplier with all information in his possession that it reasonably considers necessary for the project. The Purchaser is also to make available any further information requested by the Supplier within the timescale stated in the Contract Particulars. Additionally if the Purchaser is engaged pursuant to another contract, it is to make available to the Supplier information from the other contract relating to the performance of the service but may omit commercial and pricing information (3·1). Responses to requests and approvals are also to be made within the timescale stated in the Contract Particulars.
- There is provision to insert a completion date and for completion by sections.
- The Supplier is expected to complete the service in accordance with the contract (Article 1). The Supplier is responsible for the delivery of the service in accordance with the contract and for the performance of its supply chain (4·2). The Purchaser is to carry out the services in accordance with the contract to the reasonable satisfaction of the Purchaser, with personnel and plant necessary for safe, efficient and timely completion.

JCT CE 2011

- The Purchaser is to certify completion after satisfactory inspection and/or completion tests and commissioning. The Completion Date is defined as the date when in the opinion of the Purchaser the Services or Services within any relevant section were completed (3·7).
- If Part 1 of the Contract Particulars appoints the Supplier to prepare the Project Programme, the Supplier will be responsible for the update of the programme, showing amendments and sequencing of events or the likely time for any events and also identify key decision events that will require the decision of the Purchaser or Purchaser Representative (4·19·1).
- The Supplier would also coordinate any proposed changes to the Project Programme by members of the Supply Chain and where necessary meet with the Purchaser (Client) to explain the proposed changes and how they would affect the completion date, including measures to ensure the original completion date is achieved. However, where the completion date is to be changed as a result of changes to the programme the written consent of the Purchaser, referred to as the Client in this section of the contract, must be followed (4·19·2).
- All amendments to the Project Programme shall be sent to all supply chain members and cascaded to all Project Participants. This clause reiterates that any amendment or proposal indicating a change in completion date would require the prior approval of the Client (Purchaser) (4·19·2).

Control

- The Purchaser is to provide access to the site necessary to enable the Supplier to perform his obligations (3·4). The Purchaser is to appoint a representative who shall be the first point of contact for the project and act on behalf of the Purchaser. The Purchaser Representative may be replaced for good reasons after the Supplier has been notified (3·5).
- The initial members of the Project Team are set out in 2·3, however this may be modified or changed by contrary provisions in a Project Teams Agreement. Subject to such contradictory agreement, the Project Team will be responsible for guiding the successful delivery of the project from design to construction (2·4).
- The Supplier is to use reasonable endeavours to engage the Supply Chain using CE 2011 or in terms that fully reflect the principles of CE 11. Where contracts other than CE 11 are used the Supplier is to provide the Purchaser with a copy of the terms and advice on the differences. The Supplier is to avoid terms placing onerous obligations on the Supply Chain.
- The Supplier is expected to work together with and fully involve the Project Team in the delivery of the service. As appropriate the Supplier is expected to include members of

JCT CE 2011

the supply chain and other relevant Project Participants in project planning, risk, value engineering and other relevant matters (4·16).

- Goods and Materials to be provided by the Supplier are to be of good quality, conform to the contract and devoid of deleterious materials (unless these are instructed by the Purchaser). The Supplier is expected to give due consideration to environmental and sustainability issues in providing goods (4·11, 4·12).
- The Supplier is to comply with all reasonable instructions from the Purchaser or Purchaser's representative that are in writing and relate to the project (4·14).
- Notices under the contract are to be in writing and deemed as served when delivered by hand or registered post to the address stated in the contract particulars. Where no address is provided, Notices are to be sent to the last known principal address. The contract suggests that oral notices may be given on immediate health and safety risk issues but that this is to be confirmed by a written notice within three working days (1·7). The footnote explains that if there is to be service by email a specific protocol would have to be agreed.
- The Supplier grants the Purchaser an irrevocable assignable and royalty-free licence to use, copy and reproduce all designs and related documents prepared in connection with the Service for any purpose related to the project including extension of the project but not to reproduce the design for the purpose of the extension of the project (4·10). Copyright is to remain with the Supplier or the relevant member of the supply chain. The Supplier shall also pay a royalty for any patent or related processes and indemnify the Purchaser against any claims on account of intellectual property infringement by the Supplier (4·11).
- Key members of the Supply Chain are to be identified in the Contract Particulars Table A part 4. While the Supplier may replace any of the persons named in that schedule they may only do so with approval of the Purchaser, such approval which is not to be unreasonably withheld. Any replacement is expected to be suitably qualified to perform the relevant role (4·15).
- Where the Contract Particulars indicate that the Supplier will organise the progress meetings, the Supplier will be expected to schedule the meetings, coordinate attendance and ensure that the meeting records are kept. Where the Contract Particulars do not indicate the Supplier as responsible for the progress meetings, the Supplier shall attend all meetings he has been invited to.
- Where the Risk Register is to be prepared by the Supplier (this is to be indicated in the Contract Particulars), the Supplier is expected to investigate the risks that may occur in the project, the probability of the risks eventuating, financial estimate of the likely consequence and possible risk mitigation techniques to adopt (5·1). Where the Risk Register is to be prepared by another project, the Supplier is to

JCT CE 2011

give all necessary information. The same rules will apply to the Supplier in terms of updating the Risk Register.

- Where the Risk Allocation Schedule applies, the additional financial liability of the Purchaser is dependent on the full expenditure of amount allocated for the risk and similarly any additional time liability to be carried by the Purchaser is dependent on the full use of the time allocated in the schedule for the risk (5·3). Also the risk of the parties set out in the Risk Allocation Schedule is fixed and can only be changed by an agreement in writing.
- The Supplier's liability may be limited by a stated sum if the parties indicate same in the Contract Particulars.
- The Relief Events set out in the contract include instructions from the Purchaser to change the Service, an act or omission from the Purchaser or anyone for whom he is responsible, suspension due to non-payment which affects the completion date, the occurrence of any risk referred to in the Risk Allocation Schedule to the extent that the risk is not allocated to the Supplier and also where although the risk had been allocated to the Supplier the consequences of the risk have exceeded the costs and time allocated for it or allocated as being the responsibility of the Supplier and finally the occurrence of any event not envisaged by the Risk Allocation Schedule, which is beyond the control of the Supplier and could not have been reasonably foreseeable at the date of the contract. This excludes any act, omission, insolvency of the Supplier or members of his team, supply chain and sub-suppliers (5·7).
- It would also be a Relief Event where the Purchaser instructs the Supplier to open up for inspection or carry out testing on any of the Services, such instruction will only be a Relief Event where the inspection and tests had not already been provided before the contract or where the tests/inspections fail to disclose that the work and/or materials did not comply with the contract.
- Either party is to notify the other on knowledge that a Relief Event is about to occur or has occurred and they are expected to work collaboratively in dealing with such events and reducing the consequences of its occurrence (5·9).
- Not later than 14 days after the notification (or any other period agreed by the parties) of the Relief Event, the Supplier is expected to provide the Purchaser with a statement (with as much details as possible) of the effect of the Relief Event on the costs of performing the Services and/or date or dates for completion (5·11).
- The parties are to work together to agree on the likely effect of a Relief Event as presented in a statement prepared by the Supplier, and to work together on actions to minimise the adverse effect of the Relief Event. All reasonable efforts are to be used in reaching an agreement. Also any changes to the costs of performing the Services or Date of Completion or Risk Allocation Schedule are to be agreed in writing (5·13).

JCT CE 2011

- Where the Supplier fails to notify the Purchaser of a Relief Event or fails to issue a statement of the likely event of such an event, the Purchaser is expected to carry out an assessment of such event and notify the Supplier accordingly. The delay in the notification of the Relief Event is to be accounted for and any additional costs or time disruption caused by such delay is to be ignored in the assessment of the Relief Event (5·15, 5·16).

Money

- There are two payment options – the parties may choose either a target cost option or a lump sum option in the Contract Particulars.
- Where the Target Cost option is preferred, the Purchaser is expected in Part 7 of the Contract Particulars to indicate the minimum set of documents the Supplier should maintain for Allowable Cost (see below for description of Allowable Cost).
- The Contract Particulars will indicate the Target Cost (which is the cost set by the parties under which the parties share gain and above which parties share pain), the Suppliers margin (which could be described as central office and site office overheads and profit element), the Guaranteed Maximum Price – this is optional (this could be described as the final and firm cost of the Services above which the risk of excess is the sole liability of the Supplier), Allowable Cost (this excludes costs of defective works, Supplier Margin and other costs excluded by the parties).
- Where the Target Cost option is the preferred payment option, the Supplier is expected to keep a fully auditable and detailed record of allowable costs which can be inspected by the Purchaser. The parties as stated above would specify in part 7 of the Contract Particulars the records that the Supplier is to keep (7·2). The Purchaser is also to have direct access to original receipts and books of accounts (7·3).
- The Supplier is to provide on a monthly basis a breakdown of the Allowable Costs and the Supplier Margin. Each statement will also indicate the sum the Supplier considers due on the relevant due date, the basis on which the calculation has been made along with additional information that may be requested by the Purchaser (7·4).
- The Purchaser may disagree with the basis of the costs provided by the Supplier on two grounds, the first being the inclusion of Excluded Costs in Allowable Costs calculation. The second is that the cumulative Allowable Costs exceeds the Target Cost in which case only the portion of excess assigned to the Purchaser in the Contract Particulars is payable or it exceeds the Guaranteed Maximum Cost in which no additional Allowable Cost is recoverable. If the parties fail to agree on the estimate, a meeting may be held to resolve the differences (7·5).
- The due date for payment of the Allowable Costs and Suppliers Margin is five days after the issue of the Supplier breakdown (7·6). The final date for payment is 15 days from the due date (7·7).

JCT CE 2011

- Within five days of the Due Date the Purchaser is to issue a statement to the Supplier stating the amount he considers due and the basis for the calculation of that amount. If the Purchaser fails to give this notice, the Supplier breakdown becomes a payment notice and this amount will be due for payment by the final date of payment unless the Party from whom payment is due issues a Pay Less Notice.
- The party from which payment is due may, five days before the final payment date, issue a notice of its intention to pay less and basis for the calculation of this amount. Where a Pay Less Notice is served, the amount to be paid on the final date for payment shall be the sum stated in the Pay Less Notice (7·9).
- If any additional amount falls due to the Supplier in accordance with section 5, the amount of those additional sums will be added to the Target Cost and the Guaranteed Maximum Cost (if any) and those cost headings will be amended accordingly (7·14).
- Changes may be made to the Suppliers Margin; such changes should be in writing and would amend the contract on signing by the parties. Unless the Supplier Margin is expressed as a percentage of the Target Costs, increases and/or decreases would not automatically apply.
- After the completion of the Services, the Allowable Cost for completing the project, the Suppliers Margin, the Final Cost and Final Guaranteed Maximum price (if any) shall be calculated and included in the next breakdown of costs to be issued by the Supplier.
- Where the Allowable Cost of completing the Services is less than the Target Cost, the difference between the two figures will be shared by the parties in the relevant portions set out in the Contract Particulars (7·11).
- Where the Allowable Cost is greater that the Target Cost but less than or equal to the Guaranteed Maximum Cost, the Supplier shall receive the portion of the excess set in the Contract Particulars as the share of the Purchaser in such circumstances (7·12).
- Where the Allowable Cost is greater than the Guaranteed Maximum Cost, the portion of the cost in excess of the Guaranteed Maximum Cost shall be borne solely by the Employer.
- Where the lump sum Contract Sum Option is preferred, the parties are to set out the dates for which periodic payments are to be made. This may be when a specific relevant activity or milestone has been completed. On the dates of completion of the relevant activity or the reaching of the relevant milestone, the Supplier will make an application for payment to the Purchaser. The application would show the sum the Supplier considers due and how it was calculated, the total sum previously paid and a statement confirming that the relevant activity or milestone has been reached (7·16).

JCT CE 2011

- The Supplier shall provide any extra information required by the Purchaser (7·17). The Purchaser may also dispute that a relevant event has been completed or that a milestone has been reached. In such circumstances the parties may meet to settle such a difference in opinion (7·18).
- The due date for payment shall be five days after the Supplier's application and the final date for payment shall be 15 days after the due date (7·19, 7·20).
- Not later than five days after the due date, the Purchaser is expected to give a Payment Notice to the Supplier indicating the amount it thinks due the Supplier on the due date and the basis for its calculation (the contract prescribes the basis of calculation as the sum claimed in the Suppliers Application for Payment, if different the amount agreed by the parties or in the absence of an agreement, the amount the Purchaser considers due). This is the sum to be paid on the final date of payment unless a Pay Less Notice is issued (7·121). If the Purchaser fails to issue a Payment Notice, the Supplier Application becomes a Payment Notice.
- The Purchaser may issue a Pay Less Notice five days before the final date of payment stating his intention to pay a lesser sum than indicated in the Payment Notice and the basis of calculation of that amount. The amount on the Pay Less Notice becomes the amount due on the final date for payment.
- The Supplier, apart from being entitled to interest on late payment (7·27), may also, on the failure of the Purchaser to pay an amount due by the final payment date, issue a seven days notice of suspend if the Purchaser fails to keep to its payment obligations (7·28). The Supplier is entitled to suspend some or all of his obligations if the non-payment continues after the expiry of the seven days' notice. Where the Supplier exercises this right of suspension, it is entitled to reasonable costs incurred as a result (7·28). Applications for such costs are to be made to the Purchaser and the Supplier is entitled to payment within 20 days of such application.
- Where the liquidated damages clause is activated from the Project Particulars, the Supplier would be liable to pay same on failure to complete on the relevant Date for Completion of either the services or a section of it. Also where the Bonus for Early Completion clause had been activated in the Contract Particulars, the Supplier will be due a bonus on completing before the relevant Date for Completion. Both payments are to be within 20 days of notification being sent to the other party.

Statutory obligations

- The Supplier is expected to comply with statutory requirements and have regard to the code of practice relevant to his trade.
- The Supplier may be appointed the Principal Contractor for the purposes of the CDM Regulations 2007 and also for the purpose of the SWMP Regulations (4·18).

JCT CE 2011

Insurance

- A schedule of risks to be covered by insurance and the amount of minimum cover and minimum period is created (8·1).
- The types of insurance cover required for the project, the level of cover, the minimum amount of cover, minimum period of cover and the party responsible for maintaining each type of insurance are all to be set out in the Contract Particulars.
- There is also a provision in the Contract Particulars to limit the liability of the Supplier to a specified sum.

Termination

- The Purchaser may terminate the contract of the Supplier if the following occur: the Supplier fails to rectify any breach duly notified, 14 days after such notification; the supplier becomes insolvent, where the Purchaser's (where the Supplier is a sub-supplier) contract is terminated (10·2).
- The Supplier may terminate the contract on the occurrence of any of the following: if payment remains unpaid 28 days after the final payment date, if the Supplier notifies a breach of contract to the Purchaser which is not remedied 14 days after such notification, if the Purchaser is insolvent (10·3).

Miscellaneous

- Rights of third parties under the (Rights of Third Parties) Act 1999 are specifically excluded except as provided for in the contract (1·6). The Supplier may be required to grant Third Party Rights or collateral warranties as set out in the Contract Particulars.
- The Supplier is to indemnify the Purchaser for any expense with regards to liability for the death or injury of any person due to its or those engaged by the Supplier negligence/default in connection with providing the Service (8·3). The Supplier is similarly to indemnify the Purchaser for any injury or damage to property caused by its carrying out the Services due to any negligence/default on its part or persons engaged by it (8·5). Where the Contract Particulars include a limitation of liability amount, the liability of the Supplier except in relation to death and personal injury shall be limited to the amount stated.
- Where the parties choose in the Contract Particulars to include key performance indicators (measurement of performance) in the contract. Both parties throughout the period of the performance of the Services are to measure each other against the agreed key performance indicators and share feedback during regular reviews. The Supplier is to keep a written record of all performance reviews carried out under the contract and to provide the Purchaser with copies on reasonable notice (6).
- The contract is to be governed by the laws of England and Wales amendments would be required if it is to be used in Scotland or Northern Ireland (1·8).

JCT CE 2011

- Part 9 allows the parties to include any Supplementary Conditions required for the contract. Public authorities may wish to use this section to include conditions relating to release of information (Freedom of Information and also Official Secrets Act among others) and such other specific items not catered for in the contract conditions.

Disputes

- One of the dispute resolution stages is negotiation between the senior executives. Parties are expected to indicate which senior executive would be representing their side should a dispute occur in the Contract Particulars.
- The Contract Particulars set out the insurance requirements for the contract and the party responsible for each type of insurance. The Supplier is expected to provide details of its insurers and the terms of the policies for the approval of the Purchaser (8·2).
- The Parties are to endeavour to notify each other of any anticipated dispute so that it can be avoided by negotiation (11·1). Where a dispute arises, the parties are to endeavour to resolve by negotiation in good faith between senior executives nominated in the Contract Particulars (11·2). Either party is free to refer any dispute to adjudication in line with the relevant Scheme for Construction Contracts Regulation (11·3). Litigation is provided as the final tribunal for the resolution of disputes.
- Either party also has a right to request that evidence of that insurance are in force and adequate premiums are being paid are provided within 14 days of such request.

JCT CE 2011

This contract?

If considering using JCT CE 2011 remember that:

JCT CE can be used for procurement of construction works and construction-related services. It is drafted to allow for adaptation throughout the supply chain including the provision of professional services. It is particularly aimed at collaborative and integrative working and a suitable contract to be used for partnering.

JCT CE can be used for Supplier Design and it is suitable for works that are to be carried out in sections.

It also offers the flexibility of using either a Target Costs payment method or a Lump Sum payment method.

Related matters

References

JCT Constructing Excellence Construction Contract 2011
Guide to JCT Constructing Excellence Construction Contract 2011
The Stationery Office

GC/Works/1 (1998)

The Stationery Office

GC/Works/1 With Quantities (1998)

Background

GC/Works/1 first appeared in 1973 as a form intended for use almost exclusively by central government departments. GC/Works/1 (1998 Edition) is a direct successor and is published for use in major civil engineering or building projects, under traditional, design and build, or management procurement. It can also be used by non-central government agencies and private clients.

The use of GC/Works has declined over the years. As noted earlier the UK Government endorsement of collaborative contracts such as the NEC3 and JCT Constructing Excellence has led to their widespread use in Government projects. Although contracts in the GC suite are still being used sparingly in some projects, its decline in importance is best exemplified by the fact that it has not been updated to comply with current legislation.

GC/Works/1 is available in six versions as follows:

GC/Works/1: With Quantities (1998)
GC/Works/1: Without Quantities (1998)
GC/Works/1: Single Stage Design and Build (1998)
GC/Works/1: Two Stage Design and Build (1999)
GC/Works/1: With Quantities Construction Management Trade Contract (1999)
GC/Works/1: Without Quantities Construction Management Trade Contract (1999)

GC/Works/1 contracts are for use on major building and engineering projects. The range of contracts under the GC/Works label is comprehensive and further includes:

GC/Works/2: for building and civil engineering minor works (1998)
GC/Works/3: for mechanical and electrical engineering works (1998)
GC/Works/4: for building, civil engineering, mechanical and electrical small works (1998)
GC/Works/5: for the appointment of consultants (1999)
GC/Works/5: framework agreement for consultancy services (1999)
GC/Works/6: for a daywork term contract (1999)
GC/Works/7: for measured term contracts (1999)
GC/Works/8: for a specialist term contract for equipment maintenance (1999)
GC/Works/9: for operation, repair and maintenance of plant, equipment and installations (1999)
GC/Works10: for facilities management (2000)

GC/Works/1 (1998)

GC/Works/1 (1998) With Quantities is a particularly complete publication and can be adapted to suit a wide range of applications. It is similar in structure to its immediate predecessor and even uses the same numbers for most of the Conditions. There are fundamental differences, however, in the text which are not always immediately apparent. The earlier published form was intended almost exclusively for use by government departments and reflected the methods and procedures of contract administration then used by them. The form was not intended to be even-handed in all matters, and the Project Manager was afforded absolute authority with many of his or her decisions being 'final and conclusive'. The current form is claimed to be adaptable enough for use by non-central government employers (for example local authorities, educational institutions, housing associations, NHS Trusts, etc.) and by private sector employers. To facilitate this an attempt has been made to produce a form which strikes a fair balance between the interests of the Employer on the one hand and those of the contractor on the other. A 'fair dealings' clause has been introduced, and there is recognition of the fact that the Project Manager's decisions are now open to adjudication.

The last amendment of the form took account of the recommendations in the Latham Report, and complied with the conditions of the Housing Grants, Construction and Regeneration Act 1996 (Part II). Amendment 1, applicable to GC/Works/1 design and build forms only, was published in 2000 to take account of the Government's 'Achieving Excellence' initiative, and includes clauses to cover risk management, value engineering and whole life costing. It must be noted that this contract has not been updated to comply with the amendments to the Housing Grant, Construction and Regeneration Contract 1996 as amended by LDEDC Act 2009, therefore it would require extensive amendments of the payments sections at the very least for it to be used on projects commencing in England after 1 October 2011 (1 November 2011 for Scotland).

Nature

The document runs to over 80 pages. There is an introduction and contents list, followed by the Conditions which are set out in a clear graphic style using straightforward language and well established terminology. Also included are a Schedule of Time Limits (useful summary for contract administrators); a detailed alphabetical index; the customary Abstract of Particulars but with an Addendum for entries about information yet to be supplied; and the tender forms. The Contract Agreement is in two versions so that the contract can be under Scots law, or under the law of England, Wales and Northern Ireland.

Use

The form is intended for use in major building or civil engineering works.

The Conditions include:

- design by the contractor and sub-contractors;

GC/Works/1 (1998)

- professional indemnity insurance for design;
- incentive bonus for early completion;
- finance charges;
- mobilisation payments;
- payments to the contractor on the basis of stages, milestones or valuations;
- performance bonds;
- parent company guarantee;
- collateral warranties.

The factual details relating to a particular contract and the incorporation of option provisions will be determined on how the Abstract of Particulars is completed. The Abstract is detailed and among other things requires the names of the Project Manager and Planning Supervisor (who may be the Project Manager) to be entered. There is also space for the adjudicator and the arbitrator to be named in this document. It is recommended in the notes that the same adjudicator and arbitrator are named in all the Employer's related contractual documents, whether with the Contractor, consultants or others. This could be problematic if the disputes are not related.

A Contract Agreement is to be executed in duplicate and the date entered. Government contracts are not normally executed under seal, but there is space for attestation if required.

Synopsis

1 Intentions

- There is a fair dealing clause which requires both parties to act in good faith and in a cooperative and open relationship (1A).
- The contractor is to execute the Works with diligence, in accordance with the Programme, with all reasonable skill and care, and in a workmanlike manner. If any part of the Works does not conform with the contract and is rejected by the Project Manager, then it must be replaced by the contractor at its own expense (31[6]). The terms 'the Works' and 'Things' are defined (1[1]).
- The contractor may be required to undertake responsibility for design work in respect of such work carried out by himself, or by a sub-contractor or supplier. The contractor's liability can be either that of the professional duty to exercise reasonable skill and care (10 – Alternative A) or to give a fitness for purpose warranty (10 – Alternative B).
- The contractor is deemed to have satisfied itself about the conditions under which he works (7[1]). No additional payment is allowed except for unforeseeable ground conditions (7[5]).
- The quality of 'Things' for incorporation is to conform to the requirements of the Specification, bills and drawings and be fit for their intended purposes (31[2]).

GC/Works/1 (1998)

The contractor must be prepared to satisfy the Project Manager in respect of the execution of the Works, and that it is using the skill and care expected of an experienced and competent contractor.

- The 'contract' means the Contract Agreement, Conditions, Abstract of Particulars, Specification, drawings, bills of quantities, Programme, tender, and the Employer's written acceptance (1[1]).
- If discrepancies occur between Specification and drawings, or between drawings, the contractor is to draw the Project Manager's notice to any discovered (2[3]). The Conditions prevail where documents conflict with them (2[1]).
- Bills of quantities are to be prepared in accordance with the method of measurement identified, except where stated otherwise (3[1]). Any errors or omissions in the bills are to be rectified by the Employer (3[3]).
- The contractor is to receive a copy of drawings issued 'during the progress of the Works' in a form which the Project Manager considers suitable for reproduction (2[5]).

2 Time

- The contract period will be stated in the Abstract of Particulars (34[1]). The Employer will notify the contractor when it may take possession of the site or parts of the site. All notices under the contract are to be in writing (1[3]).
- The contractor is required to proceed with diligence and in accordance with the Programme, or as the Project Manager instructs (34[1]). The whole of the Works or any relevant Section must be completed in accordance with the contract, and to the satisfaction of the Project Manager by the date for completion (34[1]).
- The date for completion is set out in or ascertained from the Abstract of Particulars (1[1]). This envisages practical completion (although not called such) and includes clearing of rubbish and all Things not incorporated (34[2]).
- The contractor is required to submit a Programme prior to acceptance of the tender, for it to be agreed by the Employer (1[1]). The Programme is to be for the whole period for completion, and must show sequence and other specified information (33[1]).
- Regular progress meetings are to be held (35[2]), and the contractor is obliged to submit a written report on progress, including requests for extensions of time and re-programming proposals, at least five days before each meeting (35[3]). If notice is given, or if the Project Manager is already aware of likely delay, he or she shall consider whether or not to award an extension (36[1]). The causes for which an extension may be awarded are listed (36[2]), and the Project Manager is to indicate whether the award is interim or final. The Project Manager is to keep interim decisions under review until a final decision is possible (36[3]). It is interesting that weather is not recognised as a cause of delay.

GC/Works/1 (1998)

- The Project Manager is required to issue a written statement of progress within seven days after each progress meeting (35[4]).
- Acceleration of completion is possible upon direction by the Employer, subject to acceptance of contractor's priced proposals (38). The contractor may also choose to submit priced proposals and Programme amendments for the Employer to consider.
- The Project Manager shall issue a certificate when the Works, or any Section, are completed in accordance with the contract (39).
- Failure to complete the Works or a Section (which includes clearance) by the relevant Date of Completion makes the contractor liable to the Employer for liquidated damages (55). There is no reference to a certificate of non-completion.
- The Maintenance Period will be stated in the Abstract of Particulars (21[1]). The contract accepts that there might be more than one Maintenance Period. The contractor is obliged to make good defects at his own cost and to the satisfaction of the Employer. Any arguments about liability and reimbursement must wait until after defects have been rectified.
- There is provision for completion of the Works by Section if specified in the Abstract of Particulars (1[1]).
- There is provision for the Employer to take early possession of any part of the Works, and this also relates to completion by Sections (37).

3 Control

- The contractor is not allowed to assign or transfer the contract or any interest without written consent of the Employer (61). Sub-letting is also barred without prior consent of the Employer or the Project Manager (62[1]).
- In any sub-contract, the contractor is required to ensure certain terms (62[2]). The contractor is responsible for seeing that sub-contractors comply with all obligations imposed upon them. The Main Contractor must see that sub-contract works are completed (62[4]).
- Sub-contractors or suppliers may be nominated on the basis of a Prime Cost sum (63[1]). The contractor is entirely responsible for the performance of any nominated sub-contractors, except that if optional clause 63A is stated to apply, the Employer will bear the losses due to insolvency. In the event of determination of a nominated sub-contract the Employer may renominate a replacement or direct the contractor to complete the work (63[7]). There are no stated procedures and no requirement to use a particular form of contract. The contractor is given right of reasonable objection (63[6]).
- Instructions from the Project Manager must be in writing (40[3]) except for a few (listed) which can be oral and confirmed later. The contract sets out what instructions are empowered (40[2]).

GC/Works/1 (1998)

- Instructions can be given by the Project Manager or delegated to his or her representative (4), and the contractor must comply forthwith. Instructions requiring a variation are termed 'VIs'. The Project Manager may require the contractor to submit a quotation of the full cost of complying with a VI within 21 days of the instruction (40).
- In the event of failure to comply with the Project Manager's instruction, the Employer may have the work done by others at the contractor's expense (53). This right extends to rectifying defects (21[3]).
- The Project Manager is to provide the contractor with information necessary for setting out the Works, and the contractor is solely responsible for the correctness of the setting out (9).
- The contractor shall employ a competent agent (5) who is to supervise the Works, be in attendance at site during all working hours, and supply the Project Manager with returns (15). A clerk of works or Resident Engineer may be appointed, and the Project Manager or quantity surveyor may appoint representatives to exercise their respective powers – which must be listed (4).
- The Project Manager may inspect, examine or have tests carried out (31[4]). Independent experts may be brought in to test fitness or suitability of Things, and if their findings disclose non-compliance with the contract, then the contractor must bear the cost of rectification and any necessary further tests (31[5]).
- The Employer has power to execute other works (which may or may not be in connection with the Works) during the execution of the contract (65).

4 Money

- The Contract Sum is defined (1[1]) and may be adjusted as provided for in the contract.
- Provisional sums require instructions in writing from the Project Manager before work under these items begins (64). Valuation is as provided for in the contract (42).
- Valuation of Project Manager's instructions (40) may be by acceptance of a lump sum quotation. If there is no agreement, the quantity surveyor will value on the basis set out (41) or (42[5]) in the case of a variation instruction, or (43) in the case of other instructions. Prolongation or disruption costs may be included as part of the valuation.
- The right to prolongation and disruption expenses generally is limited (46[1]). The matters are set down in the Conditions. Interest and finance charges are expressly excluded (46[6]). Recovery of expenses depends on written application from the contractor made to the Project Manager in time (46[3]). The application must meet the requirements set down.
- Finance charges may be payable to the contractor only for limited reasons, and for stated periods (47[1] and [3]). The rate is to be stated in the Abstract of Particulars (47[2]).

GC/Works/1 (1998)

- Progress payments, termed 'advances on account' (48), are based on either Stage Payments, Milestone Payments or Valuations (50[2]). Payments will include for work executed to the satisfaction of the Project Manager, and the contractor is entitled to 95 per cent of the relevant sum, plus 100 per cent of certain other sums and certain adjustments (48[2]). Stage Payment Chart and Milestone Payment Chart are defined (1[1]).
- After completion of the Works, the contractor is entitled to be paid the amount estimated by the Employer as the Final Sum, less half the retention. The quantity surveyor shall send a copy of the final account to the contractor within six months of certified completion (49[2]). The contractor must notify agreement or otherwise within three months. The other half of any retention is released when the Final Certificate is issued at the end of the last Maintenance Period, and when the contractor has complied with making good defects.

5 Statutory obligations

- The contractor is to give all statutory notices required, obtain any consents necessary, and pay fees and charges arising. The Employer will reimburse fees or charges properly incurred. An obligation on the contractor acting as Principal Contractor to comply with the CDM Regulations is expressly stated (11).
- The contractor is also required to conform to any occupier's rules or regulations (if stated in the Abstract of Particulars) relevant to the site or the premises within which he is working (22).
- The contractor is required to comply with all statutory requirements which govern the storage and use of all Things brought on to the site (13[2]).

6 Insurance

- The contractor is required to maintain for the duration of the Contract and the longest Maintenance Period: employers' liability insurance; insurance against loss or damage to the Works and Things for full reinstatement value; insurance against personal injury or damage to property (8). The evidence can be required within 21 days from acceptance of tender (Alternative A). The contractor may be required to maintain insurance in the joint names of the Employer, the contractor and all sub-contractors in accordance with details attached to the Abstract of Particulars (Alternative B).
- Where so stated in the Abstract of Particulars, and in connection with a contractor's design obligation, the contractor may be required to take out and maintain professional indemnity insurance cover (8A).
- The contractor is responsible for loss or damage to the Works and even extending to any Things not for incorporation in the Works (19[6]). This is in respect of any loss or damage, but where this arises because of 'accepted risks', defined in (1[1]), unforeseeable ground conditions or unforeseeable circumstances beyond the control

of the contractor, the contractor will be reimbursed by the Employer. There is an absolute obligation on the contractor to reinstate, replace or make good to the satisfaction of the Employer (19).

- The contractor is to take precautions needed to take care of the site and the Works against loss or damage from fire, and any other cause, and shall take all reasonable steps for security and protection of the site and Works including lighting and watching (13[1]).

7 Termination

- The Employer may determine the contract at any time by giving notice to the Contractor. This is a discretionary power which can be 'at will', and not conditional upon some default by the contractor (56).
- In addition, the Employer has the right to determine the contract for specific defaults by the contractor including insolvency (56[6]).
- The contractor may determine the contract on various stated grounds, and matters following determination by the contractor are covered in Condition 58.
- Matters following determination by the Employer (eg payment, completion, removal, transfer of sub-contracts) are dealt with in Condition 57. The quantity surveyor shall ascertain and the Project Manager certify the cost to the Employer of completion of the Works.

8 Miscellaneous

- A list of definitions is included (1[1]).
- There appears to be no express condition to contract out from the Contracts (Rights of Third Parties) Act 1999.
- The Project Manager is to certify unforeseeable ground conditions (7(4)).
- The contractor is to give the Project Manager reasonable notice before covering up work (17) and shall not lay foundations until the Project Manager has examined the excavations (16).
- The Project Manager may order the replacement of the contractor's site staff, including the agent (6[1]). The Project Manager has power to control the admittance of certain persons to the site (26).
- Security measures such as a requirement for passes (27), the taking of photographs (28), and awareness by all employees of the Official Secrets Acts (29) may be an obligation, where stated in the Abstract of Particulars.
- The contractor has express obligations relating to the protection of the Works (13), the prevention of nuisance (14) and the removal of rubbish (34[2]).

GC/Works/1 (1998)

- There is provision for the discovery of antiquities (32[3]).
- There is an extremely wide provision for recovery of sums where money is owed by the contractor or to the Contractor, under this or any other contract with the Employer (51).

9 Disputes

- There is provision for adjudication for the resolution of any dispute arising during the course of the Works (59[1]). There are precise requirements for the notice of referral and the procedures. A decision may normally be expected within 28 days of the notice. The adjudicator's decision is binding until the dispute is finally determined by legal proceedings or by arbitration.
- Arbitration is included in addition to adjudication as a means of dealing with disputes (60[1]), and the arbitrator is given wide powers under the contract.

GC/Works/1 (1998)

This contract?

If considering using GC/Works/1 remember that:

This was the major form for lump contracts originally drafted for use by central government, but it was substantially revised in the 1998 edition to allow for a much wider application, including use by private sector employers. However, it is still intended primarily for use by government departments or Crown agencies. There is a version for use with quantities, another for use without quantities. It has not been updated to comply with current regulations and therefore may not be suitable for use on a new project commencing after 1 October 2011 unless it is substantially amended.

It can be used for work in England and Wales, and for work in Northern Ireland or Scotland. In the latter cases Condition 60 deals with the differences in arbitration resulting from the contract being subject to Northern Ireland law and Scots law. There are relevant references to statute law which applies to these countries, and a different Contract Agreement for use under Scots law is included. Fuller helpful information is given in the Commentary under 'Legal Background'.

It can include completion in stages, design by the contractor with professional indemnity insurance, security measures, early possession, acceleration and cost savings, bonuses, nomination of sub-contractors or suppliers, mobilisation payment, alternatives for advances on account, and bonds in lieu of retention. The wording is clear, with a good graphic layout. The procedures are logical, and there are many interesting features in the provisions, for example, that the contractor is to provide regular progress reports for comment by the contract administrator, and that the contractor bears any losses resulting from failures on the part of nominated sub-contractors. On the whole the form places more risk on the contractor than the JCT SBC.

When completing the contract details, the Abstract of Particulars is a vital document with which to tailor the particular contract to the intended works.

If acting as Project Manager, contract administration should be relatively straightforward. The obligations and responsibilities are clearly stated, the person concerned is given considerable authority, and the procedures are not arduous. However, it is necessary to keep a careful watch on the Schedule of Time Limits.

The 1994 Latham Report recommended that government departments then using GC/Works/1 should begin to change to the New Engineering Contract. The current 1998 GC/Works/1 family of forms may be seen as a robust response to that suggestion. It has emerged as a versatile and well structured document which embodies many of the Latham Report's points for 'an effective form of contract in modern conditions'. Amendments to the design and build versions were published in 2000, to introduce some of the recommendations of 'Achieving Excellence'.The Government Central Advice Unit also publishes some excellent Information Notes from time to time.

6 Traditional procurement: standard lump sum forms

GC/Works/1 (1998)

Related matters

Documents

GC/Works/1 With Quantities (1998) General Conditions

GC/Works/1 Without Quantities (1998) General Conditions

GC/Works/1 Model Forms and Commentary

GC/Works Sub-Contract

NEC3

The Institution of Civil Engineers
New Engineering Contract Documents

Engineering and Construction Contract Third Edition

Background

This form is placed under the heading of Traditional Procurement and Lump Sum Forms because it is a major form of contract. It is part of a system which was a bold and major initiative in the drafting of construction contracts. This resulted in a form which is adaptable and suitable for use in lump sum, design and build, or management procurement, and for both civil engineering and building works.

The NEC3 is a Third Edition development of what was first called the New Engineering Contract (NEC). This was an entirely new 'clean sheet' approach to drafting construction contracts undertaken for the Institution of Civil Engineers. It was prepared by a panel of engineers and lawyers chaired by Dr Martin Barnes of Coopers and Lybrand, London.

The NEC offers:

1 Flexibility: by making one all purpose document suitable for traditional procurement, design and build, or management contracts. It is suitable for most types of civil engineering and building work, from large-scale projects down to domestic-scale work. In practice, it has been used mainly in high-value, large-scale projects, eg construction of the London Olympic Games stadium. Drafted as a head contract, it is for use under UK law and also overseas.

2 Clarity: This form aims to be clear and easily understandable, and therefore likely to lead to fewer disputes. It was drafted with plain language, with relatively short clauses to achieve this purpose.

3 Good management on the part of all parties: it was felt that there should be an end to adversarial posturing by bringing into the contract an obligation for frank and open discussion of problems as they arose, thereby minimising the risk of disputes escalating to the point where time and costly overruns became inevitable. It was further thought desirable to introduce incentives for good performance and early completion.

Sir Michael Latham bestowed high praise on the original New Engineering Contract in his 1994 report. After listing what he considered to be desirable features which should be present in all modern construction contracts, he stated that 'the approach of the New Engineering Contract is extremely attractive' and that it contains 'virtually all these assumptions of best practice'. He went on to advocate certain changes to the New Engineering Contract, some of which were as follows:

- that the name should be changed to New Construction Contract (hence the change to NEC);
- that there should be provision for a secure trust funding;
- that there should be prompt payment provision for sub-contractors;
- that there should be affirmation by the parties that all dealings were to be on a fair basis;
- that core clauses should be left unamended and only compatible sub-contracts used;
- that terms of appointment for consultants and adjudicators should interlock with the contract;
- that consideration should be given to a short and simpler minor works variant (now available).

The Latham Report also recommended that 'Government Departments should begin changing to the NEC' and that 'the use of NEC (amended) by private sector clients should be strongly promoted'.

Since the Latham Report the NEC has been taken up widely, and has been used on projects in various sectors of construction and engineering in various parts of the world. An example of this is that the English National Health Service required that an amended version of NEC2 was used on its Procure21 projects.

The third edition introduced some significant changes to the suite. New concepts such as the use of a risk register, 'Key Dates', key performance indicators and third party rights were introduced. The number of secondary options was also increased. With changes in UK legislation in summer 2011, it was imperative that NEC3 be amended to bring it in line with the law. The amendments, which are available online, concentrate on the clauses of the contract affected by the new legislation, such as the Adjudication and Payment provisions.

Nature

The New Engineering Contract is an interlocking family of contracts, the Engineering and Construction Contract is the main construction contract, the Engineering and Construction Sub-Contract supports sub-contracting using this form, the Engineering and Construction Short Contract is the minor (small project) version of the main contract and is complemented by the Engineering and Construction Short Sub-Contract. Other contracts in the family include a supply contract and supply short contract, professional services contract, an adjudicator's contract, a term services contract, and a framework agreement, together with relevant guidance notes and comprehensive flow charts. NEC3 is intended as a reference document, and contains Core clauses and Optional clauses.

NEC3

The Core clauses are set out in nine Sections, and apply in all contracts. The core clauses allow for a flexible amount of contractor design, enabling the form to be used in traditional and design-build procurement. The Main Option clauses constitute six sets of clauses A to F, and one set will be added to the Core clauses to adapt the document to the type of contract required (for example Priced Contract With Quantities or Activity Schedule; Target Contract; Cost Reimbursable Contract; Management Contract). These Main Option clauses relate to the pricing and payment system. For convenience, versions of NEC3 with the core clauses merged with each of the six Main Options are published separately. Chapter 10 will consider in detail the Target Cost provision of the NEC3 contract.

There are also Secondary Option clauses which may be incorporated or not as required. Some can only work in conjunction with certain Main Option clauses. There are 22 headings (X1–X20, Y(UK)2 and Y(UK)3) which can be incorporated as required to allow for performance bonds; partnering; key performance indicators; advance payment; sectional completion; limitation of contractor's liability for design; fluctuations; retention; bonus for early completion; delay damages; low performance damages, etc. This gives great opportunity to tailor the conditions to the intended works.

The NEC was a novel piece of drafting in 'simple language' using non-traditional terminology. The use of the present tense throughout the contract has been criticised by some commentators.

Some concepts in this contract are different to those used in more traditional standard forms, for instance Compensation Events replace such concepts as variation and extension of time provisions.

In an attempt to stimulate good management, emphasis is laid on the contractual importance of effective programming, sound management, and the need for early warnings by both the Project Manager and the contractor in order that matters which have implications for progress and additional costs can be properly considered at the earliest possible time. The risk register introduced by the third edition is a further tool to encourage the early identification and management of potential problems.

Use

First, it is necessary to select the appropriate Main Option. Then the Secondary Options can be considered and incorporated as desired. It is necessary to determine the make-up of the contract content before completing the statements of Contract Data. The Core clauses are relatively brief, and the information carried in the Works Information and the Contract Data therefore becomes extremely important. Part One of the latter consists of information to be provided by the Employer, and Part Two is data provided by the Contractor. Because of the number of options available, and the fact that data will be related to the selected options, completion of the Works Information and the Contract Data needs to be precise and approached with great care.

NEC3

Synopsis of Core clauses

1 Intentions

- The intentions of the parties as indicated in the Contract Documents should be evident from the Core clauses, the choice of Option clauses and the Contract Data provided by the Employer.
- The contractual spirit of mutual trust and cooperation is expressed in the 'General Section' (10·1) of the Core clauses.
- There are clear rules relating to communications (eg instructions, certificates, submissions, records, etc) (13).
- Early warning is a significant requirement in the contract (16).
- A register of risks is set up at the start of the project and included in the Contract Data. The register may be added to during the course of the project, and the contractor or Project Manager may require a risk reduction meeting to discuss the noted risks (16).
- Instructions are required from the Project Manager to resolve any ambiguities or inconsistencies (17).
- The contractor is obliged to notify the Project Manager of work which he feels is either impossible to execute or illegal (18).
- The contractor's main obligation is to provide the Works in accordance with the Works Information (20), defined in clause 11·2. It is important therefore to make certain that this information is full, clear and accurate.
- The contract allows for design by the contractor (21) and questions of copyright are dealt with (22).
- The contractor is responsible for cooperation over providing information, and the sharing of working areas is a contractual obligation (25).
- Title to plant, equipment and materials is normally vested in the Contractor, but may pass to the Employer where the Supervisor marks goods and materials as being 'for the contract' (70). The subject of title is allocated a complete Section of the Core clauses.

2 Time

- Starting and completion arrangements are straightforward (30). Possession of the site, access and use is subject to conditions (33).
- Programmes should be identified in the Contract Data, or otherwise submitted to the Project Manager by the contractor. If the contractor fails to produce a programme, 25 per cent of any amount that would otherwise be due to the contractor is retained until the contractor complies (50·3). The detail to be included is described (31). Programmes may be revised subject to conditions (32).

NEC3

- The Project Manager is empowered to issue instructions that work stops, or that it is not started until instructed (34).
- The contract may stipulate 'Key Dates' by which defined operations must be complete. This allows the work of one contractor engaged under NEC3 to be dovetailed with that of another. Cost incurred by the Employer through failure to meet a key date can be claimed against the contractor in default (25·3).
- Procedures for using or taking over part of the Works early by the Employer are subject to conditions. Possession of any part of the Works, or the whole site, is dependent upon certification by the Project Manager (35).
- The Project Manager can require the contractor to submit a quotation for accelerating the Works in order to achieve completion ahead of the contract completion date (36).
- Where delay occurs due to certain intervening events, these may constitute Compensation Events (60). There are 19 listed, and for weather in particular, precise requirements can be included in the Contract Data. The contractor is obliged to notify the Project Manager of such events, and the Project Manager will decide whether compensation is due (61). Obviously the 'early warning' requirement will be taken into account. Compensation Events are afforded a complete Section 6 in the Core clauses.
- The Project Manager may instruct the contractor to submit a quotation to deal with the monetary losses associated with the delays (62).
- Assessment of Compensation Events is a matter for the Project Manager in accordance with certain rules and procedures (63 and 64). The Project Manager must notify the contractor of his or her decision.

3 Control

- The early warning obligation can constitute a control mechanism (16).
- The Project Manager and the Supervisor are both given considerable powers, and both may delegate. The Project Manager is empowered to issue instructions to the contractor relating to changes of Works Information or a Key Date (14).
- The contractor must submit names, qualifications and experience of key people. Replacements are subject to acceptance by the Project Manager (24).
- The Project Manager may order the removal of an employee from any further connection with the particular contract (24·2).
- The contractor must arrange for access to Works, materials and plant in store, for the Project Manager, Supervisor and others notified by the Project Manager (28).
- The contractor must obey instructions from the Project Manager and the Supervisor, authorised under the contract (27·3).

NEC3

- The contractor is wholly responsible for the work of all sub-contractors. All sub-contractors are subject to acceptance by the Project Manager (26).
- Tests and inspections carried out by the contractor may be observed by the Supervisor, who may also order the contractor to carry out tests, and carry out his own tests (40).
- The Supervisor may instruct the contractor to search for defects (42) and whether or not the Supervisor notifies him the contractor is obliged to correct defects before the end of the Defects Correction Period (43).
- Where Works have been taken over by the Employer, the Project Manager is to arrange access for the contractor to correct defects. Where it is agreed that defects need not be corrected, then there may be changes to Works Information and a cost reduction (44).
- The contract makes no reference to assignment, other than the contractor's obligation to assign the benefit of contracts on termination of his employment (96).

4 Money

- An Addendum Y(UK)2 has been issued (essential for all contracts on NEC3 in the UK), it has been amended to take account of the amendment of the Housing Grants, Construction and Regeneration Act 1996 by the Local Democracy Economic Development and Construction Act 2009 and this affects the provisions for payment as set out in Section 5 of the Core clauses.
- The Project Manager must assess the amounts due to the contractor at each assessment date. The intervals are included in the Contract Data (50).
- The Project Manager certifies a payment on or before the date on which a payment becomes due, and each certified payment is made on or before the final date for payment (51).
- The Project Manager's certificate is the notice of payment to the contractor and sets out the amount due on the relevant payment due date (the notified sum) and the basis on which the amount was calculated (Y2.2).
- The date on which payment becomes due is seven days after the assessment date, and the final date for payment is 21 days after the date on which payment becomes due (Y2.2).
- If either party intends to pay less than the notified sum, that party will issue a Pay Less Notice not later than seven days (the prescribed period) before the final payment date, stating the amount he considers due and the basis for calculating it. No amount shall be withheld under this contract unless a party has issued a Pay Less Notice (Y2.3).
- Interest is payable on amounts due but unpaid, and in respect of a Project Manager's

certificate which is due but issued late. The interest rates are to be stated in the Contract Data (51).

- Suspension of performance by the contractor in the event of the Employer's failure to make proper payment is treated as a Compensation Event (60·7, incorporated by Y2.4).
- There can be price adjustments for inflation (ie fluctuations) under Supplementary Option X1 (applicable only for Main Options A–D) calculated on the basis of a Price Adjustment Factor.

5 Statutory obligations

- The contractor is obliged to notify the Project Manager if he becomes aware of anything in the Works Information which would be illegal (8).
- If the Project Manager corrects the Works Information so that it complies with Statute, this may be a Compensation Event.

6 Insurance

- The standard risks to be carried by the Employer are itemised, and any additional risks to be carried by the Employer may be entered in the Contract Data (80).
- Risks not itemised as being carried by the Employer are to be carried by the contractor (81).
- Each party indemnifies the other in respect of claims, proceedings, compensation or costs arising from an event which is at risk of the party concerned (83).
- Insurance responsibilities are tabled and as stated in the Contract Data. Policies are to be taken out in joint names, and in the case of the contractor policies and certificates are subject to acceptance by the Project Manager. If the contractor fails to submit, then the Employer may insure and charge to the contractor (85 and 86).
- Where the Employer insures, policies and certificates must be submitted to the Contractor. If the Employer fails to submit, then the contractor may insure and charge to the Employer (87).
- Details of insurance obligations and cover are to be stated in the Contract Data.

7 Termination

- Valid reasons for termination by the Employer and by the contractor are set out in a Termination Table (90·2).
- In the event of termination the Project Manager issues a Termination Certificate and within 13 weeks certifies final payment (90).
- Following the certificate, termination procedures are implemented as set out in the Termination Table.

NEC3

- The Employer may elect to complete the Works himself or employ another contractor, and may use any plant or materials to which he has title (92).
- Payments which may be due on termination are as set out in the Termination Table (93).

8 Miscellaneous

- Main Option clauses can include Activity Schedules (for A or C), or bills of quantities (for B or D).
- Use of the NEC engineering and construction sub-contract and the professional services contract seem to be required regardless of which Main Options are incorporated.
- Secondary Option clauses can be incorporated to make provision for price adjustment for inflation (X1); changes in the law (X2); multiple currencies (X3); parent company guarantee (X4); sectional completion (X5); bonus for early completion (X6); delay damages (X7); partnering (X12); performance bond (X13); advanced payment to the contractor (X14); limitation of contractor's design liability to using reasonable skill and care (X15); retention (X16); low performance damages (X17); limitation of liability (X18); key performance indicators (X20) and additional conditions of contract (Z) may be incorporated, in which case they should be stated in the Contract Data (option Z).

  Option Y(UK)3 should be incorporated into the Contract Data for all contracts to which the law of England and Wales, and Northern Ireland applies, and is a contracting out of third party rights under the Contracts (Rights of Third Parties Act) 1999.

9 Disputes

- Alternative provisions for adjudication are set out in Options W1 and W2. Option W2 must be used when the Housing Grants, Construction and Regeneration Act 1996 applies to the contract.
- Under Option W1 the parties to the contract and the Project Manager are to follow the detailed procedures as set out, including the limits on timing as set out in the Adjudication Table. Option W2 is a procedure which complies with the Act. Option W2 has been amended to bring it in compliance with amendments to the Construction Act. The changes include the addition of an express term that the adjudicator in his discretion is to allocate his fees and expenses between the parties (W2.3 (8)) and another term, that the adjudicator may, within five days of giving his decisions to the parties, correct any clerical or typographical error in the decision (W 2.3 (12)).
- The adjudicator may be named in the Contract Data.
- The adjudicator's decision is final and binding unless and until referred to a further 'tribunal'. Whether this is to be arbitration or legal proceedings will presumably be stated in the Contract Data. If arbitration, the procedures to be followed appear not to be stated in the contract and would presumably be for the parties to agree.

NEC3

This contract?

If considering using the NEC3 remember that:

It is important to remember that the NEC3 is built around the idea of Core clauses to which selected Optional clauses and Secondary Option clauses may be added .

The Contract Data and Works Information are essential components of the NEC3. The former is not to be changed once the contract is entered into. The Works Information supplied by the Employer and by the contractor can be presented in a variety of formats, and is information necessary at tender stage.

There are no stated restrictions on the use of NEC3, but the law of the contract, the language of the contract, and the currency of the contract should be entered in Part One of the Contract Data. Changes in the law of the country in which the site is located might be a Compensation Event if Option X2 is incorporated. Additionally Addendum Y(UK)2 as amended takes account of the Housing Grants, Construction and Regeneration Act 1996 as amended, and Addendum Y(UK)3 takes account of the Contracts (Rights of Third Parties) Act 1999. Addendum Y(UK)2 will be applicable for England and Wales, Northern Ireland and Scotland, and Y(UK)3 will be applicable only to England and Wales and Northern Ireland.

The key persons are the Project Manager, who manages the procurement of the Works for the Employer; and the Supervisor, who exercises certain responsibilities relating to quality assurance on site for the Employer with whom he or she has a contract for services.

Completion of the form requires selecting or assembling the appropriate options, and making relevant entries to 13 pages of Contract Data. Attestation is by a separate document.

Contract administration requires attention to communications, early warnings, changes in Works Information, and Compensation Events in particular. A cooperative and non-adversarial attitude is essential with NEC3, and there is a strong emphasis on best practice management.

NEC3

Related matters

Documents

Engineering and construction contract
Engineering and construction contract A: Priced contract with activity schedule
Engineering and construction contract B: Priced contract with bill of quantities
Engineering and construction contract C: Target contract with activity schedule
Engineering and construction contract D: Target contract with bill of quantities
Engineering and construction contract E: Cost-reimbursable contract
Engineering and construction contract F: Management contract
Engineering and construction contract: Guidance notes
Engineering and construction contract: Flow charts
Engineering and construction subcontract
Engineering and construction short subcontract
Engineering and professional services contract
Engineering and professional services contract: guidance notes and flow charts
Engineering and construction short contract
Engineering and construction short contract: guidance notes and flow charts
Adjudicator's contract
Adjudicator's contract: guidance notes and flow charts
Term services contract
Term services contract: guidance notes
Term services contract: flow charts
Framework contract
Framework contract: guidance notes and flow charts
Procurement and contract strategies

Frances Forward
Guide to NEC3
RIBA Publishing 2011

CIOB CPC 2012

The Chartered Institute of Building

Complex Projects Contract 2012 (Review Edition)

Background

Although it is in its review edition, this contract is being critiqued in this section because it represents a major step towards more computerised operations in the construction industry. The CIOB Complex Projects Contract Review Edition was released in May 2012. It aims to bring construction contracts into the 21st century by supporting fully computerised operations and use with the Building Information Model (BIM). It envisages active management and engagement from stakeholders in a project. It is amendable to three procurement routes, ie Employer design, Employer design contract but with aspects of contractor design and also design and build contracts including turnkey projects.

Nature

The Contract is for use with complex projects. It defines Complex Projects as those having one or more of the following features:

- Complex MEP services
- Civil engineering nature
- More than one building
- Any building of 50 feet high
- Accommodation below ground
- Production involving the management of
    - Construction period in excess of 12 months
    - Design work to be completed during construction
    - Multiple prime contractors
    - Multiple possessions and/or access dates
    - Short period of possessions
    - Multiple key dates and/or sectional completion dates

The contract is made up of three documents: The contract agreement, the conditions and the Contract Appendixes. The contract envisages that the parties would include project-specific matters that take precedence over general conditions in the Special Conditions.

The conditions of contract comprises of 64 clauses, starting with definitions and interpretation and concluding with Issue Resolution and Dispute Resolution. The Contractor and the Employer are to appoint their representatives who shall act with the full authority of either party on all matters relating to the contract. Where the need

CIOB CPC 2012

arises for a replacement (where the original appointee is unable to act or in the case of the Contractor's representative there is a reasonable objection from the Employer or Contract Administrator) the relevant party will make a replacement appointment within five business days informing the other party, the Contract Administrator (CA) and Listed Persons of the details and qualifications of the replacement (12).

Synopsis

Intention

- The parties are to work together and cooperate in the spirit of trust and good faith and in compliance with the contract (5·1).
- The Contractor is to comply with all applicable laws, including the laws of other countries other than the law of the country the site is situated, where aspect of the work is carried out in that second country. Failure to comply will be a Contractor's risk for which he shall indemnify the Employer against all expenses and loss including third party action (5·3).
- The Contract documents are to be read together, however in the event of discrepancy between their provisions, an order of priority is set out with the Contract Agreement and Special condition at the top of the list and the Contractor's pricing document and the Contractor's design at the bottom of the list (3·3).
- Where the contract requires that any communication (instructions, decisions) be made, it shall be in writing (except otherwise provided) and delivered either by hand, special delivery or by electronic mail (4·2). The contract provides for when information delivered by hand or electronically is deemed received (4·3).
- Unless the Special Conditions provide differently, the Contractor shall have access to the site on the access date and commence construction in a good and workmanlike manner and complete the works on the date stated for substantial completion (5·4).
- The approval, acceptance or instructions by the CA or Listed Persons shall not relieve the Contractor of its obligation under the contract (6·5).
- The Contractor is to ensure that it does not put the Employer in breach of connected contracts (5·7).
- If at any time the Employer, Contract Administrator or Listed Persons become aware of any event likely to occur or occurring that will affect the progress of the Works, the person is to notify the Contractor of such event (34·1).
- The Contractor on becoming aware of any event likely to occur or occurring (including those notified by other person as envisaged under 34·1), it shall prepare an Early Warning notification to the CA and other listed persons, describing the event and its likely effect on progress (3·42).

CIOB CPC 2012

Time

- The Employer is to grant the Contractor access and possession on access dates as provided in the appendix to the contract or by sections, if sectional possession is envisaged (5·2).
- Where it is stated in the appendix to the contract (Appendix B), that the Contractor shall complete the works in sections, the Employer shall ensure that the Contractor is given access to each section on the Section Access Date stated in the contract appendix and the Contractor is expected to commence work and complete same on the date for sectional completion set out in the contract (5·5). Parts of the work slated for completion on a key date is to be completed on the said date (5·6).
- The Contractor may request for a decision or determination from the Contract Administrator including a request for approval, release of further information, supply of anything provided in the contract for the Employer to provide, supply of drawings (6·1). Such request is to be made at least 10 business days before the Logical Date by which the Contractor requires a response from the CA (6·3).
- The CA is to provide a response to the Contractor's request within the timescale provided under the contract. The options available include 10 business days from the receipt of the request, the Logical Date identified in the latest Working Schedule by which the contractor requires the information; the date stated in the specification for the relevant supply is to be made among others. The latest occurring of the options available is set as the deadline for response by the CA (6·4).
- Where the contract requires the Contractor to submit anything to the Contract Administrator, Project Time Manager, Design Coordination Manager or Valuer for acceptance or approval, the submittal is to be made 10 business days before the logical date that the Contractor requires a decision on the submittal (7·1).
- Any such submittal is to be deemed accepted within 10 business days of the submittal unless the Contractor is responded in the negative by the Listed Persons. The contract sets out possible responses (7·2).
- Submittals may be accepted in part within the timescale set out in clause 7·2, in such cases the Contractor is expected to resubmit the rejected portions within a specified date (7·3).
- Where a submission is rejected or deemed rejected, the Contractor is expected to resubmit a compliant submission. The time and costs risks associated with such resubmission are to be borne by the Contractor (7·4).
- The Contract Administrator is to keep a database of all submissions for the project and to issue a copy of same to Listed Persons before each progress meeting (7·5).

CIOB CPC 2012

- The Contractor is not to implement any submission until it has been approved or deemed approved (7·6). Where the Contractor believes that any rejection, approval or decision is in conflict with the contract or amounts to a variation, it is expected to submit the matter for Issue Resolution within five business days of receipt of the relevant communication; otherwise it shall be deemed to have accepted it (7·7).

Control

- Unless otherwise stated in the Special Conditions, the Contractor is not expected to verify the accuracy of any design not produced by it (3·5).
- The Contractor is expected to notify the Contract Administrator (CA) at the earliest opportunity of any inconsistency in the contract documents and/or between the contract documents and the law (3·4).
- The conditions represent the entire agreement between the parties and override any earlier communication or agreement (3·1). The Contract also provides for severability, therefore if any clause becomes inapplicable, the rest of the contract will continue to have effect.
- The service of notice or other communication is to be to the Contract Administrator and listed persons. The Contract makes provisions for electronic communication and common areas where stakeholders may view communications (2·3·7).
- Within 10 business days of the receipt of notification under 3·4, the CA is to give instructions which shall be valued as a variation except, the inconsistency would be resolved by relying on the position under a higher priority document or where the inconsistency refers to the contractor design or any documents submitted by the Contractor (3·6).
- Although an instruction for inconsistencies in documents is to be valued as a variation, where the current Working Schedule indicates that the activity to be affected by such instruction is to take effect within 20 business days of the date of the notice, any delay, expenses or costs of such activity shall be at the Contractor risk unless the instruction relates to inconsistencies in Employers design documents as provided under 3·5.
- The Party providing information in a native file transfer, or hosting the File Transfer Protocol or Common Data Environment shall ensure that the latest version of the software is used and maintain the integrity and security of such platforms, indemnifying all other authorised users in the event of loss or corruption of information (4·4).
- The Contractor is to ensure the compatibility and coordination of all materials and goods to be integrated into the project and their compatibility with parts of the works (5·8).

CIOB CPC 2012

- The Contractor warrants that it would use the skills and diligence of a specialist in the type of construction covered by the contract to ensure that it does not specify or use deleterious materials or materials not in conformity with local laws or standards (5·9).
- The Employer is on reasonable request from the Contractor to provide evidence that it has the finance to fund the project within 10 business days of such request (5·10). The Employer is also to provide the Contractor with details of any material changes to the source of funding for the project before embarking on such change (5·10).
- If the Employer fails to provide the information as required under 5·10, the Contractor may suspend some or all of its obligations on service of a 10 day notice to suspend. Such notice should spell out the activities the Contractor intends to suspend (5·11). The same rule as in 5·10 and 5·11 applies to a Contractor that receives a request by the Employer to be furnished with evidence of the Contractor's financial capability to continue to fulfil its obligations to complete the works.
- The Contractor is expected to have and retain all intellectual property rights on all design contained in the Contractor Design Portion of the contract and to indemnify the Employer in the event of loss or expenses on account of the design infringing any third party intellectual property (8·1).
- The Contractor is expected to grant the Employer irrevocable, non-exclusive and sub-licensable right to use the designs of the Contractor for all purposes connected to the works including facilities management and repairs and alteration of the works which may be carried out by another Contractor (8·2).
- Where the Employer provides the Contractor with information relating to the physical ground conditions, subsurface conditions or geology, it shall have the status assigned to it in the Special Conditions. Where no status is assigned, the Contractor is expected to rely on the information (8·5).
- Except where covered by clause 8·5, the Contractor is expected to carry its own investigation of the site prior to commencing works (8·6).
- The Contractor is expected to use reasonable skills and care of a registered professional experienced in such work. The work is to comply with relevant standards and laws and be of good quality. Additionally the work should incorporate the requirements and benefits of the design preceding it. The design is also expected to facilitate safe construction and be fit for the purpose required by the contract. The design should include all works reasonably inferred from the specification as well as design not referred to in the specification but which is required to complete the works or which is necessary for the works to fit the purpose set out in the contract (8·7).
- The contractor is to ensure that there are no clashes or inconsistencies or ambiguities in its design or between its design and the design of other parts of the works (8·8).

CIOB CPC 2012

- Unless stated otherwise in the specification or instructed by the Contract Administrator, the Contractor shall not commence any Design Stage unless the previous design stage has been approved (8·9).
- At the completion of each Design Stage, the approved design shall be signed by the parties with a copy provided to the CA (8·10). The Contractor will update the design when changes occur due to variations and to reflect the as-built information (8·11). The Contractor is expected to publish its designs at various intervals stated in the contract and at the request of the CA (8·12). Except in relation to the Contractor's design for Building Information Modelling (BIM), the Design Coordination Manager is expected to maintain a database of the Contractor's design submission with a copy of the database being provided to the CA and Listed Persons five business days before the Progress Meeting (8·13).
- Where the contract is used as a design and build contract, the Contractor is to provide the CA with a Design Execution Plan which would set out the design process, timing of submittals and other relevant matters (8·14·1). On the issue of the Certificate of Substantial Completion of Works, publish its corrected design recording how the works were actually built.
- Unless otherwise stated in the contract or against local laws, goods and materials are to become part of the Works as soon as they are incorporated into the work or the value for them is added to the payment notice (whichever occurs first) (13·2).
- Where the CA becomes aware that any person engaged by the contractor is performing below standard or is not complying with health and safety rules or damaging the environment, it shall bring it to the notice of the CA. If the action complained persists, the CA is entitled to require the Contractor to exclude such person from the Works and where necessary require the appointment of a competent replacement (14·2).
- Where the specification requires that samples of goods and materials be supplied to the CA for approval, the Contractor shall provide such samples along with all necessary technical information before incorporation into the Works (14·4).
- The Contractor is to carry out all tests and completion tests set out in the specification in the presence of the CA and any other persons (14·8). Where the specification requires that the CA be present at a testing, the CA will be notified of the testing five business days before the date of the testing (14·9). The Contractor is to forward to the CA duly certified reports and certificates of the tests; where the CA is satisfied that the tests meet the standard required by the specification, the CA is expected to endorse the Contractor's certificate or issue a certificate stating same (14·11).
- Where the CA is of the opinion that any goods, materials and/or Permanent Plant is defective, it may order its reopening and retesting, or its removal from site and

CIOB CPC 2012

replacement, to the extent that any goods, materials and/or Permanent Plant is found to be defective, the Contractor bear the costs of any replacement as well as the time and costs of the tests (14·16).

- Where the Contractor is not satisfied with the decision in 14·16 it may refer it for Issue Resolution within two business days; failing which it shall be deemed that the Contractor accepts the CA decision (4·17).
- The Contractor shall not assign its rights or benefits in the contract except on prior approval of the CA, however where the assignment is for the purpose of security in favour of a bank or lending institution and covers monies due to that will be due the Contractor under the contract, such approval is not required. The Contractor is to notify the Employer promptly of such assignment (17·1).

Building Information Modelling (BIM)

- Where the specification requires that the works be designed using a Building Information Model (BIM), it is to be prepared in a Common Data Environment with both parties and all relevant stakeholders having access to it (9·1).
- Unless a contrary intention is expressed in the specifications the Building Information Model and all drawings and information extracted from it, is owned by the Employer. The extent and purpose of information extracted from the model is stated in the appendix to the contract (Level of Development – LOD), a use beyond this will be at the sole risk of such user. Unless, specifically authorised design contributors are not to modify, transmit or use the Building Information Model (BIM) for any other purposes except the works.
- Where the contract requires the Contractor to prepare the Building Information Model (BIM), the Contractor will be expected to appoint the design coordination manager, provide the Common Data Environment and remain entirely responsible for the suitability and integrity of the preferred software and of any information from the model. The Contractor shall maintain and update the model as required by the CA and also obtain the digital signature of the Employer and Contractor at the completion of each Level of Development (9·2).
- Where the Contractor is to make a Design Contribution, the Design will be to the Level of Development specified in the Appendix and shall maintain and update such contribution as required by the CA. The Contractor is also expected to indemnify other Design users against any liability (direct or consequential) arising from the Contractor's Design. The contractor is also expected to notify the CA and the Design Coordination Manager of any clashes or inconsistencies between the Contractor's design and that made by other designers (9·3).
- The Contractor is to carry out all temporary and ancillary work necessary for or in connection with the Works (10).

CIOB CPC 2012

Money

- The CA is to issue a Notice of Payment Due to the Employer and each Listed Person no later than the Notice Date (which shall be set out in the Appendix to the Contract) (55·1). A notice of payment shall identify the final date of payment and the amount due to be paid (the items to be considered in calculating this amount are set out in the contract) (55·2). If the aggregate sum of the amount due exceeds the Predicated Cost, the CA is to notify the parties of the amount due from the Contractor to the Employer (55·3).
- Where the CA fails to issue a Notice of Payment Due by the Notice Date, the Contractor may issue a Notice of Payment Due to the Employer, copied to the CA, the Notice shall include the sum it considers due, basis of its calculation and the basis for claiming that the payment is due (56).
- Where the Contractor issues a Notice of Payment Due, the final date of payment shall be postponed by the number of days between the Notice Date and the date on which the Contractor issued such notice (57·2).
- Where the Notice of Payment Due requires the Employer to pay the Contractor, the Employer shall make payment on or before the final payment date stated in Appendix B to the Contractor of amount notified in the Notice of Payment Due (57·3).
- Where the Intention to pay a lesser sum, and unless contrary to local laws, the Employer shall notify the Contractor no later than five business days prior to the Final Payment Date of its intention to pay less and the basis for the calculation of that amount (57·3·2). Similar rules apply where the payment is due from the Contractor to the Employer (57·4).
- Where payment is not made in full by the final date for payment, the Contractor may suspend all or any of its obligations on the issuance of 10 business days' notice, until such time full payment is made the Contractor shall not recommence the Works. The notice should identify the obligations the contractor intends to suspend (57·3·3).
- Parties are also entitled to interest on late payment at the rate stated in Appendix B (58).
- Unless stated otherwise in the specification, the contractor is not to sub-contract the works without the approval of the CA, such approval not to be unreasonably withheld (17·3). Where the Employer nominates a list of sub-contractors, the Contractor shall at its sole discretion select a sub-contractor (17·3).
- Irrespective of the appointment of sub-contractors, the Contractor shall remain wholly responsible for carrying out and completing the Works (17·4).
- Progress meetings are to be held according to a schedule set out in the appendix to

CIOB CPC 2012

the contract and are to be attended by the Contractor, CA, Project Time Manager and other persons requested to attend by the CA. The minutes of the meeting will be distributed by the three business days after the meeting; the minutes shall be deemed to be agreed unless there is any objection within five business days of the issue of the minutes (18).

- The CA is to issue all instructions required by the contract. Instructions from the CA may include such matters as Prime Cost/Provisional Costs expenditure or omission, suspension of the contractor's obligation and any necessary instruction for safe, timely and cost-effective completion of the Works (20·1).
- The CA prior to the issue of the Certificate of Substantial Completion may instruct a Variation. As soon as reasonably practical after receiving such instruction the Contractor is to provide a calculation of the time and cost effect (if any) of the Variation prepared in accordance with contract.
- Within five business days of receiving an Early Warning, the CA is to update the risk register and hold a risk management meeting with relevant stakeholders where mitigation of the risk will be discussed and appropriate instructions issued (35).
- The contract provides detailed clauses for calculation of the effect of Early Warning events on time and also costs (36, 37).
- After the receipt and due consideration of the Early Warning, the Project Time Manager shall within 10 business days of the receipt of this information advise the CA on the impact of the Early Warning as provided under the contract as well as alternative instructions to reduce the time lost to the event (38).
- Within five business days of receiving such advice, the CA may extend the time by fixing a new Relevant Completion Date or issue other instructions as appropriate (38·2).

Statutory obligations

- The Contractor is to maintain sufficient health and safety procedures on site including keeping to local laws and appointing necessary personnel who shall have the authority to give instructions on health and safety issues and keep records. Any incidents are to be reported to the CA within two business days, failing which the CA may require the Contractor to suspend performance of the contract to allow for investigation. The cost of such suspension is to be borne by the Contractor.
- The Contractor shall comply with all instructions given by the CA within the time stated in such instruction and the absence of time stipulation within reasonable time (20·2). Where an instruction from the CA will render the Contractor's design in conflict with law and/or inconsistent with design of other parts, the Contractor is to notify the CA with a copy to the Employer. The CA is expected to amend, retract or affirm the instruction after which the Contractor is to comply with it (20·3).

CIOB CPC 2012

- Where the Contractor fails to carry out an instruction given by the CA, the CA may at any time notify the Contractor of the default which would entitle the Employer without further notice to engage others to execute the instruction and work incidental to it. In such circumstances the Contractor shall bear the risk in time and costs as well as any loss or expenses incurred by the Employer.
- Unless there is a contrary provision in the Special Conditions, the Contractor is to obtain all permits and licences required for it to perform its obligations under the contract. The Employer is to use reasonable endeavours to assist the Contractor in obtaining the permits and licences where requested (16).

Miscellaneous

- Defined Terms are capitalised terms which are used frequently all through the contract and have their meanings set out in Appendix A of the contract (1).
- The Interpretation clause makes the law applicable to the contract and the currency of payment dependent on the entry made by the parties in the relevant appendix.
- All communication shall be in the English language (4·1).
- Construction is to be carried out on business days and within normal hours as stated in the specifications except where ordered otherwise by the CA or where the work is needed for health and safety reasons or to protect the works or adjoining properties. In the latter case the Contractor is to inform the CA within two business days of the nature and quantity of the work and the reason for it. Where the Contractor fails to inform the CA within the timescale envisaged, the CA may require that the Contractor suspends further performance of the Works until the issue is properly investigated and recorded; the Employer may also pay other persons to carry out the investigations. The time and costs of such process is to be borne by the Contractor (13·5).

Insurance

- Each party is expected to take out and maintain insurances as stated in the Special Conditions (27·1).
- Each party may request to see evidence of the insurance the contract requires the other party to maintain. Where such evidence is not provided, the other party may take out the required insurance. If this is done by the Contractor it will be treated as a Variation and if by the Employer, appropriate deductions will be made from payments due the Contractor to cover cost of the insurance (27·2).
- The Contractor shall be liable and identify the Employer against loss and expenses arising from personal injury or death during the course of the Works except the death or injury is due to an act or omission of the Employer or persons engaged by it. The same rule applies to injury and damage to real and personal property (27·3).

CIOB CPC 2012

Termination

- The Employer is entitled to terminate for convenience on the issue of a notice to terminate to the Contractor not later than five business days before the Termination Date, the notice is to be copied to the CA and Listed Persons (59·1).
- The Penultimate valuation on termination on this ground is to place within 60 business days and is to include value if work properly completed at the Termination Date, the cost of removal from site of any Contractor's Plant, Temporary Work or Welfare Facilities, the value of any of these equipments to be left on site and any expenses incurred by the Contractor as a result of termination (59·3).
- Payment on this heading specifically excludes any for compensation including loss of profit on uncompleted work or damages under this clause (59·4).
- For a period of 300 business days following termination under this clause the Employer is not, without the Contractor's consent, to engage another person to carry out any work forming part of the contract except for the purposes of making good defects and securing the safety of the works, property or persons (59·6).
- If work is recommenced without the Contractor's consent during the 300 business days period, the Contractor shall be entitled to compensation for any loss of profit on uncompleted work.
- The Employer may terminate for Contractor's default at any time before the issue of the certificate of Substantial Completion for the Works. Contractor default may include insolvency, refusal to comply with CA instructions, failure to comply with the law, bribery and corruption and health and safety breaches (60·1).
- The CA is to notify the Contractor within 10 business days of the Contractor's Default stating the nature of the breaches, the date of its occurrence and action required to remedy the breach if it is amendable to remedial (60·1). If the Contractor fails to remedy the default within 10 business days, the Employer may give five business days' notice of termination to the Contractor copying the CA and Listed Persons and stating the Termination Date.
- If the CA specifies in the notice that the breach is not capable of remedy, the Contractor may nevertheless propose a solution within five business days of the notice to the Employer copied to the CA and Listed Persons (60·3). The proposal may either be accepted or rejected or further information may be required (60·3).
- Where the Contractor fails to provide further information as requested or the proposal is rejected, the Employer may by five business days' notice copied to the CA and Listed Persons terminate the Contract, stating the Termination Date (60·4).
- Where the Contractor's remedy is accepted for a specified default, if the Contractor repeats the default, the Employer within 15 business days' notice of such repetition

serve on the Contractor notice of termination identifying that the notice is issued under the clause and stating the Termination Date (60·5).

- Where Termination is at the default of the Contractor, the Contractor shall vacate the site and the Employer shall take whatever steps reasonably necessary to secure the site (60·6).
- Within 100 business days of termination for contractor's default or 60 business days of the Substantial Completion of the Works, whichever is later, the Valuer shall issue the CA with the Penultimate Valuation which will include works properly completed at the Termination Date, including value of Temporary Work, Contractor's Plant or Welfare Facilities not returned to the Contractor less the cost of the Employer completing the Works and the Contractor shall not be entitled to loss of profits, loss of opportunity, etc (60·7). Within 10 business days of a Penultimate Valuation, the CA shall issue a Notice of Payment Due.
- Termination may also be on account of an Employer's breach. An Employer breach includes failure to make payment, interference with the issuance of certificates under the Contract. Failure to comply with local laws on bribery and corruption and health and safety, bankruptcy among others (61·1). On the occurrence of any of the issues listed as Employer's default, the Contractor shall within 10 business days notify the Employer copying the CA, setting out the nature of default, date of occurrence and action required to remedy the default (61).
- If the Contractor fails to remedy the notice within 10 business days of the notice, the Contractor may give a five business days' notice of termination to the Employer copied to the CA and Listed persons and stating the Termination Date.
- If at any time the Employer repeats the default, the Contractor may within 15 business days after such repetition serve the Employer a termination notice (61·3).
- Calculation of payment on termination under this heading includes work properly completed at the Termination Date, overhead costs and profit for the works stated in the Contractor's Pricing Document, any costs or loss and/or expenses arising directly from the termination (61·5). Payment is to be made within 20 business days of receipt of the Contractor's Notice of Payment Due or within 60 business days of the Termination Date, whichever is later.
- Either Party may terminate if part or the whole of the works is suspended by reason of any events Appendix F for a continuous period of 120 business days or more. Such Termination will be by notice and state that if the suspension continues for a further five business days it intends to terminate the Contractor's employment under the contract (62·1).
- Within 60 business days of Termination, the Valuer is to issue the CA a Penultimate Valuation which shall include the Work properly completed at the Date of

CIOB CPC 2012

Termination, value of all Temporary Work, Plant or Welfare facilities less any amount previously certified for payment (62·4).

Dispute resolution

- Except in circumstances where a timescale is prescribed by the contract, either party may within 20 business days of the occurrence of an issue arising give notice to the other of any issues they wish resolved (63·1). All notices requiring Issue Resolution are to be served electronically (63·2).
- As a pre-step to Issue Resolution, the parties' representatives and failing that senior management are to meet to resolve the issue (63·3).
- If the attempt at a negotiated resolution fails, or within 10 days of a party giving notice of an issue requiring resolution, the Principal Expert shall be appointed to resolve the issue. The procedure is set out in the Appendix to the contract (63·4). The Principal Expert is to issue its determination within 20 business days of being appointed (63).
- If the Principal Expert fails to deliver a Determination within the time allowed, the party is entailed to treat such matter as a dispute (64·3).
- The Contracts sets up mediation as the first step in dispute resolution (64·1).
- Adjudication is also set up as means of dispute resolution and its primacy in some jurisdictions such as the UK is acknowledged (64·7).
- The final tribunal for dispute resolution is arbitration in accordance with rules set out in detail in Appendix B of the contract.

CIOB CPC 2012

This contract?

If considering using CIOB CPC 2012 remember that:

The CIOB CPC is for complex projects and may not be suited for a contract of a simple nature.

The Contractor particularly has to be aware of the range of responsibilities placed on it by the contract, for instance the contractor is expected to ensure that it does not put the Employer in breach of connected contracts. The Appendix to the contract is an important document that should be completed carefully and read in conjunction with the main contract.

This contract provides well drafted clauses for modern contract using electronic communications and Building Information Modelling (BIM).

Related matters

Documents

CIOB Complex Projects Contract 2012
CIOB Complex Projects Contract

Traditional procurement 7

Shorter lump sum forms

The Joint Contracts Tribunal Ltd
Intermediate Building Contracts 2011

The Joint Contracts Tribunal Ltd
Minor Works Building Contracts 2011

The Joint Contracts Tribunal Ltd
Repairs and Maintenance Contract (Commercial) 2011 Edition

Association of Consultant Architects
ACA Form of Building Agreement 1982 (Third Edition 1998, 2003 Revision)

The Stationery Office
Form GC/Works/2 (1998)

The Stationery Office
Form GC/Works/4 (1998)

The Institution of Civil Engineers
NEC Document
Engineering and Construction Short Contract (June 2005) with 2011 amendments

The Joint Council for Landscape Industries (JCLI)
Agreement for Landscape Works 2012

Chartered Institute of Building
CIOB Forms of Contract

Scottish Building Contract Committee (SBCC)
SBCC Forms of Contract 2011

Just what constitutes a shorter form is arguable. For the purposes of this book, contracts which are comparatively brief and easy to handle in terms of administration are included under this heading. This need not necessarily imply that they are solely for smaller works nor indeed only suitable for lump sum contracts.See also Chapter 8 below, in which short forms which are more likely to be categorised as consumer contracts are covered.

JCT IC11/ICD11

The Joint Contracts Tribunal Ltd

Intermediate Building Contracts 2011

Background

With the introduction of a then new and more sophisticated edition of The Standard Form of Building Contract (JCT80), many architects felt that they lacked a contract suitable for middle range jobs. The RIBA expressed this concern, and in October 1981 the JCT set up a working party to prepare an 'intermediate' form. With considerable input from constituent bodies, in particular the RIBA, the Association of District Councils and the Association of Metropolitan Authorities, the Intermediate Form appeared in September 1984.

IFC84 was the subject of 12 Amendments, the last of which was to meet many of the recommendations made in the Latham Report of 1994. Incorporation of Amendment 12 ensured compliance with Part II of the Housing Grants, Construction and Regeneration Act 1996 in respect of adjudication and payment provisions.

The development of this form continued with publication of the 1998 edition, which consolidated the various amendments to IFC84. Further refinement was undertaken in the 2005 edition, which was released in two versions, one with aspects of the design to be undertaken by the Contractor and one where the Contractor responsibilities did not include design. The 2005 edition incorporated many significant changes while retaining popular provisions like naming sub-contractors.

The 2011 edition was published primarily in response to the amendment of the Housing Grants, Construction and Regeneration Act 1996 by the Local Democracy, Economic Development and Construction Act 2009 which came into force on different dates throughout Great Britain and Northern Ireland starting on 1 October 2011 in England and Wales. The changes in this edition concentrate on the payment provisions, payment certificates, definition of insolvency and an update of drafting around terrorism cover.

Nature

The Intermediate Building Contract continues to be published in two versions, one 'with contractor's design' which has provision for the contractor to design an identified portion of the Works (ICD11), and one which does not (IC11). In all other respects the versions are identical, therefore the points raised below can be assumed to apply to both versions, unless indicated otherwise.

Both versions of the form now run to over 80 pages. There are ten Recitals in the ICD11 version and nine Articles. The Conditions are arranged under nine headings, in line with SBC. There is a contents list at the front which gives clause and page numbers. Contract Particulars (to be completed by the parties) are also included at the front, and the Conditions are followed by four Schedules dealing with insurance options, named sub-contractors, forms of bonds (in relation to advance payment, and off-site materials and goods), and fluctuations.

The Intermediate Building Contract has the virtue of relative brevity, a clear layout and commendably easy cross-referencing. The Conditions should be adequate for the foreseeable circumstances of most middle range projects.

Use

The inside front cover of IC11 (not part of the text) lists three criteria for suitability. These refer to building works of simple content and without complex services installations, where the works are designed by or on behalf of the Employer and the Employer is to provide the Contractor with drawings, specifications and schedules that define the quantity and quality of work and finally where the Employer intends to engage an Architect/Contract Administrator and a Quantity Surveyor to administer the conditions. It is a lump sum contract, to be priced entirely by the Contractor, and therefore the job must be fully designed and billed or specified at tender stage.

ICD11 lists an additional criterion for suitability, ie that the form is suitable where the contractor is to design a discrete part or parts of the Works, and the requirements for that design have been detailed by or on behalf of the Employer.

The guidance note states clearly that it is not suitable for design and build procurement. The Employer is required to appoint an Architect/Contract Administrator (Article 3), and to name whoever is appointed to undertake the duties required of a Quantity Surveyor (Article 4). The CDM Coordinator and Principal Contractor for CDM and SWMP Regulations will be identified in entries to Articles 5 and 6.

Clause 1·1 identifies the Contract Documents as being the Contract Drawings, and either the Priced Document or the Specification. Where a sub-contractor is named, the NAM documents are also to be included. For the ICD version, the Contract Documents also include Employer's Requirements, Contractor's Proposals and a CDP Analysis.

The fourth Recital (fifth in ICD) allows the contractor to tender either by pricing the itemised bills, Specification or Schedules (Option A), or to state just a lump sum based on a Specification which is not itemised for pricing (Option B). If the latter then the Employer will require the contractor to submit a Schedule of Rates, or a Contract Sum Analysis. The Employer might be wise to stipulate a Contract Sum Analysis option. The Employer might also require it to be in a preferred format, and perhaps this should be prepared by the quantity surveyor for completion by the tenderers.

There is a provision for sectional completion, and if partial possession before practical completion is required, then clause 2·25 provides for this.

JCT IC11/ICD11

Synopsis

1 Intentions

- The contractor is obliged to carry out and complete the Works in accordance with the Contract Documents and with the Health and Safety Plan and statutory requirements (2·1). The contractor must complete the design of the Contractor's Designed Portion, and comply with all instructions of the Architect relating to the integration of the Portion with the rest of the Works (2·1, ICD only).
- The quality and quantity of work included in the Contract Sum is clearly defined (4·1) and is related to the documents used.
- The contractor is required to submit drawings and other documents it prepares in relation to the design as reasonably necessary to explain the Contractor's Proposals (2.10.2, ICD only). These are to be provided 'as and when necessary' or as stipulated in the Contract Documents (2.10.3, ICD only).
- Materials, goods and workmanship are to be to the standard set out in the Contract Documents (2·1 and 4·1), including the Employer's Requirements or Contractor's Proposals as relevant. If stated to be to the Architect's satisfaction, they are to be to the Architect's reasonable satisfaction. Where no standard is set out, they are to be a standard appropriate to the Works (2·2).
- The Contract Documents are to be read as a whole and the printed Articles, Conditions and Appendix have priority (1·3).
- In the case of inconsistencies or errors in or between documents (including the tender particulars for a named sub-contractor) corrective instructions must be given (2·13·1).
- Contract bills, except where specifically stated otherwise, must be prepared in accordance with the Standard Method of Measurement 7th Edition (2·12·1).
- If applicable, the contractor must be provided with two copies of the information referred to in the Information Release Schedule by the stated times (Third/Fourth Recital and clause 2·10). The contractor must also be issued with further drawings as reasonably necessary to complete the Works (2·11). Use of them is limited and confidentiality of rates is to be respected (2·8·3).
- There is no reference to a contractor's programme.
- The CDM Regulations oblige the Employer to nominate a CDM Coordinator and where relevant a Principal Contractor both for CDM regulation and SWMP Regulations. This becomes a contractual obligation also (Articles 5 and 6 and clause 3·18) and any need to appoint a replacement is also covered (3·19).

JCT IC11/ICD11

2 Time

- Dates for possession and completion must be entered in the Contract Particulars. The contractor must proceed regularly and diligently and complete on or before the completion date (2·4).
- There is provision for dividing the Works into Sections, and setting separate commencement and completion dates, and rates of liquidated damages for each section. All provisions relating to timing, for example extending the date for completion, apply separately to each section, except that there is only one Final Certificate.
- An option clause for deferring possession not exceeding six weeks may apply subject to an entry in the Contract Particulars (2·5).
- Notice of delay must be given in writing by the contractor as soon as the Works (on any Section) appears likely to be delayed. The contractor must supply any information reasonably necessary (2·19·4). The Architect is to consider a new completion date and to notify the contractor of his or her decision, in writing, as soon as he or she is able to see the effect on completion (2·19·1). Although no time limit is stated, this must be within a reasonable time. Relevant 'events' are listed for which the Architect is empowered to make an extension (2·20). Review of extensions up to 12 weeks beyond practical completion is discretionary (2·19·3).
- If the contractor fails to meet a completion date, this fact must be certified (2·22). Liquidated damages may be deducted or otherwise recovered by the Employer (2·23).
- Practical completion is certified by the Architect (2·21).
- The contractor is obliged to rectify defects (2·30) unless the Employer decides otherwise and takes an appropriate deduction instead.
- There is provision for partial possession (2·25).
- Where the Employer wishes to occupy part of the uncompleted Works for storage etc, this is possible subject to proper insurance arrangements (2·6).

3 Control

- The bar to assignment without written consent refers to 'the Contract or any rights thereunder' (7·1). Sub-letting any part of the work requires the Architect's written consent (3·15).
- The contract provides for collateral warranties to be provided by the contractor to funders and purchasers/tenants, and by sub-contractors to the purchasers/tenants, funders, and the Employer (Section 7). The requirement to enter into warranties must be set out in the Contract Particulars, the relevant persons and sub-contractors identified, together with information regarding limits to the contractor's liability.
- All sub-contractors are domestic. There is provision for requiring a 'named' sub-

contractor to execute identified parts of the work (3.7). The provisions relating to named sub-contractors are set out in Schedule 2, and require the use of the standard form sub-contract ICSub/NAM/A. Two methods are available, through naming the sub-contractor in the Contract Documents, or in an instruction regarding a provisional sum. Both require the use of standard forms of tender ICSub/NAM/IT and ICSub/NAM/T.

- There is no provision for a list of three names, and such a practice should not be necessary. However, the NBS Small Jobs Version does offer suitable clauses, although care should be taken to state that this is a 3·6 sub-contract and not under clause 3·7.
- Architect's instructions must be in writing (3·8). Instructions empowered include for variations (3·11), postponement (3·12) and expenditure of provisional sums (3·13).
- The contractor is required to have a competent person-in-charge on the Works at all reasonable times (3·2) and to permit the presence of the Employer's clerk of works (3·3) who has no prescribed authority.
- Where work or materials do not conform to the contract, the Architect may order their removal from the site (3·16). Instructions are empowered concerning inspection and testing (3·14) and there is a particularly helpful provision concerning similar work elsewhere which may be suspect following established failure (3·15).
- The Employer is entitled to carry out work not forming part of the contract during the time that the contractor is in possession subject to certain conditions (2·7).

4 Money

- The Contract Sum is VAT-exclusive (4·3) and may only be adjusted as provided for in the contract (4·2).
- The contract may include for fluctuations (4·15 and 4·16). These are limited to tax etc (Schedule 4).
- Where provisional sums have been included, instructions must be given on how to use them (3·13).
- Applications for reimbursement of loss and/or expense must be made in writing by the contractor (4·17). The grounds for a valid application are set out (4·18) and include only matters over which the contractor has no control and which occur because of action or failure by the Employer. The procedures must be followed precisely. Other rights at common law are preserved.
- Interim payments to the contractor are to be at pre-arranged stages. The contract provides different timescales for the calculation of the due date for interim payments, for instance unless otherwise agreed by the parties, the due date for interim payment from commencement of works up to practical completion is at the monthly dates set out in the Contract Particulars; also the due date for interim payment after practical completion, is a date not later than 14 days from date of practical completion

JCT IC11/ICD11

(4·7·1). Retention is five per cent unless an alternative rate is entered in the Contract Particulars (note IC does not use the term 'retention').

- The Architect/Contract Administrator is required to issue an interim payment certificate not later than five days from the due date for interim payment. The certificate should state the amount the Architect/Contract Administrator considers due on the relevant due date and the basis on which the amount was calculated (4·7·2).
- In relation to interim payment, the contractor may not later than seven days before the due date for interim payment make an application to the Quantity Surveyor stating the sum he considers will be due him on the relevant due date and the basis on which the sum was calculated (4·10). This application becomes a payment notice if the Architect/Contract Administrator fails to issue an interim certificate in accordance with the contract.
- Where no application for payment had been made and the Architect/Contractor Administrator fails to issue an Interim Certificate, the Contractor may at any time after the expiration of the five day period from the due date, issue a payment notice to the Quantity Surveyor, stating the sum the Contractor considers due on the relevant due date and basis for the calculation of the sum (4·10·2).
- The final date of payment on the interim certificate is 14 days from its due date. Unless a Pay Less Notice is issued the Employer is to pay the sum stated in the interim certificate (4·11·2) on the final date of payment.
- Where the Architect/Contract Administrator fails or neglects to issue an interim certificate in accordance with 4·7·2, then the Contractor's Interim Payment Notice under clause 4·10 applies, and subject to the service of a Pay Less Notice, the Employer shall pay the sum stated in the Contractor's Payment Notice (4·11·3) on the final date for payment.
- Where the Contractor's Payment Notice is issued after the expiration of the five day period after the due date, then the final date for payment is postponed by the same number of days after such period that the Payment Notice was issued (4·11·4).
- If the Employer intends to pay less than the sum stated in the interim payment certificate or Contractor's Payment Notice, it is required to, not later than five days from the final date of payment, issue a Pay Less Notice stating the sum he considers due to the Contractor on the date of the issue of the notice and the basis on which it was calculated (4·11·5, 4·12·1). It must be noted that the Employer is not entitled to withhold or deduct any amount from monies due the Contractor unless the proper Pay Less Notice has been issued.
- Failure to pay by the final date for payment will attract simple interest on the overdue amount (4·11·8), and can give the contractor a right to suspend work some or its entire obligation with a right to recover reasonable costs and expenses incurred as a

JCT IC11/ICD11

result of such suspension. Suspension is to be preceded by the service of a seven day notice and may only progress where there is a failure to remedy the non-payment after the seven day period (4·13).

- There is a precise timescale for the preparation of a final account after practical completion. Issue of the Final Certificate is within 28 days of sending the final account to the Contractor, or certifying that defects have been made good, or the end of the rectification period, whichever is the later (4·14·1).
- The due date for final payment shall be the date of issue of the final certificate, or where the certificate has not been issued, the last day of the 28 day period referred to in 4.14.1, and the final date for payment is 28 days from the due date (4·14·3).
- Similar rules as those discussed above for the Interim Certificate apply in respect of the Final Certificate with regard to notices (4·14).

5 Statutory obligations

- It is the contractor's duty to comply with all statutory obligations and give all required notices (2·1). The contractor is entitled to recover fees and charges not otherwise provided for (2·3).
- The contractor is to notify the Architect if it finds any conflict between statutory requirements and the Contract Documents (2·15·1). The Architect must issue an instruction (2·15·2). The contractor is not liable for any non-compliance if it results from having carried out work in accordance with the Contract Documents or any instruction (2·15·3).
- The contractor is empowered to carry out limited work for emergency compliance and this will be treated as a variation to be valued accordingly (2·16).
- The contractor is contractually obliged to comply with the CDM Regulations and particularly, where the project is notifiable, to comply with duties in relation to the Construction Phase Plan and the Health and Safety File (3·18).

6 Insurance

- What a particular contract includes will depend to a large extent on the entries in the Contract Particulars (eg whether option clauses are to apply, minimum amount of cover required, etc). The Architect may be obliged to issue instructions, call for documentary evidence and pass policies to the Employer for checking.
- The contractor is to indemnify the Employer in respect of personal injury or death, and injury or damage to property other than the actual Works (6·1 and 6·2). This is to be backed by insurance, and an entry will state the minimum cover.
- If instructed, the contractor is to take out joint names insurance for the Employer against risk of claims arising due to legal nuisance. There is a list of exceptions, and

JCT IC11/ICD11

damage must not be attributable to any negligence by the Contractor. An entry in the Contract Particulars will indicate whether cover may be required and the amount of cover to be provided (6·5).

- Insurance of 'the Works' is for all risks where new buildings are concerned and should be for full reinstatement value. It can be taken out either by the contractor (Schedule 1 Option A) or by the Employer (Schedule 1 Option B).
- Insurance of existing structures and the contents is a matter for the Employer (Schedule 1 Option C) and is limited to specified perils. New work in existing buildings, although still a matter for the Employer, requires all risks cover.
- The contractor is required to carry professional indemnity insurance to cover its liability for design, details of which should be set out in the Contract Particulars.
- An entry in the Contract Particulars will show whether the Joint Code of Practice on the Protection from Fire of Construction Sites is to apply (6·12, 6·13) and if so, both the Employer and the contractor must comply with it. In the event of non-compliance the insurers can specify remedial measures which have to be taken.
- The 2011 edition of the contract has extensive provisions for insurance to cover various acts of terrorism (6·10 and 6·12).

7 Termination

- The Employer is allowed to terminate the employment of the contractor by reason of specified defaults (8·4) or in the event of the insolvency of the Contractor (8·5) or in the event of bribery (8·6). Where termination is for defaults set out in 8·4, a 14 day warning notice is required before the actual notice of termination by the Employer which to take place within 21 days after the expiration of the 14 days.
- The consequences of termination based on the contractor's default or insolvency or bribery is set out in clause 8·7, and makes the contractor liable for costs and expenses incurred by the Employer in completing the project using another contractor and in securing the site and materials and any other expenses arising from the termination..
- The contractor is allowed to terminate its own employment for specified defaults of the Employer (8·9) or in the event of the insolvency of the Employer (8·10).
- Either party can terminate the employment of the contractor for listed neutral causes (8·11).
- The respective rights and duties of the parties concerning payment, removal and completion following termination under clauses 8.10 or 8.11 are set out in detail in clause (8·12).

JCT IC11/ICD11

8 Miscellaneous

- Definitions are included (1·1).
- There is a contracting out of third party rights under the Contracts (Rights of Third Parties) Act 1999 (1·6).
- There is no reference to access for the Architect, but this would normally be implied.
- There is power to exclude persons from the Works (3·17).
- There is no provision for antiquities.
- Contract Sum Analysis (Second Recital) is defined (1·1), and JCT Practice Note 23 (original series, green cover) gives a useful explanation.
- The use of Sub/NAM/ITandT where a person is to be a named sub-contractor is confirmed (Schedule 2·5).

9 Disputes

- Subject to the right of either party to refer any matter at any time to adjudication, mediation is suggested by the contract as an appropriate first instance dispute resolution method (9·1).
- Part II of the Housing Grants, Construction and Regeneration Act 1996 as amended gives either party a statutory right to refer any difference or dispute arising out of the contract to adjudication. Article 7 provides for this.
- The adjudication procedures are those of the Scheme for Construction Contracts, subject to certain provisions regarding the appointment and qualifications of the adjudicator (9·2)
- The adjudicator's decision is binding on the parties at least until the dispute is finally determined at arbitration or by legal proceedings.
- Arbitration may be selected as the agreed method for final determination of disputes (Article 8).
- The appointment of the arbitrator is subject to clause 9·4, and the arbitrator's powers are clearly defined (9·5).
- The parties agree that either may appeal to the courts on a question of law (9·7).
- Arbitration is to be conducted in accordance with the JCT 2011 Edition of the Construction Industry Model Arbitration Rules and the provisions of the Arbitration Act 1996 shall apply.
- Where the Contract Particulars do not indicate that Article 8 (arbitration) is to apply, then Article 9, legal proceedings, will automatically apply.

JCT IC11/ICD11

This contract?

If considering using IC11 or ICD11 remember that:

It is intended for building work of a simple content, without specialist installations, and where the work is adequately specified or billed before tender. The Employer is required to appoint a contract administrator and a quantity surveyor.

If used for work in Northern Ireland an Adaptation Schedule should be incorporated. The form is not suitable for use in Scotland, and where the site of the Works is in Scotland, the appropriate SBC form should be used.

The ICD version allows the contractor to design an identified part of the Works. This depends on detailed Employer's Requirements being issued at tender stage. Although the contractor is to submit further design information before work is carried out, the Employer would be sensible to set out exactly what information is required and when in the Requirements. It should also be noted that ICD11 does not include the detailed design submission procedure set out in DB11 and is therefore not suitable for a design and build contract.

The contract accommodates partial possession and sectional completion. There are also provisions for the contractor and/or its sub-contractors to provide collateral warranties on JCT standard forms to purchaser/tenants, funders and to the Employer. Rights under the Contract (Rights of Third Party) Act 2009 are specifically excluded.

It allows for sub-contractors to be named, and there are two procedures. The first requires the naming to be pre-contract and may seem inflexible but brings greater certainty. The second allows for naming during construction and is covered in the contract by a provisional sum. In both cases the sub-contractors are domestic and the responsibility of the main Contractor. Use of dedicated documents is mandatory with named sub-contractors. As the main contractor is not responsible for named sub-contractor design, employers should be advised to use an ICSub/NAM/E agreement for each named sub-contractor involved in some design relating to their work.

When completing the form, decisions are required relating to matters including deferment of possession; bonds (for advance payment, 'listed items'); insurance of the Works; Joint Fire Code; liquidated damages; fluctuations; and electronic communications. Caution is needed over naming a quantity surveyor – this should not be left blank, and even if the Employer does not agree to appointing a quantity surveyor, the mechanism of the contract still requires a name to be entered to fulfil this role (usually that of the Architect).

If acting as contract administrator note that while the procedural rules are less demanding than those for SBC11, care is needed to make sure that action is taken within a reasonable time even though no time limit is stated. This is particularly so concerning named sub-contractors.

The RIBA publishes contract administration forms for IC11 and ICD11.

JCT IC11/ICD11

Related matters

Documents

Intermediate Building Contract
Intermediate Building Contract with contractor's design
Intermediate Sub-contract Agreement
Intermediate Sub-contract Conditions
Intermediate Sub-contract with sub-contractor's design Agreement
Intermediate Sub-contract with sub-contractor's design Conditions
Intermediate Named Sub-contract Tender and Agreement
Intermediate Named Sub-contract Conditions
Intermediate Named Sub-contractor/Employer Agreement
Contractor Collateral Warranty for a Funder
Contractor Collateral Warranty for a Purchaser or Tenant
Sub-contractor Collateral Warranty for a Funder
Sub-contractor Collateral Warranty for a Purchaser or Tenant
Sub-contractor Collateral Warranty for Employer

References

Intermediate Building Contract Guide
Intermediate Building Sub-contract Guide

Commentaries

Sarah Lupton
Guide to IC11
RIBA Publishing (2011)

David Chappell
IC11 Contract Administration Guide
RIBA Publishing (2011)

JCT MW11/MWD11

The Joint Contracts Tribunal Ltd

Minor Works Building Contracts 2011

Background

The Agreement for Minor Building Works first appeared in 1968, and was intended for minor building operations and maintenance work for which the JCT Standard Form of Building Contract (then JCT63) was clearly inappropriate. It was just five pages long, compared with nearly 40 pages of the full Standard Form. It was not for use with bills of quantities, and was stated as being suitable where the Contract Sum did not exceed £8,000.

In the 1970s the RIBA, conscious of certain deficiencies in both the 1963 Standard Form and the Minor Works Agreement, set out proposals for a new, simpler 'short form' of building contract. RIBA Council approved this proposal with acclamation in June 1978. The aim was for a four-page contract with conditions written in plain English and structured logically under eight headings. The JCT accepted the proposal in principle, but the response of their working group was to draft a new 1980 version of the Minor Works form. It was a significant advance, however, and this was the first time that Conditions in JCT Forms were arranged under Section headings. Incidentally the 'short form' concept was later to resurface in the drafting of IFC84.

MW80 was the subject of 11 Amendments, the last of which was to take account of the Housing Grants, Construction and Regeneration Act 1996. The 1998 Edition of the Agreement for Minor Building Works was basically a consolidated version of MW80.

In 2005 the Agreement for Minor Building Works was revised along with all the other JCT standard forms, and two new editions were published, entitled the Minor Works Building Contract, and the Minor Works Building Contract with contractor's design. The most significant change is, of course, the introduction of the new version allowing for the main contractor to undertake a limited amount of design. This new version will no doubt be very welcome, as it is frequently the case in practice that even on smaller projects some design input from the contractor is needed, and previously there had been no suitable form within the JCT suite.

The 2005 editions also contained some other changes. The format, sequence, clause numbering and terminology had been revised, and the language used had been clarified throughout. A Contract Particulars section was introduced at the start of the Form. The Scheme for Construction Contracts was also adopted into JCT, and legal proceedings, rather than arbitration was made the default mechanism for the final resolution of disputes.

JCT MW11/MWD11

The 2011 edition of the contract was issued for the primary purpose of ensuring that the Contract continues to comply with the provisions of the Housing Grants, Construction and Regeneration Act 2011 as amended by the Local Democracy, Economic Development and Construction Act 2009. The changes concentrate mainly on the payment and payment certification provisions.

Nature

The Minor Works Building Contract is in two versions, one 'with contractor's design' which has provision for the contractor to design an identified portion of the Works (MWD11), and one which does not (MW11). In all other respects the versions are identical, therefore the points raised below can be assumed to apply to both versions, unless indicated otherwise.

Both versions of the form are over 30 pages long, but the contract Conditions take up only around half of these. The Agreement includes four Recitals (seven in MWD11) and eight Articles, and the Conditions are set out under Section headings.

A two-page Contract Particulars Section at the start of the form requires entries of information relating to the project. There are two schedules at the back of the form. Schedule 1, incorporated by clause 7·3, covers adjudication, and Schedule 2, incorporated by clause 4·11, is a fluctuations option. A Guidance Note is also included at the back of the form.

Use

The form is relatively brief, and apparently simple. However, it should be remembered that what is expressly stated might not be the entire picture. Terms might be implied by common law, and the form needs to be used with thought and treated with care.

A note as to appropriate use appears on the inside of the front cover of both versions, and further advice is set out in the Guidance Notes. These give a clear reminder that it is to be used only where the client has engaged a professionally qualified person to act as the Architect/Contract Administrator in administering the terms. It is for use where minor building works of simple character are to be carried out for an agreed lump sum. The form is not for use with works for which bills of quantities are required, or where the duration is likely to be such that full labour and materials fluctuations provisions are required. There is no provision in the form for the Employer to nominate or name sub-contractors for specialist work.

The 'with contractor's design' version, unlike SBC11 and IC11, contains very brief provisions relating to that design, and does not include requirements for approving design information, nor for the contractor to carry Professional Indemnity Insurance. MWD11 should therefore only be used where the design input is limited, and should never be used for design-build procurement.

JCT MW11/MWD11

There can be 'Contract Drawings', a 'Contract Specification' or Schedules which are also Contract Documents (Second Recital). The contractor will price a detailed contract document, or may provide a lump sum price supported by a Schedule of Rates (Second Recital). There are no supplements published to extend the range of this contract.

In many instances where the Minor Works Agreement is used for domestic work, the Housing Grants Construction and Regeneration Act as amended may not apply and the contract will therefore not be subject to the statutory requirements relating to adjudication and payment provisions. Nevertheless, the forms include the requirements for adjudication and certain procedures relating to payment. If not required by statute, they may be removed but only after taking legal advice.

If used as a contract direct between consumer and contractor of the type to which the Unfair Terms in Consumer Contracts Regulations 1994 (SI 1994/3159) might apply care should be taken to explain the terms to the consumer, or the consumer should take legal advice. The JCT now has other contracts specially drafted for use by consumers in connection with work on their homes, whether or not a consultant has been engaged, which may be more suitable (these contracts are covered in later chapters).

Synopsis

1 Intentions

- The contractor is obliged to carry out and complete the Works in accordance with the Contract Documents, the Health and Safety Plan where applicable and the statutory requirements (2·1).
- The contractor is to complete the design of the Contractor's Designed Portion (2·1·1, MWD11 only).
- The contractor is to provide further information relating to the Contractor's Designed Portion as is reasonably necessary (2·1·5, MWD11 only).
- The Architect is obliged to issue any further information necessary to enable the contractor to carry out the Works (2·3 or 2·4 in MWD11).
- Inconsistencies in or between Contract Documents shall be corrected and this may be treated as a variation instruction (2·5·1).
- The printed agreement or these conditions take precedence over other Contract Documents (1·2).
- Each party undertakes to the other that it will comply with the requirements of the CDM Regulations (3·9). The Architect is to act as CDM Coordinator unless the name of another person is interested in Article 5.

2 Time

- The Works may be commenced on and shall be completed by dates to be inserted in the Contract Particulars (2·2 or 2·3).

JCT MW11/MWD11

- The contractor is to notify the Architect if completion by the stated date is unlikely, for reasons which are not within the contractor's control (2·7 or 2·8).
- The Architect is empowered to make such extension of time as may be reasonable (2·7). (Note: no specific grounds are listed.)
- If the contractor fails to complete by the date, the Employer is entitled to liquidated damages (2·8 or 2·9) and the rate is to be stated in the Contract Particulars. (Note: there is no reference to a non-completion certificate.)
- Practical completion is certified by the Architect (2·9 or 2·10).
- Following this the contractor is obliged to rectify defects. (The Rectification Period is three months, although a longer period may be stated.) A certificate is to be issued by the Architect when this obligation has been discharged.
- There is no provision for deferring possession, nor for partial possession, nor for sectional completion.

3 Control

- The bar to assignment without written consent refers to 'this Contract or any rights thereunder' (3·1). Written consent to sub-contract is required (3·3).
- The contractor's 'competent person' is to be on site at all reasonable times (not constantly) (3·2). There is no provision for a clerk of works.
- There is no provision for naming a sub-contractor, and no provision for including a list of approved firms. Note however that neither is there anything which prevents this, and the NBS Small Jobs Version suggests suitable ways of achieving this.
- Architect's instructions are to be issued in writing (3·4 or 3·4·1) but may be oral and confirmed in writing. Instructions may include variations (3·6·1) and this would presumably allow for postponement, as no specific reference is made elsewhere. Where after a seven day notice the Contractor fails to comply with an instruction, the Employer may engage other persons to give effect to the instructions and the Contractor will be liable for all additional costs incurred by the Employer in this process (3·5).
- There is no provision for testing, or opening up of work. In the event of failure to meet the contract standards, and problems over remedial works, refusal to certify leading to non-payment would seem to be the ultimate sanction.

4 Money

- The Contract Sum is VAT-exclusive (4·1).
- The contract is fixed price (4·10) except for limited fluctuations (tax, etc) provided for by Schedule 2 (4·11). A percentage addition entry is required in the Contract Particulars. (If none, NIL is entered.)

JCT MW11/MWD11

- Instructions must be given if provisional sums are included (3·7). The cost of variations is either to be agreed in advance or valued (3·6).
- Direct loss and/or expense is limited to variations or provisional sum work, and included in the valuation (3·6·3).
- The due dates for interim payments to the contractor from commencement of works up to practical completion are at intervals of four weeks calculated from the date of commencement (4·3). The due date for interim payment after practical completion shall be seven days after the date of practical completion. After the initial practical completion due date, interim certificates should be issued at two month intervals up to the expiry of the rectification period (4·4).
- The Architect/Contract Administrator is required to issue an interim payment certificate not later than five days from the due date for interim payment. The certificate should state the amount the Architect/Contract Administrator considers due on the relevant due date and basis on which the amount was calculated (4·3, 4·4).
- The final date of payment on the interim certificate is 14 days from its due date. Unless a Pay Less Notice is issued, the Employer is to pay the sum stated in the interim certificate (4·5).
- Where the Architect/Contract Administrator fails or neglects to issue an interim certificate in accordance with 4·4, then the Contractor may at any time after the expiration of the five day period issue a Payment Notice to the Architect/Contract Administrator, stating the sum he considers due on the relevant due date and basis for calculating it, subject to the service of a Pay Less Notice, the Employer shall pay the sum stated in the Contractor's Payment Notice on the final date for payment (4·5·2).
- Where the Contractor's Payment Notice is issued after the expiration of the five day period after the due date, then the final date for payment is postponed by the same number of days after such period that the Payment Notice was issued (4·5·3).
- If the Employer intends to pay less than the sum stated in the interim payment certificate or Contractor's Payment Notice, the Employer is required to, not later than five days from the final date of payment, issue a Pay Less Notice stating the sum it considers due to the Contractor on the date of the notice and the basis it was calculated (4·4). It must be noted that the Employer is not entitled to withhold or deduct any amount from monies due the Contractor unless the proper Pay Less Notice has been issued.
- Failure to pay by the final date for payment will attract simple interest on the overdue amount (4·6), and can give the contractor a right to suspend some or its entire obligation with a right to recover reasonable costs and expenses incurred as a result of such suspension. Suspension is to be preceded by the service of a seven day notice and may only progress where there is a failure to remedy the non-payment after the seven day period (4·7).

JCT MW11/MWD11

- There is a precise timescale for the preparation of a final account after practical completion. The issue of the Final Certificate is within 28 days of either the receipt of documentation from the Contractor or the date specified in the certificate of making good under clause 2·11, whichever is the later (4·8).
- The due date for the final certificate shall be the date of issue of the final certificate, and the final date of payment shall be 14 days after the due date (4·8·2).
- Similar rules as those discussed above on Interim Certificate apply in respect of the Final Certificate with regard to notices (4·8, 4·9).

5 Statutory obligations

- It is the contractor's duty to comply with all statutory obligations, including giving all required notices (2·1).
- The contractor is to notify the Architect in writing if it finds any conflict between statutory requirements and his other contractual obligations. Having done that, it will not be liable to the Employer under this contract (2·5 or 2·6).
- The contractor is obliged to comply with the CDM Regulations and particularly, where the project is notifiable, to comply with duties in relation to the Construction Phase Plan and the Health and Safety File (3·9).

6 Insurance

- The contractor indemnifies the Employer in respect of personal injury or damage to property (5·1 and 5·2). He is required to arrange insurance to back this (5·3). The minimum cover as a contractual obligation requires an entry in the Contract Particulars (5·3).
- The contractor is obliged to arrange insurance of new works in joint names against damage by perils specified in clause 5·4A. The percentage to cover professional fees should be inserted.
- There is no provision for the Employer to insure new works.
- Joint names insurance of existing structures, and any new work which is part of an alteration or conversion, is to be arranged by the Employer. The contractual requirement is for cover against specified perils (5·4B). There is also a provision for insurance of existing structures by the Employer in his own name (5·4C).

7 Termination

- The Employer may terminate the employment of the contractor if it fails to proceed satisfactorily with the Works, or if it fails to comply with its obligations under the CDM Regulations, or if it becomes insolvent (6·4 and 6·5). The Architect may issue a warning notice, but notice of termination is a matter for the Employer.

JCT MW11/MWD11

- The contractor may terminate his own employment for Employer defaults and Insolvency (6·8 and 6·9).
- Either party may terminate the employment of the contractor if the Works are suspended due to stated neutral event (6·10).
- The respective rights and duties of the parties following determination are set out in the Conditions (6·7 and 6·11).

8 Miscellaneous

- The Architect may order the exclusion of any person from the Works (3·8).
- There is no reference to antiquities, terrorism cover, etc
- There is a contracting out of third party rights under the Contracts (Rights of Third Parties) Act 1999 (1·5).

9 Disputes

- Subject to the right to refer to adjudication, mediation is suggested as the first instance process for dispute resolution (7·1).
- Part II of the Housing Grants, Construction and Regeneration Act 1996 as amended gives either party a statutory right to refer any difference or dispute arising out of the contract to adjudication. Article 6 of MW11 provides for this.
- Adjudication is to be conducted according to the procedures set out in the Scheme, except that the adjudicator and the nominating body may be stated in the Contract Particulars.
- There is an optional provision for arbitration (Article 7), and if disputes are required to be resolved by arbitration then the Contract Particulars must state that Article 7 and Schedule 1 apply.
- The appointment of the arbitrator is subject to Article 7, and his or her powers are defined in Schedule 1.
- Arbitration is to be conducted in accordance with the JCT 2011 Edition of the Construction Industry Model Arbitration Rules.

JCT MW11/MWD11

This contract?

If considering using MW11 or MWD11 remember that:

It is intended for small building work of a simple 'one-off' nature, and is not suitable for jobbing or maintenance type work. There are two versions, one for use where some design input is required from the contractor, and one where it is not. It can only be used where the Employer has engaged a professional consultant to act as contract administrator. There is no provision for bills of quantities and although a quantity surveyor may be named, it is with no specific role under the Conditions.

If used for work in Northern Ireland an Adaptation Schedule should be incorporated. The form is not suitable for use in Scotland, and where the intended work is in Scotland, the SBC Scottish Minor Works form is available.

There is no provision for phased completion, naming of sub-contractors, or design by the contractor. The form is drafted to include compliance with the CDM Regulations, and with the Housing Grants, Construction and Regeneration Act 1996 as amended, whether or not these apply in full to the particular contract. When completing the form decisions are required relating to insurance of the Works and damages for non-completion.

If acting as contract administrator, note that although the Conditions are likely to prove adequate for most situations, should the nature of the work require it, then it might be advisable to clarify the procedural rules pre-contract, especially if working with a contractor for the first time.

The RIBA publishes contract administration forms for MW11/MWD11.

For slightly larger projects, or those which require more comprehensive conditions, then IC11 might be a safer choice. For work on projects where the Client is a residential homeowner who intends to reside in the project, perhaps consumer contracts, like the JCT forms for homeowners, might be more applicable. The Minor Works Agreement has featured in a surprising number of court cases, often due to use beyond its intended limits or because of careless administration, and a RIBA expert has commented that although it appears to be a favourite with the profession, at the same time it appears to be little understood. It has limitations, particularly concerning the design insurance and determination provisions, and needs to be treated with respect and administered with diligence.

7 Traditional procurement: shorter lump sum forms

JCT MW11/MWD11

Related matters

Documents

Minor Works Building Contract
Minor Works Building Contract with contractor's design
Short Form of Sub-Contract

References

Practice Note JCT: Deciding on the Appropriate JCT Form of Contract (2011)

Commentaries

Sarah Lupton
Guide to MW11
RIBA Publishing (2011)

David Chappell
MW11 Contract Administration Guide
RIBA Publishing (2011)

JCT RM11

The Joint Contract Tribunal Ltd

Repair and Maintenance Contract (Commercial) 2011 Edition

Background

The Repair and Maintenance Contract (Commercial) 2006 (RM06) is intended for use on 'individual, substantially defined, programmes of repair and/or maintenance on specified buildings or sites'. It is derived from the JCT Conditions of Contract for Building Works of a Jobbing Character (JA/C 90), which was originally introduced in 1990.

The form is for Employers who have a building stock which requires small jobs undertaken from time to time, in the nature of repairs and maintenance, and who would be reasonably experienced in commissioning such work. It is not intended for use by homeowners, and it does not provide for the role of a contract administrator.

Nature

The form is intended for defined small projects, but is not to be used as a term contract, for which the Measured Term Contract would be more appropriate. It allows for three different bases for pricing, either as a lump sum contract, or as a re-measurement contract, or as a mixture of the two with defined work being priced as a lump sum and additional work measured using an agreed schedule of rates.

The form is relatively short, running to 18 pages in total. It contains a form of Invitation to Tender, and a form of Tender. It also includes Contract Particulars, and a guidance note, together with six pages of conditions arranged under seven Sections.

Use

The form is intended for use by local authority or commercial clients, who will be experienced in placing orders for such work, and in dealing with contractor's accounts.

All the details regarding the work to be carried out and the information required under the Contract Particulars must be sent to the contractor at time of tender. In particular, the contractor must be told on which basis it is to price the work, as a lump sum and/or a schedule of rates, and the start and completion dates for the Works.

The contract will come into existence after the contractor has completed and returned the Tender form, and the Employer has accepted that tender. The completed tender, signed by the Employer and returned to the Contractor, is the evidence that agreement has been reached, and there is therefore no need for recitals, articles or an attestation. As an alternative, as explained in the Guidance Note, the RM11 conditions may be

JCT RM11

incorporated by reference in an Employer's order, in which case the relevant parts of the form should be marked 'not used'.

It should be noted that the form does not include any reference to health and safety, or to the CDM Regulations, although there might be occasions when these will apply, either in full, or to the extent that Regulation 13 affects design.

The 2011 edition of the contract is generally compliant with the Housing Grants, Construction and Regeneration Act 1996 as amended. It should be noted that the form allows for payment at a single stage for projects with durations of less than 45 days and falling outside the scope of the Act and also makes provision for stage payments for projects lasting for more than 45 days (Article 3).

Synopsis

1 Intentions

- The contractor is obliged to carry out the Works 'in a regular, diligent and competent manner, in accordance with all applicable legislation' (2·1).
- As there are no articles, the Works to be carried out are identified in the invitation to tender and the Contract Particulars.
- The Employer is obliged to issues any further information the contractor may reasonably require to carry out the Works (2·3).
- The conditions and the accepted Tender prevail over any other document (1·2·1).
- There is no reference to discrepancies, these would have to be resolved by discussion and agreement.

2 Time

- The work may be commenced, on or shall be completed by dates that are entered in the Contract Particulars (2·2).
- The Employer must fix a new completion date if the contractor is delayed for a reason beyond its control (2·4).
- The contractor must use reasonable endeavours to prevent delay (2·4).
- There is no provision for liquidated damages.
- There is no requirement for a statement of practical completion, and the rectification periods runs for six weeks after the completion of the Works.

3 Control

- The Contractor shall not assign the benefit of the contract and also shall not sub-contract the Works or part of it without the prior written consent of the Employer, such consent not to be unreasonably withheld (3·1·4, 3·1·5).

JCT RM11

- There is no provision for naming or listing approved firms, although a list could be included in the specification.
- The Employer may appoint a representative (3·2).
- The Employer may issue instructions which shall be in writing and where issued orally shall be confirmed in writing (3·3). Instructions requiring variations may be issued by the Employer, although the scope of these is limited to those of 'a nature and scale that is reasonable relative to the scope of the Works' (3·4).

4 Money

- The contract price is exclusive of VAT.
- The contract may be let on a lump sum basis, or as a measurement contract, or as a combination of these.
- Variations are to be valued by agreement between the parties, or failing agreement by the Employer on a fair and reasonable basis, using agreed rates where applicable, and including an amount for any loss and/or expense suffered (3·5).
- Payment may be by instalments or by a single payment. If instalments are used, the contractor is to invoice at the agreed stages, and the Employer must pay within 14 days of the invoice (4·3, 4·5).
- On completion of the Works, the contractor sends the Employer an itemised invoice (4·4, 4·5), which must be paid within 14 days.
- If the Employer intends to pay less than the sum stated in the invoice, the Employer is required to, not later than five days from the final date of payment to issue a Pay Less Notice stating the sum it considers due to the Contractor on the date of the notice and the basis on which it was calculated (4·6). It must be noted that the Employer is not entitled to withhold or deduct any amount from monies due the Contractor unless the proper Pay Less Notice has been issued.
- Failure to pay by the final date for payment will attract simple interest on the overdue amount (4·7), and can give the contractor a right to suspend some or all of its entire obligation with a right to recover reasonable costs and expenses incurred as a result of such suspension. Suspension is to be preceded by the service of a seven day notice and may only progress where there is a failure to remedy the non-payment after the seven day period (4·8).
- There is no provision for retention, therefore nothing is withheld over the rectification period.
- There is no provision for fluctuations.

5 Statutory obligations

- Unlike other forms in the JCT suite, 'Statutory Requirements' are not defined, instead

JCT RM11

the contractor is required to carry out the Works in accordance with all applicable legislation (2·1).

- The reference to 'all applicable legislation' (2·1) would include the CDM Regulations, although there is no specific mention of these in the conditions.

6 Insurance

- The contractor is to indemnify the Employer in respect of personal injury or death, or damage to property other than the Works caused by its own negligence (5·1 and 5·2). This is to be backed by insurance, and an entry in the Contract Particulars will state the minimum cover (5·4·2).
- Unless otherwise agreed, insurance of the Works is the responsibility of the contractor under a joint names 'all risks' policy (5·4·1).
- Insurance of existing structures against listed perils is the responsibility of the Employer.

7 Termination

- Each party is entitled to terminate the contract immediately if the other party becomes insolvent, or after a seven day warning notice has been issued if the other party is in material breach (6·1).
- The Employer may terminate the contractor's employment in the event of any corruption (6·2).

8 Miscellaneous

- The contractor must take all reasonable steps to ensure that employees, sub-contractor's etc are registered cardholders under the Construction Skills Certification Scheme.
- There is no reference to access for the Employer's representative, but this is probably implied.

9 Disputes

- Disputes may be resolved through mediation, or through adjudication under the Scheme for Construction Contracts.
- There is no arbitration clause, therefore either party would have the right to pursue a claim through litigation.

JCT RM11

This contract?

RM11 is an attractive option for employers who wish to contract direct for small works, and do not require a contract administrator.

The form is flexible, allowing for use with its incorporated forms of invitation and tender, or by means of a works order. It also allows for a variety of methods of pricing, reflecting the reality of commissioning work of this nature.

The form does not contain any provisions for liquidated damages or for retention, and there is nothing to cover the situation where the contractor may be undertaking any design. It will therefore be most suited to experienced employers on very short, one-off jobs. For longer commercial projects MW11 or MWD011 should be considered, and where a series of jobs is anticipated, MTC11 may be more appropriate. If the Employer is the residential occupier of the property on which the work is to be carried out, the home/owner occupier contracts may be used.

Related matters

Documents

Repair and Maintenance Contract Commercial 2011 Edition (includes a Guidance Note)

ACA Form

Association of Consultant Architects

ACA Form of Building Agreement 1982 (Third Edition 1998, 2003 Revision)

Background

The ACA Form was seen at inception as providing an alternative to the relatively complex procedures of the newly introduced JCT80. However with the publication of IFC84 by the JCT and in more recent years the NEC3 short contract and other forms it seems more appropriate to categorise the form as a short form lump sum contract rather than an alternative to the more complex JCT Standard Building Contract. The first edition took two years and 11 drafts to produce. The new agreement was presented as suitable for use on a very wide range of jobs of various sizes and types.

At the outset the ACA contract working party made it known that their intention was to produce a form which was 'a flexible and fairly balanced contract for an efficient architect working with an efficient contractor for an efficient client'. Early criticism was that the form was drafted unilaterally without any contribution from contractors. However, it has been used successfully on a wide variety of jobs, including fast-track projects. Major client bodies appear to have used the form without problems, and the British Property Federation cooperated over a version of the form suitable for use under the BPF System of procurement which was not withdrawn until 1998.

The second (1984) edition included a number of significant improvements. The form is kept under review, and revised from time to time. The Third Edition appeared in 1998, with amendments needed to take account of the Housing Grants, Construction and Regeneration Act 1996 (Part II).

The form has not yet been updated to take account of changes in legislation especially the amendment of the Housing Grants, Construction and Regeneration Act 1996 (Part II) by Part 8 of the Local Democracy, Economic Development and Construction Act 2009. Therefore the contract in its current state may not be suitable to use for new projects commencing in the UK unless it is amended.

Nature

The total document runs to over 30 pages. There is a contents page which lists the Sections in which the clauses of the Conditions are grouped. This is followed by the Agreement which includes alternative clauses relating to the contract administrator appointed; who will be responsible for the preparation of further drawings and details; and whether the Works are to be completed in Sections.

Flexibility is a feature of the form, made possible by the use of alternatives both in the Agreement and also at various points throughout the Conditions. The parties execute

ACA Form

the document either as a deed, or not as a deed, at the end of the Conditions. The expressed intention was to produce a form which was plainly worded. However, some of the terminology used is peculiar to the ACA form, and might cause confusion. The administrative procedures are relatively straightforward, although there is little clear guidance on their detailed use.

Examples of where the terminology differs from most other forms include:

- completion date: the alternative clauses for extensions of time, possible possession or taking over in parts, and possible acceleration;
- extra costs: the production by the contractor of his estimate of the cost implications of an architect's instruction, for agreement, before complying with it;
- information: the attempt to establish systematically within the contract a schedule for the supply of information to be produced;
- design: the attempt to establish within the contract the extent to which Architect and contractor are each liable for the design of the Works.

To help in making this feasible, there are Schedules which follow after the Conditions. The Time Schedule offers Alternative 1 where the job is to be completed as one operation, or Alternative 2 where the job is to be completed in Sections. A further Schedule provides for detail on the issue of information; what this is to be, who is to be responsible, and when it is to be supplied. A final Schedule provides stage payment information.

Use

There is no suggested limit on cost or type of job for which the form is thought to be suitable. It can be used with or without a bill of quantities and where no quantity surveyor is appointed. It can be used where the Employer is private or is a local authority, and where contract administration is by an Architect or by a supervising officer.

The contract can be fixed price, or fluctuations based on an ACA index can be incorporated. The form may be used as a traditional work and materials contract, or the contractor may be required to accept a measure of responsibility for design and the provision of drawings. The flexibility in the document is made possible only by the introduction of alternative clauses, and great care is needed to ensure that the intended alternatives are clearly evident.

The Third Edition takes account of the Housing Grants, Construction and Regeneration Act 1996 (Part II).

Synopsis

1 Intentions

- The contractor is obliged to execute and complete the Works. This must be done in strict accordance with the Contract Documents (1·1). The contractor is required to use skill, care and diligence (1·2).

ACA Form

- What constitutes 'the Contract Documents' will be defined in clause C of the Agreement, and incorporated by clause D.
- The provisions of the printed form will prevail, unless there is anything to the contrary such as documents listed under clause 1·3.
- The drawings may be supplied solely by the Architect (2·1 Alternative 1) or may be supplemented by drawings and details for which the contractor takes responsibility (2·1 Alternative 2). This will also be evident under Alternative 1 or 2 in clause F of the Agreement.
- The contractor is responsible for the accuracy of drawings and other information prepared by him, and warrants compliance with performance specifications and fitness for purpose (3·1).
- The contractor is to permit others engaged directly by the Employer to carry out work which does not form part of the contract, whilst he has possession (10·1).

2 Time

- Time Schedule entries set out the important dates. Alternative 1 is used for a single phase job. Alternative 2 allows for possession in parts and/or completion by Sections.
- The Employer is to give the contractor possession to the date or dates stated in the Time Schedule, and the contractor is to commence immediately and proceed regularly and diligently (11·1).
- The contractor's entitlement to extensions of time will be subject to Alternative 1 or Alternative 2 of clause 11·5. The first alternative includes solely delay caused by the Employer, his architect or persons appointed under the CDM Regulations. The second is wider, and includes for neutral causes. The Architect has 60 days in which to notify the contractor of his or her decision, and decisions are subject to review within a reasonable time of taking over (11·6 and 11·7).
- The Architect is also empowered to issue an instruction to accelerate or postpone the dates set out in the Time Schedule. This is an unusual provision, although it may be subject to the test of reasonableness. There must of course be a fair and reasonable adjustment to the Contract Sum as a result, and a revised Time Schedule is required (11·8 and 11·9).
- The onus is on the contractor to notify the Architect when the Works are ready for taking over by the Employer. The contractor may also produce a Contractor's List of outstanding items. The Architect may then issue a Taking Over Certificate, or issue an architect's list of items which need attention before taking over. Taking over is possible even though there are outstanding items, and in this respect it differs from the notion of practical completion in JCT forms (12·1).

ACA Form

- Where the contractor has failed to have the Works ready for taking over by the agreed dates, this fact is certified by the Architect (11·2). Damages may then become payable (11·3 Alternative 1 or Alternative 2).
- Outstanding work at taking over, repairs, replacements and defects may be carried out as instructed by the Architect either during or immediately after the Maintenance Period (12·2).
- The contractor may be requested to allow the Employer to take over any part of the Works or any Section prior to the issue of a Taking Over Certificate (13·1).

3 Control

- Assignment of rights and obligations by either party requires the written consent of the other, but money is expressly excluded from this (9·1).
- The sub-contracting of work by the contractor requires the written consent of the Architect (9·2).
- Sub-contractors may be named in Contract Documents. This may be by way of a single name, a list, or a provisional sum. If this arises out of an architect's instruction, the contractor is given a right of reasonable objection (9·3, 9·4 and 9·5). The contractor is responsible for all sub-contractors, including those named (9·9). This extends to all matters of design, compliance with performance specification, and design coordination (9·8).
- The contractor is clearly made responsible for all management of the Works , and this includes inspection, supervision, planning and superintendence (5·1). The contractor must appoint as full-time site manager a person approved by the Architect. This person's duties are clearly listed (5·2 and 5·3).
- Facilities are to be provided for access and visits by the Architect, both to the Works and workshops (4·1 and 4·2).
- Instructions and notices given by the Architect must be in writing (23·1) although the contract does allow for oral instructions in an emergency, provided these are confirmed in writing (8·3). Matters on which the Architect is empowered to issue instructions are conveniently listed, and include removal of work or materials from the site, dismissal from the Works, opening up and testing, variations, and 'any matter connected with the Works'. Immediate compliance by the contractor is generally required (8·1).

4 Money

- The Contract Sum may be adjusted in accordance with the terms of the contract, and will become the 'Final Contract Sum' – both are exclusive of VAT (clause B of the Agreement, and 15·1).

ACA Form

- A quantity surveyor, if appointed, is named in the Conditions, and his or her duties may be defined (15·2 and 15·3).
- The contract may include for fluctuations based on the ACA index. Deleting this option will make the contract literally 'fixed price' (18·1, 18·2 and 18·3).
- Provisional sums may be included (16·6) although these appear to be only for work or materials in connection with sub-contractors or suppliers.
- Valuations of Architect's instructions will take into account loss and/or expense. Estimates are to be provided by the contractor before compliance. If agreement is not reached, compliance can still be instructed and valuation made based on the Schedule of Rates (if appropriate) or otherwise on a fair and reasonable basis (17·1, 17·2, 17·3 and 17·5).
- Interim payments to the contractor will be either on the basis of monthly valuations (Alternative A) or by stage payments (Alternative B) (16·1).
- Under both Alternative A and B the contractor is to present the Architect with an application for payment stating the total due, and supported by documentary evidence as applicable (16·1).
- The Architect is to issue an Interim Certificate within 10 working days of receipt of the application, stating the amount due and the basis of calculation (16·2).
- If the Employer proposes to withhold or deduct any sum, he must give the contractor written notice showing the amount and grounds for such action not later than five working days before the final date for payment (16·5).
- The contractor is otherwise entitled to payment of the amount certified. The final date for payment is 10 days from the date of the Interim Certificate (16·3).
- Retention of five per cent will normally be retained by the Employer, and in the case of private employers will be placed in a separate bank account without obligation to the contractor for interest gained (16·4).
- The contractor has 60 working days following the expiry of the Maintenance Period within which to submit a final account (19·1). The Architect is required to issue the Final Certificate within 60 days after the contractor has discharged all his obligations under the Agreement (19·2).
- The Final Certificate must show the amount due and the basis on which the calculation is made. The final date for payment is 10 working days following the issue of the Final Certificate (19·3).

5 **Statutory obligations**

- Unless instructed to the contrary, the contractor is required to comply with statutory requirements and to make applications, give notices and pay fees (1·7).

ACA Form

- If there is any apparent conflict between the Contract Documents and statutory requirements, the contractor must notify the Architect, who will issue an instruction (1·6). Where the contractor is responsible for supplying drawings, he also assumes responsibility for ensuring compliance with statutory requirements (2·5).
- The Contractor, where also appointed Principal Contractor, has particular contractual obligations in addition to statutory duties relating to health and safety (26). These include cooperating with the Planning Supervisor, and in respect of the Health and Safety Plan, and the Health and Safety File.

6 Insurance

- In respect of personal injury or death, and damage to property other than the Works, the contractor gives the Employer an indemnity. This will be reduced proportionately to the extent that the Employer has contributed to the injury or damage (6·3).
- The contractor will take out insurance cover against these indemnified risks to no less than the sum included in the contract, although of course this will not limit his liability (6·3).
- Insurance of the Works may be by the contractor (Alternative 1) or by the Employer (Alternative 2). Insurance is to be in joint names. The Conditions do not appear to state specifically what risks are to be covered (6·4).
- Additional insurance may be a requirement for an agreed sum against damage to property (other than the Works) where there is no negligence, etc by the Contractor, eg legal nuisance (6·5).
- There is provision for the contractor to take out design indemnity insurance (6·6).

7 Termination

- The contract includes for termination by the Employer for stated reasons of default. The last one is simply where the contractor 'shall otherwise be in breach' of the agreement (20·1). The Employer is to serve a default notice, which may be followed by a termination notice. A dispute over this may be referred to adjudication (20·1).
- The contract also includes for termination by the contractor for stated reasons of default by the Employer. A default notice may be issued to be followed by the termination notice. Adjudication may be used where there is a dispute (20·2).
- Either party is given the option of terminating the contractor's employment on grounds of insolvency. It is not automatic determination (20·3).
- Either party is given the option of terminating the contractor's employment for neutral causes (21).
- The consequences of termination, and action to be taken (eg payment, possession of site, sub-contracts) is dealt with in detail (22).

ACA Form

8 Miscellaneous

- There is an optional provision for dealing with adverse ground conditions or obstructions on the site (2·6).
- Clause J of the Agreement states that third party rights under the Contracts (Rights of Third Parties Act) 1999 will not apply, but a marginal note states that clause J may be deleted and a clause substituted which lists parties who may be given rights under the contract.
- Confidentiality of documents is assumed (3·3).
- Any drawings provided by the contractor are his responsibility entirely irrespective of comments or advice by the Architect (3·4).
- Statutory undertakers are to be given access to site (10·3).
- Antiquities etc are deemed to be the property of the Employer (14·1). The contractor must report any finds to the Architect immediately (14·2).

9 Disputes

- The Agreement allows for disputes to be resolved by four methods. There is first conciliation (25A), then adjudication (25B), and finally provision for either litigation (Alternative 1) or arbitration (Alternative 2) (25C).
- There are alternative provisions relating to litigation and arbitration depending on whether the proper law of the contract is English law or Scots law (25·11).
- Conciliation can mean reference to a person named in the Agreement, or as otherwise agreed by the parties. Where the parties sign any written agreement on the terms of a settlement, then this is to be regarded as final and binding (25·3).
- Under the Housing Grants, Construction and Regeneration Act 1996 (Part II) the parties have the right to refer any difference or dispute to adjudication. The adjudicator may be named in the Agreement, or be otherwise appointed in accordance with the CIC Model Adjudication Procedure (25·5).
- Adjudication is to be conducted according to the CIC Model Adjudication Procedure, and the adjudicator's decision will be final and binding at least until the dispute is finally determined by arbitration or in the courts (25·7).
- Arbitration is subject to the provisions of the Arbitration Act 1996 if under English law, or its counterpart if under Scots law. If the parties do not agree over the name of the arbitrator, the appointor is to be the President of the Chartered Institute of Arbitrators (25·9).

ACA Form

This contract?

If considering using the ACA Form remember that:

It requires amendment to bring it up to date with legislation in the UK.

It is intended for lump sum contracts, and can be used regardless of sector although certain clauses may need to be deleted if the Employer is a local authority. It may be used with or without a bill of quantities. Work needs to be fully designed and reasonably well documented at tender stage, although there is alternative provision for further detailing by either the Architect or the Contractor. Possession and completion may be in respect of a single contract period or for sectional completion in accordance with a Time Schedule. The Employer is required to appoint an architect or Supervising Officer, and may appoint a quantity surveyor.

The form is stated to be suitable under Scots law, and there are alternative clauses relating to litigation and arbitration. There is no reference to its suitability under the law of Northern Ireland.

A notable feature of this form is the range of alternative clauses available to cover most situations, for example relating to responsibility for further necessary information including drawings; priority of Contract Documents; adverse ground conditions; insurance of the Works; liquidated damages; grounds for extensions of time; payment periodic or by stages; dispute resolution; possession and completion by Sections. The form appears to deal in a very simple way with naming of sub-contractors, design by sub-contractors, and the procedures are kept to a very minimum. This flexibility can be achieved all within the one document, and without the need for supplements. The only bolt-on document is the ACA Conciliation Procedure 1998.

Completing the form requires particular care over selecting the appropriate combination of alternatives, and in completing the Schedules. The form has a logical structure and the language used is straightforward English. However, some of the terms used may be unfamiliar to regular JCT users.

The contract administrator is given considerable authority. The procedural rules are straightforward. ACA publishes standard forms and certificates for use with the ACA Form.

This is a different form for traditional procurement, attractive, concise and modern.

7 Traditional procurement: shorter lump sum forms

ACA Form

Related matters

Documents

ACA Form of Building Agreement 1982; Third Edition 1998 (2000 Revision)
ACA Form of Sub-Contract 1982; Third Edition 1998 (2000 Revision)
ACA98 Appointment of a Consultant Architect

Notes

Guide to the ACA Form of Building Agreement.

GC/Works/2

The Stationery Office

GC/Works/2 (1998)

Background

This is sub-titled as a Contract for Building and Civil Engineering Minor Works, but it is more in the nature of an intermediate form standing between the major works GC/Works/1 form and the GC/Works/4 small works contract. It is intended for contracts of between £25,000 and £200,000 in value, and for demolition works of any value. It replaces the former GC/Works/2 (1990) and the old small works C1010 (1990).

It is published as a two volume package, General Conditions, and Model Forms and Commentary. The former includes a disk (Word Perfect 6.1) of the 18 Model Forms.

The form is for use with lump sum tenders invited on the basis of Specification and drawings only – without provision for bills of quantities, and with the optional requirement for the contractor to submit a Schedule of Rates to enable fair valuation of any variations.

Nature

The General Conditions run to some 45 pages and follow the well established GC/Works pattern of clear graphic style, straightforward language and standard terminology. The Introduction and contents list are followed by the Conditions of which there are 48, structured under nine headings.

In common with other GC/Works forms, there is a very useful Schedule of Time Limits and an alphabetical index. Use of the Model Forms is essential. Model Form 1 contains the Abstract of Particulars and Addendum; Model Form 2 is an Invitation to Tender and Schedule of Drawings; Model 3 is a Tender and Tender Price Form; Model Form 4 carries details of Insurance Documents; Model Form 5 is a Performance Bond; Model Form 6 is a Parent Company Contract Performance Guarantee; Model Form 7 relates to the Appointment of an Adjudicator; and Model Form 8 is an 'Order to Proceed'. The latter is in effect an instruction to the contractor to proceed with the Works on a specified date. There is no separate Contract Agreement.

Use

GC/Works/2 has relatively limited provisions, but almost certainly adequate for the kind of operations intended. As stated in the Commentary it is necessary when considering a choice of this form compared with, say, GC/Works/1, to establish whether certain features (eg sectional completion) are contractual requirements. If so, then this less comprehensive document might not prove suitable. The choice must be determined by the circumstances, the nature of the project, and the balance of risks to be covered.

7 Traditional procurement: shorter lump sum forms

GC/Works/2

As there is no formal Contract Agreement, a contract will be brought into existence when the Employer signifies acceptance of the contractor's tender. This should be in writing to bring certainty to the arrangement, particularly as the result will almost invariably be a 'construction contract' as defined in the Housing Grants, Construction and Regeneration Act 1996 (Part II). GC/Works/2 makes no provision for a quantity surveyor, but a Project Manager and Planning Supervisor should be named in the Abstract of Particulars, and the name of an adjudicator and an arbitrator may also be entered.

Synopsis

1 Intentions

- A fair dealings provision is included (1A).
- The contractor is to carry out the Works in accordance with the Contract Documents (2), and instructions of the Project Manager (25). The Works are as described in the Specification and shown on drawings, and will include all modified or additional works to be executed under the contract (1). They are to be executed in a workmanlike manner and to the satisfaction of the Project Manager (19).
- The contractor is deemed to have satisfied himself about all matters which might affect carrying out the Works. No additional payment will be allowed because of misunderstanding (4).
- All 'Things' selected by the contractor for incorporation in the Works, will be as described in the Specification and drawings and must conform to the requirements of the contract (19[2]).
- The 'Contract' means the written agreement concluded by tender, acceptance, Conditions, Abstract of Particulars, Specification and drawings, etc, all taken together (1). In case of discrepancy, there is a detailed hierarchy (2).
- Further drawings, details, instructions etc may be issued by the Project Manager from time to time during the Works (25).

2 Time

- Possession is given to the contractor by written order to proceed. He must thereupon commence on a certain date, and 'proceed with diligence' and complete by the Date for Completion (21[1]).
- A reasonable extension may be awarded by the Project Manager, only for circumstances wholly beyond the contractor's control (23).
- The Works must be cleared of rubbish and delivered up to the Project Manager's satisfaction by the Date for Completion (21[4]).

GC/Works/2

- Defects which appear in the Maintenance Period stated in the Abstract of Particulars must be made good to the satisfaction of the Employer at the contractor's expense (9).

3 Control

- The contractor cannot assign the contract or any interest without written consent of the Project Manager (44). Sub-contracting requires the written consent of the Project Manager.
- There is no provision for sub-contractors and suppliers to be nominated by the Employer or Project Manager.
- The Project Manager may issue instructions on any matter necessary, including variations (25). Notices must be in writing, and oral instructions confirmed in writing. The contractor must comply forthwith.
- Instructions which result in a variation will be valued wherever practicable by prior quotation and agreement, or a relevant charge for daywork, or by the Project Manager, on fair rates and prices, and will include for disruption or prolongation costs (26).
- There is no reference to setting out, nor to the contractor's person-in-charge.
- The Project Manager and his representative are empowered to order tests, and the cost will be borne by the contractor where things are not in accordance with the contract (19).
- The Employer may carry out work directly during the time the contractor is in possession (46).

4 Money

- The Contract Sum is defined (1), and the 'Final Sum' will be adjusted in accordance with the contract.
- The Project Manager must give written instructions before provisional sum work is commenced (45). It will be valued as provided for in the contract (26).
- The Contractor, following certification by the Project Manager, shall be entitled to monthly payment of advances on account (30). Valuations will be prepared by the contractor and, if agreed by the Project Manager, the sum due will be certified by him.
- The contractor may have to allow credit for old materials. 97 per cent of the value of work executed and value of Things for incorporation will be paid during progress of the Works (30).
- On completion, the contractor can expect to be paid what the Employer estimates the Final Sum to be, less half the retention (31[1]).

GC/Works/2

- The Project Manager will send the contractor a draft final account within six months after completion, which is certified by the Project Manager. The Final Sum will be paid when the Project Manager certifies that the Works are in a satisfactory state following the Maintenance Period (31).
- The contract fully complies with the Housing Grants, Construction and Regeneration Act 1996 provisions concerning payment procedures.

5 Statutory obligations

- The contractor is required to give all notices, pay any fees and charges, and make and supply all drawings required to support such notices, arising from statutory obligations (6). This includes the CDM Regulations.
- The contractor is required to comply with any statutory regulations relating to storage and use of all things brought on the site (7[2]).
- The contractor is required to comply with applicable occupier's rules and regulations in respect of the site (10).

6 Insurance

- The contractor is required to take out and maintain employer's liability insurance in respect of his employees on site, and is advised to insert a similar provision in sub-contracts (5[1]).
- The contractor shall insure in joint names against all risks damage to the Works and Things for which the contractor is responsible. This will be for full reinstatement value plus professional fees (5[2]).
- The contractor indemnifies the Employer in respect of injury to persons, loss or damage to third party property, loss of profits or use, and will cover this by insurance (5[2] and 8).
- The Employer is to bear the certain specified risks arising from work to existing structures, and may elect to take out insurance (5[6] and 8).

7 Termination

- The Employer has the right to determine the contract for specified grounds including insolvency of the contractor (38).
- Matters following determination (payment, completion, removal, etc) are dealt with in Condition 39. The Project Manager must certify the cost of completion.
- The contractor may determine the contract for specific grounds, including insolvency of the Employer (40).
- Either party may determine the contract following suspension of the whole or substantially the whole of the Works (41).

GC/Works/2

8 Miscellaneous

- A full list of definitions is included (1).
- There is no express reference to rights of third parties, or to contracting out of the Contracts (Rights of Third Parties) Act 1999.
- The contractor has obligations concerning watching, lighting and protection (7) and for removal of rubbish (21[4]).
- Security matters such as admission to the site (14), taking photographs (16), passes (15), and Official Secrets (17) may give rise to relevant obligations.

9 Disputes

- There is provision for adjudication for the resolution of any dispute arising out of the contract (42). There are precise requirements for the notice of referral and the procedures to be followed. The adjudicator may be named in the Abstract of Particulars, and his decision is binding on the parties, at least until finally determined by arbitration.
- Arbitration is given as the forum for final resolution of disputes and the arbitrator is given wide powers under the contract (43).

7 Traditional procurement: shorter lump sum forms

GC/Works/2

This contract?

If considering using GC/Works/2 remember that:

This contract has not yet been updated to comply with changes in the Construction Act and may require amendments.

It is intended for use when lump sum tenders are being invited on the basis of drawings and a Specification only. Its use is no longer confined to central government departments. The Employer is required to appoint a Project Manager who is given considerable powers to act for the Employer, subject to excluded matters which may be listed in the Abstract of Particulars. There is no requirement for a quantity surveyor, and functions normally ascribed to him are the responsibility of the Project Manager.

The form may be used in England and Wales, or under the law of Northern Ireland, or under Scots law. The arbitration provisions appropriate to the latter are set out in Condition 43.

The Conditions are general, and the Abstract of Particulars allows for some flexibility in tailoring the contract to the nature of the intended work. There is no provision for sectional completion. There is no provision for nomination of sub-contractors or suppliers by the Employer. The two volume presentation is comprehensive, and the Model Forms should be used as some of them carry information which is supplemental to the Conditions. The Commentary is practical and particularly informative.

Contract administration should be straightforward, always provided that the administrator takes the trouble to become thoroughly conversant with the terminology, the procedures, and the time limits. Rather unusually but very sensibly, progress meetings become contractual obligations, although there is no requirement for a programme.

This is an attractive form which has many features not found in other short forms. The result is a fairly substantial document which can cover a wide range of work which is too complex for GC/Works/4, but not justifying use of GC/Works/1. It may also be seen as an alternative to using JCT forms Minor Works and Intermediate forms.

Related matters

Documents

GC/Works/2 (1998) Contract for Building and Civil Engineering Minor Works in two volumes: General Conditions; Model Forms and Commentary

GC/Works/4

The Stationery Office

GC/Works/4 (1998)

Background

This is sub-titled as a Contract for Building, Civil Engineering, Mechanical and Electrical Small Works, and obviously intended as a general purpose document to cover small works of a varied nature. It is intended for contracts of up to £75,000 in value, and replaces Form C1001 (1990).

It is published as a two volume package; General Conditions and Model Forms and Commentary. The former includes a digital version of the 13 Model Forms.

The form is for use with lump sum tenders invited on the basis of Specification and drawings only, without provision for bills of quantities.

Nature

The General Conditions run to some 18 pages and are set out in clear graphic style, straightforward language and GC/Works terminology. There is a contents list followed by the Conditions of which there are 31 structured under seven headings.

As with other GC/Works forms, there is a Schedule of Time Limits. Use of the Model Forms is essential. Model Form 1 is the Abstract of Particulars; Model Form 2 is an Invitation to Tender and Schedule of Drawings; Model Form 3 is Tender and Tender Price Form; Model Form 4 is the Adjudicator's Appointment; Model Form 5 is the Order to Proceed; Model Forms 6 to 13 are contract administration forms.

Use

GC/Works/4 has provisions which should be sufficient for most small contracts where services installations also form part, but choice should ultimately depend on the nature of the intended works. The form accepts that either all the CDM Regulations will apply, or that only CDM Regulations 7 and 13 will be applicable This contract has not be updated to comply with the provisions of the Housing Grants, Construction and Regeneration Act 1996 (Part II) as amended. Therefore it may not be suitable for use on a project commencing after 1 October 2011.

Brief synopsis of Conditions

- A fair dealings provision is included (1A).
- Conditions of contract prevail in the event of discrepancy, except where special supplementary conditions are included in the Abstract of Particulars (2·1).
- Specification takes precedence over drawings unless otherwise instructed (2·2).

GC/Works/4

- Contractor responsible for care of site and Works, including sole responsibility for protection, security, lighting, and watching over the site and Works (5).
- Contractor indemnifies Employer in respect of any loss or damage which arises out of work under the contract (6). There is no provision for insurance in this contract.
- Making good defects in the Maintenance Period will only apply if stated in the Abstract of Particulars (7).
- The usual GC/Works provisions for matters such as occupier's rules, site admittance, passes, photography and Official Secrets, are included in a truncated form.
- The contractor's dates for commencement and completion will be stated in the Abstract of Particulars and subject to the order to proceed (15).
- The Works must be cleared of rubbish and delivered up to the Project Manager's satisfaction on completion (15).
- A reasonable extension of time may be awarded by the Project Manager, but only for circumstances beyond the contractor's control.
- The contractor cannot assign or sub-let without the written consent of the Project Manager (30).
- There is no provision for provisional sums.
- The Project Manager may issue instructions on any matters necessary, including variations (17).
- Valuation of variation instructions whenever practicable will be by prior quotation and agreement, or by the Project Manager on the basis of fair rates and prices (18).
- There are no contract provisions relating to progress meetings.
- There is no provision for prolongation and disruption.
- The Employer may carry out work direct during the time the contractor is carrying out the Works (31).
- The contract price (tender as accepted) may be adjusted in the final account (21).
- Payment to the contractor will be after completion, unless the Abstract of Particulars states that there will be advances on account (20). This will mean one-third payable after one-third of the work completed, with the remainder after completion. Applications must be made by the contractor to the Project Manager, and are subject to certification by the Project Manager (22).
- In the event of failure to complete to time, the contractor may be liable for liquidated damages, or damages at large as stated in the Abstract of Particulars (26).

GC/Works/4

- The Employer has the right to determine the contract for specified grounds, including insolvency of the contractor (27).
- The contractor has no rights to determine the contract.
- Adjudication is the only provision for resolving disputes (28). The decision of the adjudicator is binding until finally determined by arbitration, but the form does not include for arbitration. Alternatively the parties may agree to accept the decision of the adjudicator as final determination.
- There is no express reference to rights of third parties or to contracting out of the Contracts (Rights of Third Parties) Act 1999.

This contract?

If considering using GC/Works/4 remember that:

It is important to note that it has not been updated to bring it in compliance with current legislation.

It is intended for use when lump sum tenders are being invited on the basis of drawings and a Specification only. Its use is no longer confined to government departments, although some provisions will obviously not be relevant to the private sector client (for example the recovery of sums by the Crown under Condition 24). The Employer is required to appoint a Project Manager, but there is no stated function for a quantity surveyor.

The form may be used under the law of England and Wales, or under the law of Northern Ireland or under Scots law. The adjudication provisions appropriate to the latter are covered by Condition 29.

The Conditions are relatively brief and although limited, are adequate for most small works. The Abstract of Particulars becomes an important document. The two volume pack is attractively presented although perhaps a trifle over-sophisticated for this class of work. The Model Forms should be used.

Contract administration should be straightforward, and the procedures are simple. The terminology is typical GC/Works but clear.

An interesting basic alternative small Works Contract, particularly where services installations form part of the Works. Likely to appeal most to those already familiar with other GC/Works contracts.

Related matters

Documents

GC/Works/4 (1998) Contract for Building and Civil Engineering, Mechanical and Electrical Small Works in two volumes: General Conditions; Model Forms and Commentary

NEC3 (Short Contract) 2011 amendments

The Institution of Civil Engineers

New Engineering Contract Document

Engineering and Construction Short Contract 3 (with 2011 amendments)

Background

Although the New Engineering Contract of 1993 was at first promoted as a contract which could be used across the whole spectrum of projects, the Latham Report stated the need for 'a simpler and shorter minor works document'. Such a document, the Engineering and Construction Short Contract was published in July 1999 as one of the NEC family. The form was republished as part of the NEC3 suite of documents along with a useful guide and flow charts.

Nature

The form is obviously a derivative of the ECC contract, but it has been very thoughtfully structured. It is much more than simply a paired down version of the major document. The important material peculiar to a particular contract is placed right up-front (the converse of the major document) and comprises:

- Contract Data: dates; damages; interest on late payments; limit of contractor's liability; insurance obligations; name of adjudicator and arbitration procedures (if relevant). Additional Conditions may be incorporated and if so they are to be listed.
- Contractor's Offer: which will indicate whether this is a lump sum or a remeasurement contract.
- Employer's Acceptance: signed and dated. The offer and acceptance bring about the contract of course.
- Price List: a schedule of the quantity, rates and prices of items.
- Works Information: description of the Works which the contractor is to carry out, and any work which the contractor is to design; list of drawings; list of specifications applicable; constraints on the contractor such as sequence, timing, methods, and conduct of work; requirements for a Programme, such as form, content, submission and updating; and services to be provided by the Employer.
- Site Information: ground conditions, access, position of adjacent structures etc

The Conditions of contract, which occupy only 11 pages, are set out in a similar

NEC3 (Short Contract) 2011 amendments

although not identical way to those in the major form. The clauses are of necessity briefer than those in the major contract, and some provisions are omitted entirely, such as testing, health and safety compliance etc There is no express provision for a contract administrator or Project Manager, but the Employer may delegate the authority for taking empowered actions.

The language used in the form has attracted a 'Clear English Standard' award, the terminology is consistent with other documents in the NEC family, and the balance is generally attractive. The only provisions which stand out as being particularly demanding in terms of management expertise are those which concern the Compensation Events, which are almost as complex as those in the major form.

The Contract has been amended to include additional conditions where the Housing Grants, Construction and Regeneration Act 1996 as amended applies.

Use

This short contract has been specifically produced for use with straightforward work, for which sophisticated procedures are not necessary, and where the risks are relatively low. There is no restriction on the value of contract work for which it might be suitable, and it is the nature of the intended work which must be the determining factor.

Brief synopsis of Conditions

1 Intentions

- The parties act in a contractual spirit of mutual trust and cooperation (10·1).
- The terms used in the contract are helpfully and fully defined (11).
- Communications are to be in writing, and if a period for reply is stated in the Contract Data, then within that period (12).
- The Employer may give instructions which change the Works Information (13·2).
- The contractor must obey empowered instructions issued by the Employer (13·1).
- The Employer must allow the contractor access and use of the site (note: not necessarily possession), and provide the services stated in the Works Information (14).
- Early warning is a significant requirement in the contract (15).

2 Time

- Starting date and completion date are entered in the Contract Data. The contractor may not start before, and completion may be on or before the completion date (30·1).
- The contractor must submit a forecast of the date for completion to the Employer each week (30·2).

NEC3 (Short Contract) 2011 amendments

- The Employer may instruct the contractor to stop or restart work (30·4).
- The contractor must submit a Programme as required in the Works Information (31).
- Where delay occurs due to certain intervening events, these may constitute Compensation Events (60). There are 13 listed, mostly arising from action or inaction by the Employer, but also including some neutral causes. These are for weather (measured in ratio of days lost against contract period); physical conditions beyond those which could reasonably have been expected; and an event which delays completion by more than two weeks and which could not normally be expected to occur. This would presumably not allow for strikes or lock-outs.
- The procedures for notifying Compensation Events, quotations for changes to prices or rates and the mechanism for assessing the events are almost as full for this short contract as those in the major form (62 and 63).

3 Control

- The early warning obligation can constitute a control mechanism (15).
- The contractor cannot start work on which he has designed, before the Employer has accepted that the design complies with the Works Information (20).
- The Employer may delegate any actions, and may cancel any delegation (13·4).
- The Employer may instruct the removal of an employee (21·3).
- The contractor must provide access for the Employer and others to work and to stored plant and materials (22).
- There is no consent required for sub-contracting, but the contractor remains wholly responsible (21).
- There is no provision for testing.
- The Employer may instruct the contractor to search for defects (40·1) but whether or not the Employer notifies the contractor of a defect, he is obliged to correct them (41).
- After completion the contractor is to correct notified defects before the end of the Defects Correction Period (stated in weeks in the Contract Data) (41·2), and the Employer is to issue a Defects Certificate (41·3).
- Uncorrected defects permit the Employer to engage others to carry out remedial work, the cost of which can be charged to the contractor (42).
- Until the Defects Certificate has been issued, the contractor is liable for replacement in the event of loss of plant or materials, and damage to the Works (43·1).

NEC3 (Short Contract) 2011 amendments

4 Money

- The contractor is to make application for payment by the assessment day (that is the date stated in the Contract Data) once a month (50·1).
- The payment due date for an application for payment is set at the assessment day which follows receipt of that application (1·1).
- The Contractor's application for payment is the notice of payment specifying the sum the Contractor considers to be due at the payment due date (notified sum, the basis on which the amount has been calculated and details of how the amount has been calculated.
- The final date for payment of the notified sum is three weeks after the payment due date (1·1). Interest becomes payable on late payments (51).
- If the Employer intends to pay less than the notified sum he is to inform the Contractor of the amount he considers due on the date of the notice and the basis for the calculation no later than seven days before the final date for payment.
- A party is to pay the notified sum unless it has served a valid Pay Less Notice.
- Retention is held according to the percentage stated in the Contract Data, half is released on completion and the remainder after the Defects Certificate is issued (50·6).
- If the Contractor exercises its right to suspend performance on account of non-payment of sums due, this will be deemed a Compensation Event.

5 Statutory obligations

- There are no express obligations relating to statute or regulations, but these would be implied. In the event of a breach of statutory duty by the Employer, the contractor is indemnified against claims or proceedings and costs arising (81·1).
- In particular there is no express reference to health and safety and the CDM Regulations, other than providing a reason for termination by the Employer if the contractor substantially breaks a regulation (90·3).

6 Insurance

- The contractor is to provide in joint names the insurances stated in the Insurance Table (82·1).
- The Employer may provide insurance where this is stated in the Contract Data, and where this occurs it is not provided by the contractor (82·1).
- The insurance is for replacement cost in respect of loss or damage to plant, materials and the Works, and extends from starting date to Certificate of Completion in the case of plant and materials, and Defects Certificate in the case of the Works.

NEC3 (Short Contract) 2011 amendments

- Insurance may also be required in respect of the contractor's liability for damage to property other than the Works, and injury or death to persons for the minimum cover as stated in the Contract Data.
- The contractor's liability for loss or damage to the Employer's property is limited to the amount stated in the Contract Data (80·1).

7 Termination

- Both the Employer and the contractor have the right to determine (and this presumably means the contract, although not expressly stated).
- There are eight reasons stated which allow for termination, including insolvency of the other party (90·2). The Employer may also terminate 'for any other reason' (90·6).
- The Employer must issue a Termination Certificate, after which the contractor must cease work (90·1).
- On termination the contractor must leave the site (91·1) and the Employer may have the Works completed by others.
- Amounts due on termination are as stated, according to the reasons which apply (92).

8 Miscellaneous

- Use of the NEC Engineering and Construction Short Sub-contract would seem to be necessary.
- The Addendum Y(UK)2 is not applicable for use with the short contract, but payment provisions no doubt could be adapted and incorporated by reference in the Contract Data.
- The Addendum Y(UK)3 on third party rights is stated as being suitable for use with the short form.
- Clauses 93 to 95 on dispute resolution in the short form should be replaced by clauses 93UK to 95UK, for use in the UK where the Housing Grants, Construction and Regeneration Act 1996 applies.

9 Disputes

- Settlement of disputes is to be by reference to adjudication (93).
- The adjudicator may be named in the Contract Data.
- A party may issue to the other party a notice of intention to refer a dispute to adjudication at any time and is to refer such dispute to an adjudicator within one week of the notice.
- The notice at his sole discretion will allocate the costs of his fees between the parties.

NEC3 (Short Contract) 2011 amendments

- The adjudicator within five working days of its decision may correct clerical and other typographical errors in the decision.
- The adjudicator's decision is final and binding unless and until referred to a further 'tribunal'. The Contract Data should state whether arbitration is the tribunal, and if so, what the arbitration procedure is to be.
- Where the adjudicator's decision changes an amount notified as due, payment of the sum due will be no later than seven days from the decision or the final date of payment, whichever is later.

This contract?

If considering using the ECC short contract remember that:

It is intended for use as a lump sum or remeasurement contract for minor building and engineering works. Care is needed at the outset to establish that the Conditions, which are short but generally commensurate with work of this nature, will be adequate for the intended works. The agreement is based on the Offer and Acceptance near the front of the contract form. Contract Data and Works Information are particularly important and require full entries and careful checking by both parties.

The law of the contract is that applying to where the site is. There is no express reference to the law of Northern Ireland or to Scots law; this is in keeping with the international ethos of this form. Consequential amendments necessary to the Conditions in different jurisdictions would be included in Contract Data.

The contract continues with the NEC3 tradition of using the present tense, the form is short, and well written,

This form is a useful addition to the category of short contracts.

Related matters

Documents

Engineering and Construction Short Contract (June 2005)
Addendum Y(UK)3 (June 2005)
NEC Partnering Option, Option X12 (June 2005)
Engineering and Construction Short Sub-Contract

Notes

Engineering and Construction Short Contract Guidance Notes and Flow Charts
NEC3 Contracts. September 2011 amendments.

JCLI Agreement

The Joint Council for Landscape Industries (JCLI)

JCLI Agreement for Landscape Works 2012

Background

The JCLI originally had two standard forms for landscape works based on JCT63 With and Without Quantities. In 1978 these were replaced by a single form modelled on the then current JCT Minor Works Agreement 1968. Their new form adopted a Section headed format (two years ahead of the JCT) and incorporated additional clauses of specific relevance to landscape works. These included such matters as the failure of plants, malicious damage and theft, and additional retention to cover plants dead at practical completion. The form also contained provisions for partial possession, Prime Cost sums, objections to nomination, delays by the Employer and full fluctuations, none of which were included in the JCT Minor Works form. This form was considerably revised in 1987, again in 1989, and is currently in a 2002 revision of a 1998 edition. Landscape contracts will mostly be 'construction contracts' and need to take account of the Housing Grants, Construction and Regeneration Act 1996 provisions.

The Housing Grants, Construction and Regeneration Act as amended has previously been mentioned and the JCLI have issued new editions of its form in response to these legislative changes. The JCLI Agreement for Landscape Works 2012 suite have two versions, one with Contractor design and the other with no design responsibility for the Contractor.

JCLI also publishes a JCLI Agreement for Landscape Maintenance Works 2012 for use where the landscape contractor is to be responsible for the care of trees, shrubs and grass after practical completion. The JCLI Agreement for Landscape Works is suitable for contracts of a simple nature where the design work is to be undertaken by the Employer or its consultant. Where named specialists or detailed control procedures are required the contract may not be suitable for use. Also where the contractor is to design discrete parts of the works, it is recommended that the JCLI Landscape Contract with Contractor Design should be considered.

The Contract commences with Contract Particulars and is divided into seven sections starting with Definition and Interpretation, Carrying out the Works to Termination and Settlement of Disputes.

The Agreement is a bipartite agreement between the Employer and the Contractor and a Landscape Architect/Contract Administrator to manage the works.

The works contract is a relative short contract with 36 pages including schedules.

JCLI Agreement

Synopsis

1 Intentions

- The Contractor is to carry out and complete the works in proper and workmanlike manner, in accordance with the contract and complying with all statutory requirements including the issue of notices where required. Where the contract provides that materials or standards of workmanship is to be in the opinion of the Landscape Architect/Contract Administrator (LSA/CA), such quality and standards are to be the reasonable satisfaction of the LSA/CA (2·1).
- The recitals are used to set out a brief description of the works and the documents where the Employer's design are contained. It also confirms that the Contractor has provided the Employer with either the priced Contract Specification or Work Schedules or Schedule of Rates.
- The Contract Particulars are used to define the project and project expectations in more detail. The Contract Particulars are to be used to specify the date for commencement of works, date of completion, liquidated damages provision and rectification period.
- Article 2 of the Contract Particulars is for the parties to set out the contract sum while Article 4 is to be used to name the appointed LSA/CA.
- The contract is to be read as a whole however priority is given to the conditions of agreement (JCLI WC) over other contract documents including drawings, contract specification and Framework Agreement (1·2).

2 Time

- The Works is to commence and be completed on the dates stated in the Contract Particulars (2·2). The LSA/CA is to issue all instructions necessary for the project to progress as well as all certificates required under the contract. There is provision for sectional completion.
- The Contractor is to notify the LSA/CA at any time it becomes apparent that the date for completion set out in the contract will not be met. The LSA/CA is to grant the Contractor an extension of time where the reason for delay is beyond the control of the Contractor (including instructions by the LSA/CA that were given not because of a default by the Contractor but which have resulted in delay) (2·7).
- Circumstances that are under the control of the Contractor include any default by the Contractor, including default of those employed or engaged by the Contractor and these shall not entitle the Contractor to an extension of time (2·7).
- Where completion has not been achieved by the Contractor on the date of Completion as set out in the Contract Particulars (and amended from time to time by extension of time under 2·7), the Employer shall have the right to levy liquidated damages on the Contractor at the rate set out in the Contract Particulars. The liquidated damages

JCLI Agreement

shall be levied from the date for completion (which was not met) until practical completion is achieved. The liquidated damages may be deducted from the monies due the Contractor after the service of the relevant notices or recovered as a debt (2·8).

- There are two alternatives in the management of defect and establishment care of plants by the Contractor. Both provide that in the event of defects, shrinkages and other faults the LSA/CA shall inform the Contractor not later 14 days after the expiry of the Rectification period the Contractor shall repair the fault at his own costs. The Alternatives differ because where 2·10A provides for a separate agreement with the LSA/CA to manage the and care for trees, shrubs and other plants after practical completion, 2·10B on the other hand provides that the Employer shall cater for trees, shrubs and other plants after practical completion and will bear the costs of replacement of defective trees.
- Where the Employer wants to take possession of a section of the works before practical completion, the Employer is do so with consent of the Contractor which shall not be unreasonably withheld. Before such takeover of possession, it is expected that the parties would have confirmed from their insurers that such possession will not prejudice the insurance. The date of possession of the Relevant Part by the Employer shall the Date of Completion of the relevant Part and the Contractor will be expected to have complied sufficiently with its duty under the CDM Regulations in relation to a health and safety file for the Relevant Part.
- Also liquidated damages for the project as a whole will be reduced by a value equal to the value of the Relevant Part (2·12).

3 Control

- All instructions are to be in writing and are properly served when delivered to the address the parties set out in the agreement or an alternative address notified by a party. Where the address of a party is unknown, service will be deemed to have been made when it is delivered to the last known address or where it is a company to the registered or principal office.
- Instructions are to be issued in writing by the LSA/CA, where oral instructions are issued they are to be confirmed within two days by the LSA/CA (3·4).
- Where an instruction has not been promptly implemented by the Contractor, and if after seven days of receipt of a notice from the LSA/CA, the Contractor fails to comply with the instructions, the Employer is entitled to employ other persons to carry out the instructions and the costs of such engagement would be charged to the Contractor (3·5).
- Where the Contractor becomes of aware of any divergence between Statutory Requirements and the provisions of the contract documents or instructions of a LSA/CA, the Contractor is issue a notice to the LSA/CA stating the divergence (2·5·1). To

JCLI Agreement

the extent that the Contractor keeps to the provisions of 2·5·1, it shall not be liable for any inconsistencies between the works and the statutory requirements where the works have been constructed in compliance with the contract documents or instructions from the LCA/CA (2·5·2).

- Inconsistencies in contract documents provided by the Employer (Contractor Drawings, Contract Specifications and Works Schedules) shall be corrected by the LSA/CA and where it leads to an omission or addition, it shall be treated as a variation (2·4).
- It is expected that Provisional sums in the contract are be extended to cover theft and malicious damage not within the control of the Contractor that occur before Practical Completion (2·13).
- Neither party shall without the consent of the other assign the contract or its rights under it (3·1).
- The Contractor is expected to ensure at all reasonable times that a competent person is at site that may receive instructions given by the LSA/CA. Any instructions given to that person shall be deemed given to the Contractor (3·2).
- Practical Completion is said to be where in the reasonable satisfaction of the LSA/CA, Practical Completion has been achieved and the Contractor has fulfilled his duties under CDM and other regulations (2·9).
- The LSA/CA is entitled to issue instructions varying the works (3·6·1). The price to carry out such variation instructions is to be agreed with the Contractor. In absence of an agreement on the price for carrying out the varied work, the LSA/CA is entitled to value the works reasonably using information provided in the priced Contract Schedules/Contract Specification/Schedule of Rates. Such assessment is expected to include loss and/or expense incurred due to the disruption to the Contractor's schedule in carrying out the variation instruction (3·6).
- The LSA/CA may issue an instruction excluding from the site any person employed on it, such instruction is be given fairly and reasonably (3·8).
- The Contractor is not expected to sub-contract without the consent of the LSA/CA which may not be unreasonably withheld or delayed. However, a Contractor who sub-contracts remains liable to carry out all of the works in accordance with the contract, instructions of the LSA/CA and in keeping with statutory requirements (3·3·1).
- The contract provides some conditions for sub-contracting, this include sub-contract conditions that the contract terminates on the termination of the main contract with the Employer, that the parties shall apply with the CDM Regulations where applicable and that where the final date of payment under the sub-contract has been missed without payment, the contractor shall in addition to the outstanding sum be liable to pay interest at a rate equivalent to that set out in the main contract.

JCLI Agreement

- Except for personal injury or death arising from the negligence of the Employer or persons employed or engaged by it, the Contractor indemnifies the Employer for all costs and expense arising from personal injury or death of any person arising out of the course of or caused by carrying out the Works (5·1). Liability on similar terms is on the Contractor for injury or damage to property (5·2). The Contractor is expected to take out and maintain insurance to cover liability in 5·1 and 5·2 (5·3).

4 Money

- Calculation of payments under this contract are exclusive of VAT, which shall be paid as appropriate (4·1).
- The due dates for interim payment up to practical completion shall be dates occurring at four week intervals from the date of commencement. Within five days of the due date LSA/CA is required to issue an interim certificate of the amount due the contractor on the relevant due date and the basis of calculation. The contract stipulates the calculation should take cognizance of work properly executed to date and materials and goods that have been properly brought to site for the purpose of the works and discount from these, the total sums stated in previous interim certificates, total sums notified on any Contractor Payment notices as may be varied by any Pay Less Notice and the total difference 'between a valuation on a notice given against an interim certificate under clause 4·5·4 and the Valuation on the relevant interim certificate' (4·3·1).
- After practical completion, the due date for interim payment shall be seven days after practical completion and the LSA/CA is expected to issue an interim payment not later than five days after the due date (4·4).
- Other interim notices which are issued after practical completions are to be issued within three month intervals from the date of practical completion up to the expiry of the Rectification Period.
- The final date of payment on all interim certificates shall be 14 days from the due date (4·3·3, 4·4·2·3).
- Save for Pay Less Notices to be issued by the LSA/CA the sum to be paid on the final payment date is the sum stated on the interim certificate.
- If the LSA/CA fails to issue an interim certificate five days after the due date, the Contractor at the expiration of the five day period may issue a payment notice to the LSA/CA (with copy to the Employer) stating the sum the Contractor considers due at the relevant due date and basis for the calculation and taking into consideration the outline of calculation set out in 4·3 and 4·4 (4·5·2).
- Where the Contractor issues a payment notice, the final date of payment is postponed by the number of days after the five day period that it took the Contractor to issue the payment notice (4·5·3).

JCLI Agreement

- If the Employer intends to pay less than the sum stated on either the interim certificate or the Contractor's payment notice, the LSA/CA shall issue a Pay Less Notice stating the Employer's intention not later than five days before the final payment date. The notice shall state the sum the employer considers due to the contractor at the date of the notice. The sum stated on the notice shall be the sum paid on the final payment date (4·5·4).
- Where the Employer fails to make payment on the final payment date, the Contractor shall be entitled to interest on the overdue amount at the rate of 5% over the dealing rate of the Bank of England current at the date the payment becomes overdue. Payment of the interest stated above does not preclude the Contractor from his rights to the full sum or to claim other rights arising from such default (4·6).
- The Contractor shall have a right to suspend performance of some or all of its duties on the failure of the Employer to keep to its payment obligations. Such right may only be activated after a seven day notice to the Employer of the intention to suspend and the reason for such suspension. After the expiry of the seven days notice, if the situation is not remedied, the Contractor may suspend (4·7·1).
- Reasonable costs and expenses incurred as a result of such suspension is to be paid by the Employer (4·7·2) and applications in respect of such costs are made to the LSA/CA and are to be included in the next and subsequent interim certificates.
- Within the period stated in the Contract particulars the Contractor is to provide the LSA/CA all necessary documents for the calculation of the final payment. The due date for final payment shall be 28 days after the receipt of the document or if later, the date stated in the Certificate of making Good under clause 2·11 (4·8·1). Not later than five days after the due date the LSA/CA shall issue the final certificate, stating the amount due, the party to whom it is due and how the sum was calculated.
- The final date for payment is 14 days from the due date (4·8·2).
- If the party who is expected to make the final payment intends to pay less than the certified sum, the Contractor or the LSA/CA on behalf of the Employer, issues a notice of its intention to pay less not later than five days before the final date of payment, the notice is to state the sum due and how it was calculated. The amount on the Pay Less Notice becomes due on final payment date (4·8·3).
- Where a final certificate is not issued in accordance with the Contract, the Contractor may, after the expiration of the five day period, issue a final payment notice to the LSA/CA with a copy to the Employer, stating the sum he considers due and the basis for the calculation. The final date of payment is consequently postponed by the number of days it took the contractor to issue the final payment certificate.
- If the Employer intends to pay less than the sum stated in the final payment certificate, it may issue a notice (Pay Less Notice) under clause 4·8·3, stating the amount it

JCLI Agreement

considers due and basis for the calculation, this amount then becomes the amount to be paid on the final payment date (4·8·4).

- Where no Pay Less Notice is issued, the payer will be liable to pay the sum stated in the Final Certificate or Final Payment Notice (4·8·5). A failure to pay the amount on the final payment date attracts interest on the overdue sum (4·9).

5 Statutory obligations

- Where the CDM Regulations apply, Article 4 is for the appointment of a CDM Coordinator, default position is for the appointment of the Landscape Architect/ Contract Administrator as the CDM Coordinator, appoint another person to the role.
- Article 5 provides as a default that the Contractor is appointed the Principal Contractor in terms of the CDM Regulations; however there is an option to appoint another person to the role.
- Rights of third parties under the Contract (Rights of Third Parties) Act 1999 are specifically excluded except as provided for in the contract (1·5).
- The parties agree to comply with their roles under the CDM Regulations (3·9). Also the Employer is to notify the Contractor of the name and address of any new CDM Coordinator and Principal Contractor for the purpose CDM that may be appointed by the Employer as replacement to those named under the Contract Particulars.
- The Contractor is to pay all fees required by law. Such fees will not be refunded by the Employer except there is an agreement to this effect by the parties (2·6).

6 Miscellaneous

- The definition of day excludes public holidays but admits Sundays. Where a period of specified days is to be reckoned from a particular date, the period shall begin a day after this date (1·4).
- The default position is for the laws of England and Wales to govern the Contract. The footnote advises that changes may be made to suit another jurisdiction if the Contract is to be used outside England and Wales (1·7).

7 Insurance

- There are three options in the insurance section: if the Contract Particulars chose clause 5·4A the Contractor is take out and maintain all risks insurance with insurers approved by the Employer in a joint name policy. The policy is over full reinstatement value of the works plus a percentage to cover professional fees. The insurance is to be in place until practical completion or termination by the Employer, whichever comes earlier (5·4A).
- The Employer in the alternative in 5·4B is to take out and maintain the joint name insurance policy to cover existing structures, contents owned by him and the full

JCLI Agreement

costs of reinstatement and repair up to Practical Completion. The Contractor is to authorise all payments to be made to the Employer in the event of damage (5·4B).

- The last option is for the Employer to maintain the insurance in his own name (5·4C).
- Where the Contractor maintains the insurance, he is expected to produce evidence of same on reasonable request from the Employer.
- Where damage occurs, the Contractor shall authorise that payment should be made to the Employer and shall with all due diligence pursue the restoration of the damaged work.

8 Termination

- The Termination section sets out the different instances of insolvency relevant for termination (6·1). Notice of termination is not to be unreasonably issued. Termination is to take effect on receipt of notice and such notice or notices are to be delivered by hand or by delivery post (6·2).
- Irrespective of the grounds of termination, the Contractor may be reinstated on terms agreed by the parties (6·3).
- Where the Contractor defaults by failing to carry out the works diligently, or by suspending all or substantial aspects of the works without reasonable cause and/or fails to comply with its duties under CDM Regulations (6·4·1), the Employer may issue the Contractor with a seven day notice to rectify the specified default. If this is not rectified within that period, the Employer by a further notice within 10 days of the expiration of the seven day notice may terminate the Contractor's employment (6·4).
- In the event of the insolvency of the Contractor, the Employer may, by notice at any time, terminate the employment of the Contractor (6·5). As from the date of insolvency the Contractor is relieved of its obligation in Article 1 to carry out and complete the works, all payments from the Employer to the Contractor are restricted in accordance with the provisions of clause 6·7.
- The Employer may take reasonable steps to secure the Site and Materials on Site on Termination (6·5·2). The Employer is also entitled to terminate by notice for corruption (6·6).
- If the Contractor employment is terminated under clauses 6·4, 6·5 and 6·6, the Employer shall take possession of the site and may engage others to complete the works. No further sums shall be due to the contractor other than amounts under clause 6·7·4; and no outstanding sum shall be due for payment if the LSA/CA has issued the relevant Pay Less Notice under clause 4·5·4, or if the Contractor has become insolvent after the last date that the notice should have been given (6·7·2).
- After the completion of the works and the making good of defects or instructions (otherwise 2·11A or 2·11B), the LSA/CA shall within three months issue a certificate

JCLI Agreement

(or in the alternative the Employer shall issue a statement). The certificate/statement shall calculate the difference between loss and expenses incurred by the Employer arising out of employing other persons to complete the works, securing the site and any other direct loss and/or damage arising as a result of the termination and other losses for which the Contractor is liable added to this amount should be the total amount of payments made to the contractor, the sum of these two headings is then subtracted from the total amount agreed by the parties as the contract sum (6·7·3).

- Where the agreed contract sum is less than the expenses incurred by the Employer, the difference shall be a debt payable by the Contractor to the Employer and vice versa.
- The Contractor's right to terminate is dependent on defaults by the Employer and the LSA/CA. Such defaults include: failure to pay by the final date of payment in accordance with clause 4·5 and/or any VAT properly chargeable on such amount, interference with the issuance of any certificate due under the contract, failure to keep to his responsibilities under the CDM, suspension for a continuous period of one month or more due to LSA/CA instructions on inconsistencies in contract document provided by the Contractor, or any impediment, or prevention or default by the Employer, LSA/CA or persons engaged by the Employer (the clause excludes Force Majeure events, actions from statutory authorities, loss or damage due to Specified Perils, civil commotion among others, 6·8·1, 6·8·2).
- On the occurrence of the default outlined in 6·8·1 and 6·8·2 the Contractor is entitled to give the Employer a notice specifying the defaults. If seven days after the receipt of the notice, the default continues, the Contractor may by another notice issued within 10 days of the expiry of the seven days terminate the contract (6·8·3).
- The Contractor may terminate by notice in the event of the Employer's insolvency. On the Employer's insolvency, the Contractor's obligation under Article 1 to carry out and complete the works is suspended (6·9).
- Either party may terminate if work is stopped for a continuous period of one month or more because of Force Majeure (Act of God, ie natural disasters – flash flooding), LSA/CA instructions on inconsistent documents and/or variation which is a result of the negligence of the undertaker, loss and damage occasioned by Specified Perils (this is defined in Section 1 of the contract and includes fire, lightning, earthquake, etc), civil commotion and/or threat of terrorism, exercise of statutory powers by the government which affects the execution of the works. On the occurrence of any of the above events either party may upon the expiry of the one month suspension period, give notice that unless the suspension ceases within seven days of the receipt of the notice, he would terminate. Failing the cessation of suspension after the seven day period, the notifying party may by further notice terminate the contract (6·10).

JCLI Agreement

- The Contractor is precluded from giving notice under Specified Perils where the loss or damage to the works occasioned by the Specified Perils was due to the negligence and/or default of the Contractor or those engaged by it (6·10·2).
- On termination either on the Employer's default (including insolvency) or for reasons beyond the reasonable control of the parties (Force Majeure, Specified Perils, Statutory Actions), the Contractor shall prepare an account setting out the total value of work properly executed at the date of termination, all amounts due to the Contractor under the contract, the costs of materials and goods properly ordered for the works which the Contractor has paid or is bound to pay (6·11·1, 6·11·2).
- Where the termination was due to the Employer's default (including insolvency) and also where the termination is because of loss and damage due to Specified Perils caused by the negligence of the Employer or those engaged by it, the account should also include any direct loss and/or damage caused by the termination (6·11·3).
- With due consideration to the amounts previously paid to the Contractor, the Employer is to pay any outstanding amount on the account within 28 days of the receipt of the account. Any payment with respect to site materials in based on the materials becoming the property of the Employer (6·11·4).

9 Dispute resolution

- Articles 6–8 deal with dispute resolution. An acknowledgment of each party's right to refer any dispute to Adjudication is recognised under Article 6; Article 7 provides arbitration has the default final tribunal for settlement adopting the JCT 2011 Construction Industry Model Arbitration Rules. Issues relating to the Construction Industry Scheme or VAT, as well as disputes over the enforcement of an adjudicator's decisions are to be excluded from the terms of reference for the arbitration panel.
- Article 8 provides for legal proceedings in court both as a necessary bridge in terms of issues specifically excluded from arbitration as noted above and also as an alternative to arbitration.
- Section 7 is concerned with settlement of dispute. The mediation clause presupposes negotiation between the parties that has been unsuccessful and advises parties to seriously consider mediation if suggested by either party (7·1).
- The contract adopts the JCT style of allowing its adjudication procedure to be determined by the relevant scheme of construction contracts (7·2).
- Where the Contract Particulars indicate Arbitration as the final tribunal, an appropriate procedure is set out in schedule 1 of the contract (7·3).

JCLI Agreement

This contract?

If considering using the JCLI Agreement remember that:

It is intended for new landscape work, both soft and hard landscaping. It covers work up to practical completion, but maintenance is a matter for the JCLI Agreement for Landscape Maintenance Works. It is for use in either private or public sectors. There is provision for bills of quantities. The Employer must appoint a Landscape Architect or a Contract Administrator.

There is provision for phased completion, however landscape design by the Contractor is handled in the alternative JCLI Landscape Agreement with Contractor Design. There is provision for partial possession, nomination of sub-contractors, and clauses dealing with the failure of plants, malicious damage or theft, and post-practical completion care. The form is drafted to include compliance with the CDM Regulations although it is envisaged that some contracts let under it may not fall within the coverage of this legislation and the Housing Grants, Construction and Regeneration Act 1996 as amended.

When completing the form decisions are required relating to insurance of the Works, damages for non-completion, and post-practical completion care.

If acting as contract administrator, a non-expert in landscape operations might find difficulties over practical completion, defects liability obligations and staggered release of retention. The procedural rules in general are straightforward but if the agreement is used in parallel with building work being carried out on the same site by a Principal Contractor, care is advisable over coordination of contract periods, Defects Liability Periods, health and safety documents, indemnity and insurance.

The JCLI issues loose-leaf revisions and Practice Notes which give useful advice on matters peculiar to landscape work such as plant specification, watering, frost damage, temporary protection, liability for plant failures and multiple Defects Liability Periods.

The wording of the Conditions closely follows those of the JCT form MW11 and therefore the structure, language and terminology will be familiar to many. For large hard landscape work it might be worth considering the use of the JCT form IC 2011 suitably modified as an alternative.

Related matters

Documents

JCLI Agreement for Landscape Works 2012
JCLI Agreement for Landscape Works with Contractor's Design 2012
JCLI Agreement for Landscape Maintenance Works 2012
Maintenance Works

CIOB Forms

Chartered Institute of Building

CIOB Forms of Contract

Background

The Chartered Institute of Building was originally established in 1834 as the Builders Society. It now has a wide range of membership which includes contractors, consultants and clients. In 2002 it assimilated the membership of the Architecture and Surveying Institute (ASI). The ASI at that time published a range of standard forms of contract and the CIOB consequently took over their publication. The current range of forms are virtually identical to those previously published as ASI contracts, with some minor changes to the text and terminology. All three versions now include a Section for completion at the start of the form, rather than requiring entries in the conditions or an appendix as the ASI versions had done.

CIOB forms exist to cover a wide range of building operations as befits an Institute which counts contractors, architects, architectural technicians and all branches of the surveying profession among its members. The three main contracts have each been approved by the British Institute of Architectural Technologists. These forms are for use with traditional methods of procurement, taking a lump sum as the contract basis. The CIOB also publish a standard form for facilities management, which is beyond the scope of this book.

Nature

All CIOB forms are plainly worded, and in the main are commendably free from legal jargon. Both contracts and sub-contracts are structured to a common pattern, with the clauses in the main contract Conditions grouped under 11 headings. The contracts currently published are as follows:

CIOB Building Contract (2004 Edition): suitable for all types of works, but primarily intended for larger or complex jobs of all types. It may be used either with or without bills of quantities. CIOB domestic sub-contract forms and nominated sub-contract forms are available.

CIOB Small Works Contract (2011 Edition): This contract is intended for use on a small project of a value not exceeding £250,000 or less (at 2011 prices) and lasting no longer than six months. The project is to be fully designed and described by drawings and/or a specification/schedule of works. It is not suitable for use with bills of quantities.

CIOB Minor Works Contract (2004 Edition): for use with straightforward jobs or minor works of a relatively simple character carried out on a lump sum basis. It is not suitable for use with bills of quantities or where it is intended to nominate sub-contractors.

CIOB Forms

CIOB Mini Contract: in two versions, for Home Improvement Agencies and General Use (2011 Editions).

The forms referred to in this Section are the four main contracts listed above. See Chapter 8 below for details of the CIOB Mini forms of contract.

Use

CIOB forms are suitable for use in the private sector or by local authorities. A contract administrator is needed in all cases, but that person may be an architect, surveyor or engineer. The contract administrator is referred to in the Conditions as 'the Architect' in the Building Contract and Small Works Contract, and 'the Adviser' in the Minor Works Contract – regardless of profession!

All the forms commence with entries which identify the parties and date of the contract. There are brief Recitals, and the Agreement in which details relevant to the particular contract must be entered. There is provision for attestation to be under hand and not as a deed, or as a deed. Each form has appendices peculiar to the specific contract, and each has an index list of clauses.

None of the 2004 published forms have been updated to comply with the provisions of the Housing Grants, Construction and Regeneration Act 1996 as amended and would therefore require amendments before they are used for new projects. The Small Works Contract 2011 has been drafted to comply with the Act and can be used as it is.

Brief synopsis of forms

CIOB Building Contract (2004)

- A headnote indicates that the form is intended for larger or complex jobs, and for use with or without bills of quantities.
- Contract documents are drawings, and bills of quantities or Specification. If the latter then the contractor must supply a Schedule of Rates.
- Details relating to the particular contract are to be entered in the Agreement.
- The person appointed by the Employer as contract administrator is referred to as 'the Contract Administrator'. If that person is 'Surveyor/Engineer' this will be an entry in the Recitals and the wording of the Conditions is deemed to have been changed.
- The obligations of the contractor and the role of the contract administrator are well described (1 and 2).
- The contractor must submit a Programme/progress chart within three weeks of entering into the contract (4·11).

CIOB Forms

- Key contract dates are entered in the Agreement, and the contract administrator may award at his or her absolute discretion extensions of time for listed admissible causes of delay (4·4).
- The contract requires practical completion (the date 'shall be discussed with and approved in writing by the Contract Administrator', 4·2) and can also accommodate Part/Sectional Completion as the 'Employer may require or agree with the Contractor' (4·6).
- Failure to meet the completion date will result in payment of liquidated damages, as confirmed in writing by the contract administrator (4·5).
- The Employer may appoint a Clerk of Works empowered to issue directions, but which must be confirmed as contract administrator's instructions (2·6).
- Domestic sub-contracting is permitted, subject to approval by the contract administrator (5·1).
- There is provision for nominated sub-contractors and Prime Cost suppliers, subject to stated conditions (5·3 and 5·4).
- The Contract Sum is VAT-exclusive. Fluctuations in scheduled rates and prices for labour and materials may be included, or there can be adjustment by use of formula rules. Otherwise only changes in statutory charges will be allowable (7·3).
- The contract administrator is empowered to order variations, and the order will also stipulate the basis for valuation (ie either according to the priced document; or rates approved by the contract administrator; or a quotation approved by the contract administrator; or as daywork). Note that if there is no quantity surveyor, then measuring is the responsibility of the contractor (7·2).
- Architect's Interim Certificates are normally issued at monthly intervals, with payment by the Employer due within 14 days (6·3). Amounts payable to nominated sub-contractors must be identified in the Certificates, and the contractor must provide proof of payment. Failure to comply means direct payment by the Employer (6·81).
- Architect's Final Certificate is to be issued 'as soon as practicable' after any defects have been made good following the end of the Defects Liability Period – normally six months (6·9).
- No certificate is to be taken as conclusive evidence that work, materials or goods are in accordance with the contract (6·91).
- The contractor must comply with all legal and statutory requirements, including giving necessary notices and paying fees and charges legally demandable (1·3). If changes from Contract Documents become necessary for reasons of statutory compliance, the contract administrator must receive written notice from the contractor (1·31).
- Compliance with health and safety CDM Regulations becomes a contractual obligation as well as a statutory one (Agreement A1 and 1·3).

CIOB Forms

- Insurance of new work in joint names, against risk of damage by listed perils, is by the contractor (8·1), although the Employer may elect to carry this insurance. Insurance of existing buildings against risk of damage by listed perils is at the sole risk of the Employer (8·2).
- There is provision for determining the employment of the contractor for listed reasons of default on the part of either Employer or Contractor. The procedures are clearly set out, and if determination occurs then actions required in respect of removal from the site, completion of the Works, and settlement of claims, are all described (9·1 and 9·2).
- Disputes or differences are to be submitted to the contract administrator initially for his or her decision (10·1). If not resolved then the dispute may proceed to arbitration (10·2). The contract lists the several methods and rules which can apply, including a shortened arbitration procedure (10·3). There is also a Section on the right of parties to refer a dispute to adjudication and the procedures relating to the appointment of an adjudicator and conduct of the adjudication (11).

CIOB Small Works Contract (2011)

- A headnote indicates that the form is intended for smaller works at values of £250,000 or less (at 2011 prices). It should not be used for complex operations.
- The works is described in R1 with further documents to identify it appropriately (specification/Schedule of works/drawings) set out in Appendix 2.
- The contractor is to carry out and complete the works as described in the contract documents and Construction Phase Plan (A1).
- The contract sum is exclusive of VAT (A5) and is stated in Memorandum of Agreement at A4.
- The Contractor is to undertake the role of the Principal Contractor for all matters of Health and Safety as defined in the CDM Regulations.
- The Contract is to be administered by a Contractor Administrator which is to be named in A6 and where it is a notifiable project the CDM Coordinator is to be named in A7.
- The Agreement is to take priority over other contract documents (A9).
- The Contractor is to comply with the construction programme set out in Appendix 2 and proceed with the Works diligently, expeditiously and will be held liable for any delays except where those delays were beyond the control of the contractor (2·1·1).
- Without prejudice to their contractual rights, the Employer and the Contractor are to act fairly and in a spirit of trust and mutual cooperation in the performance of their obligation. And to help each other resolve problems that occur during the project (2·5).
- The commencement date and the completion date for the project are set out in the contract (2·1·2).

CIOB Forms

- The Contractor is to inform the Contract Administrator in writing as soon as it becomes apparent that the Completion Date will not be achieved. It will be at the sole discretion of the Contract Administrator to grant an extension of time and this will be done in writing (2·1·4).
- Liquidated damages are to be paid for non-completion (2·2).
- Practical Completion is to be certified by the Contract Administrator when in his opinion practical completion has been achieved.
- Except otherwise provided by the parties the defect period is to be for six months commencing from the date of practical completion.
- The contractor is to serve all notices and comply with all legal and statutory requirements including building regulations (3·3).
- The Contractor is not to carry out any additional work or incur expenses unless authorised in writing by the Contract Administrator (3·4).
- The Contractor is to notify the Contract Administrator of any discrepancies found in the contract documents. The Contract Administrator is to determine the appropriate action and issue the necessary instructions which shall be carried out by the Contractor at his own expense (4·2).
- The Contractor shall be responsible for setting out the Works and shall rectify all errors at his own expense (4·3).
- The duties and powers of the Contract Administrator are set out in clause 5 and include issuing instructions which shall be in writing (5·3·1) and rejecting work not in accordance with the contract (5·2).
- Where the Contractor fails to comply with the Contract Administrator instruction after relevant notice there is provision to employ another contractor to carry out the instruction with the Contractor liable for expenses incurred in that process (5·3·1).
- The Contract Administrator may issue instructions requiring a variation. Parties are to come to an agreement on the costs of such variation, failing that the Contract Administrator shall value it on a fair and reasonable basis (7).
- Payment is either a single payment when the duration of the contract is less than 45 days or stage payments where the duration is more than 45 days and therefore under the ambit of the Construction Act (8).
- Where stage payments apply, the Contractor is required to issue to the Employer and the Contract Administrator an interim payment certificate at intervals set out in Appendix 1, indicating the amount the Contractor considers due at the interval and the basis for calculating it (8·3). The due date for payment shall be the date the Employer receives the certificate.

CIOB Forms

- The Final Date for payment is 14 days from the due date (8·3). No later than five days after the due date, the Employer or Contract Administrator shall issue a written notice specifying the payment proposed, what the sum relates to and how it was calculated (8·4·1). This amount will be due for payment on the final payment date unless a Pay Less Notice is issued by the Employer in accordance with 8·4·3.
- If the Employer fails to issue the notice in 8·4·1 it shall be liable to pay the amount stated in the Contractor's Interim Payment Notice on the final date of payment (8·4·3) unless a notice under 8·4·3 is issued.
- If the Employer intend to pay less than the sum stated in its written notice issued under 8·4·1 or where applicable the Contractor's interim payment certificate, it shall no later than five days before the Final Date of Payment, issue a Pay Less Notice, indicating the sum it considers due to the Contractor at the time of the notice and the basis of how it was calculated (8·4·3).
- The Contractor (or where appropriate the Employer) will be entitled to interest payment on any overdue amount not paid in full by the Final Payment Date (8·8). The Contractor also has the right to suspend some or its entire obligations if a default on payment continues after a seven day notice and is entitled to reasonable costs and expenses incurred as a result of such suspension (8·5).
- There are detailed and similar provisions for the final certificate (8·7).
- Neither party may assign or otherwise dispose of its rights and obligations under the contract without the prior written consent of the other except such prohibition shall not affect assignment by way of security and assignments to subsidiary or associated companies within the same group of companies.
- The Contractor is to insure in the joint names of both parties for the works, goods on site and other related risks while the Employer is to insure for existing structures and works. Parties are allowed to vary the insurance provisions by agreement (10).
- Determination of the contract may be by the Employer (11·1) for specified defaults of the contractor and insolvency or by the Contractor (11·2) for specified defaults of the Employer and insolvency or either party may terminate for neutral causes (11·3), the consequences of such determination are covered under clause 12.
- The Contracts (Rights of Third Parties) Act 1999 is specifically excluded (14).
- Disputes are to be resolved by adjudication and the final tribunal for resolution is the courts (15).

CIOB Minor Works Contract (2004)

- A headnote indicates that this form is intended for 'minor' works on a lump sum basis. No bills of quantities and no nominated sub-contractors.

CIOB Forms

- Contract documents are drawings and a Specification or Schedule of Work, and Health and Safety Plan.
- Details relating to the particular contract are to be entered in a schedule at the start of the Conditions.
- The person appointed by the Employer as contract administrator is referred to as the 'Adviser'.
- The obligations of the contractor (1) and the role of the Adviser (2) are briefly described.
- Key contract dates are to be entered in the Conditions (4·1). The Adviser may award, in his absolute discretion, an extension of time if the circumstances warrant it.
- The contract requires practical completion to be approved by the Adviser, and followed by a defects period – normally of six months (4·2).
- Failure to meet the completion date will result in payment of liquidated damages (4·1).
- Sub-letting is not permitted without the written consent of the Adviser (5·1).
- The Contract Sum is VAT-exclusive (A·3). The contract is fixed price except for changes in statutory payments (7·3).
- The Adviser may order variations, and the order will also stipulate the basis for valuation (7·1).
- Adviser's Interim Certificates will be issued from time to time at the discretion of the Adviser (6·2), with payment by the Employer due within 14 days (6·3).
- Adviser's Final Certificate will be issued after proper completion of the work and making good the defects after the end of the defects period (6·5).
- The contractor must comply with all statutory requirements and pay all fees and charges legally demandable (1·3).
- Insurance of new work in joint names against specified perils is by the contractor (8·1). Insurance of existing buildings against specified perils is at the 'sole risk' of the Employer (8·2).
- The contract provides for determination of the employment of the contractor for listed reasons on the part of the Employer or the Contractor. There is very terse reference to actions which might follow (9·1 and 9·2).
- Claims or disputes are to be submitted to the Adviser initially for his decision (10·1). If not resolved, they may proceed to arbitration (10·2). There is also a Section on the right of parties to refer a dispute to adjudication and the procedures relating to the appointment of an adjudicator and conduct of the adjudication (11).

CIOB Forms

This contract?

If considering using CIOB Forms remember that:

The intended scope of the contract is carried in a headnote on each of the forms. They are all for lump sum contracts, and for private or local authority use. They are obviously for use by CIOB members, but non-members might also find them of considerable interest and may use them. It is important to note that only the Small Works version has been updated to comply with current legislation.

The Building Contract and Small Works Contract both state that the law of the contract is English law, but the Minor Works Contract is silent on this point. All three forms refer to adjudication procedures being subject to the law of England and Wales. The forms would therefore not appear to be suitable for use under Scots law.

Contract administrators should first be certain that the provisions adequately cover the nature of the intended work, and should check in particular that the provisions for Practical Completion Certificates, insurance, determination and adjudication satisfy their requirements. They are somewhat limited, and probably best used for traditional work. Certainly as far as payment is concerned the forms seem to be light on detail required by the Housing Grants, Construction and Regeneration Act 1996 and might be subject to the Scheme for Construction Contracts. There is no provision for design by the Contractor, but nomination of sub-contractors and suppliers is provided for except in the Minor Works Contract. CIOB sub-contracts are available for nominated and domestic sub-contracts.

Completing the forms is straightforward, with details entered in a Section at the start of the form.

The contract administrator is given considerable authority, and contract administration should prove a straightforward and conventional operation. There is a full range of CIOB standard contract administration forms available.

Three compact and interesting forms, traditional in scope, clearly set out and structured, and plainly worded. Likely to appeal to clients, and certainly to smaller building firms.

Related matters

Documents

Building Contract 2004 Edition
Small Works Contract 2011 Edition
Minor Works Contract 2004 Edition
Domestic Sub-Contract 2004 Edition
Nominated Sub-Contract 2004 Edition
Contract Administration Forms
(eight in number, available in pad form)

Agreement for Appointment of Professional Adviser
Agreement for Appointment of Planning Supervisor

Notes

CIOB Contracts Guide – Guide Notes on their use

SBCC Documents

Scottish Building Contract Committee (SBCC)

SBCC Forms of Contract

Background

Scots law for historical reasons, differs markedly from the law of England and Wales. Also, with the establishment of the Scottish Parliament, not all laws made by Great Britain and Northern Ireland Westminster Parliament apply to Scotland. Historically sources of law in Scotland are not the same as those of England, and the influence of Roman law and Canon law over time has resulted in a unique legal system, courts structure, and distinctive terminology. Close continental links in the past have also helped to produce what one commentator has described as an 'intermediate between Civil law and Common law'.

There are, however, many similarities and legislations such as the Housing Grants, Construction and Regeneration Act 1996 as amended applies equally in both jurisdictions. However, because of the differences it is important that parties take account of the significant differences in legislation, and in the law relating to property, delict (broadly speaking the equivalent of the English law of tort) and of course contract.

In the past, building contracts in Scotland were often based on an exchange of letters rather than formal documents, and were direct trades contracts. The Emmerson Report of 1962 highlighted the different circumstances in Scotland and concluded that the existing trade by trade basis was unsuitable for main contracting in the building industry. It recommended that closer links should be established with London, and that a working party be appointed in Scotland, which duly resulted in the McEwan Younger Committee. A report from that committee, with the initiative of the Royal Incorporation of Architects in Scotland, resulted in the formation of the Scottish Building Contract Committee (SBCC) in 1964. The SBCC has now been restructured as a limited company. The SBCC Ltd board is advised by a Consultative Committee drawn widely from representative bodies from within the building industry in Scotland as follows:

- Royal Incorporation of Architects in Scotland;
- Scottish Building;
- The Royal Institution of Chartered Surveyors in Scotland;
- Scottish CASEC;
- Convention of Scottish Local Authorities;
- National Specialists Contractor's Council – Scottish Committee;
- Association of Consulting Engineers (Scottish Group);
- Scottish Executive, Building Division;
- Confederation of British Industry;
- Association of Scottish Chambers of Commerce.

This is obviously a wide representation compared, for example, with the JCT Ltd.

SBCC Documents

The Banwell Report, issued in March 1964, included a recommendation that 'a common form of contract for all construction work covering England, Scotland and Wales was both desirable and practicable'. Implementation of this report resulted in the Joint Contracts Tribunal inviting the Scottish Building Contracts Committee to join the Tribunal, and this invitation was accepted in 1966 'subject to the right of the SBCC to issue Tribunal forms in a manner which conformed with Scots law and practice'.

SBCC Ltd is therefore primarily responsible for the adaptation of JCT documents for use in Scotland. It is also responsible for amending and publishing such forms, advising on the interpretation of these contracts, promoting best practice, drafting and publishing guidance and practice notes, nominating arbiters, mediators or third party tribunals, and attending national and other committees including those at the JCT. SBCC Ltd is now the 'Relevant College' for the Scottish Construction Industry within JCT Ltd, and takes an active part in providing input to drafting where Scots law and practice dictate.

Nature

The SBCC has published 2011 editions of its forms to comply with the changes in the Housing Grants, Construction and Regeneration Act 1996 as amended by the Local Democracy, Economic Development and Construction Act 2009 which became effective in Scotland on 1 November 2011. The 2011 editions of the SBCC forms mirror the releases by the JCT of the JCT 2011 Contracts. The 2011 editions include:

- Standard Building Contract With Quantities for use in Scotland
- Standard Building Contract Without Quantities for use in Scotland
- Standard Building Contract With Approximate Quantities for use in Scotland
- Design and Build Contract for use in Scotland
- Minor Works Building Contract for use in Scotland
- Minor Works Building Contract with Contractors Design for use in Scotland

Use

The SBCC forms are to be used for the same type of projects that similar JCT contracts would be suitable for in England and Wales. Therefore a relatively complex project which requires extensive control procedures is best let under the Standard Building Contract for use in Scotland (which is available in the same three versions as the JCT – with quantities, with approximate quantities and without quantities) while a Design and Build contract would be suited to the Design and Build Contract for use in Scotland.

The most significant difference is that attestation is to be made in accordance with Scots law. The SBCC issues guidance on attestation procedures. Another difference concerns dispute resolution. The Arbitration (Scotland) Act 2010 applies in Scotland, the Act is broadly speaking similar to the legislation in England and Wales.

Architects undertaking work in Scotland who are not familiar with Scots law would do well to seek legal advice.

SBCC Documents

Synopsis of MW/Scot11 and comparisons with JCT MW11

The SBC Minor Works Contract (MW/Scot11), and Minor Works Contract with contractor's design (MWD/Scot11) are closely modelled on MW11 and MWD11, respectively. The differences between the JCT and SBCC versions of the forms may be summarised as follows:

1 Intentions

- MW/Scot05 provides for the optional use of bills of quantities (second recital, third in MW/Scott11 and MWD/Scot11, respectively) and the appointment of a Quantity Surveyor (Article 4).
- There is an additional Article 10 on Registration: 'parties consent to registration hereof for preservation and execution'.
- Applicable law is stated to be the law of Scotland (1·7).

2 Time

- The wording of the clauses is identical, save for some clause number cross references.

3 Control

- Covered under Section heading 3 in MW11, but under Section heading 4 in MW/Scot11 due to a provision for bills of quantities under Section 3 of MW/Scott 11.
- Wording of the provisions is mainly the same in both forms, but MW/Scot11 provides for listed sub-contractors.
- The main contractor may choose a domestic sub-contractor from a list of not less than three names as set out in the Contract Documents. There is a mechanism for maintaining the list at three, and a fall-back provision where this proves impossible (4·3·2 and 4·3·3). This is similar to the SBC11 clause 3·8.

4 Money

- Covered under Section heading 4 in MW11, but Section heading 5 in MW/Scot11.
- The wording of the clauses is identical, save for some clause number cross references.

5 Statutory obligations

- The wording of the clauses dealing with statutory requirements is identical.

6 Insurance

- Covered under Section heading 5 in MW11 but Section heading 6 in MW/Scot11. The wording of the clauses is identical in both forms, except for some minor cross references.

SBCC Documents

7 Termination

- Covered under Section heading 6 in MW11 but Section heading 7 in the SBC versions. The wording of the provisions is identical in both forms, except for an additional provision dealing with proceedings in other jurisdictions (7·1·5) and adjustments to take account of Scottish legislation (7·6).

8 Miscellaneous

- Schedules are the same for both forms in respect of 1: Arbitration and 2: Fluctuations The wording of Schedule Part 2: adjudication is different to take account of Scottish legislation. There is an additional Schedule Part 3: Contract Documents under which the parties are required to list all the documents forming the contract.

9 Disputes

- Part II of the Housing Grants, Construction and Regeneration Act 1996 as amended applies to Scotland, and either party has a statutory right to refer any difference or dispute arising under the contract for adjudication.
- The procedures and rules for adjudication in clause 8·2 are identical to those in MW11.
- Arbitration in Scotland is not subject to the Arbitration Act 1996 but the Arbitration (Scotland) Act 2010, and Schedule Part 1 sets out the relevant procedures and Codes which will apply. This will not apply unless it has been selected in the Contract Particulars.
- The alternative of court proceedings is referred to in clause 8·4 and the court is given rights in relation to opening up and reviewing certificates and decisions.

SBCC Documents

This contract?

If considering using MW/Scot11 remember that:

It is intended for building works of a simple straightforward nature, and is not suitable for work of such duration that full fluctuations provisions are required. It can only be used where the Employer has engaged a professional consultant to act as contract administrator. There is provision for bills of quantities, and a quantity surveyor may be appointed.

This contract is the only standard form for minor building works in Scotland. The form is drafted to ensure compliance with the CDM Regulations, and with Part II of the Housing Grants, Construction and Regeneration Act 1996 as amended.

As with JCT MW11, there is no provision for phased completion. Unlike the JCT form, this SBCC contract provides for the naming of sub-contractors by way of a list of three names and there is also a dedicated SBCC sub-contract available.

When completing the form, decisions are required relating to insurance of the Works and damages for late completion. Appropriate deletions will indicate whether the final resolution of disputes is by arbitration or court proceedings.

If acting as contract administrator, the Conditions are likely to prove adequate for most situations. The procedural rules are simple.

This SBCC form can be seen as more of a middle range contract for all work where use of the full SBC version of SBC11 cannot be justified. There is no SBCC equivalent of the JCT IC11 form.

Related matters

Documents

SBCC Minor Works Contract 2011 Edition
SBCC Minor Works Contract with Contractors Design 2011 Edition

Notes

SBCC Guidance Notes upon Dispute Resolution in Scotland

Traditional procurement 8

Consumer contracts

The Joint Contracts Tribunal Ltd
2005 Building Contract for a Home Owner/Occupier revision 2009

The Joint Contracts Tribunal Ltd
2005 Contract for Home Repairs and Maintenance revision 2009

Chartered Institute of Building
Mini Form of Contract 2011 Edition

These are contracts between 'consumers' (ie a natural person entering into a contract for purposes outside business, in particular a person wishing to have work carried out on his or her own house) and a 'contractor' (ie a supplier of goods or services in the course of their business).

The law seeks to protect consumers so that they are not put at a disadvantage. The Unfair Terms in Consumer Contracts Regulations 1994, Unfair Terms in Consumer Contracts Regulations 1999 and Cancellation of Contracts, etc Regulations 2008 are some of the regulations that apply to contracts which have not been individually negotiated (eg this would generally include all standard forms of building contract and those for professional services), and require that there must be no unfair terms on the consumer and also allows the consumer a cooling-off period within which they may cancel the contract without liability. Terms which are deemed to be unfair are those which might cause a significant imbalance in the parties' rights to the detriment of the consumer and such terms will not be binding on the consumer. The Regulations also require contracts to be expressed in plain, intelligible language.

The forms in this chapter will normally be classed as consumer contracts.

JCT HO/B, and HO/C & HO/CA

The Joint Contracts Tribunal Ltd

Building Contract for a Home Owner/ Occupier who has not appointed a consultant to oversee the work

Building Contract and Consultancy Agreement for a Home Owner/ Occupier

Background

It used to be thought that whilst home improvements might prove lucrative for smaller builders, such work for the most part was not of interest to professional consultants. However, the boom in housing improvements in recent years and the potential for engagement in this market have shown the need for forms of contract appropriate to this kind of work.

The JCT has two forms of building contract for homeowners or occupiers intending to carry out domestic building work. They are both packaged in a folder, there are counterpart copies of the forms for customer and the builder, and guidance notes. They are written in a refreshing style commendably free from jargon and legalist language which has gained for them the Crystal Mark for Clarity approved by the Plain English Campaign. They are marketed widely through retail outlets such as book shops directly to customers.

The first form published in 1999 was the Building Contract for a Home Owner/ Occupier, suitable for use where the customer chose to deal directly with a builder for home improvements, small extensions or repairs. Obviously this promised a significant improvement over oral arrangements or poorly worded letters, and encouraged the parties to consider methodically and agree the important points before concluding the deal.

The second form published in 2001 was the Building Contract and Consultancy Agreement for a Home Owner/Occupier who has appointed a consultant, and it followed the same attractive format for packaging and presentation. This could prove to be a more appropriate form for much of the larger-scale domestic work now attracting the involvement of architects and building surveyors, than the JCT Minor Works Contract which is perhaps more suited to smaller work of a commercial nature.

JCT HO/B, and HO/C & HO/CA

It can be used only where a consultant is appointed to act on the customer's behalf, and the document folder includes a JCT Consultancy Agreement for professional services which is dedicated for use with this building contract. It is likely to prove more appropriate in these circumstances than agreements published by the professional bodies. Both forms were republished in 2005 and revised in 2009.

Nature

The Building Contract for a Home Owner/Occupier is just 13 pages long, and is in two parts. First there is a questionnaire in duplicate which when completed sets out the arrangements for the work. Secondly there are the contract Conditions clearly and simply worded under 12 headings (also two copies). The customer is provided with an enquiry letter to send to a potential builder, a sheet of helpful guidance notes and a Cancellation form in the event he seeks to cancel the contract seven days after entering into it.

The Building Contract and Consultancy Agreement for a Home Owner/Occupier is rather more formal in appearance. There is a Building Contract which has two parts; Part 1 is the arrangements for the work, and Part 2 is the Conditions set out under 14 headings. The Consultancy Agreement is also a two-part document; Part 1 is the consultant's services and Part 2 is the Conditions set out under 11 headings, a total of just 13 pages of text. There are copies of each for the customer and the Contractor, and Guidance Notes and cancellation forms.

Use

Both forms are simple and easy to understand. They are only suitable for construction contracts to which Part II of the Housing Grants, Construction and Regeneration Act 1996 Act 1996 as amended does not apply. The CDM Regulations will not apply.

The Building Contract for a Home Owner/Occupier must not be used where a consultant is employed. There is no stated cost limit, but as will be obvious from the excellent tick box approach used for the arrangements document, and the basic contract Conditions, it is for very small domestic work only. Incidentally, for architects who are involved in a partial service for domestic work but whose clients nevertheless ask for advice about appointing a builder, this form would be a sound recommendation.

The Building Contract and Consultancy Agreement is for a home owner/occupier who intends to appoint a consultant to deal directly with the builder. Note that it is suitable only for a homeowner. If the work is being carried on as a business venture, then one of the commercial contracts should be used.

Brief synopsis

1 **Building Contract for a Home Owner/Occupier 2005 revised in 2009**

- Lump sum contract. Note that contractor's quotation is VAT-inclusive.
- Drawings and/or Specification or other documents. No bills of quantities.

JCT HO/B, and HO/C & HO/CA

- Either customer or contractor may deal with applications for planning permission, building regulations and party wall consents. The Contract price is deemed to include the costs of such applications if the Contractor is applying for it.
- Facilities for Contractor, as ticked, to be provided free of charge by the customer.
- Contractor's responsibilities include storing equipment at the end of each day, regularly disposing of rubbish, and leaving all clean and tidy after finishing the work.
- Payment may be single payment or by agreed instalments. Customer to pay on invoices within 14 days, 95 per cent of amounts due.
- Working period may be by agreed duration, or start and completion date entered. Working hours may be specified.
- Only customer can change work details. Contractor to submit a price before work goes ahead.
- Customer can extend work period if contractor is delayed for limited stated reasons.
- Insurance provisions limited to customer's household insurance, contractor's all risks cover for damage to work and unfixed materials, and public liability cover.
- Customer is to indicate if the premises will be ocuupied (lived in) during the duration of the works. If the premises are unoccupied during the time of construction, the contractor to provide practical and common sense precautions to deter intruders.
- Either customer or contractor can bring contract to an end for stated reasons.
- The customer has a right to cancel the contract for any reason by giving the contractor a notice in writing within seven days of signing the contract. The main position is that all payments made (or monies disbursed) by the customer are returned to it, however where the customer had agreed in writing that the contractor provide certain types of goods and services within the seven day period, he may be required to pay for those goods and services (examples include perishable goods).
- Defects period is three months, and customer will pay remaining five per cent of money due within 14 days of contractor putting right any faults promptly reported by the customer.
- If disputes arise, either party can start court proceedings, or may opt for adjudication.

2 **Building Contract and Consultancy Agreement for a Home Owner/Occupier 2005 revised in 2009**

- Description of the work is detailed in contractor's quotation /consultant's drawings/ consultant's specification. No bills of quantities, but 'other documents' may be included.

JCT HO/B, and HO/C & HO/CA

- Lump sum contract. Contractor's price is VAT-inclusive. contractor to itemise this and show details of VAT chargeable.
- Price includes for 'unexpected problems' which should have been foreseen by the contractor from the documents or a site visit. Contract figure can only be changed up or down if changes to the work are instructed.
- A start and completion date should be entered, or a contract period stated. Working hours may be specified.
- The customer can expect to receive the benefit of any product guarantees.
- The contractor's responsibilities include carrying out work carefully, competently and 'as the consultant instructs' and to be 'at the premises regularly to carry out the work' and to 'keep to all his legal duties and responsibilities'.
- The customer's responsibilities include providing access to the premises throughout the working period, keeping working areas clear of obstructions, and allowing the contractor to carry out work in an order which he considers necessary to complete on time.
- The consultant will act for the customer in giving instructions, extensions of time, and in issuing certificates. There are only two types of certificates, first on completion of the work or stage of the work, and second after the contractor has rectified faults at the end of the defects period of three months. Although there are no monetary certificates, the consultant must be satisfied that the contractor's invoices are correct. The contract states that in the event of any disagreement with the consultant's decisions, the contractor must take this up directly with the customer.
- Changing the work details can be ordered only by the consultant. Where an increase in work is likely, the contractor must quote the extra cost and time involved before work can be authorised. Where change amounts to a reduction of work, the contractor will make an appropriate deduction.
- The consultant can make a fair and reasonable extension if the contractor is unable to complete to time for reasons beyond his control. If delay is caused by the consultant or the customer the contractor may also be entitled to costs.
- Consultant is responsible for planning permission, building regulations and party wall consents, however the costs of these are not included in the consultant's fee and must be paid separately by the customer. (Consultants acting for the customer in serving party wall notices should make sure that they have written authorisation, otherwise their capacity to act might be challenged.)
- Welfare facilities to be provided for contractor free of charge by customer are as ticked.

JCT HO/B, and HO/C & HO/CA

- The contractor is to take all practical steps to prevent or minimise health and safety risks to the customer and other occupants, to minimise environmental disturbance, nuisance or pollution. In return the customer undertakes to take notice of warnings by the contractor and not knowingly allow occupants or visitors to be exposed to dangers.
- Payment may be a single payment or by instalments as agreed. Customer to pay 95 per cent of total amount due. If stage payments are selected, they should be clearly defined and amounts stated.
- Customer is expected to pay 95 per cent within 14 days after completion has been certified by the consultant. There is a three month Defects Liability Period, at the end of which the consultant will issue a list of any faults. When these have been rectified the remaining five per cent will be due within 14 days after completion has been certified.
- Insurance provisions are minimal, and limited to householder's insurance, contractor's all risks cover for full cost of damage to work and unfixed materials (no perils stipulated) and public liability cover. The contract liability cover figure is to be entered.
- Provisions for occupation and security of premises are limited. If remaining in residence the customer should be made aware of the inconvenience and disruption which might result, and the contractor should allow for temporary protective measures as appropriate. If the customer is vacating the premises, house insurance policies should be checked, as most suspend cover where premises are left unoccupied beyond a stated period and special arrangements might become advisable. Also the contractor's obligation to adopt 'practical and common-sense precautions' might require something more specific in the Specification.
- Both contracts may be brought to an end by the parties to them (customer/contractor and customer/consultant) for specified reasons and the customer retains the right to cancel either contract within seven days of signing it in keeping with the Cancellation of Contracts, etc Regulations 2008.
- If disputes arise, either party can start court proceedings or may opt for adjudication. In the latter event the contractor may not apply to the National Specialist Contractors Council to be appointor.
- Other rights and remedies are not extinguished by the contract provisions.

JCT HO/B, and HO/C & HO/CA

This contract?

If considering using JCT Homeowner Contracts remember that:

Each form is intended for use only with work for home owners/occupiers. If the customer wishes to appoint a consultant, then the only one to be used is the version which gives a role for the consultant. In such cases the dedicated Consultancy Agreement must also be used. This document takes a very practical and clear approach to defining the services and the conditions which will apply.

Neither of the forms is suitable for use in Scotland; the SBCC publishes Homeowner Contracts for use in Scotland.

Completing the forms should be straightforward, but care is needed to make sure that duplicate copies carry identical entries.

Problems could exist over possession and occupation, work sequence, design responsibility particularly relating to services installations or other specialist work, and insurance.

Helpful guidance notes are provided for each contract, and they should be read carefully, particularly in the case of the version where a consultant is appointed. As yet there are no dedicated contract administration forms available, but letters should be clearly identified as certificates where they are intended to serve as such.

Each of these forms adopts a completely fresh and friendly approach which will initially be unfamiliar to most contract administrators. The presentation and packaging is novel and customer orientated. The terminology is straightforward and the forms are commendably written in plain English. As one commentator has noted: "This little form is a beauty".

Related matters

Documents

JCT Building Contract for a Home Owner/Occupier 2005 revised 2009
JCT Building Contract and Consultancy Agreement for a Home Owner/Occupier 2005 revised 2009

References

JCT Guidance Notes included for each of the forms

JCT HO/RM

The Joint Contracts Tribunal Ltd

JCT Contract for Home Repairs and Maintenance

Background

The JCT first published this contract for home care and repair works in 2002, to ensure that there was a form for all situations. It was presumably intended to cover the type of very minor works for which even the Home Owner/Occupier Contracts might seem overly long. The JCT republished the document in a 2006 edition with a slightly revised format, and it is now available in an edition published after a 2009 update. It may be downloaded free from the JCT website.

The form provides a most useful service in bringing consumers and builders to think about, and commit to writing, those essentials of the contract which in the past have too often been left as vague assumptions.

Where the contractor is previously unknown to the customer, but quite ready to enter into an agreement such as this, it could also signify that this is probably a reputable firm.

Nature

This must be the shortest standard form for building work ever produced. The contract is just five pages long, including a cancellation form, with an additional page of guidance notes. The Conditions are minimal but appropriate for this kind and size of operations, clearly worded and set out in 12 short Sections. As with other JCT contracts for homeowners, this one also comes with the Crystal Mark of the Plain English Campaign.

Use

The guidance notes suggest that repairs and maintenance might, for example, cover electrical rewiring, plumbing installations or even painting and decorating. The form is not intended for use with building work which might involve structural alterations, nor where more than one trade is likely to be involved.

An important point emphasied is that the customer should let the contractor know at the time of requesting a quotation that this contract will be used. This will then reduce the likelihood of the contractor submitting a quotation which is subject to the small print of his own terms.

Brief synopsis

- A two line description of the intended work is followed by a tick box indicating whether the premises will be in occupation at the time.

JCT HO/RM

- Details of the work are given in documents that are to be ticked, including a 'specification' prepared either by the customer or the contractor, and the contractor's quotation.
- The contractor's price is inclusive of VAT, and may be a fixed lump sum or an hourly rate.
- Facilities to be provided by the customer free of charge are shown in tick boxes.
- Payment is not made until the work is completed, and within 14 days of receipt of the contractor's itemised invoice.
- The contractor must carry 'enough insurance' to cover full costs of damage and materials on site, in addition to public liability insurance.
- A start date and the contract period are entered, together with the agreed daily hours of working.
- The contractor's obligation is to carry out the work 'competently and carefully', and to leave the work areas clean and tidy each day.
- Sub-contracting is permitted, but requires the customer's permission.
- The contractor is responsible for health, safety and environmental matters.
- The customer has the right to cancel the contract within seven days of entering the contract and all payments are to be returned except where the customer has agreed in writing to provisions of services or certain goods (ie perishable goods) within the seven day period.
- Third party rights are excluded, but the contract does not rule out other legal remedies open to either party.
- There is no provision for loss or expense, but the contract accepts that the parties may claim from each other in the event of failure to keep to the contract.
- Disputes can be referred to adjudication, and the right to litigation is preserved.

JCT HO/RM

This contract?

If advising using JCT Home Repairs Contract remember that:

It is intended for repairs and maintenance work, to which Part II of the Housing Grants, Construction and Regeneration Act 1996 will not apply. The work will almost certainly not be subject to the full CDM Regulations.

It is not for use in Scotland.

It is a modest form, but it must provide a more business-like way of dealing than just relying on a contractor's estimate, whether written or oral. The intended repair works may be simple, but the cost could seem a relatively large expense to the customer and should be covered by a proper agreement.

There is no role under the contract for construction professionals, but they might be approached for advice on a suitable form and if so this should be a safe recommendation. It might also help to protect customers from the so-called 'cowboys' of the industry!

Related matters

Documents

JCT Contract for Home Repairs and Maintenance 2006 revised 2009

References

JCT Guidance Notes for customers included in the printed form

CIOB Mini Forms

Chartered Institute of Building

Mini Form of Contract (General Use)

Mini Form of Contract (Home Improvement Agencies)

Background

In 1998 the CIOB took an innovative step and produced a document which they neatly styled a Mini form of contract. Before this it was impossible to find a standard form appropriate for very small jobs, which also provided for the client to appoint an architect or other professional to act as a contract administrator. At the time the Mini had no real competitors. As with the other ASI standard forms, this is now published by the CIOB.

The form is produced in two versions, one for general use and the other developed in collaboration with Care and Repair England for use with residential works. Both forms have now been revised and were republished in 2011 by the CIOB in association with Dickinson Dees LLP and Northumbria University.

Nature

In appearance and structure the forms are somewhat conventional construction format and may not be very user friendly. Having said that, they are written in plain English and require the minimum of effort to complete.

The General Use version has six pages of Conditions, and the Home Improvements Agencies version has seven pages. Both versions of the form come with a dedicated Letter of Invitation, form of tender and letter of acceptance in an appendix. The appendix also includes an Insurance Backed Warranty Cover that protects the Employer in the event that the Contractor ceases to trade or refuses to complete the work or remedy a defect or major damage and detailed provisions on fees were the Works admits stage payments.

Use

They are recommended for use in contracts up to the value of £20,000 at 2011 prices, and both require the Employer to appoint an 'Adviser' to act as contract administrator.

Whilst the form for general use might well constitute a construction contract to which Part II of the Housing Grants, Construction and Regeneration Act 1996 as amended applies, the version for residential work would certainly not. Whether or not the CDM Regulations applied in full would depend on the nature, scale and duration of the intended works, and the forms include optional clauses to cater for this.

CIOB Mini Forms

Brief synopsis

1 CIOB Mini Form of Contract (General Use)

- The works are described in R1 and further explained in the Contract Documents (specification/Schedule of works/drawings) set out in Appendix 2. The Contract Documents are prepared by the Contract Administrator named in the contract on behalf of the Employer.
- The Contract Documents are to be signed by the parties to the contract.
- The contractor is to carry out and complete the Works as described in the Contract Documents (A1). The Contractor is expected to be a TrustMark registered firm.
- The contract sum is exclusive of VAT (A5) and is stated in a Memorandum of Agreement at A3.
- Where the project is notifiable the necessary appointment of a CDM coordinator and Principal Contractor are to be made.
- The Agreement and Conditions are to take priority over other Contract Documents (A6).
- The Contractor is to proceed diligently, expeditiously with the Works (2·1).
- The commencement date and the completion date for the project are set out in contract (2·2).
- The Contractor is to inform the Contract Administrator in writing as soon as it becomes apparent that the Completion Date will not be achieved. It will be at the sole discretion of the Contract Administrator to grant an extension of time and this will be done in writing (2·3).
- Liquidated damages are to be paid for non-completion and delay not covered by an extension of time (2·4).
- Unless otherwise provided by the parties the defect period is to be for three months commencing from the date of practical completion (2·6).
- Practical Completion is to be certified by the Contract Administrator when in his opinion practical completion has been achieved (2·7).
- The Contractor is not exempted from latent defects that may occur subsequently (2·8).
- The Contractor is to be given sufficient access to the Site to carry out the Works (3·2).
- The Contractor is not to carry out any additional work or incur expenses unless authorised in writing by the Contract Administrator (3·3).
- The Contractor is to safeguard the Works generally and ensure the safety of people on site (3·4).

CIOB Mini Forms

- The duties and powers of the Contract Administrator are set out in clause 4 and include issuing instructions which shall be in writing (4·2) and rejecting work not in accordance with the contract (4·3).
- The Contract Administrator may issue instructions requiring a variation. Parties are to come to an agreement on the costs of such variation, failing that the Contract Administrator shall value it on a fair and reasonable basis (6).
- Payment is either a single payment after the Contract Administrator has certified rectification of all defects as required by clause 2·7 or at stages set out in Appendix 1 (7).
- Where stage payments apply the parties are expected to adhere to Part 2 of Appendix 1 strictly. Appendix Part 2 provides that the Contractor is required to issue to the Employer and the Contract Administrator an interim payment certificate at intervals set out in Appendix 1 Part 1, indicating the amount the Contractor considers due at the interval and the basis for calculating it. Due date for payment shall be the date the Employer receives the certificate.
- The Final Date for payment is 14 days from the due date. No later than five days after the due date, the Employer or Contract Administrator shall issue a written notice specifying the payment proposed, what the sum relates to and how it was calculated. This amount will be due for payment on the final payment date unless a Pay Less Notice is issued by the Employer.
- If the Contract Administrator fails to issue the notice, it shall be liable to pay the amount stated in the Contractor's Interim Payment Notice on the final date of payment unless a Pay Less Notice is issued.
- If the Employer intends to pay less than the sum stated in its written or where applicable the Contractor's Interim Payment Certificate, it shall no later than five days before the Final Date of Payment, issue a Pay Less Notice, indicating the sum it considers due to the Contractor at the time of the notice and the basis of how it was calculated.
- The Contractor (or where appropriate the Employer) will be entitled to interest payment on any overdue amount not paid in full by the Final Payment Date. The Contractor also has the right to suspend some or its entire obligations if a default on payment continues after a seven day notice and is entitled to reasonable costs and expenses incurred as a result of such suspension.
- There are detailed and similar provisions for the final certificate.
- Neither party may assign or otherwise dispose of its rights and obligations under the contract without the prior written of the other except such prohibition shall not affect assignment by way of security and assignments to subsidiary or associated companies within the same group of companies. The Contractor is not to sub-let any part of the work without the written consent of the Contract Administrator.

CIOB Mini Forms

- The Contractor is to insure in the joint names of both parties for the works, goods on site and other related risks, if the Employer is to insure for existing structures and works. Parties are allowed to vary the insurance provisions by agreement (9).
- The Works is to be covered by the insurance backed warranty which protects the Employer against insolvency of the Contractor, or rogue behaviour of a contractor who abandons the works without cause.
- Determination of the contract may be by the Employer (10·1) for specified defaults of the contractor and insolvency or by the Contractor (10·3) for specified defaults of the Employer and insolvency or either party may terminate for neutral causes and the consequences for all typed of determination are covered under clause 10.
- The Contracts (Rights of Third Parties) Act 1999 is specifically excluded (12).
- Contract is governed under English Law and English Courts have jurisdiction. Disputes are to be resolved by adjudication and the final tribunal for resolution is the courts (11).

2 CIOB Mini Form of Contract (Home Improvement Agencies)

- The wording of the Conditions in this version of the form are virtually identical with those of the form for General Use, with the following exceptions:
- The agreement requires that the Contractor commits no offence under the Bribery Act 2010 or the Local Government Act 1972 (4).
- There is a change in the numbering of the clauses from clause 5. The equivalent of the same clause on Contract Administrator's duties in the form for general use is clause 4.

CIOB Mini Forms

This contract?

If considering using an CIOB Mini Form remember that:

It is intended only for very small domestic work valued at £20,000 at 2011 prices. Projects under this contract may not always be subject to Part II of the Housing Grants, Construction and Regeneration Act 1996 as amended. However, it is important to note that the contract has adopted adjudication as the initial dispute resolution procedure and incorporated the procedure of the Scheme for Construction Contracts as amended. The contract also envisages that the Employer will appoint a Contract Administrator who shall assist in the preparation of the contract documents as well as administer the contract.

The form is suitable for use in England and Wales.

The provisions are probably adequate for most work of this nature and the form is plainly worded.

The dedicated Letter of Invitation, Form of Tender and Letter of Acceptance should be used, because the last two become Contract Documents. When completing the documents, entries are also to be made in the text of the Conditions.

If acting as contract administrator note that the procedural rules are relatively simple and the Contract Administrator is given considerable discretion and authority.

The CIOB deserve credit for being the first to produce such forms, which also provide for a consultant to act as contract administrator. The forms are more conventional than the more consumer friendly JCT forms.

Related matters

Documents

Mini Form of Contract (General Use) 2011
Mini Form of Contract (Home Improvement Agencies) 2011

Traditional procurement 9

Measurement forms

The Joint Contracts Tribunal Ltd
Standard Form of Building Contract 2011 Edition
With Approximate Quantities

The Association for Consultancy and Engineering and the Civil Engineering Contractors Association
ICC Conditions of Contract Measurement Version (August 2011)

The Association for Consultancy and Engineering and the Civil Engineering Contractors Association
ICC Conditions of Contract for Minor Works Version (August 2011)

The Joint Contracts Tribunal Ltd
Measured Term Contract 2011 Edition

For the purposes of this chapter, contracts which are not based on a lump sum figure and which provide for a substantial amount of remeasurement have been included as measurement contracts. It is acknowledged that most lump sum contracts accept remeasurement to some degree, and that measurement rules provide for 'an approximate quantity' (which of course is not the same thing as 'approximate quantities'). With measurement contracts the nature and extent of the work is broadly known before work is started.

JCT SBC11/AQ

The Joint Contracts Tribunal Ltd

Standard Building Contract With Approximate Quantities 2011

Background

There is often insufficient time (even when the scope of the work is reasonably definable and measurable right from the outset) to complete the drawings and Specification in sufficient detail to allow the quantity surveyor to fully measure, work up and collate measurements in order to prepare bills of quantities on behalf of the Employer for the purpose of obtaining lump sum tenders. In such circumstances the JCT Standard Building Contract With Approximate Quantities may be appropriate.

This version of the standard JCT form was first produced in 1979 in response to pressure from property developers. They wanted a traditional method of building procurement, with as early a start on site as possible. It was thought that this could still be achieved if work could be described in accordance with the relevant measurement rules, even though the quantity of work could not be accurately determined. It has now been revised and updated as part of the JCT 2011 suite of contracts.

Nature

This contract allows parties to commence work without a commitment to a firm price.

Use

The headnote to the Approximate Quantities edition states that the form is for use 'for larger works designed and/or detailed by or on behalf of the Employer . . . where detailed contract provisions are necessary and with a approximate bill of quantities to define the quality and quantity of the work, which are to be subject to remeasurement, as there is insufficient time to prepare the detailed drawings necessary for accurate bills of quantities to be produced'.

Reference is made to bills of quantities setting out 'a reasonably accurate forecast of the quantity of work to be done'. The form should not be used where only certain Sections of the Works are approximate. In such cases the Standard Form With Quantities should be used, and the relevant items might be marked 'Provisional' or, subject of 'an approximate quantity'.

JCT SBC11/AQ

Brief synopsis

- As might be expected the text of the With Approximate Quantities version follows very closely that of the With Quantities version. The wording of the First and Second Recitals differs, and Article 2 and clause 4·2 refers to an Ascertained Final Sum instead of a Contract Sum.
- The With Approximate Quantities version differs from SBC/Q in clauses 5·6 (valuation rules) to take account of the fact that all quantities in the bill are approximate.
- In clause 2·29·5 work whose quantity was not reasonably accurately forecast in the Contract Bills is included as an additional relevant event justifying an extension to the contract period.
- The list of matters for which loss and expense may be payable under clause 4·24·4 refers to work 'for which the quantity included in the Contract Bills is not a reasonably accurate forecast'.
- Interim Certificates cover 'all work measured and valued by the quantity surveyor'. Valuations are always required under the Approximate Quantities form, and are to the usual valuation procedures. All documents and computations are to be sent to the quantity surveyor by the contractor for the Final Sum.
- The use of price adjustment formulae for fluctuations (Option C) is not included.

JCT SBC11/AQ

This contract?

If considering using SBC11 With Approximate Quantities remember that:

It is intended for use in substantial contracts where it is not possible to prepare full quantities at tender stage. It permits a certain amount of fast tracking, but the design needs to be well developed and main detail worked out before approximate quantities are taken off. This allows for some design development in parallel with construction work, but if the approximate quantities in the bills are not reasonably accurate there can be penalties in both cost and time. As with the other SBC11 forms the Employer is required to appoint a contract administrator and a quantity surveyor.

If used for work in Northern Ireland an Adaptation Schedule should be incorporated, while for work in Scotland the Scottish Building Contract version of the form should be used.

The form has the same basic structure as the other SBC11 versions, using the same language and terminology. The main difference is the use of an ascertained final sum instead of a contract lump sum. The procedures relating to valuation are simpler than those in the other versions, but otherwise the payment provisions are similar.

It can include for partial possession, deferment of possession, sectional completion and for a contractor's designed portion. It allows for sub-contractors to be chosen by the contractor from a list of not less than three names.

When completing the form decisions are required relating to matters including deferment of possession; bonds (whether in lieu of retention, advance payment or 'listed items'); insurance of the Works; Joint Fire Code; liquidated damages; advance payment and fluctuations. Care is needed to ensure that the relevant Supplements are used, and option clauses selected.

If acting as contract administrator note that some of the procedural rules are detailed and likely to prove time-consuming.

The RIBA publishes contract administration forms for SBC11.

This form is probably the least risky remeasurement option for the Employer, and allows a measure of control not found in cost plus contracts. However, successful use depends very much on how full and accurate the approximate quantities are in the first place.

9 Traditional procurement: measurement forms

JCT SBC11/AQ

Related matters

Documents

Standard Building Contract With Approximate Quantities
Standard Building Sub-contract Agreement
Standard Building Sub-contract Conditions
Standard Building Sub-contract with sub-contractor's design Agreement
Standard Building Sub-contract with sub-contractor's design Conditions
Contractor Collateral Warranty for a Funder
Contractor Collateral Warranty for a Purchaser or Tenant
Sub-contractor Collateral Warranty for a Funder
Sub-contractor Collateral Warranty for a Purchaser or Tenant
Sub-contractor Collateral Warranty for Employer

David Chappell
SBC11 Contract Administration Guide
RIBA Publishing (2011)

References

Standard Building Contract Guide
Standard Building Sub-Contract Guide
JCT Practice Note: Deciding on the Appropriate JCT Form of Contract (2011)

Commentaries

Sarah Lupton
Guide to SBC11
RIBA Publishing (2011)

ICC Conditions

The Association for Consultancy and Engineering and the Civil Engineering Contractors Associations

ICC Conditions of Contract Measurement Version (August 2011)

Background

The Infrastructure Conditions of Contract (ICC) are based on the former ICE Conditions of Contract. These conditions are sponsored by the Association of Consultancy Engineering (ACE) and the Civil Engineering Contractors Association (CECA). The use and review of the contracts under this family is undertaken by the Infrastructure Conditions of Contract Development Forum (ICoCDF) which comprises representatives from the two sponsoring associations, Employer representatives and legal experts.

The ICC Measurement Version is based on the traditional pattern of engineer-designed works with the Contractor engaged to build the works with valuation admeasurement. The Conditions show that the form is not appropriate for lump sum contracts. The Contract supports the modern ethos of team working and incorporates an early warning procedure for circumstances that may result in additional time or costs.

Nature

The document is over 70 pages long and comprises the Conditions of Contract; a Form of Tender with an Appendix in two parts, the first of which is to be completed prior to tendering, and the second of which is to be completed by the Contractor; and a Form of Agreement. The latter identifies the documents which form part of the Contract and may be drawings, the Specification, and the priced bill of quantities, in addition to the Conditions.

Also included is a Form of Default Bond, and the Contract Price Fluctuations for Civil Engineering Work and Structural Steelwork.

The Conditions are contained in 72 clauses and reference is made relatively easy for the uninitiated because there is a Table of Contents and a particularly detailed Index.

Use

The Form of Agreement identifies the Contract Documents, and entries in the Appendix to the Tender will show detail such as commencement date, contract period, completion by Sections, liquidated damages, payment and retention, insurance requirements etc

The key person for contract administration is 'the Engineer', who must be named, and in the event of his or her being unable to act the Employer is obliged to nominate a successor.

9 Traditional procurement: measurement forms

ICC Conditions

Synopsis

1 Intentions

- The contractor undertakes to construct and complete the Works as specified in or inferred from the contract (8).
- The contractor is responsible for all site operations and methods, but not the design of permanent works (unless expressly provided in the contract), nor for the design of temporary and permanent works designed by the Engineer. Any design responsibility of the contractor is limited to using reasonable skill, care and diligence (8).
- The contractor is to work in strict accordance with the contract, and to the satisfaction of the Engineer. The Contractor is to comply with and adhere strictly to the Engineer's instructions on any matter whether mentioned in the contract or not (13).
- The definition of 'the Works' includes both temporary and permanent work. The 'Agreement' comprises the Tender and written acceptance of it, drawings, the ICC conditions of contract, Specification, and priced bill of quantities. The documents are to be taken as being mutually explanatory and in the event of ambiguities or inconsistencies, the Engineer shall explain and resolve same and may issue appropriate instructions in writing (5).
- The quantities in the bill are estimated only, and remeasurement will establish the actual quantities (55).
- The contractor is expected to inspect and examine the site and its surroundings before tendering. The rates and prices he quotes will be in the bill of quantities, and only if matters which could not have reasonably been foreseen are encountered is additional payment possible (11 and 12).
- The contract allows for further necessary drawings, Specifications and instructions to be supplied by the Engineer from time to time (7).
- The contractor is required to submit a Programme for approval by the Engineer, and to revise it within 21 days if the Engineer instructs (14).
- All materials and workmanship shall be as described in the contract, and as instructed by the Engineer. There is provision for samples and testing (36).
- Facilities must be afforded by the contractor for work not in the contract but ancillary to the Works undertaken by other contractors employed by the Employer (31).
- The duties and authority of the Engineer, the Engineer's Representative, and named assistants, are all clearly defined (2).

ICC Conditions

2 Time

- The contract may prescribe that possession of the site is to be given to the contractor in portions (42).
- The contractor is to commence as soon as possible after the Works Commencement Date as stated in the Appendix to the Form of Tender, or within 28 days after the contract is entered into, or other agreed date. The contractor is then to proceed with expedition (41).
- The time for completion is to be stated in the Appendix to the Form of Tender. Completion by Sections may be required (43).
- Interim extensions of time may be awarded. The contractor must inform the Engineer within 28 days after the cause of the delay, and supply detailed particulars. The Engineer must respond to all claims upon receipt of particulars, and may award an extension in the absence of a claim. The overall extension of time awarded is subject to final review after completion (44).
- Where the Engineer thinks that progress is too slow and no extension of time is possible, written notice can be given to the contractor to expedite matters. The contractor will not be entitled to additional payment for taking such steps as may be necessary (46).
- The Employer will be entitled to liquidated damages if the contractor does not complete to time (47).
- The Engineer will issue a Certificate of Completion when the whole of the Works are substantially completed and have passed any final tests required by the contract (48).
- The outstanding work and defects period runs from the date of substantial completion, and is stated in the Appendix to the Tender as the Defects Correction Period. The contractor is obliged to finish any work outstanding, to deal with repair, amendment, reconstruction, rectification and making good of defects either within the period or as soon as may be practicable. A Defects Correction Certificate is to be issued by the Engineer when he or she is satisfied, although this in no way relieves the contractor of any liability (61).

3 Control

- The contractor is prevented from assigning the contract or any benefit or interest under it without the written consent of the Employer (3).
- The contractor may not sub-contract the whole of the works without the written consent of the Employer. Sub-contracting of any part of the work or design is permitted on the condition of a written notice to the Engineer indicating the extent of work to be sub-contracted and the details of the sub-contractor not later than 14 days prior to the sub-contractor's entry to the site (4).

ICC Conditions

- Sub-contractors may be nominated, although the contractor is given the right of objection (59). There is a detailed set of provisions for dealing with nomination and, as is normal, the Employer is required to bear some of the risk where defaults occur. If any design obligation rests with the sub-contractor, then this must be stated in the contract and the sub-contract (58[3]).
- The contractor is wholly responsible for the accurate setting out of the Works and, unless incorrect information was given by the Engineer, must rectify any error at his own cost (17).
- The Engineer is empowered to suspend any part of the Works (40) and to order variations, subject to their being of the type defined in the contract (51).
- The contractor is obliged to give the Engineer a reasonable opportunity to inspect work before it is covered up (38).
- The Engineer is empowered to instruct the removal from the site of any materials not in accordance with the contract, and the proper re-execution of work (39).
- The contractor is obliged to provide necessary superintendence, and a competent agent or representative must be constantly on the Works (15).

4 Money

- Because this is not a lump sum contract, there is reference to a 'Tender Total' (ie total of the priced bill of quantities or estimated total value of the works) and a 'Contract Price' (ie sums to be ascertained and paid in accordance with the contract) (1[1j]).
- VAT will not have been allowed for in the Tender, and will be additional to the Tender Total (70[1]).
- Provisional sums and Prime Cost items are both defined (1[1]), and work or goods which are the subject of provisional sums and Prime Cost items may be ordered by the Engineer (58).
- Variations may be ordered by the Engineer (51). Wherever possible quotations should be agreed in advance of the order. Otherwise variations are valued at the rates in the contract if applicable, or otherwise at rates fixed by the Engineer, as the Engineer considers reasonable (52). Daywork is to be used as a basis if the Engineer thinks it necessary or desirable, and the rates will be as set out in the daywork schedule included in the contract (56[4]).
- Payment is on the basis of a monthly statement submitted to the Engineer (60[1]). The Engineer must issue a certificate within 25 days of delivery of a statement. Amounts for nominated sub-contractors are listed separately. The certificate must show the amount due and the basis of calculation. If the Employer intends to pay less than the amount stated on the certificate he must notify the contractor not less than one day before the final date for payment, and state the sum the Employer

ICC Conditions

considers due on the date the notice served and the basis for calculating it. Final date for payment by the Employer is 28 days after delivery of the contractor's monthly statement to the Engineer. If the Engineer fails to issue a certificate as provided for in the contract, the Contractor's monthly statement given under clause 60(1) becomes a payment notice or where the Contractor had not submitted a monthly statement, then the Contractor may at any time give the Employer a notice with a copy to the Engineer of the sum the Contractor considers due at the relevant payment date and the basis of the calculation of that amount.

- Where the Employer fails to make proper payment on time, then the contractor is entitled to interest on the overdue amount (60).
- Rate of retention, and the limit of retention will be as entered in the Appendix Part 1 (60[5]).
- Half the retention is released within 14 days of the issue of the Certificate of Substantial Completion, and the other half within 14 days of the end of the Defects Correction Period (60[6]).
- Not later than three months after the date of the Defects Correction Certificate, the contractor is to give the Engineer a final account and supporting documents. The Engineer then has up to three months to issue the Final Certificate which states the amount due. Payment is required within 28 days of certification (60[4]).

5 Statutory obligations

- The contractor is obliged to give all notices and pay all fees required by legislation. These might relate to temporary works. If the Engineer certifies it, then the contractor will receive repayment of all sums involved (26).
- Whilst the contractor indemnifies the Employer against the consequences of any breach of statutory obligations, this will not apply if it arises because of compliance with instructions given by the Engineer. There is no express obligation on the contractor to check whether documents or instructions by the Engineer conform to statutory requirements, but if they are found not to, the Engineer must issue instructions (26).
- The CDM Regulations 1994 place statutory obligations on both employer and contractor, particularly in respect of the Health and Safety Plan and the Health and Safety File. The Employer is obliged to appoint a Planning Supervisor and a Principal Contractor. Through incorporation of these provisions into the contract, the statutory duties also become contractual obligations (71).
- The New Roads and Street Works Act 1991 is given detailed attention (27). There is also particular reference to legislation on damage to highways (30) and unnecessary interference to roads and footpaths (29).

ICC Conditions

6 Insurance

- The contractor is to take full responsibility for the care of the Works and materials for incorporation, from the date of commencement until the Engineer has issued the Certificate of Substantial Completion. The risk covers damage from any cause whatsoever, except where the damage is due to the Employer, or is a defined Excepted Risk, or is due to faulty design of the permanent works (20).
- The contractor is to insure in joint names, against the risk of damage to the Works for the full replacement cost plus an additional 10 per cent. The policies are subject to approval by the Employer before Works Commencement Date, and it may be prudent for the Employer to state the kind of cover required at tender stage (21).
- The contractor indemnifies the Employer against all losses and claims arising from death or injury to any person, and damage to property other than the Works. There are certain stated exceptions (22).
- The contractor is required to be insured against many of the risks in respect of which the Employer has been indemnified (23).
- The contractor's obligations concerning the safety of workmen is reinforced, and the Employer is indemnified in respect of any claims (24).

7 Termination

- The Employer is given the right to terminate the employment of the contractor in the event of the contractor's insolvency, or because of specified defaults by the Contractor. The Employer is entitled to take possession of the site, have the work completed, and postpone any settlement of accounts until the Defects Correction Period has expired (65).
- The contractor is given the right to terminate his own employment for specified defaults by the Employer, or if the Employer becomes insolvent (64).
- Termination of nominated sub-contracts is dealt with separately (59).

8 Miscellaneous

- Definitions are included (1).
- The Engineer can require the removal of contractor's employees (16).
- There is provision in the event of discovery of fossils, antiquities, things of archaeological interest, etc (32).
- The Engineer is to have access to the Works, the site and workshops (37).
- Matters relating to possession of site and site access, beyond that prescribed in the contract, are largely the contractor's responsibility (42), although extensions of time and additional costs may be applicable in the event of failure to give adequate possession.

ICC Conditions

- No equipment owned by the contractor is to be removed from the site without written consent of the Engineer, consent not to be unreasonably withheld (54).
- The rights and obligations of the parties on the outbreak of war are fully stated (63). There is a provision contracting out of the Contracts (Rights of Third Parties) Act 1999 (3[2]).
- Special conditions can be properly incorporated and should be numbered consecutively as a continuation (72).

9 Disputes

- As soon as either party becomes aware of any circumstance that if not resolved shall become a dispute, it shall inform the other party with a copy to the Engineer. No later than seven days after such notice and at the earliest possible time, the parties shall meet with the aim of resolving the issue. The Engineer may be invited to the meeting. If the parties fail to reach an agreement within a reasonable time, they are expected to set out in writing the areas still in dispute (66).
- The contract sets out clauses 66A, 66B and 66C as alternative/complementary dispute resolution procedures.
- Clause 66A provides the parties the option by agreement to seek resolution of a dispute under the ICE Conciliation Procedure (1999) or the ICE Construction Mediation Procedure 2002 (66A).
- Since the Housing Grants, Construction and Regeneration Act 1996 (Part II) as amended came into force, parties to the contract have the right to refer any dispute to adjudication at any time. Therefore notwithstanding the provisions of clause 66 or 66A, either party is entitled to refer a dispute to adjudication, the conditions envisage that a notice of adjudication is to be given, and adjudication is to be conducted in accordance with the ICE Adjudication Procedure (1997) (66B).
- All disputes may be finally determined by reference to arbitration (other than disputes on giving effect to the decisions of an adjudicator). The party seeking arbitration must serve a notice to refer. Arbitration is to be under the Arbitration Act 1996, and conducted in accordance with either the ICE Arbitration Procedure (1997) or the Construction Industry Model Arbitration Rules (66C).

ICC Conditions

This contract?

If considering using ICE Conditions of Contract remember that:

This is a contract most suitable for major civil engineering works, on the basis of measurement.

The form is for use under the law of England and Wales, and may also be adapted for use in Northern Ireland and under Scots law. If the law of the contract is that of Scotland or Northern Ireland, then clause 67 (1), (2) and/or (3) shall apply. If used outside Great Britain and Northern Ireland, the contract is to be construed and interpreted in accordance with the local laws of such jurisdiction.

The Conditions are comprehensive, and relatively flexible, ie with regards to commencement and completion, nomination of sub-contractors, valuation of variations, and design by the Contractor.

Completing the form is confined to entries in those documents which follow the Conditions, in particular the Appendix to the Tender and the Form of Agreement.

Parties are also expected to use Special Conditions to include particular arrangements specific to their projects.

Amendments of the conditions itself is discouraged, because changes in one clause may affect the balance of risks in other related clauses.

In terms of contract administration the Engineer is given greater authority than is usually the case with contract administration under building contracts.

The contract continues the ICE forms' traditional self-contained approach, without the need for supplements.

Related matters

Documents

ICE Conditions of Contract: Measurement Version (August 2011)

ICC Minor Works

The Association for Consultancy and Engineering and the Civil Engineering Contractors Associations

ICC Conditions of Contract: Measurement Version (August 2011)

Background

The Infrastructure Conditions of Contract for Minor Works Version is sponsored by the Association of Consultancy Engineering (ACE) and the Civil Engineering Contractors Association (CECA).

Nature

This contract is suitable for use where the risks are small, the contract period is not expected to exceed six months, there are no nominations, design of the Works is essentially complete at the point of inviting tenders, the contractor has no responsibility for design of the permanent works except for works of a specialist nature, and the contract value does not exceed £500,000. It is a form suitable for straightforward and simple jobs.

The form is about 20 pages long, and this includes the Conditions, an Appendix, and a Form of Agreement. The Conditions are set out under 15 headings, and are commendably clear and an easy read. They are prefaced by a full Index, and helpful Guidance Notes. An October 2011 update brought its terms in compliance with the amendments to the Housing Grants, Construction and Regeneration Act 1996.

Use

The form is suitable for lump sum contracts, or with measurement contracts using a priced bill of quantities, valuation based on a Schedule of Rates or a Daywork Schedule, or as a cost plus form. An Appendix entry will show which is applicable.

The Employer is required to appoint an Engineer to administer the terms of the contract. The form also provides for the appointment of a Planning Supervisor. A starting date is to be entered in the Appendix, together with a period for completion. Completion of the Works can be in phases.

Synopsis

1 Intentions

- The Employer must appoint an Engineer, who is to be named in the Appendix (2·1).
- The Engineer may appoint a named Resident Engineer, and delegate any powers except those dealing with some areas of its powers including suspension of works,

ICC Minor Works

determination whether a particular event deserves an extension of time on grounds of being unforeseeable among a few others (2·2).

- The contract comprises of the Contractor's Tender, the Conditions of Contract, the Appendix, to the Conditions of Contract, drawings, Specification, and the alternate of either priced bill of quantities, Schedules of Rates or Daywork Schedules, and other documents listed under 'extra documents' in the Form of Agreement (Article 3).
- The contractor undertakes to perform and complete the Works (3·2). He takes full responsibility for the care of the Works from commencement until 14 days after the issue of the practical completion Certificate (3·3).
- The contractor is liable for design only where expressly stated in the contract, and in respect of temporary works other than those designed by the Engineer (3·9). The standard expected is that of all reasonable skill, care and diligence.
- The Engineer must provide any necessary instructions, drawings or other information (3·8).
- Other persons engaged direct by the Employer are to be given reasonable facilities (3·11).

2 Time

- The starting date is entered in the Appendix; if not, then the Engineer must give written instructions within 28 days after acceptance of the tender (4·1).
- The contract period will be stated in the Appendix (4·2).
- If required, the contractor must provide a programme within 14 days of the starting date (4·3).
- An extension of time may be granted where progress is delayed for reasons stated in the Conditions (4·4). The contractor is expected to take all reasonable steps to avoid or minimise the delay.
- Substantial completion occurs when the Works are fit to be taken into use or possession by the Employer. The Engineer is to certify Substantial Completion, or must advise the contractor in writing what remains to be done to achieve it. Partial possession is possible (4·5), as is completion by Sections identified in the Appendix.
- Liquidated damages will be payable where the contractor fails to complete by the completion date (4·6).
- A Defects Correction Period follows practical completion. The duration of this will be stated in the Appendix (5·1).
- Completion is to be certified by the Engineer after the defects have been made good and the Defects Correction Period has expired. Certification is in response to a request by the Contractor, and shows that the contractual obligations have been discharged to the Engineer's satisfaction (5·3).

ICC Minor Works

3 Control

- Instructions which the Engineer is empowered to issue are listed. These include variations, testing, suspension of work, removal of work not in accordance with the contract and exclusion of persons (2·3).
- Each of the parties is bound by every instruction or decision of the Engineer, unless it concerns a matter referred for dispute resolution (2·7).
- The contractor cannot assign the contract or any rights under it without the written consent of the Employer (8·1). The Employer equally requires the contractor's written consent.
- The contractor may not sub-contract any part of the Works without the consent of the Engineer (8·2).
- There is no reference to nominated sub-contractors or suppliers, but the Guidance Notes suggest that approved sub-contractors and suppliers can be named and listed by the Engineer in the Specification.
- The contractor accepts full responsibility for setting out and for the stability and safety of his operations and methods (3·7).
- The contractor is to notify the Engineer of the person who is authorised to receive instructions (3·6).

4 Money

- More than one basis of payment can be used on any one contract. The Appendix requires deletion of methods not used. Options are for lump sum, measurement on priced bill, valuation on a Schedule of Rates, valuation on a Daywork Schedule and cost plus.
- VAT is not included in the tender figure.
- The contractor may be entitled to additional payments due to unforeseeable adverse conditions (3·10) or because of delay or disruption to progress (6·1).
- The contractor is to submit a monthly statement giving the value of work executed and materials or other items to be included (7·2).
- The Engineer is to issue an Interim Certificate, within 25 days of delivery of the monthly statement (7·3). The Appendix may include a minimum figure for any Interim Certificate. Every Certificate shall show the amount due and the basis on which it was calculated. Payment by the Employer becomes due on certification, with a final date for payment 28 days after delivery of the monthly statement. If the Employer intends to pay less than the amount stated in the certificate, he must notify the contractor not less than one day before the final date for payment, stating the sum it considers due on the date the notice is served and the basis the sum is calculated (7·8).

ICC Minor Works

- Where the Engineer fails to issue an interim certificate as provided under this contract, the Contractor's monthly statement – clause 7·2 will become a payment notice, where the Contractor had not served a monthly notice, the Contractor may at any time to issue a payment notice to the Employer with a copy to the Engineer, stating the sum it considers due and basis for calculation of that sum.
- In such cases the final date of payment shall be postponed by the same number of days after the due date, that the Contractor issued the payment notice (7·7).
- Within 28 days after the Engineer has certified completion, following making good of any outstanding work at the expiry of the Defects Correction Period, the contractor shall submit a final account. Within 42 days of receipt of this the Engineer should issue the Final Certificate. The amount payable is due upon certification, and the final date for payment is 14 days later (7·4).
- Interest may be added to overdue payments (7·6).

5 Statutory obligations

- The contractor is required to comply with all relevant statutory obligations, give all notices required, and pay all fees and charges (9·1).
- Responsibility for any consent, approval, licence or permission for permanent works rests with the Employer. This would include planning consent and also presumably matters of land law including party walls consents (9·2).
- The contractor's liability does not extend to breach where this has occurred because instructions from the Engineer have been followed (9·3).
- The CDM Regulations 1994 place statutory obligations on both Employer and Contractor. Unless stated otherwise, the Employer nominates the Engineer to act as Planning Supervisor and the contractor as Principal Contractor. There are requirements under the Regulations concerning the Health and Safety Plan and the Health and Safety File, and these obligations become contractual as well (13).

6 Insurance

- If insurance of the Works is to be the responsibility of the contractor an Appendix entry is required. The contractor is then obliged to take out joint names insurance in respect of temporary and permanent works. Unfixed materials and construction plant are included. Cover is for full value against all loss or damage, bar Excepted Risks as defined in the contract Conditions (10·1).
- The contractor gives the Employer an indemnity against loss and claims for injury or damage to persons and property. This liability will be reduced proportionately to the extent that the Employer or those for whom he is legally responsible contributed to the cause (10·2).

ICC Minor Works

- There are further exceptions to the contractor's liability for matters beyond his control and in respect of which he does not indemnify the Employer (10·4).
- Insurance required under the contract is subject to approval by the Employer (10·6).

7 Termination

- There is provision for termination where circumstances outside the control of the parties renders it impossible or illegal for either party to fulfil its obligations under the contract. In such circumstances the work will be deemed abandoned on the service of notice by one party to the other (14·1).
- The Employer may also at any time by written order (Termination Order) require the Contractor to cease work (termination for convenience) (14·2).
- Either Party may terminate on insolvency of the other, refusal of the other party to perform its obligations and unauthorised assignment. Termination is by seven days' notice in writing to the defaulting party.
- On abandonment or termination, the Engineer in preparing the final certificate shall consider the amount due to the Contractor on work actually done, the value of any unused or partially used materials and goods under the control of the Employer. Additionally where the Employer had terminated for convenience, cost reasonably incurred or committed by the Contractor in expectation of completing the works including a reasonable percentage to cater for profit is to be included in the payment certification.

8 Miscellaneous

- Definitions are included as part of the Conditions of contract (1).
- There is a contracting out of rights of third parties in accordance with the Contracts (Rights of Third Parties) Act 1999 (8·1).

9 Disputes

- As soon as either party becomes aware of any circumstance that if not resolved shall become a dispute, it shall inform the other party with a copy to the Engineer. No later than seven days after such notice and at the earliest possible time, the parties shall meet with the aim of resolving the issue. The Engineer may be invited to the meeting. If the parties fail to reach an agreement within a reasonable time, they are expected to set out in writing the areas still in dispute (11).
- The contract sets out in the Addendum options A, B or C as alternative/complementary dispute resolution procedures.
- Option A provides the parties the avenue by agreement to seek an amicable resolution of their dispute under the ICE Conciliation Procedure (1999) or the ICE Construction Mediation Procedure 2002 (66A).

ICC Minor Works

- Since the Housing Grants, Construction and Regeneration Act 1996 (Part II) as amended came into force, parties to the contract have the right to refer any dispute to adjudication at any time. Therefore notwithstanding the provisions of clause 11 or option A, either party is entitled to refer a dispute to adjudication, the conditions envisages that a notice of adjudication is to be given, and adjudication is to be conducted in accordance with the ICE Adjudication Procedure (1997) (66B).
- All disputes other than failure to give effect an adjudicator's determination, shall be finally determined by reference to arbitration. The party seeking arbitration must serve a notice to refer. Arbitration is to be under the Arbitration Act 1996, and conducted in accordance with either the ICE Arbitration Procedure (1997) or the Construction Industry Model Arbitration Rules (66C).

This contract?

If considering using the ICE Minor Works Form remember that:

It is intended primarily for minor engineering works, with short duration, and a value not exceeding £500,000. It is for lump sum with or without a bill of quantities, or for measurement contracts. The Employer is required to appoint an Engineer to be contract administrator. The contract is for use under the law of England and Wales, and is suitable for use in Northern Ireland or under Scots law as provided for in clause 12.

It is a truly short but balanced form which allows for phased completion. The Conditions are succinctly and clearly worded. Sub-contractors may be listed in the Specification.

Completing the form is straightforward, with entries required in the Agreement and the Appendix.

Contract administration should not be demanding as the Engineer is given considerable authority, and the procedures are straightforward.

A pleasing and neat form for low risk projects.

Related matters

Documents

ICC Conditions of Contract Minor Works Version (2011)

JCT MTC11

The Joint Contracts Tribunal Ltd

Measured Term Contract 2011 Edition

Background

The Standard Form of Measured Term Contract was introduced in 1989 for use by Employers in both public and private sectors who have building stock in need of planned regular maintenance and minor improvement work. It is obviously tiresome and wasteful having to enter into separate contracts for each small job, and in some cases a contractor might be needed to undertake repair work at short notice. In all such circumstances it is usually preferable to deal with one contractor appointed to handle all such work under one contract for a specific period, on terms previously agreed.

Competitive tenders may be invited on the basis of rates taking into account the nature of the intended works, the geographical area to be covered, and the duration of the contract. MTC 2011 offers a flexible medium to long term agreement and is generally appropriate for contract periods of one year or more. It contains optional provisions for the revision of rates, and also contains a break clause. Under this contract, orders are placed on an agreed basis and the contractor fulfils them with payments calculated on a schedule of rates or a schedule of hourly rates. The contract offers flexibility to the Employer because it does not create exclusivity over his projects and does not hold it contractually to a minimum number of orders.

Nature

The total document is over 48 pages and contains a Contents table, Articles of Agreement with six Recitals and eight Articles, Contract Particulars, an Attestation, and Conditions set out under nine Section headings, all following the pattern of other JCT forms such as SBC11.

The First Recital refers to the nature of the intended work as being 'maintenance and minor'. It also requires the 'Contract Area' to be defined. The Employer is required to appoint a contract administrator, a person who has special significance under this contract because each separate job within the period of the contract must be initiated by an order issued by the contract administrator. The Fourth Recital also refers to CDM Regulations compliance in respect of each separate order.

The Second Recital embodies the offer by the contractor to carry out work under the contract to agreed terms of payment set out by the contract administrator, and acceptance of this offer by the Employer.

Article 3 identifies the name of the person or firm acting in the capacity of contract administrator, and requires that any replacement needed must be nominated within 14 days. Article 4 identifies the CDM coordinator and Article 5 the Principal Contractor.

JCT MTC11

Entries in the Contract Particulars are particularly important with this type of long term arrangement.

Details should be given of the types of work for which orders may be issued, a list of properties in the Contract Area which may be included within the contract, and an indication of the estimated value of work which may be anticipated (although not guaranteed). There is opportunity to assign a priority code to each anticipated order, for example an 'A' Code could require response within four hours. The duration of the contract period, which will normally be for a minimum of one year, should also be entered. The terms for measurement, valuation and payment are under items 8 to 12 of the Contract Particulars.

By nature the Measured Term Contract differs from a lump sum contract in that there can be no precise amount of work established at the outset and no Contract Sum. It is an enabling document, which allows for the issue of specific orders over a given period, to be valued according to rates, prices and percentages as entered in the Appendix.

Use

After the identity of the parties and the date of the Agreement, the Recitals require an entry which states the 'Contract Area'. There is no reference to drawings or documents other than the accepted terms of payment. The contract administrator must be named under Article 3. The term 'Architect' is not used at all in the contract.

The form can be executed under hand and not as a deed, or as a deed.

The Contract Particulars require an entry stating the minimum and maximum value of any one order to be issued, together with an approximate total figure or figure per annum. A priority coding for orders may be introduced, which would signal the need for rapid response by the contractor to specific orders such as emergency repairs within stipulated minimum periods.

Note that for payment it is necessary to identify whether payment is based on the National Schedule of Rates, or some other Schedule of Rates. The contract can be fixed price as far as rates are concerned, or subject to fluctuations. MTC 2011 incorporates changes to payment and payment certificate introduced by the amendments to the Housing Grants, Construction and Regeneration Act 1996 as amended.

Responsibility for measurement and valuation can rest with either the contractor or the contract administrator. The Contract Particulars should indicate whether the contractor is to undertake all measurement and valuation, or conversely, that the contract administrator is to be responsible. Alternatively it can be shown that only orders above a stated value will be the responsibility of the contract administrator for measurement and valuation.

With a contract of relatively long duration, it is desirable that there should be a break provision. The period of notice required to bring this about is 13 weeks unless a different period is entered in the Contract Particulars.

JCT MTC11

Synopsis

1 Intentions

- The definitions in this contract have a particular significance, because of their context (1·1).
- The printed Articles, Conditions and Appendix entries prevail in the event of any conflict with Schedules, Specification or drawings (1·2).
- The contractor is obliged to carry out work when issued with an order. The work is to be executed in a good and workmanlike manner, in accordance with the Contract Documents, empowered instructions, and any relevant Health and Safety Plan. The contractor does not have exclusive right to all work within the Contract Area and the Employer can use other contractors or his own labour force if desired (2·1 and 2·3·1).
- The Employer has the right to supply direct any materials, plant or equipment needed for carrying out work, and the contractor will have responsibilities concerning these (2·3).
- If supplied by the Employer, materials and goods are to be of the kinds set out in the Schedule of Rates, and the contractor is not liable for any losses resulting from any failure to comply (2·3·6).
- If the Employer replaces the CDM Coordinator or the Principal Contractor, the contractor must be notified (3·10·2).

2 Time

- The duration of the contract and its starting date are entered in the Contract Particulars (item 2). There may be a priority code imposed.
- The starting date and reasonable completion date for work included under an order shall be stated in each order (2·6).
- A Programme must be provided by the contractor where the contract administrator requests one (2·7).
- Where matters beyond the control of the contractor cause delay, an extension to the time for completion for each order may be given by the contract administrator on a fair and reasonable basis (2·10).
- The contractor is required to make good any defects appearing within six months of the Order Completion Date.

3 Control

- The bar to assignment without written consent extends to the contract, or any part share or interest (3·1). Sub-contracting in any order is restricted to the extent that previous consent in writing of the contract administrator is required (3·2).

JCT MTC11

- The contractor is obliged to employ a competent representative (3·3). (Note: there is no reference to his or her being constantly or otherwise upon the Works.)
- Access to the site, which can be a complicated issue in work of this nature, lays a considerable burden upon the contract administrator. The contractor is obviously entitled to a degree of possession sufficient to enable it to carry out the work under any order. Where access is restricted, unproductive time may be charged on a daywork basis (3·4).
- Variations may be instructed by the contract administrator, and what constitutes a variation under this contract is defined (3·5).
- An order, although issued, may be cancelled in writing by the contract administrator. The contractor will be entitled to direct costs already incurred (3·6).
- The contract administrator has the power to order the exclusion of any person from the site (3·7).
- If the contractor does not comply with written instructions from the contract administrator, then, after proper notice, other persons may be brought in by the Employer to give effect to the instruction at the contractor's expense (3·8).

4 Money

- The work covered by each order is subject to measurement and valuation in accordance with the agreed Schedule of Rates (5·3·1). If daywork is the appropriate basis, the Schedule of Hourly Charges is used to value the Order (5·4·1). Where neither are appropriate, then fair rates or prices shall apply. In the event that agreement is still required, this shall be between the parties, or as a last resort it shall rest with the contract administrator, who must consult with the contractor (5·5).
- If the contractor's progress is interrupted because of an instruction issued by the contract administrator, then agreed lost time or other unproductive costs are valued on a daywork basis (5·8).
- Responsibility for measurement and valuation rests with the person designated in the Contract Particulars (5·2). It is possible to set a value limit whereby in the case of orders below an estimated value responsibility rests with the Contractor. Above this figure, unless there is anything to the contrary, responsibility will rest with the contract administrator.
- Most work carried out under an order will be subject to Part II of the Housing Grants, Construction and Regeneration Act 1996 as amended, and the contract provisions relating to payment take account of this.
- All payments are VAT-exclusive, where any order comprises of work estimated to take more than 45 days to complete or the total value of the order is above the amount entered in the Contract Particulars as the cap amount (where no amount has been stated, the default position is any amount above £2,500) progress payment shall apply (4·1, 4·3).

JCT MTC11

- Where progress payments apply the Contractor is to make application to the Contract Administrator for payments at intervals of not less than one month from the date of commencement, the application should state the amount the Contractor considers will become due at the relevant due date and should take into cognizance any amount previously certified, the sums stated should be up to a date stated in the application which should not be more than seven days before the date of application (4·3·1·2).
- The due dates for payment shall be 10 days after receipt of the application from the Contractor or if later the one month interval from the commencement date (4·3·2).
- The Contract Administrator shall not later than five days after the due date, issue an interim certificate stating the amount due the Contractor of the relevant due date and basis it was calculated.
- There are two options for a valuation of the final payment, either the Contract Administator measures or values the order or the Contractor is in charge of valuation. The parties make this choice in the Contract Particulars.
- Where the Contract Administrator does the valuation, the due date shall be 65 days from the order completion date (4·4·1). The Contract Administrator not later than five days after the due date is to issue a certificate stating the total sum he considers due to the Contractor for the Completed Order less any amounts previously certified and any payments made in pursuant of the Contractor's payment Notice and stating the basis on which the sum has been calculated (4·4·2). If the Contract Administrator does issue a certificate in accordance with 4·4·2 the Contractor may make an application for payment stating the amount it considers due and basis for the calculation (4·4·3).
- Where the Contractor is to value the Order, the Contractor shall after the date of Order Completion make an application to the Contract Administrator, stating the sums the Contractor considers due and basis it was calculated (4·5·1). The due date for payment shall be 28 days of the receipt of the application from the Contractor. No later than five days after the due date the Contract Administrator shall issue a certificate stating the sums he considers due to the Contractor the basis it was calculated (4·5·2). If the Contractor fails to make an application 56 days after the date for Completion of the Order, the Contract Administrator may at any time give the Contractor a notice, that an application be made within 28 days failing which the Contract Administrator shall arrange for valuation (4·5·3).
- Where the Contractor fails to make an application within the notice period set out in 4·5·3 the Contract Administrator shall arrange for valuation and the due date for payment shall be 35 days from the expiry of the date for the Contractor to make an application.
- No later than five days after the due date the CA shall issue a certificate stating the amount due (including deductions of the amount spent on hiring independent valuation) and the basis it was calculated.

JCT MTC11

- In any of the previous paragraphs Contract Administrator fails to issue the certificate as required, the Contractor may at any time, after the expiration of the five day period, make an application stating the amount it considers due and the basis for the calculation.
- The final date of payment of all amounts under 4·3 progress payments and 4·5 final payments, shall be 14 days from the relevant due dates. The final date of payment will be extended where the Contractor has to make an application on the failure of the Contract Administrator to issue a certificate. The extension covers the same number of days that it took the Contractor to make its application at the expiry of the five day period (4·6·5).
- Subject to the Employer issuing a Pay Less Notice, the amount to be paid at the final payment date will be the sum stated in the relevant certificate or payment application where the later applies (4·6·2).
- If the Employer intends to pay less than the amount stated in the certificate or application, the Employer is to issue a notice to the Contractor stating the amount it considers due to the Contractor on the date of the notice and the basis it was calculated. The sum on the notice becomes payable on the final payment date (4·6·5).
- Interest shall be payable on any amount outstanding after the final date of payment (4·6·6) and the Contractor reserves the right to suspend some or all of its obligations if non-payment persists after a seven day notice following non-payment on the final date for payment. Where the Contractor exercises this right, the Employer shall be liable for all reasonable costs arising from such suspension (4·7).

5 Statutory obligations

- It is the contractor's duty to comply with all statutory obligations and give all required notices (2·1). He is entitled to recover fees and charges not otherwise provided for (2·9). These duties arise in respect of any work undertaken in response to an order.
- The contractor is to notify the contract administrator if he finds any conflict between statutory requirements and an order. The contract administrator must issue an instruction which will be a variation. The contractor is then not liable for non-compliance resulting from the order or a subsequent variation (2·8).
- The respective obligations of the Employer and the Contractor, with regard to the CDM Regulations applying to an order, and in particular Construction Phase Plans and Health and Safety Files, become contractual as well as statutory duties (3·9).

6 Insurance

- The contractor is to indemnify the Employer in respect of death or injury to persons or damage to property other than the Works, which arises from carrying out an order (6·1 and 6·2). This indemnity is to be backed by insurance, and an entry against item 13 of the Contract Particulars will state the minimum cover required.

- Insurance of existing structures and contents which might be affected by an order is the responsibility of the Employer (6·7). Cover will be for the full cost of reinstatement, repair or replacement after loss or damage due to one or more of the stated perils. Where the Employer does not wish to insure the existing structures, amendments will need to be made to the form, which should be agreed between the parties prior to entering into the contract.
- All risks insurance of work or supply instructed under orders is the responsibility of the Contractor. It will most likely be covered by an annual all risks policy, but this must be a joint names policy. Cover for each order is required up to the Order Completion Date (6·9).
- There are extensive terms covering terrorism cover (6·15).

7 Termination

- The Employer is allowed to terminate the employment of the contractor for given reasons (8·4). Termination will affect the contract as a whole, although the default may arise only in respect of an order. The clause refers to work being 'materially' suspended, disrupted or delayed, and minor or trivial instances would clearly be excluded by the words 'but not unreasonably or vexatiously' (8·4). A warning notice is required before the actual notice of determination by the Employer. In the case of insolvency, termination is no longer automatic (8·5·1).
- The contractor is allowed to terminate its own employment for stated reasons, which include failure by the Employer to pay amounts properly due by the final date for payment (8·7).
- Common law rights are preserved whether termination is by employer or contractor, and the grounds stated in the contract are without prejudice to any other rights or remedies.
- The respective rights and duties of the parties concerning outstanding payments and any direct loss and/or damage arising from determination are set out in detail (8·9, 8·10).

8 Miscellaneous

- The contract includes break provisions, which allow for determination of the contractor's employment by either party after six months. Such action could become necessary on a long-running contract because of changes to the Employer's building programme or due to a fluctuating workload. Thirteen weeks' notice (or lesser period if previously agreed) is required (7·1).
- Rights of third parties under the Contracts (Rights of Third Parties) Act 1999 are expressly excluded (1·5).

JCT MTC11

9 Disputes

- Either party has a right to refer any dispute or difference arising under the contract to adjudication (Article 6 and clause 9·2).
- Where Article 7 is stated to apply, arbitration is the agreed method for final determination of disputes (9·4·1). Written notice of reference is required.
- The conduct of the arbitration and appointment of the arbitrator are clearly defined (9·1·3 and 9·5). The parties agree that there may be appeal to the courts (9·1·7).
- The JCT has adopted the 2011 JCT Edition of the Construction Industry Model Arbitration Rules, and the provisions of the Arbitration Act 1996 shall apply.
- Unless it is stated that Article 7 applies, then the final determination of disputes is to be by legal proceedings and not by arbitration (Article 8).
- There is a reference in clause 9·1 to 'mediation'. This means of resolving disputes may be particularly appropriate to the relatively low cost and short duration of work carried out under individual orders. It will not remove the statutory right to adjudication, nor a contractual agreement to arbitration or legal proceedings.

JCT MTC11

This contract?

If considering using MTC11 remember that:

It is intended for maintenance and small works programmes of between one and three years' duration, and the approximate value of work to be carried out is given as a sum either per annum or relating to the contract period. There is only one version for both private and public sector use. The Employer is required to appoint a contract administrator. The form avoids the need for numerous separate contracts, but the appointed contractor may only carry out each separate job when initiated by an order issued by the contract administrator.

The applicable law of the contract is the law of England, there the form may be used as printed for work in England and Wales. A footnote to clause 1·7 refers to use under other laws.

The form includes break provisions, commencement and completion of orders, arrangements for site access, and cancellation of an order. Orders are subject to a minimum and maximum value as entered in the Contract Particulars. Contract documents comprise the Articles, Conditions and Schedule of Rates. There is one contract period and orders are given commencement and completion dates. All work is subject to measurement and valuation, and this can be made the responsibility of the contractor or the contract administrator. Fluctuations provisions may apply or the contract may be fixed price.

When completing the form, entries in the Contract Particulars are required on matters including list of properties; description of types of work; value of works; contract period; priority coding; payment provisions; and the break provision.

If acting as contract administrator, this responsibility will extend to all work carried out under the orders. This will include the issuing of orders, and may include issue of instructions, variations, certificates for Progress Payments, extension of time, and cancellation of an order.

This is the only JCT standard form of contract published specifically for term contract working. The Conditions are clearly worded and Section headed.

Related matters

Documents

Measured Term Contract 2011 Edition

References

Measured Term Contract Guide (2011)

Traditional procurement 10

Cost plus and target cost forms

The Joint Contracts Tribunal Ltd
Standard Form of Prime Cost Contract 2011 Edition

New Engineering Contract
Engineering and Construction Contract Option C

Cost plus procurement allows the Employer to proceed on an indication only of the price, and agrees to pay the actual cost of labour, materials and plant, plus an amount for the contractor's overheads and profit. Target Cost is a variant of the Cost plus method. The distinguishing aspect of it is the setting of a target price, below which parties share the savings at pre-agreed ratio and above which parties share the pain of the excess amount. This focuses attention on effective cost management.

JCT PCC11

The Joint Contracts Tribunal Ltd

Standard Form of Prime Cost Contract 2011 Edition

Background

PCC 2011 is a cost-reimbursable contract. It allows for an early start at the site without the need to define completely the extent and nature of the work. Originally intended for use in cases of repairs or alterations to damaged or old buildings where there are uncertainties as to the precise requirements of the work. The contract has however found wider use; it is often used at the early phases of a project with a lump sum of remeasurement contract used for later phases. The contract indicates that it is appropriate for contracts designed by or on behalf of the Employer where it is not possible to prepare full design information before the works commence.

The contract like others in the JCT suite requires the appointment of an Architect/Contract Administrator and Quantity Surveyor to administer the conditions. It also contains strict control of expenditure provisions. The Contract makes no provision for any aspect of the work by the Contractor, it however provides for sectional possession and completion.

The main changes in the 2011 edition are with regards to the payment and payment certificate provisions. Other changes includes the extension of the role of the Principal Contractor to cover the SWMP Regulations, the revision of the provision on terrorism cover and minor changes in the definition of insolvency and terminal payment rules.

The contract has more than 86 pages including options for collateral warranty, Rights of Purchasers and Tenants.

Nature

This is a heavyweight document over 150 pages long, including an Appendix, with an Annex 1 to the Appendix relating to bonds, an Annex 2 to the Conditions relating to EDI provisions, Supplemental Provisions in respect of VAT, and Modifications necessary for Sectional Completion under Article 7. These Modifications are quite extensive, and clauses throughout the contract which are affected as the result of including Sectional Completion are identified by small letter 's' in the margin. This arrangement of printing Sectional Completion provisions in the body of the text, although convenient in many ways, does make for a rather bulky document and arduous cross-referencing.

The Articles of Agreement include seven Recitals and nine Articles, and the Agreement may be executed under hand not as a deed, or as a deed if required.

JCT PCC11

The contract Conditions are set out under nine Section headings, helpfully indexed in a Contents page at the front of the form. A key feature essential with this kind of contracting is the provision of eight Schedules. These are very important components, on which a great deal of reliance is placed. The Schedules are as follows:

First Schedule:	description of the nature and scope of the Works, and list of drawings (if any);
Second Schedule:	definitions of the Prime Cost – relating to general items, labour, site staff, materials and goods, plant and services, sundry costs, sub-contract works etc;
Third Schedule:	Contract Fee – fixed fee or percentage fee;
Fourth Schedule:	estimate of the Prime Cost of items of work;
Fifth Schedule:	items of work to be executed by domestic sub-contractors listed in the Specification;
Sixth Schedule:	items of work to be executed by nominated sub-contractors;
Seventh Schedule:	materials and goods to be supplied by nominated suppliers;
Eighth Schedule:	items of work to be executed by the Employer or others direct.

These schedules should be fully and carefully completed because the nature of the intended work is likely to mean that the contract will be let on minimal information. There may or may not be drawings to accompany the Specification, and the contents of the Schedules are therefore vital for both tendering and valuation purposes.

Use

In the Recitals, after stating in general terms the nature of the Works (also to be described as clearly as possible in the First Schedule), reference is made to a Specification and any drawings (which if used, are to be listed in the First Schedule). The Architect/contract administrator responsible for the preparation of these is the person named in Article 3. The quantity surveyor is the person named in Article 4.

The contractor undertakes to carry out and complete the Works (as described in the First Schedule) together with other items as instructed by the Architect (although presumably the scope of the contract may not be materially altered).

The Employer undertakes to pay the contractor the Prime Cost (hence the importance of the definitions in the Second Schedule) and the Contract Fee (Third Schedule). There is provision for the fee to be revised if alterations in the nature or scope of the Works justifies this.

The Employer is afforded (C1·5·1) in that the Architect is empowered to disallow costs where the contractor does not carry out the work as economically as possible, or uses a greater number of operatives than is reasonably required.

JCT PCC11

Synopsis

1 Intentions

- The contractor is obliged to carry out and complete the Works in all respects in accordance with the Contract Documents and empowered instructions of the Architect (1·5).
- Protection for the Employer against wasteful use of labour and materials is a provision (1·5).
- Quality and standards, so far as procurable, are to be as described in the Specification (3·10).
- The contractor must be provided with such further drawings or details as are reasonably necessary to explain and amplify the Specification (1·6). There are limits to the use of the Specification and all drawings, and the confidentiality of rates must be respected (1·9).
- There is provision for correction of discrepancies in or between documents (1·10).

2 Time

- Dates for possession and completion are to be entered in the Appendix. There is provision for deferment of possession for up to six weeks. The contractor is to proceed regularly and diligently and complete on or before the completion date.
- Notice of delay must be given by the contractor in writing (2·5). The Architect is empowered to award an extension of time should completion be delayed beyond the completion date, provided the reason is one or more of the Relevant Events listed. The Architect is to make in writing a fair and reasonable extension within 12 weeks of receipt of the notice and particulars.
- Failure by the contractor to complete within the contract period is to be certified by the Architect (2·2). Liquidated damages are then recoverable by the Employer.
- Practical completion is to be certified by the Architect (2·8).
- There is provision for partial possession by the Employer (2·9).
- The contractor is obliged to rectify defects (2·10) which are notified by the Architect within 14 days of the expiry of the Defects Liability Period.

3 Control

- The bar to assignment of the contract without written consent extends to both parties (3·1).
- The contractor may not sub-contract without written consent of the Architect (3·17).
- Sub-contractors may be named and included in a list of not fewer than three names in or annexed to the Specification (3·18).

JCT PCC11

- There is also provision for nominating sub-contractors (8A·1). There are specified forms and procedures, (ie NSC/T (PCC); NSC/W (PCC); NSC/N (PCC); NSC/A (PCC) with Conditions incorporated by reference).
- Architect's instructions must be in writing (3·3). Alteration of the nature or scope of work is not empowered.
- The contractor is required to have a competent person-in-charge on the site constantly (3·6). The Employer is entitled to appoint a clerk of works who can issue directions, although these must be confirmed as instructions by the Architect to have effect (3·9).
- There is provision for opening up, inspection and testing (3·11 and 3·12) and the familiar JCT Code of Practice relating to the fair and reasonable operation of this provision is included at the end of Section 3 of the form.
- There is provision for work to be carried out by others engaged direct by the Employer (3·13) and such items of work are best listed in the Eighth Schedule, and relevant information included in the Specification.

4 Money

- There is no Contract Sum, but Article 2 refers to a Prime Cost, Contract Fee and any direct loss and/or expense ascertained.
- The Contract Fee is to be stated in the Third Schedule, but may be adjusted (4·10).
- The contractor may make written application for reimbursement of direct loss and expense suffered under specified headings or 'matters'. Common law rights are preserved (4·13).
- Interim valuations are to be made by the quantity surveyor, and the contractor must provide the quantity surveyor with necessary details of expenditure to enable valuations to be made (4·4).
- The amounts payable under the contract are exclusive of VAT and the Employer in addition to any payment is expected to pay VAT as properly charged (4·4).
- Due date for interim payment from commencement to practical completion shall be the monthly due dates specified in the Contract Particulars. After practical completion the due dates shall be specified at two month intervals and the last due date shall be the date of the expiry of the rectification period or if later the issue of the Certificate of Making Good (4·6).
- The Architect/Contract Administrator is to issue an interim payment certificate within five days of each due date, stating the sum it considers due to the Contractor on the relevant due date and the basis on which it was calculated (4·7).
- The Contractor is expected, not less than seven days before the due date, to issue to the Quantity Surveyor an application for payment stating the sum it considers should

JCT PCC11

be due to it on the relevant due date and basis for the calculation. Where such application is made and the Architect/Contract Administrator (A/CA) fails to issue an interim certificate, the application becomes an Interim Payment Notice. Also where no application had been made and the A/CA has not issued an Interim Certificate, the Contractor may any time after the expiry of the five day period within which the A/CA was required to issue an Interim Certificate, issue a payment notice stating the amount it considers due at the relevant due date and the basis on which it was calculated (4·8). In the latter circumstance, the final date for payment is extended by the same number of days after the expiry of the period that it took for the Contractor to issue a Payment Notice (4·10·4).

- The final date of payment is 14 days from the due date (4·10·1) and except where a Pay Less Notice has been issued, the Employer shall pay the amount stated in the Interim Certificate or Payment Notice (4·10).
- Where the Employer intends to pay less than the amount stated as due from him in either the interim payment certificate or Payment notice, the Employer is required to issue a notice not later than five days before the final payment date of the amount it considers due to the Contractor on the date of the notice and the basis of calculating it (4·10·5).
- Overdue sums that remain unpaid after the final date of payment shall attract simple interest (4·10·6) and also the Contractor may after a seven day notice suspend some or all its obligations under the contract. The Employer shall be liable for all reasonable costs of such suspension (4·12).
- There are specific timescales for the receipt of documentation from the Contractor and the issuance of the final payment certificate. The process of issuance and payment for the Final Certificate contain similar rules on payment notices and certification as the ones discussed above for interim payments (4·13, 4·14) with the final date of payment being 28 days after the due date.

5 Statutory obligations

- It is the contractor's duty to comply with all statutory obligations and give all required notices (5·1).
- The contractor is to notify the Architect if he finds any conflict between statutory requirements and the documents. The Architect must issue an instruction and the contractor is thereafter not liable to the Employer under the contract for any non-compliance with statutory requirements resulting from the instruction (5·2 and 5·5).
- The contractor is empowered to carry out limited work for emergency compliance, and this will be treated as a variation and valued accordingly (5·4).
- The contractor is obliged to comply with the CDM Regulations and particularly, where the project is notifiable, to comply with duties in relation to the Construction Phase Plan and the Health and Safety File (5·20).

JCT PCC11

6 Insurance

- The contractor indemnifies the Employer in respect of personal injury or death, unless due to the Employer's negligence (6·1).
- The contractor indemnifies the Employer in respect of damage to property, provided that this is due to the contractor's negligence (6·1).
- The contractor is to maintain insurance to cover these indemnities, and the minimum cover required by contract is the sum entered in the Appendix (6·2). This does not necessarily limit the contractor's liability.
- If instructed, the contractor is to take out joint names insurance for the Employer against the risk of legal nuisance. There is a list of exceptions, and damage must not be attributable to any negligence by the contractor (6·2).
- Insurance of 'the Works' is for all risks where new buildings are concerned, and a joint names policy may be taken out by the contractor or the Employer as selected (6·3A or 6·3B).
- Insurance of existing structures and contents is for specified perils, and is to be taken out in joint names by the Employer (6·3C).
- In the event of terrorism cover ceasing to be available, the options open to the Employer are stated in clauses 6.3A, 6.3B and 6.3C, whichever is applicable.
- Where insurance is required against the Employer's loss of liquidated damages due to an extension of time following damages to the Works, then this should be entered in the Appendix (6·3D).
- An Appendix entry will show whether the Joint Fire Code of Practice on the Protection from Fire of Construction Sites is to apply. If so, both contractor and employer will need to respect it for in the event of non-compliance, the insurers can specify remedial measures which must be undertaken (6·3FC).

7 Termination

- The Employer is allowed to determine the employment of the contractor by reasons of specified defaults (7·2). A warning notice may be issued by the Architect, but the notice of determination is a matter for the Employer. In case of insolvency of the Contractor, then depending on the circumstances determination might be automatic subject to possible reinstatement, or the Employer might enter into an agreement with the contractor (a '7·5·2·1 agreement') for continuation or novation (7·5).
- Depending upon the circumstances, the Employer can have the right to make interim arrangements for certain work to be carried out during the holding period under this agreement. He may still elect to have the Works completed by a different contractor, or abandon the idea of completing the Works altogether.

JCT PCC11

- The contractor is allowed to determine his own employment for specified defaults by the Employer (7·9). The procedures must be followed meticulously. In the event of insolvency of the Employer, the contractor may elect to determine his own employment.
- Either party can determine the employment of the contractor for listed neutral causes (7·13).
- The respective rights and duties of the parties concerning payment, removal and completion are set out in detail in the applicable clauses.

8 Miscellaneous

- A full list of definitions, many of them specific to PCC98, is included (1·3).
- Special provisions apply to the keeping of records, measurements and accounts concerning the ascertainment of Prime Cost items (1·12).
- Section 8A of the form is given up to nominated sub-contractors, and Section 8B is given up to nominated suppliers.
- Access for the Architect is allowed at all reasonable times (3·8).
- Action necessary as a consequence of discovery of antiquities (3·16) is included.
- Third party rights under the Contracts (Rights of Third Parties) Act 1999 are excluded (1·25).

9 Disputes

- The Housing Grants, Construction and Regeneration Act 1996 (Part II) as amended gives either party a statutory right to refer any difference or dispute arising out of the contract to adjudication. Article 8 of PCC98 provides for this.
- Procedures for adjudication are set out in detail in clause 9A.
- Arbitration is to be the method for final resolution of disputes (unless the Appendix statement has been deleted) and is detailed in clause 9B.
- Arbitration is to be conducted in accordance with the JCT 1998 Edition of the Construction Industry Model Arbitration Rules.
- Where arbitration has been deleted as the chosen method, then clause 9C will apply and the dispute will be determined by legal proceedings.

JCT PCC11

This contract?

If considering using PCC11 remember that:

It is intended for contracts where work must be started on site ahead of full documentation, or where the nature of the intended work is such that it is impossible to prepare full information. It is published in one version for either private or public sector clients. The Recitals call for a Specification and such drawings as are listed in the First Schedule, and an estimate of the Prime Cost of the items of work as shown in the Fourth Schedule. The Contract Fee charged by the contractor may be either on a fixed or percentage basis as indicated in the Third Schedule. The Employer is required to appoint a contract administrator and a quantity surveyor.

The form is for use in England and Wales. The Scottish Building Contract Committee published its own SBC Prime Cost Contract.

PPC11 provides for partial possession, sectional completion (Modifications to facilitate this are included at the end of the contract form). There is no provision for design by the Contractor, nor for performance specified work.

Sub-contractors may be selected by the contractor from a list of not less than three names. Sub-contractors and suppliers may also be nominated, in which case the use of dedicated documents is mandatory. The procedures follow closely those for JCT11, but the prescribed NSC documents carry the affix PCC.

When completing the form, entries are required relating to decisions on matters including deferment of possession; bonds (listed items); insurance of the Works; Joint Fire Code; liquidated damages; and EDI. The eight Schedules should also be checked for completeness of entries.

If acting as contract administrator it is essential to follow carefully the procedural rules, particularly where nominations are made.

This is an attractively presented, self-contained but bulky document. The Conditions are Section headed and sub-headed, but the procedures are rather complex for administration. It seems not to have sold in great numbers, not surprising perhaps as this is a procurement method which brings considerable risks for the Employer. However, it seems to have been used without serious problems, possibly due to careful selection of the Contractor, a realistic attitude on the part of the Employer and sound practice in contract administration.

Related matters

Documents

Standard Form of Prime Cost Contract 2011 Edition

References

Guide PCC(2011)
Practice Note 5: Deciding on the Appropriate JCT Form of Contract

NEC3 Option 3

The New Engineering Contract

Main Option C Target Cost Contract

Background

The NEC3 provides for Target Costs in Main Options C and D. The main difference between the provisions of both Main options is that Option D requires the preparation of a bill of quantity. Both contracts require the Contractor to keep detailed cost records that may be inspected by the Project Manager and also used to forecast future costs. It is important that the parties set a realistic Target Price. Too high a target price removes the incentive for cost effectiveness and over-rewards the contractor. An artificially low target price is likely to lead to speculative claims and disputes. The brief synopsis below examines the main provisions of the NEC3 option C, which is the more regularly used of the two Main options on target Costs.

Brief synopsis

Target Costs is cost related, for information on other aspects of the NEC3 form refer to Chapter 6.

The Contractor is reimbursed for the costs of carrying out the works until completion when the difference between the costs of the works and the Target Price is considered.

The Activity Schedule sets out the various component parts and stages of the work and is usually priced in the tender, in Option C, the activity schedule is used only in assessing the value of compensation events.

In summary Defined Costs comprises of payment to the sub-contractor that have been properly made and costs of cost components listed in the Schedule of Costs Components less Disallowed Costs. Disallowed Costs cover such headings as costs incurred because the contractor did not give an early warning, cost of correcting defects caused by the contractor not complying with the Works Information among others.

It requires the Contractor to keep specified costs records on an open book basis, ie open to inspection and monitoring by the Project Manager (52).

During the currency of the project the Contractor is paid the 'Price of Work Done to Date' which is defined as the total Defined Cost which the Project Manager forecasts would have been paid by the Contractor before the next assessment date plus Contractor's fee (11·20 (29)). The fee is calculated from the relevant percentages included in Contract Data and is applied as appropriate for sub-contracted work and non-sub-contracted work (different percentages may apply to either work type).

A preliminary assessment of the Contractor's share is made at completion of the

NEC3 Option 3

whole works using forecasts of the final Price for Work Done to Date and the Final Total Prices (Prices are the lump sum prices for each of the activities in the Activity Schedules which may be changed during the course of the works in accordance to the contract). The difference between the two is included in the amount due following completion (53·3).

The Project Manager makes a final assessment of the Contractor's share using the final Price of Work Done to Date and the final total of the Prices. The difference is contained in the final amount due (53·4).

Where the total Price for Work Done to Date is less than the total of the Prices the Contractor is paid his share of gains/savings (the Defined Cost less than the Target Cost). Where the reverse is the case, the Contractor is to pay the Employer his share of the excess (53·2).

Compensation events may impact on the Defined Cost (63).

This contract?

If you are considering using NEC3 Option C remember that:

The setting of the Target Cost is the key to achieving success under this contract. The Target Cost should be based on an accurate as possible cost plan from where the target cost should be drawn. Another useful exercise for this type of procurement is to carry out a detailed analysis of the risk profile of the project; this would help in setting meaningful gain/pain percentages. If administered using the NEC ethos of a 'spirit of mutual trust and cooperation', the NEC3 EEC Option C provides a veritable option for incentivising cost control and effectiveness in cost-reimbursable contracts.

Design and build procurement 11

Design and build forms

The Joint Contracts Tribunal Ltd
Design and Build Contract 2011

The Association for Consultancy and Engineering and the Civil Engineering Contractors Association
ICC Design and Construct Version (2011)

The Stationery Office
GC/Works/1 Single Stage Design and Build (1998)
GC/Works/1 Two Stage Design and Build (1999)

Traditional procurement forms of contract do not, in the absence of anything to the contrary, provide for design by the Main Contractor. They are simply 'work and materials' contracts.

The wording used in some standard forms of contract expressly includes for a limited measure of design responsibility by the Main Contractor, sometimes by optional or supplemental provisions.

With one exception, this chapter is concerned only with forms of contract which have been drafted specifically for use with design and build procurement, and take full account of design responsibility by the contractor.

JCT DB11

The Joint Contracts Tribunal Ltd

Design and Build Contract 2011

Background

During the mid-1970s, a time of popular enthusiasm for industrialised approaches to building, contractor-led design and build became established as an important method of building procurement. It was recommended in the NEDO report, *Construction for Industrial Recovery*. The then Department of the Environment development management working group on value for money in local authority housing also pressed its apparent advantages. The RIBA was asked to raise with the Joint Contracts Tribunal the need for a standard form under which, for a lump sum, a contractor would design and construct the Works to Employers' stated requirements.

By this time the Department of the Environment and the National Federation of Building Trades Employers (later to become the Construction Confederation) had their own contract forms and fee scales for projects where a building was designed (sometimes using contractor-designed components) to a client's specific requirements. However, no form of contract existed for use by local authorities or the private sector which fairly apportioned the responsibilities, obligations and risks of the parties. Clearly a new form was needed which would deal with the situation where the appointment of neither an architect nor a quantity surveyor was envisaged.

Drafting the new form was protracted, and continued for six years. However, when it was finally published as the JCT Standard Form of Building Contract With Contractor's Design 1981 Edition (JCT WCD81), it was an immediate success and widely accepted within the building industry. Supplementary Provisions introduced in February 1988 greatly increased the usefulness and flexibility of WCD.

Design and build is now an established procurement method with many variants, mostly contractor-led but frequently design-led.

DB 2011 is suitable for larger works where the Employer has defined his requirements and the Contractor is expected to develop and complete the designs as well as carry out the works. The Contract envisages the appointment of an Employer's Agent who may be an external consultant to administer the project.

The main changes in the 2011 edition are with regards to the payment and payment certificate provisions. Other changes includes the extension of the role of the Principal Contractor to cover the SWMP Regulations, the revision of the provision on terrorism cover and minor changes in the definition of insolvency and terminal payment rules.

JCT DB11

Nature

DB 2011 continues with the risk format of its predecessor DB 05, and has been released to bring the form into compliance with changes in legislation.

The total document runs to over 100 pages. The Articles of Agreement include five Recitals and nine Articles, and may be executed under hand not as a deed, or as a deed.

Seven Schedules are included at the back of the form, which cover such matters as the design submission procedure, insurance options, bonds and fluctuations.

Article 1 states the express obligation of the contractor as being to 'complete the design for the Works and carry out and complete the construction of the Works' (note that the obligation is to complete the design and not carry out the design). In Article 3 the Employer nominates a person to act as Employer's Agent. This agent may be an architect, surveyor, project manager or any other suitable person, and his or her duties and any limits to his or her authority should be clearly established right from the outset. (The contract wording often refers to the 'Employer' having a duty in certain matters, and depending on the agreement, this duty might or might not rest with the Employer's Agent.)

In practice the form is often used where the scheme design has been developed to a substantial extent, and it is common practice to appoint an architect and other consultants to prepare the Employer's Requirements in considerable detail, often including the production of detailed design and even some production drawings. However the role as advisor to the Employer is quite distinct from that of Employer's Agent, and the architect should ensure that his or her terms of appointment are drafted appropriately.

Although the form bears a marked resemblance to SBC11, and in parts the Conditions are similarly worded, the difference between the forms is fundamental. There is no role for a contract administrator to act fairly as between the parties. The basis of the agreement is the compatibility between the Employer's Requirements on the one hand and the Contractor's Proposals on the other.

By the Second Recital, the contractor is obliged to submit proposals, and a tender figure. The contractor is also obliged to produce a Contract Sum Analysis. The Third Recital places on the Employer the obligation to examine the Contractor's Proposals. The wording falls short of a warranty by the Employer, but this obligation must be treated cautiously because it is the Contractor's Proposals which prevail in the event of a conflict. (The form is frequently amended to reverse this.) Where the Employer accepts some divergence, the Employer's Requirements should be amended before the Contract Documents are signed. This does not relieve the contractor of its obligation to satisfy the Employer's Requirements in terms of design, selection of components and materials, and standards of workmanship – particularly where these are covered by performance specification only.

JCT DB11

The Contractor's Proposals should respond to and be consistent with the Employer's Requirements, indicating where amendment or amplification is advisable. They should not include Prime Cost or provisional sums unless the Employer agrees to this, in which case the Requirements must be amended. They should include any necessary plans, elevations, Sections and typical details, information about the structural design, services layout drawings, and specifications for materials and workmanship not already provided in the Employer's Requirements, although specifically requested in those Requirements.

This is a lump sum contract payable in stages or periodically based on the contractor's valuation. The Conditions make no reference to bills of quantities or a Schedule of Rates. The Contract Sum Analysis will therefore be used for valuing changes in the Employer's Requirements, valuations for interim payments, and for calculating the reimbursement of increased costs by the Formula Rules. The Contract Sum Analysis is to be submitted with the tender, and the Employer's Requirements might stipulate the format and headings to be used, possibly as prepared by the Employer's quantity surveyor consultant.

Use

The form places on the contractor the same design responsibility as that of an architect or other appropriate professional designer (2·17). This of course is to use reasonable skill and care. It is not an absolute warranty except to the extent that housing designs must satisfy the provisions of the Defective Premises Act 1972. There is now a requirement in the form for the contractor to take out professional indemnity insurance to back this warranty. Details of the cover required, including the period for which it must be taken out, are entered in the Contract Particulars.

Liability for consequential loss occurring as the result of design failure by the contractor may be limited to an amount to be entered in the Contract Particulars (2·17). Opinion is divided on the worth of this, and what an appropriate figure might be. As each set of circumstances is different, the Employer should take advice from insurance experts.

The form, as used, sometimes places responsibility for the complete design on the contractor. It also permits design input by the Employer because the contractor's design warranty is only applicable 'insofar as the design of the Works is comprised in the Contractor's Proposals'. There can be problems where the Employer has a substantial design input, because in the event of failure the boundaries of responsibility become blurred.

The Employer's Requirements may therefore be anything from a simple written statement of performance requirements to a completely developed scheme design, with outline specification and drawings indicating spatial arrangements, materials and finishes, which may have received full planning permission already. However, there is no provision for design input from the Employer after completion of the tender

JCT DB11

documents, except by way of a variation or 'Change', as this form terms it. Where this occurs the Employer must bear the full cost of such variation, including any consequential expense to the contractor. Valuation is in the hands of the contractor.

The fact that there is no place for an architect or contract administrator in the contract can leave the problem of quality control unresolved. The Employer's Agent or other person acting with the authority of the Employer or his Agent is to be allowed access to the Works, but there is no inspection in the traditional sense. The contractor might have engaged its own architect to prepare designs and assist with production drawings, but many contractors consider the architect's work to be finished once he or she has completed the drawings. Some contractors choose to retain an architect for site duties to help ensure that drawings are being correctly interpreted, or to see what substitutions can be accommodated without injurious consequential effects. Others regard any questions raised by their architect about workmanship and materials as unwarranted interference, and consider that the inspection of work on site is best left to their site agent and contracts manager. Therefore it might be highly desirable for the Employer to take advantage of clause 3·1 and appoint an architect or clerk of works to inspect and report back, to ensure that the standards of workmanship and the quality of materials is in accordance with the Requirements.

Synopsis

1 Intentions

- The documents are to be read as a whole, and the printed Articles, Conditions, Appendices and Supplementary Provisions prevail in the event of any conflict (1·3).
- The contractor is obliged to carry out and complete the Works referred to in the Contract Documents (the Employer's Requirements, the Contractor's Proposals, the Contract Sum Analysis and the printed Conditions) (2·1·1). There is express reference to completing the design for the Works, and to reliance upon the contractor for materials, goods and workmanship otherwise necessary but not referred to in the documents (2·2·1).
- Kinds and standards will be either those referred to in the documents and if the Employer has specified these in the Requirements, then this will reduce liability on the contractor. If not, then the contractor will be wholly liable in the event of failure (2·1 and 2·2).
- The Contractor's Proposals are to be accompanied by a Contract Sum Analysis (Second Recital) and the Employer needs to examine both carefully, because the assumption is that he is satisfied that they meet the Employer's Requirements (Third Recital).
- There is no means within the contract of dealing with a mismatch between the Requirements and the Proposals. Where a discrepancy is found within the Requirements, the Proposals prevail. Where there is a discrepancy within the Proposals, the Employer

JCT DB11

is to be notified and he must make a decision about the discrepancy and proposed amendments (2·14·2). This might constitute a Change.

- The contractor is liable for its own design work to the extent that it warrants reasonable care and skill (2·17·1). However, where the contract is for housing work which is subject to the terms of the Defective Premises Act 1972, the limit of liability in clause 2·5·1 will not apply (2·17·2).
- The contractor's design warranty includes for consequential loss not covered by liquidated damages (eg loss of use, loss of profit, etc) and can be limited to an amount entered in the Appendix (2·17·3).
- The contractor is required to submit drawings and other documents it prepares in relation to the design (the 'Contractor's Design Documents'), as set out in the Contract Documents, or as reasonably necessary. The submission is to follow a procedure set out in Schedule 1 (2·8).
- The Employer is to respond by returning the design documents marked either 'A Action', 'B Action' or 'C Action'. The contractor is to execute work marked 'A Action' or 'B Action', in the case of the latter it must incorporate comments by the Employer. The contractor must revise drawings marked 'C Action and return for approval before executing any work' (Schedule 1: 5).
- No comments of the Employer relieve the contractor of any of its responsibility for design (Schedule 1: 8·3).
- The contractor is obliged to supply 'as-built' drawings after completion, and before commencement of the Rectification Period. These may or may not comprise part of the Health and Safety File, according to the circumstances.
- The CDM Regulations require the appointment of a CDM Coordinator and Principal Contractor, and under Articles 5 and 6 and provision 3·18, the CDM obligations on both employer and contractor become contractual as well as statutory.

2 Time

- Dates for possession and completion should be entered in the Contract Particulars. The contractor must proceed regularly and diligently and complete on or before the completion date (2·3).
- An option for deferment of possession not exceeding six weeks is available, subject to an entry in the Contract Particulars (2·4).
- There is provision for dividing the Works into Sections, and setting separate commencement and completion dates, and rates of liquidated damages for each section. All provisions relating to timing, for example extending the date for completion, apply separately to each section, except that there is only one Final Certificate.

JCT DB11

- Notice of delay must be given to the Employer, together with supporting information, including the contractor's estimate of the likely effect on completion (2·24). The Employer is required to notify the contractor of his decision relating to the completion date as soon as is reasonably practicable and in any event within 12 weeks (2·25·2).
- The listed Relevant Events for which an extension may be awarded includes reference to strikes etc affecting design work, delay resulting from necessary permissions or approvals, and the effect of changes in statutory requirements or terms of consents which arise after the base date entered in the Contract Particulars (2·26). The interim decision by the Employer is subject to review no later than 12 weeks following practical completion (2·25·5).
- If the contractor fails to complete the Works to time, the Employer may recover liquidated damages, provided that it issues a written notice to the contractor (2·29).
- Practical completion, to include sufficient compliance by the contractor in providing information for the Health and Safety File, is signified by a written statement from the Employer (2·27).
- After this the contractor is obliged to rectify defects unless the Employer decides otherwise and takes an appropriate deduction instead (2·35).
- There is provision for early use or occupation by the employee (2·5·1) and for partial procession (2·30).

3 Control

- The bar to assignment without written consent relates to the contract 'or any rights thereunder' is a (7·1).
- The contract provides for Third Party Rights to be assigned to purchasers/tenants and funders. The requirement to grant third party rights to identified persons, together with information regarding limits to the contractor's liability, must be set out in the Contract Particulars. The rights are set out in Schedule 5.
- The contract provides for collateral warranties to be provided by the contractor to funders and purchasers/tenants, and by sub-contractors to the purchasers/tenants, funders, and the Employer. The requirement to enter into warranties must be set out in the Contract Particulars, the relevant persons and sub-contractors identified, together with information regarding limits to the contractor's liability.
- The warranties to purchaser, funder and tenant are to be on the JCT standard forms CWa/P&T, CWa/F, SCWa/F and SCWa/P&T. The JCT also publish SCWa/E for use in relation to the Employer, although this is not referred to in the form.
- There is a requirement for written consent to sub-contracting which refers not only to the carrying out of work, but also to matters of design (3·3). It is a condition of

JCT DB11

any sub-letting that the sub-contract shall contain certain provisions (3·4).

- There is no facility for naming or nominating sub-contractors or suppliers in the Conditions, but named sub-contractors may be part of the Employer's Requirements under Schedule 2 Supplemental Provision 2·1.
- Employers' instructions must be in writing, although this can mean written confirmation of oral instructions (3·7). The Conditions clearly define what instructions are empowered and these may include a Change (3·9·1) and postponement of any construction work or design (3·10). The Employer cannot order a Change which modifies the design of the Works without the contractor's consent.
- The contractor is required to have a competent person-in-charge on the site full-time (3·2).
- The contract requires all work to be carried out in a proper and workmanlike manner, and in accordance with the Health and Safety Plan (2·1·1).
- The contract allows for work under the direct control of the Employer to be carried out during the time that the contractor is in possession (2·6).
- Where work or materials do not comply with the contract, the Employer may instruct the contractor to remove them from site (3·13·1). The Employer may also order any consequential Changes necessary, which will not attract any extension of time or addition to the Contract Sum. It may order tests and inspections (3·12) and the likelihood of any non-compliance in similar work elsewhere is covered (3·13·3 and Code of Practice).

4 Money

- The contractor is required to provide Priced Statements; there are strict timescales to aid cash flow; and non-payment to time can be a valid reason for suspending work.
- The amounts payable under the contract are exclusive of VAT and the Employer in addition to any payment is expected to pay VAT as properly charged (4·4).
- In terms of interim payments, the Contractor shall make an application (Interim Application) to the Employer stating the sum the Contractor considers due to him and the basis on which that sum was calculated (4·8·1).
- Where Alternative A applies, the Interim Application shall be made at the completion of each stage specified in the Contract Particulars for Alternative A. After application may have been made for the last stage, further applications will be at two month intervals until the expiry of the Rectification Period or if later the date of the issue of the Notice of Completion of Making Good. The due date at each stage shall be the later of the completion of the stage or the date of receipt of the Contractor's Application (4·8·2).

JCT DB11

- Where Alternative B applies, from commencement to Practical Completion, Interim Applications will be made on monthly dates specified in the Contract Particulars for Alternative B. After Practical Completion, Interim Application shall be at intervals of two months up to the later of the expiry of the Rectification Period or the date of issue of the Notice of Completion of Making Good. The due date in each case shall be the later of the specified date and the date of the receipt by the Employer of the Interim Application (4·8·3).
- The Employer is to issue a notice (Payment Notice) within five days of each due date, stating the sum it considers due to the Contractor on the relevant due date and the basis on which it was calculated (4·9 and 4·10·1).
- Where the Employer has not issued a Payment Notice, the amount due for payment on the Final Payment Date will be the amount stated as due in the Interim Application (4·9·2).
- The final date of payment is 14 days from the due date (4·9·1) and except where a payless notice has been issued, the Employer shall pay the amount stated in the Interim Certificate or Interim Application (4·9·2 and 4·9·3).
- Where the Employer intends to pay less than the amount stated as due from him in either the Payment notice or Interim Application, the Employer is required to issue a notice not later than five days before the final payment date, stating the amount it considers due to the Contractor on the date of the notice and the basis of calculating it (4·9·4). The amount stated on this notice shall be payable on the final date for payment.
- Overdue sums that remain unpaid after the final date of payment shall attract simple interest (4·9·5) and also the Contractor may after a seven day notice suspend some or all its obligations under the contract. The Employer shall be liable for all reasonable costs of such suspension (4·11).
- There are specific timescales for the receipt of documentation from the Contractor and the issuance of the final payment certificate. The process of issuance and payment for the Final Certificate contain similar rules on payment notices and certification as the ones discussed above for interim payments (4·12) with the final date of payment being 28 days after the due date.

5 Statutory obligations

- The contractor must comply with all statutory requirements and give all notices required by statute (2·1). The only exception to this contractual obligation is where in the Employer's Requirements it is stated that these are in compliance (eg planning permission, 2·1·2). All consents or permissions obtained by the contractor must be passed on to the Employer (2·1·3).

JCT DB11

- The contractor can only claim fees or charges where these are included for in the Employer's Requirements by way of a provisional sum. Otherwise there is no adjustment to the Contract Sum.
- The contractor is to notify the Employer if he finds any divergence between statutory requirements and either the Employer's Requirements or the Contractor's Proposals. The Employer's consent is required to any necessary amendments (2·15·1).
- If amendments to the Contractor's Proposals become necessary due to changes in statutory requirements after the base date, then these would normally constitute a Change in the Employer's Requirements, and would not be at the contractor's expense (2·15·2). However, where the Employer's Requirements expressly preclude this, then necessary amendments would be at the contractor's expense.
- The contractor is obliged to comply with the CDM Regulations and particularly, where the project is notifiable, to comply with duties in relation to the Construction Phase Plan and the Health and Safety File (3·18).

6 Insurance

- The contractor indemnifies the Employer in respect of personal injury or death, and damage to property other than the Works (6·1). This is to be backed by insurance (6·2).
- If instructed, the contractor may be required to take out joint names insurance for the Employer against the risk of legal nuisance. This will have been stated in the Employer's Requirements. There is a list of exceptions, and damage must not have been caused by the contractor's negligence. An entry on the extent of cover is required by the Contract Particulars (6·5·1).
- Insurance of 'the Works' follows the SBC05 provisions in clauses Schedule 3 (Insurance Options A, B or C). The full reinstatement value of work must include for the cost of the contractor's design work. Which alternative clause is to apply should be stated in the Employer's Requirements and shown by deletions in the Contract Particulars.
- In the event that terrorism cover is withdrawn and is no longer available, the situation and options open to the Employer are dealt with in clause 6·10.
- The contractor required to carry professional indemnity insurance. The amount of cover and the period of expiry are inserted in the Contract Particulars. The insurance must be taken out immediately following execution of the contract. There is provision for inserting a level of cover for pollution or contamination claims – if none is inserted, the level is the same as the level of cover inserted in the Contract Particulars.
- An entry in the Contract Particulars will show if the Joint Fire Code of Practice on the Protection from Fire of Construction Sites is to apply (6·13) and, if so, both Employer and contractor must comply with it. Any evidence of non-compliance could result in the insurers specifying remedial measures.

JCT DB11

7 Termination

- The Employer is allowed to terminate the employment of the contractor by reason of specified defaults (8·4). One reason is where the contractor suspends carrying out design work and is therefore unable to discharge his obligation to provide drawings. The Employer is first to issue a warning notice, and may follow this with the determination notice. In the case of insolvency of the contractor, the Employer may at any time terminate the contractor's employment by notice (8·5·1).
- The contractor is allowed to determine his own employment for specified defaults or if the Works are suspended for a specified period due to a default of the Employer (8·9·2). In the event of insolvency of the Employer, the contractor may elect to determine its own employment.
- Either party can determine the employment of the contractor for listed neutral causes (8·11·1). One is delay in obtaining planning permission, where the contractor is blameless.
- The respective rights and duties of the parties concerning payment, removal and completion are set out in detail (8·7 and 8·12). Note that the contractor's obligation extends to providing the Employer with copies of all drawings etc prepared, and that the Employer's obligation for payment includes design costs.

8 Miscellaneous

- A list of definitions is given (1·1).
- Third party rights under the Contracts (Rights of Third Parties) Act 1999 are excluded except as provided for in the Contract Particulars (1·6).
- Access for the Employer's Agent, and any person authorised by the Employer, is to be provided (3·1). This might be subject to reasonable restrictions as far as access to workshops is concerned.
- Discovery of antiquities etc is covered (3·15).
- Sums payable in respect of royalties are deemed to have been included in the Contract Sum, and the Employer is indemnified against infringements of copyright (2·18). However, where the contractor is complying with Employer's instructions (ie in matters not covered by the Employer's Requirements) then the contractor is not liable for infringements, and any additional sums are added to the Contract Sum (2·19).
- The Employer is wholly responsible for defining the boundaries of the site for the contractor (2·9). This could be considerably important in the context of the Party Wall etc Act 1996.

JCT DB11

- An appropriate deletion in the Contract Particulars should show whether or not the Supplemental Provisions apply. These are five in total but not every one will necessarily be relevant for all contracts. They can considerably extend the usefulness of the form, and they are as follows:

  1: the contractor may be required to appoint a site manager to act as a full-time representative on site, and should a change of person become necessary, the written consent of the Employer is required.

  2: the Employer is entitled to name a sub-contractor in the Employer's Requirements (note – not to be introduced later during the progress of the Works). The contractor is to notify the Employer when the sub-contract has been entered into.

  3: the Employer may include bills of quantities as part of the Employer's Requirements, and if they are firm bills, then the method of measurement used is to be stated.

  4: where variations or Changes of a major nature have been issued by the Employer, the contractor may be required to submit estimates of the anticipated effects in terms of cost, extensions of time and consequential expense, before work is authorised. If there is no agreement over terms, then the instruction may be withdrawn, or the matter referred to adjudication.

  5: where the contractor makes application for loss and/or expense as provided for under clause 4·19 the onus is on the contractor to include a detailed estimate in the application. The Employer may accept the estimate, or choose to negotiate, or refer the matter to adjudication.

9 Disputes

- The Housing Grants, Construction and Regeneration Act 1996 (Part II) gives either party a statutory right to refer any difference or dispute arising out of the contract to adjudication. Article 7 provides for this.
- Procedures for referral to adjudication and the appointment of an adjudicator are covered in clause 9·2. Any adjudication will be subject to the provisions of the Scheme for Construction Contracts.
- The adjudicator's decision is binding on the parties at least until the dispute is finally determined at arbitration or by legal proceedings.
- Arbitration may be agreed as the method for finally settling disputes (Article 8 and 9·3). Unless this provision is shown in the Contract Particulars to apply, then disputes are to be referred for legal proceedings (Article 9).

11 Design and build procurement: design and build forms

JCT DB11

This contract?

If considering using DB11 remember that:

It is intended for use where the contractor is to accept responsibility for design of the Works to a greater or lesser extent as the Employer requires, although completion of the design is a stated obligation. The contractor is to use reasonable skill and care in achieving this (ie not a fitness for purpose warranty). The more the contractor is responsible for design, the clearer the boundaries of design responsibility become. Whilst at first sight, this contract has many similarities with SBC11, a fundamental difference is the absence of any provision for a contract administrator or quantity surveyor to act on the Employer's behalf. The form is for use in England and Wales. The Scottish Building Contract Committee has published as part of its 2011 suite a Design and Build Contract for use in Scotland.

The Employer's Requirements and Contractor's Proposals are the core of this contract and it is important that they are in harmony. The Contract Sum Analysis should be adequately detailed in coverage. Completing the form requires care, particularly because of the number of Contract Particulars and supplementary provisions available.

The Employer would be well advised to consider incorporating the optional Supplementary Provisions, particularly those relating to named persons in Employer's Requirements, and submission of estimates by the contractor relating to the valuation of Changes and loss and expense.

If acting as Employer's Agent, any limits to authority should be clarified, and a clear understanding reached on what is empowered by the Employer under the contract. If acting as consultant advising the Employer, care is needed to stay strictly within the limits of the appointment especially once work starts on site. If acting for the contractor under a novation agreement, accountability should be clearly established and respected.

Related matters

Documents

Design and Build Contract 2011
Design and Build Sub-contract Agreement 2011
Design and Build Sub-contract Conditions 2011
Contractor Collateral Warranty for a Funder
Contractor Collateral Warranty for a Purchaser or Tenant
Sub-contractor Collateral Warranty for a Funder
Sub-contractor Collateral Warranty for a Purchaser or Tenant
Sub-contractor Collateral Warranty for Employer

References

JCT Design and Build Contract Guide
JCT Design and Build Sub-Contract Guide
Deciding on the Appropriate JCT Form of Contract 2011

Commentaries

Guide to DB11
RIBA Publishing (2011)

DB11 Contract Administration Guide: How to Complete the DB Contract and its Administration Forms
David Chappell
RIBA Publishing 2011

ICC/D&C

The Association for Consultancy and Engineering and the Civil Engineering Contractors Association

ICC Design and Construct Conditions of Contract Second Edition (2011)

Background

In the early 1990s government moved to adopt design and build as the basis for awarding contracts for road schemes costing up to £40 million. It was a further endorsement of the rapidly growing popularity of this method of procurement, and the belief that there would be a 'greater incentive to complete schemes more quickly and save money overall – even though the up-front costs may be higher'. The basic concept of a design and build contract is that the Employer sets out its requirement for a project including the design brief, construction and performance requirements and engages the Contractor to develop the requirements to a design on which the contractor will build the project.

The ICC Design and Construct Version is based on the ICE Design and Construct contract which was first introduced in 1992. This contract envisages lump sum payment although other forms of payment or combination of methods are also available.

These conditions are sponsored by the Association of Consultancy Engineering (ACE) and the Civil Engineering Contractors Association (CECA). The use and review of the contracts under this family is undertaken by the Infrastructure Conditions of Contract Development Forum (ICoCDF) which comprises representatives from the two sponsoring associations, Employer representatives and legal experts.

Nature

The document is 65 pages long, and includes the Conditions, a Form of Tender with a two-part Appendix, a Form of Agreement, a Form of Default Bond, and Fluctuation clauses.

Contractor's design obligations are for both permanent and temporary works. The Form of Agreement will be completed to show which documents are intended to be part of the contract. Among these the Employer's Requirements and the Contractor's Submission are key essentials.

The Conditions of the contract are in 72 clauses, and the sequence follows closely that which is found in the other ICC Conditions. The Contents list and Index on a clause by clause basis are particularly helpful.

11 Design and build procurement: design and build forms

ICC/D&C

Use

Entries in Part 1 of the Form of Tender Appendix will show a contractor tendering whether quality assurance or a performance bond is required, and provide detailed information such as commencement date, time for completion, completion by Sections, damages, payment provisions, CDM responsibilities and arbitration procedures. Part 2 of the Appendix will be completed by the tenderer.

The key person in terms of contract administration is the 'Employer's Representative'. He or she is to be named in the Appendix Part 1, and is given considerable authority to act within the terms of the contract. In the event of his or her departure the Employer must nominate a replacement.

Synopsis

1 Intentions

- The contractor undertakes to design, construct and complete the Works, including providing all design services, labour and materials – everything whether of a permanent or a temporary nature as specified in or reasonably to be inferred from the contract (8).
- In all design obligations the contractor exercises all reasonable skill, care and diligence (8) and this includes accepting responsibility for design work included as part of the Employer's Requirements.
- The contractor is to institute a quality assurance scheme to an appropriate extent, which must be approved by the Employer's Representative before commencement of work at both design and construction stages (8).
- The contractor is responsible for the safety of the design, and for stability and safety of all site operations and methods of construction (8).
- Definition of the Works includes both temporary and permanent work. Contract means Conditions of Contract, Employer's Requirements, Contractor's Submission and other documents as agreed by the parties (Form of Agreement: 2). The documents taken together are stated to be mutually explanatory, but in the event of discrepancies between the Contractor's Submission and the Employer's Requirements, the Employer Requirement shall take precedence. Ambiguities or inconsistencies in the Employer's Requirement is to be resolved by the Employer's Representative who shall issue appropriate instructions where necessary (5).
- The contractor is deemed to have inspected and examined the site and surroundings, and the information provided by the Employer before tendering (11). In the event of physical conditions or artificial obstructions which could not reasonably have been foreseen, the contractor is required to give written notice to the Employer's Representative, of claims for extension of time and/or additional payment (12).

ICC/D&C

- The contractor must submit all necessary design drawings to the Employer's Representative and his or her consent must be obtained before construction work is undertaken (6).
- Within 21 days of the award of the contract, the contractor must submit a programme to the Employer's Representative. Where the Employer's Representative objects to the original programme submitted by the Contractor, a revised programme is to be submitted with 14 days (14).
- The Works must be designed, constructed and completed in accordance with the contract, and materials and workmanship must be as described in the contract, or be to appropriate standards and codes of practice. There is provision for checks and testing to be carried out.
- Reasonable facilities must be provided for any other contractors employed by the Employer on or near the site of the Works (31).
- The functions and authority of the named Employer's Representative and his or her named assistants are clearly defined (2).

2 Time

- The Commencement Date will be as stated in the Appendix to the Tender, or as agreed by the parties, or otherwise a date between 14 days and 28 days after entering into the contract to be notified by the Employer's Representative to the Contractor or such other dates as agreed by the parties (41).
- The contractor must start as soon as reasonably practicable, and proceed with due expedition and without delay (41·2).
- The contract may prescribe that possession of the site will be in portions, and also determine the order of availability and order of the Works (42).
- Failure by the Employer to give possession which results in delay to the contractor can result in the award of extensions of time and expense (42·3).
- Extensions of time may also be due for reasons of ordered variations, weather, Employer's delay, impediment or default or special circumstances of any kind (44).
- The contractor should notify the Employer's Representative within 28 days of a delay and supply necessary particulars.
- The Employer's Representative is expected to consider all circumstance regarding the delay, and where it determines that the Contractor's submission is fair, grant an extension of time for Sectional or Substantial Completion of works. Also the Contractor should be informed quickly if the reverse is the case (44·3).
- The Employer's Representative is empowered, not later than 14 days after the due date or extended date for completion of the works, to award an extension of time if it thinks it appropriate and refuse to if it is not.

ICC/D&C

- If the contractor fails to complete the whole or any designated Section of the Works to time, the Employer may deduct and retain liquidated damages. These must not be a penalty, but where no limitation to liquidated damages is stated in the Appendix to the Form of Tender, then liquidated damages without limit shall apply (47).
- Where the Employer's Representative requests accelerated completion and the contractor agrees, then the terms for payment shall be agreed between the parties before action is taken (46).
- Where progress is too slow to ensure completion by the date agreed, the Employer's Representative may notify the contractor of his or her opinion, and the contractor is obliged to take such steps as may be necessary at his own expense (46).
- The Employer's Representative must issue a Certificate of Substantial Completion when in his or her opinion the whole or a designated Section of the Works is substantially completed. The contractor must notify the Employer's Representative when completion has been achieved, and the Employer's Representative issues the certificate within 21 days of notification, always provided that he or she is satisfied (48).
- The contractor is obliged to complete any outstanding work and deal with repairs during the Defects Correction Period. When the Employer's Representative is satisfied, a Defects Correction Certificate is issued, although this in no way relieves the contractor of any liability (61).
- Prior to the issue of the Defects Correction Certificate, the contractor must submit manuals and as-built drawings for the permanent works. This is a contractual obligation quite additional to material for the Health and Safety File (61).

3 Control

- Neither party may assign the contract or any benefit or interest under it without the written consent of the other (3).
- The contractor must first obtain consent from the Employer before making any change of the contractor's designer from the person named in the Appendix to the Form of Tender, Part 2 (4).
- The contractor is permitted to sub-contract any part of the construction work, but must notify the Employer's Representative prior to the named sub-contractor arriving on site (4).
- The Employer's Representative may order suspension of any part of the Works (40) and order alterations to the Employer's Requirements (51).
- The contractor is obliged to give the Employer's Representative full opportunity to inspect work before it is covered up (38).

ICC/D&C

- The Employer's Representative may instruct the removal from the site of any materials which do not comply with the contract, and the removal and replacement of materials and workmanship. This will extend to replacement of work for which the contractor has design responsibility (39).
- The contractor must provide all necessary superintendence. A Contractor's Representative will have overall responsibility and may delegate to a nominated deputy subject to the agreement of the Employer's Representative (15).

4 Money

- The Form of Tender includes for a lump sum, or such other sum as may be ascertained in accordance with the contract Conditions. The contract price will include for the design, construction and completion of the Works (1).
- VAT will not have been included in the contract price (70).
- Provisional sums and Prime Cost sums are not referred to in the contract, but a 'Prime Cost Item' means a Prime Cost sum for the supply of goods, materials or services (1). Use of Contingency and Prime Cost Items require prior consent by the Employer's Representative.
- Variations to the Employer's Requirements may be ordered, and if requested by the Employer's Representative the contractor must submit an estimate of the extra cost and delay involved. Otherwise, or if the estimate is not accepted, valuation of ordered variations will be by the Employer's Representative on a fair and reasonable basis and in accordance with the contract (52). Work ordered on a daywork basis will be valued in accordance with the Federation of Civil Engineering Contractors Schedule of Dayworks (55).
- Payment is on the basis of statements submitted periodically by the Contractor to the Engineer showing the amounts the Contractor considers due (60[1]). The Engineer must issue a certificate within 25 days of delivery of a statement. The certificate must show the amount due and the basis of calculation as set out in the contract. If the Employer intends to pay less than the amount stated on the certificate he must notify the contractor not less than one day before the final date for payment, and state the sum the employer considers due on the date the notice is served and the basis for calculating it. Final date for payment by the Employer is 28 days after delivery of the contractor's statement to the Engineer. If the Engineer fails to issue a certificate as provided for in the contract, the Contractor's statement given under clause 60(1) becomes a payment notice or where the Contractor had not submitted a periodic statement, then the Contractor may at any time give the Employer a notice with a copy to the Engineer of the sum the Contractor considers due at the relevant payment date and the basis of the calculation of that amount. If the latter circumstance occurs, the final date for payment will be postponed by the same number of days after the due date that the Contractor issues the payment certificate.

ICC/D&C

- Where the Employer fails to make appropriate payment on time, the contractor is entitled to interest payment on the outstanding amount (60).
- Retention amounts will be shown in the Appendix to the Form of Tender, and the payment of retention will be subject to the issue of the Certificate of Substantial Completion, and the end of the Defects Correction Period (60).
- Not later than three months after the date of the Defects Correction Certificate, the contractor must give the Employer's Representative a final account together with supporting documents. The Employer's Representative then has three months to verify this and to issue a Final Certificate. Final date for payment by the Employer is within 28 days of certification (60).

5 Statutory obligations

- The contractor must give all notices and pay all fees required by legislation. This might be in respect of design or construction relating to both temporary and permanent work. If the Employer's Representative certifies this, then the contractor can expect reimbursement (26).
- The contractor indemnifies the Employer against the consequences of any breach of statutory obligations, but this will not apply if this arises due to complying with an instruction given by the Employer's Representative. The contractor is not responsible for obtaining planning permission unless the contract actually requires this. If the Employer's Requirements do not conform with statutory requirements, then the Employer's Representative must issue necessary corrective instructions (26).
- The CDM Regulations 1994 place obligations on both Employer and Contractor, particularly in respect of the Health and Safety Plan and the Health and Safety File. The Employer is obliged to appoint a Planning Supervisor and a Principal Contractor. With the incorporation of these provisions into the contract, these statutory duties become contractual obligations as well (71).

6 Insurance

- The contractor takes full responsibility for the care of the Works, materials, plant and equipment from Commencement Date to Substantial Completion. The risks include any loss or damage from whatsoever cause, but do not include the Excepted Risks listed in the contract Conditions (20).
- The contractor must insure in joint names against risk of damage to both the temporary and permanent works for the full reinstatement cost, plus 10 per cent to cover additional costs (21). The terms of all insurances are for approval by the Employer.
- There appears to be no requirement for the contractor to take out insurance cover in respect of design failure.

ICC/D&C

- The contractor indemnifies the Employer against the consequences of claims for injury to persons and damage to property other than the Works. There are stated exceptions, and these remain the responsibility of the Employer (22).
- The contractor is required to cover the indemnity afforded the Employer by taking out third party insurance cover. The minimum cover required by contract will be the figure stated in the Appendix to the Form of Tender, but this will not necessarily be the extent of the contractor's liability (23).
- The contractor's obligations concerning accident or injury to work people is reinforced, and the Employer is indemnified in respect of claims (24).

7 Termination

- The Employer may give the contractor seven days' notice in the event of specified defaults, which include insolvency, and may expel the contractor without releasing him from any obligations under the contract (65).
- Procedures for completing the Works, ascertaining the value of work already done, and arranging for payments after termination, are set out in the contract (65).
- In the event of specified defaults on the part of the Employer, which include insolvency, the contractor may terminate his own employment under the contract after serving seven days' notice. If default continues for a further seven days the contractor may with all reasonable dispatch remove all equipment from the site (64).
- Following termination by the Employer, the Conditions provide for assignment of goods and materials, but do not appear to include for design drawings which might be necessary to complete the Works.

8 Miscellaneous

- The Conditions include a full set of definitions (1).
- The Employer's Representative can require the removal of employees of the contractor (16).
- There is provision in the event of discovery of fossils, antiquities and things of archaeological interest, etc (32).
- The Employer's Representative is to have access to the Works, the site and the Workshops. The Conditions refer to work in preparation, materials in manufacture, but not to offices where design information is being prepared (37).
- Matters relating to the possession of site, and site access, beyond those prescribed in the contract are mainly the responsibility of the contractor. Where there is a failure to give the contractor possession on time, extension of time and additional costs can be awarded (42).

ICC/D&C

- Contractor's plant and equipment, goods and materials brought on to the site may not be removed without the written consent of the Employer's Representative (54).
- In the event of an outbreak of war, the rights and obligations of the parties are as stated (63).
- Rights of third parties under the Contracts (Rights of Third Parties) Act 1999 are excluded (3).
- Special conditions may be incorporated, and they should be numbered consecutively after the standard Conditions of Contract (72).

9 Disputes

- As soon as either party becomes aware of any circumstance that if not resolved shall become a dispute, it shall inform the other party with a copy to the Engineer. No later than seven days after such notice and at the earliest possible time, the parties shall meet with the aim of resolving the issue. The Engineer may be invited to the meeting. If the parties fail to reach an agreement within a reasonable time, they are expected to set out in writing the areas still in dispute (66).
- The contract sets out clauses 66A, 66B and 66C as alternative dispute resolution procedures.
- Clause 66A provide the parties the option by agreement to seek resolution of a dispute under the ICE Conciliation Procedure (1999) or the ICE Construction Mediation Procedure 2002 (66A).
- Since the Housing Grants, Construction and Regeneration Act 1996 (Part II) as amended came into force, parties to the contract have the right to refer any dispute to adjudication at any time. Therefore notwithstanding the provisions of clause 66 or 66A, either party is entitled to refer a dispute to adjudication, the conditions envisages that a notice of adjudication is to be given, and adjudication is to be conducted in accordance with the ICE Adjudication Procedure (1997) (66B).
- All disputes may be finally determined by reference to arbitration. The party seeking arbitration must serve a notice to refer. Arbitration is to be under the Arbitration Act 1996, and conducted in accordance with either the ICE Arbitration Procedure (1997) or the Construction Industry Model Arbitration Rules (66C).

ICC/D&C

This contract?

If considering using the ICC/D&C remember that:

This form is intended for design and build by the contractor. It is primarily for use with civil engineering work. It may be for a lump sum or measurement. The Employer is required to appoint an Employer's Representative to act on his behalf in the project.

The contract is for use under the law of England and Wales, and is also suitable for use in Northern Ireland or under Scots law as provided for in clause 67.

The key features are the Employer's Requirements, and the Contractor's Submission. The onus is on the contractor to check design information supplied as part of the Employer's Requirements. Drawings originating from the contractor's designers must be approved by the Employer's Representative before work is commenced, but this in no way reduces the contractor's liability.

Related matters

Documents

ICC Design and Construct Conditions of Contract Second Edition (2011)

GC/Works/1 Design and Build

The Stationery Office

GC/Works/1 Single Stage Design and Build (1998)

GC/Works/1 Two Stage Design and Build (1999)

Background

GC/Works/1 Edition 3 for traditional procurement was first published in 1989. Shortly afterwards, with the demise of the Property Services Agency, government departments assumed responsibility for their own projects. Some looked to non-traditional procurement approaches, design and build in particular, which was becoming increasingly popular. In response to this interest, a version of GC/Works/1 for Single Stage Design and Build was introduced in 1993 and is currently in a 1998 revised form followed by a 1999 version for Two Stage Design and Build. In 2000 Amendment 1 was published in response to the Government 'Achieving Excellence' initiative, and is applicable to both forms. It includes provisions for risk management, value management, whole life costing and value engineering.

The Single Stage Design and Build version is obviously an adaptation of the traditional procurement GC/Works/1 contract. It is mainly a lump sum contract and does not distinguish a separate design phase. It is flexible in that it allows for varying amounts of design input by the contractor, as the contractor responds to the Employer's Requirements by developing the design outlined in these documents.

The Two Stage Design and Build version is also mainly a lump sum contract, but where the design may not be sufficiently advanced to enable the contractor to submit a realistic tender, a design fee is submitted initially together with a Schedule of Rates. This is used to quantify the construction price at the end of the design phase. Completion of the design phase will not necessarily lead to the Employer proceeding with construction.

This form has not been updated to comply with the Housing Grants, Construction and Regeneration Act 1996 as amended. Use of this form in a new project would require extensive amendments.

Nature

For the purposes of this book, comments will in the main focus on the Single Stage version of the design and build contract.

GC/Works/1 Design and Build

In common with other GC/Works forms, this comes as a two volume pack: first the General Conditions which run to over 80 pages, and secondly the Model Forms and Commentary. The General Conditions are prefaced by a Contents list, followed by an Index. Language and terminology is as that to be found in other GC/Works/1 contracts. The 65 clauses appear under the standard nine headings, and a large number are identical with those found in the traditional form. There is also a very useful Schedule of Time Limits, the essential Abstract of Particulars with an Addendum which is really a schedule of design information, an Invitation to Tender, Tender and Tender Price Form, and the Contract Agreement.

Use

The Single Stage version is without a separate design stage. The design input required from the contractor will be to the extent desired, and as indicated in the Employer's Requirements. The Contractor's Proposals will be submitted as part of the Tender together with a Programme, a Pricing Document, and details of professional indemnity insurance.

The Tender Price Form includes alternative entries depending on whether, in Condition 10, Alternative A (design liability limited to using reasonable care and skill), or Alternative B (warrant of fitness for purpose) applies.

The Two Stage version calls for a separate design stage, and the lump sum figure tendered is arrived at in two stages.

The Conditions in GC/Works/1 Design and Build provide for:

- design documents, with copyright in design and documents established;
- professional indemnity insurance for design;
- incentive bonus for early completion;
- finance charges;
- mobilisation payments;
- payments to the contractor on the basis of stages, milestones, or valuations;
- performance bonds;
- parent company guarantee;
- collateral warranties;
- as-built drawings and documents.

The factual details relating to a particular contract, and the incorporation of option provisions will be determined by how the Abstract of Particulars is completed. The Abstract is detailed and amongst other things requires the names of the Project Manager and Planning Supervisor (who may be the Project Manager). The provision of a Project Manager acting on the Employer's behalf, and given so much authority, is somewhat unusual in design and build contracts. The adjudicator and the arbitrator may also be named.

GC/Works/1 Design and Build

Synopsis (Single Stage version)

The form is one of the family of GC/Works/1 contracts. The Conditions are broadly similar to those of the traditional GC/Works/1 Form, and it is therefore unnecessary to repeat much of which appears earlier in Chapter 6.

However, the design and build forms differ in several important respects, some of which are as follows:

- The definitions include items mainly relevant to design and build, such as Employer's Requirements, Contractor's Proposals, Pricing Document, design, Design Document, etc
- The fair dealing and team-working obligation extends to the project team, including those responsible for design and costs (1A).
- In the event of discrepancy between Employer's Requirements and Contractor's Proposals, it is the Requirements which prevail (2[2]). This is the reverse of the position with JCT design and build documents.
- The professional indemnity insurance requirements relating to design are similar for both the traditional and design and build versions (8[A]), although in the former case these would apply only if stated in the Abstract of Particulars.
- The contractor is solely responsible for the correctness of setting out, and there is also a requirement on the contractor to supply full 'as-built' drawings and other relevant information within 14 days of the Date of Completion (9).
- Although a contractor's design obligation can be incorporated into the traditional form, the design obligations are slightly different from those for design and build (10).
- The Design Documents provision (10A) is peculiar to the design and build form.
- The provision on Foundations (16) in the traditional form is not included in the design and build version.
- The contractor must provide samples as are specified in the Employer's Requirements and obtain approval before commencing work (31[3]).
- The acceleration provisions differ (38).
- In the sub-letting provisions, the design and build form makes no reference to nominated sub-contractors (62). Obviously therefore, the nominated sub-contractor provision (63) in the traditional form is not used.

GC/Works/1 Design and Build

This contract?

If considering using GC/Works/1 Design and Build remember that:

This form has not been updated to comply with the Housing Grants, Construction and Regeneration Act 1996 as amended. Use of this form in a new project would require extensive amendments.

Although there is a contractor's design provision in the traditional GC/Works/1, this is the true design and build version. Depending largely on the design information contained in the Employer's Requirements, a choice between single stage or two stage tendering will determine which version of the design and build form is most applicable.

The now defunct National Joint Consultative Committee, and the present Construction Industry Board, have both produced excellent Codes for the selection of design and build contractors. Both advocate that design and build tendering is best achieved through the two stage process, and state that single stage tendering will be suitable only where the Employer's Requirements are for a well-defined design with little or no risk of further modification.

When completing the contract details in the GC/Works forms, the Abstract of Particulars is a key document. If any special supplementary conditions are incorporated, then in the event of conflict these prevail over the printed Conditions. This, of course, is the reverse of the position with JCT contracts.

The wording of the Conditions is clear and well presented. There are alternatives for design liability depending on whether this is for the professional duty to use reasonable care and skill, or for an absolute fitness for purpose.

Contract administration should be relatively straightforward and there is the customary GC/Works provision for progress meetings in Condition 35. The Model Forms are published in a separate supporting document and must be used. There are eight documents collateral to the contract, and a further 13 administration forms.

The government has recently set departments targets to become best practice clients. These cover the notions of integrated supply chain routes such as design and build, and value for money, taking into account whole life costing and value management. These 'Achieving Excellence' targets may be progressed by incorporating Amendment 1 into the Abstract of Particulars for GC/Works/1 Design and Build contracts.

This form will appeal most to those with experience of GC/Works/1, for the terminology and procedures will be familiar. It is particularly interesting because it seems to give the Employer and the Project Manager a degree of control over the contractor not usually found with design and build contracts.

11 Design and build procurement: design and build forms

GC/Works/1 Design and Build

Related matters

Documents

GC/Works/1 Single Stage Design and Build (1998) General Conditions
GC/Works/1 Single Stage Design and Build (1998) Model Forms and Commentary
GC/Works/1 Two Stage Design and Build (1999) General Conditions

Amendment 1: Achieving Excellence

Management procurement 12

Management forms

The Joint Contracts Tribunal Ltd
Standard Form of Management Contract 2011 Edition

The Joint Contracts Tribunal Ltd
Construction Management Agreement C/CM 2011

It is accepted that several major forms of building contract for traditional procurement can be adapted for use in management contracting. However, the forms included in this chapter are those exclusively for use in contracts where the principal role of the contractor is to manage the intended works, which are carried out by other persons under his or her control.

JCT MC11

The Joint Contracts Tribunal Ltd

Standard Form of Management Contract 2011 Edition

Background

For 'fast-track' projects where the Employer still wants the overall design, Specification and contract administration left in the hands of an independent professional team, management contracts are one solution. Their use in the UK became popular during the 1980s, but in recent years they seem to have lost ground to construction management. Major client bodies have become more sophisticated and well able to handle the direct involvement associated with this latter type of procurement.

In 1979 the RIBA Council, on the advice of its Contracts Committee, asked the JCT to produce a standard form of management contract. At the time, the only forms available were those devised by contracting organisations who pioneered this kind of working. These were often geared to suit the preferred working procedures of the companies, and understandably drafted with their particular interests very much in mind.

In 1987 the JCT issued the Standard Form of Management Contract (MC87) together with related documents necessary for management contracting. The main documents were the head contract between the Employer and the Management Contractor, and Works Contracts between the Management Contractor and each 'Works Contractor' carrying out a package of the work.

Nature

The documents are currently published in the 2011 Editions and the Management Contract is in familiar JCT format with Section headed Conditions.

The main contract between Employer and Management Contractor covers both the pre-construction period and the period of actual construction work. It contains a detailed Contents list and the Articles of Agreement which follow include Recitals, Articles and provision for attestation. The Conditions are followed by an Appendix in JCT MC11 two parts, Part 1 relating to information required generally and Part 2 relating to specific information which needs to be entered before construction work starts. Necessary to this kind of document are the Schedules which appear immediately after the VAT agreement.

The First Recital refers to the description of the project as entered in the First Schedule, and confirms that the Employer has appointed a professional team. The Third Recital confirms that the Management Contractor is to cooperate with the professional team,

JCT MC11

both in the Pre-Construction Period and the Construction Period in respect of services set out in the Third Schedule.

Article 1 confirms the Management contractor's agreement to perform the services defined in the Third Schedule, for the amounts which the Employer agrees to pay under Article 2.

The names of the Architect, the Contract Administrator and the quantity surveyor are to be entered in Articles 3A, 3B and 4. Other members of the professional team are to be entered in Article 5.

In Article 6 the Employer undertakes to have Project Drawings and the Project Specification, and a Contract Cost Plan prepared as soon as reasonably practicable after the date of the contract. By Article 7, the Employer undertakes to have necessary information prepared by the professional team in respect of the Works Contracts.

The appointments of the CDM Coordinator and Principal Contractor for the purposes of the CDM Regulations as well as SWMP Regulations are covered in Article 9. Article 8 confirms the rights of either party to refer disputes to adjudication, while Article 10 covers whether the final resolution of disputes is to be by arbitration or by litigation.

The contract may be executed under hand and not as a deed, or as is more likely with this type of contract, as a deed.

Use

The Management Contractor may be appointed by the Employer pre-construction, at a stage early enough to be able to contribute to the work of the professional team. For this he will expect to receive a fee. Then, assuming that the project proceeds to the construction period, the Management Contractor will appoint Works Contractors to carry out the 'work packages'. For this he will be paid a management fee and be reimbursed the Prime Costs as defined in the Second Schedule.

Management Contractors are almost invariably selected by tender and after interview. The fee is not usually the main criterion; this is above all a contract about resources and the ability to manage effectively many Works Contractors.

The Management Contractor will advise on the choice of the Works Contractors. They will normally be appointed on the basis of competitive tendering. The Management Contractor starts with a Contract Cost Plan and Programme dates. He will be responsible for the appointment of Works Contractors, their coordination, supervision, and the provision of all site services and facilities.

Tight financial control is essential, and considerable reliance is placed upon the ability of the Management Contractor to monitor the Cost Plan total, even though an independent surveyor is appointed by the Employer. The Management Contractor is under a contractual obligation to achieve completion on time, although any

JCT MC11

design developments or detailed changes in work packages which occur as the work proceeds could give rise to extensions of time. The contract still requires the Management Contractor to use 'best endeavours' and also allows for acceleration of parts of the Works.

The Contract Documents comprise the Project Drawings (listed in the Fourth Schedule), the Project Specification, a Contract Cost Plan (annexed to the Appendix Part 2), and the Articles, Conditions, Appendix and Schedules. (The fact that the work will be carried out on site by the Works Contractors is referred to in the Second Recital.)

Synopsis

1 Intentions

- The Management Contractor undertakes to cooperate with the professional team (1·4).
- Specific obligations are set out in clause 1·5 and the Third Schedule. These include preparation of Programmes, entering into Works Contracts, being responsible for the standards of the contract, and providing those site facilities and services listed in the Fifth Schedule. The Management Contractor is responsible for continuing supervision, and for ensuring that the project is carried through in an economical and expeditious manner. He is also to keep detailed records for the quantity surveyor to verify the Prime Costs (1·5).
- The Management Contractor is fully liable to the Employer for any breach of the contract, including those occasioned through breaches of Works Contracts (1·7).
- The Architect must supply the Management Contractor with further drawings and documents necessary to explain and amplify the Project Drawings and Project Specification (1·10).
- The Contract Documents will be Project Drawings, Project Specification, Articles, Conditions and Appendix, the Contract Cost Plan and the Schedules (1·3, also Articles 6 and 7).
- Quality is to be as described in the Project Specification, and in the Specification or bills of quantities for any Works Contract (3·8). There is no reference to Performance Specified Work in MC98, but there is in the Works Contract.
- The description of the Project is to be entered in the First Schedule.
- Project Drawings are to be listed in the Fourth Schedule.

2 Time

- The Management Contractor proceeds to construction of the Project only after written notice by the Employer (2·1).

JCT MC11

- At this point, the provisional dates (Appendix Part 1) are superseded by firm dates (Appendix Part 2) for possession and completion.
- The Management Contractor is given possession of the site on the date stated, and is required to secure commencement and ensure regular and diligent progress (2·3).
- Deferment of possession for up to six weeks is possible subject to an Appendix entry (2·3·2).
- Use or occupation of the site or the Project by the Employer prior to Practical Completion is provided for (2·3·4).
- Project extensions of time may be awarded to the Management Contractor by the Architect. The events or items which are relevant are few in number (2·13) and any extension requires the Management Contractor to have used its best endeavours to prevent delay (2·12).
- If the Management Contractor proposes to extend the contract period of a Works Contract, the Architect must first be notified and has the right to dissent (2·14).
- Completion of the Project may be on or before the completion date (2·3·1).
- Practical completion of the Project is certified by the Architect and is subject to his or her opinion (2·4).
- If the Management Contractor fails to complete the Project by the completion date, the Architect issues a certificate of non-completion (2·9).
- The Employer's entitlement to liquidated damages depends on the issue of a certificate of non-completion (2·10).
- Defects to be made good after the Defects Liability Period must be scheduled by the Architect and delivered up no less than 14 days after its expiry (2·5). When the defects have been rectified, the Architect issues a certificate of completion of making good defects (2·6).
- The contract provides for partial possession by the Employer, subject to the consent of the Management Contractor (2·8).
- The contract provides for the issue of instructions to the Management Contractor to accelerate the work. It is possible to establish a completion date earlier than the date stated in Appendix Part 1, provided that clause 3·6 is shown to apply (3·6).

3 Control

- The Management Contractor has to identify the management personnel employed on the Project and/or site in a list attached to the Second Schedule, and to name a site manager in the Appendix Part 2. The consent of the Architect is required to any changes (3·1 and 3·13).

JCT MC11

- The Architect is to issue written instructions to the Management Contractor as are reasonably necessary (3·3). The instructions might require Project changes or Works Contracts variations (3·4). The Architect is also to issue instructions about provisional sums in Works Contracts (3·4).
- The Architect has the power to instruct the Management Contractor to postpone any work (3·5) and, an unusual term in JCT contracts, to accelerate work, including altering its sequence under stated circumstances (3·6).
- The Architect shall provide the Management Contractor with information on levels, setting out, etc for the Project (3·7), and shall issue directions as necessary to the clerk of works (3·18).
- The Management Contractor must obtain vouchers to satisfy the Architect about the compliance of goods and materials (3·9). He must also comply with Architect's instructions concerning testing (3·10), removal from the site of work not in accordance with the contract (3·11), and the immediate making good of defective work (3·12).
- There is a bar to assignment of the contract without written consent (3·19). However, there is an option clause which if the Appendix Part 1 entry states that it is to apply, allows the Employer to transfer a right of action against the Management Contractor to persons with a subsequent interest in the completed Works (3·20).
- Items of work to be carried out by Works Contractors, and which are identified in the Contract Cost Plan or instructions, are subject to the Conditions in Section 8 of the Management Contract (8·1).
- In the control of Works Contracts, the Management Contractor's obligations in respect of the Employer and vice versa are fully set out (3·21). Alleged breaches by the Management Contractor or by Works Contractors are covered.
- The Management Contract allows for work not forming part of the contract to be carried out by persons directly engaged by the Employer whilst the Management Contractor still has possession of the site (3·23).

4 Money

- Management fee and prime cost are exclusive of VAT and VAT due is to be paid by the Employer as appropriate.
- Different due dates are set up for interim payments, for example during the pre-construction period. While from the date of possession it is to be the monthly dates specified in the Contract Particulars up to the date of Practical Completion. After Practical Completion the due date is to be set at two months intervals except otherwise agreed (4·7).
- The Architect/Contract Administrator (A/CA) is to issue an interim certificate within five days of each due date, stating the amount due to the Management Contractor of the

due date and the basis for calculation. Each Interim Certificate is to be accompanied by a statement specifying the amounts in respect of each Works Contractor (4·10·1, 4·10·2).

- If the A/CA fails to issue an Interim Certificate as set out above, the Management Contractor is entitled to give notice (Interim Payment Notice) to the Quantity Surveyor, at any time after the expiration of the five day period stating the sum he considers due him and the basis for calculating that amount (4·10·4).
- The final date of payment is 14 days from the due date (4·11·1). However the final date will be postponed where the Contractor serves an Interim Payment Notice by the number of days after the expiration of the five day period that it took the Contractor to issue the notice (4·11·4).
- Subject to a payless notice the Employer is to pay the sum stated on the Certificate or Notice (as appropriate) on or before the final date of payment (4·11·2).
- The Employer may not later than five days to the final date of payment issue a notice of his intention to pay less to the Contractor – stating the sum he considers due to the Contractor at the date of the notice and how it was calculated. When a Pay Less Notice is issued, the amount to be paid on the final date of payment shall be the amount stated therein (4·11·5).
- Any late payment shall attract interest (4·11·6) and the Contractor is entitled to suspend some or all his obligations upon service of the requisite seven day notice. Reasonable expenses of such suspension will be paid by the Contractor (4·13).
- There are detailed provisions for the final certificate, which mirrors the certification process for interim payments described above. The final date of payment, also applies in the case of the Final Certificate. The final date for payment is 28 days from the due date.

5 Statutory obligations

- The CDM Regulations require the appointment of a CDM coordinator and a Principal Contractor. Various other obligations arise, particularly concerning the Health and Safety Plan and the Health and Safety File. Provision is made for these in the contract (5·18 to 5·21).
- Responsibility for compliance with legislation and serving notices rests with the Management Contractor (5·1). If the Management Contractor finds a divergence between statutory requirements and Contract Documents or further drawings, etc he is to inform the Architect, who must issue instructions within seven days (5·2).
- The Management Contractor is empowered to take action in any emergency to ensure compliance, and subject to certain conditions, this will be deemed a variation to the Management Contract or a Works Contract as applicable (5·4).

JCT MC11

6 Insurance

- The Management Contractor indemnifies the Employer in respect of personal injury or damage to property other than the actual Works (6·7 and 6·8). This is to be backed by insurance (6·10).
- If instructed, the Management Contractor is to take out joint names insurance for the Employer against the risk of legal nuisance. There is a list of exceptions, and damages must not be directly attributable to any negligence by the Management Contractor or Works Contractors. An Appendix entry including the amount of cover is required (6·11·1).
- Where clause 6·4A is to apply, insurance of 'the Project' (ie work executed and site materials) is to be taken out by the Management Contractor in joint names (ie in his and the Employer's name), for the full reinstatement value of the Project against all risks. This must be done before any work begins on site.
- Where clause 6·4B is to apply, the requirement to take out such insurance rests with the Employer.
- In the event that terrorism cover is withdrawn and is no longer available, the situation and options open to the Employer are dealt with in clauses 6·4·10 and 6·5·4, introduced by Amendment 4.
- Where clause 6·5 is to apply, and the Project comprises alterations of or an extension to existing structures, then the Employer is required to take out a joint names policy in respect of the existing structures and contents. This is to be for the full cost of reinstatement etc in the event of loss due to Specified Perils.
- Insurance for the Employer's loss of liquidated damages is an option (6·6 and Appendix Part 1).
- An Appendix entry will show whether the Joint Code of Practice on the Protection from Fire of Construction Sites is to apply (6FC) and if so, both the Employer and the Management Contractor must comply with it.

7 Termination

- The Employer is allowed to determine the employment of the Management Contractor for reasons of default (7·2). A warning notice may be issued by the Architect, but the notice of determination is a matter for the Employer.
- In the case of insolvency of the Management Contractor, and depending on the circumstances, determination might be automatic subject to possible reinstatement, or the Employer might elect to enter into an agreement (a '7·5·2·1 Agreement') to allow continuation or novation (7·5).

JCT MC11

- The Employer is allowed to determine the employment of the Management Contractor at will (7·20). This may of course happen either before or during the Construction Period.
- The Management Contractor is allowed to determine his own employment for reasons of default by the Employer (7·9).
- Either party can determine the employment of the Management Contractor for listed neutral causes (7·13).
- The respective rights and duties of the parties concerning payment, removal and completion are set out in detail (7·6, 7·11 or 7·14).

8 Miscellaneous

- A list of definitions is included (1·3).
- Access for the professional team is assured, but subject to restrictions to protect any proprietary rights of the Management Contractor and Works Contractors (3·17).
- The Architect may order the removal of the manager from the Project and the Management Contractor must find a suitable replacement (3·14) subject to approval by the Architect.
- Where progress is disturbed because of the discovery of antiquities, the Management Contractor is obliged to inform the Architect, who must issue instructions (3·26 and 3·27).
- There is a contracting out of third party rights under the Contracts (Rights of Third Parties) Act 1999, introduced by Amendment 2.
- Section 8 also deals with relevant issues arising from the Works Contracts, in particular the terms of such contracts, nominated suppliers to Works Contractors, duties of the Management Contractor under Works Contracts, final payment and loss and expense reimbursement to Works Contractors.
- The five Schedules which form part of MC11 are very important. They are:

  First Schedule: Project description: a short statement of the scope of the project, to be completed by Employer;

  Second Schedule: definition of Prime Cost payable to the Management Contractor relating to Works Contracts; on-site staff of Management Contractor; on-site labour, materials, goods, plant, stores and services provided by Management Contractor;

  Third Schedule: services to be provided by the Management Contractor: can be selected from a list of more than 50 obligations relating to both the pre-construction period and after work starts on site;

JCT MC11

Fourth Schedule: list of project drawings, all to be signed by the Management Contractor and Employer;

Fifth Schedule: site facilities and services to be provided by the Management Contractor: to be completed before the construction of the Project, and initialled at the same time as Appendix Part 2 is signed.

9 Disputes

- Part II of the Housing Grants, Construction and Regeneration Act 1996 as amended gives either party a statutory right to refer any difference or dispute arising out of the contract to adjudication. Article 8 provides for this.
- Procedures for referral to adjudication, the appointment of an adjudicator, the powers and conduct of an adjudicator are as set out (9A).
- Article 10A establishes arbitration as the agreed method for final determination of disputes (9B) unless the Appendix entry shows that this has been deleted in favour of legal proceedings (Article 10B and 9C).

JCT MC11

This contract?

If considering using MC11 remember that:

It is intended for use where the Employer has appointed a contract administrator, a quantity surveyor and other advisers to make up a professional team, and the team has prepared project drawings and a project Specification, and later detailed drawings, Specifications and bills of quantities for works packages. The Works Contractors enter into contracts direct with the Management Contractor. JCT MC11 is not a lump sum contract, and the sum paid by the Employer to the Management Contractor is the Prime Cost of the work together with a management fee.

The management contract is in one version only, for use in the private or public sectors. The Conditions apply to both the pre-construction period, and construction period and the operative details are entered in Appendix Part 1 and Appendix Part 2 respectively. The Conditions include deferment of possession, acceleration, partial possession, performance specified work but not contractor's design. There is also a Section relating to the Works Contractors and respective obligations.

When completing the form decisions are required relating to deferment of possession; insurance of the Project; liquidated damages; acceleration; management fee; Joint Fire Code; and EDI. The five Schedules should also be checked for completeness of entries.

If acting as contract administrator it means dealing directly with the Management Contractor, who in turn will be involved in the administration of Conditions in the Works Contracts. There are nevertheless some instances when the contract administrator will be involved with the Works documents, and the procedural rules, which can become complicated, need to be meticulously observed.

It is a relatively high risk contract with imprecise cost and time elements initially. It depends on goodwill and a high degree of trust between the Employer, the professional team, and the Management Contractor.

Related matters

Documents

Standard Form of Management Contract 2011 Edition (MC11)

References

Guide to Management Contracts 2011

Commentaries

Vincent Powell-Smith and John Sims
The JCT Management Contract: A Practical Guide
Kluwer Publishing (1988)

JCT C/CM

The Joint Contracts Tribunal Ltd

Construction Management Agreement C/CM

Background

The fundamental distinction between management contracts and construction management lies in the degree to which the Client accepts a direct contractual relationship with the Contractors who carry out the work packages. With management contracting this will be achieved though the Management Contractor, and there will also be an independent team of professionals, including an architect and quantity surveyor with overall responsibility for design and contract administration.

With construction management, the Construction Manager will be the key person or firm with an overall responsibility for coordination and contract administration relating to the Trade Contracts. The Client also has a significant contribution to make, and is responsible for the engagement of a Consultant Team and nomination of a Consultant Team Leader. The Consultant Team will have a major involvement in the pre-contract period, and although likely to have some involvement during the construction period, this will not be in contract administration.

In July 1995 JCT produced draft documentation for construction management. This was referred to the constituent bodies of the JCT, but was then overtaken by the publication of the Latham Report, and the Housing Grants, Construction and Regeneration Act 1996 (Part II). The draft was developed to take account of the full implications of these, and the construction management documentation eventually appeared in 2002. The 2011 edition of the contract has been published primarily to bring the contract into compliance with the amendments of the Housing Grants, Construction and Regeneration Act 1996 (Part II) as amended.

Nature

The documentation consists of an Agreement (C/CM) between the Client and the Construction Manager, and a Trade Contract (TC/C) between the Client and each of the Trade Contractors. There is also an Invitation to Tender, a Tender document, and warranties by a Trade Contractor to a purchaser or tenant, and funding organisation for the Project.

The Agreement (C/CM) between the Client and the Construction Manager is an attractively presented document, logically structured and with particularly clear layout making referencing relatively straightforward.

There are four Recitals, the first of which refers to the building works being phased,

JCT C/CM

and a deletion is needed if this is to be a single stage operation. The Client undertakes to appoint the Consultant Team, and to have prepared an Initial Brief and preliminary Project Cost Plan. The other Recitals refer to the fact that the full CDM Regulations will apply; the services to be performed by the Construction Manager; and that the work will be carried out under contracts directly between the Client and Trade Contractors.

There are five Articles, which refer briefly to the obligations of the Construction Manager and the Client; the identity of the Planning Supervisor and Principal Contractor; and the methods for resolving disputes.

The Conditions are relatively short and Section headed as follows:

1. Intentions of the Parties
2. Obligations of the Construction Manager
3. Obligations of the Client
4. Assignment and Sub-contracting
5. Payment
6. Insurance and Indemnities
7. Termination of Engagement of Construction Manager
8. Proper Law and Disputes

Probably the most significant parts of the document are the Schedules (taking up 35 pages in total). These act as reference points for much of what is carried in the Conditions, and are:

- First, Description of the Project;
- Second, Insurance and Indemnities;
- Third, Definition of Reimbursable Cost;
- Fourth, Model Services to be provided by the Construction Manager;
- Fifth, Construction Manager's Personnel;
- Sixth, Site Facilities and Services to be provided by the Construction Manager;
- Seventh, Construction Management Fee;
- Eighth, Consultant Team;
- Ninth, Cost Planning and Control;
- Tenth, Adjudication;
- Eleventh, Arbitration.

JCT C/CM

Some of the Schedules contain essential detailed information, and others call for entries to be made. They amplify many of the provisions found in the Conditions, and are at the very heart of the agreement.

Perhaps surprisingly for a form more suited to major projects, attestation may be under hand or as a deed.

The nature of construction management procurement makes it likely to be of interest only for major building works undertaken by experienced client bodies. Although the Construction Manager is largely responsible for the management and coordination of Trade Contractors, this still leaves the client with considerable executive responsibility on a day-to-day basis for the duration of the pre-construction and construction stages of the Project.

Use

Any role for architects will be as members of the Consultant Team to which they might be appointed under a 'Consultancy Agreement'. They might also be named as Consultant Team Leader particularly for design stages at pre-construction, but much will depend on the nature of the work.

In the Eighth Schedule Part A the Client is to name the Team Leader, and to summarise the scope of the work of each member. A copy of the Client's Initial Brief and the Client's Preliminary Cost Plan will be developed into the Project Brief and the Project Cost Plan. The client must also identify the 'Client's Representative' and the 'Cost Consultant'. The measure of consultation between Construction Manager and the Consultant Team Leader is set out in commendable detail in Part C with clauses conveniently referenced. The involvement of the Consultant Team during the Pre-Construction and Construction Periods, which should be covered in any consultancy agreement, is clearly described in Part D of the Eighth Schedule.

Brief synopsis of Conditions

(although consultants are not involved directly in contract administration)

1 Intentions

- Subject to anything to the contrary the work will be carried out in phases (First Recital).
- Possession and control of the site is given to the Construction Manager, but this will not necessarily be exclusive to the Construction Manager (1·5).
- There is provision for the Client to use or occupy the site or the Project before completion (1·6).
- There is provision for partial possession by the Client (1·7).
- The Construction Manager is to manage the Project in accordance with the Project Brief, Project Cost Plan and Health and Safety Plan (2·1).

JCT C/CM

- The Construction Manager must provide the services set out in Fourth Schedule Part A (Pre-Construction) and Part B (Construction) (2·1), and site facilities (Sixth Schedule).
- The Construction Manager must exercise skill, care and diligence, to the extent expected of a reasonably competent Construction Manager, and must carry professional indemnity insurance as indicated in the Appendix (2·5).
- The Construction Manager is not liable to the Client for the design of the Project (Eighth Schedule item 2·6).
- The Client may appoint a Client's Representative to handle all functions ascribed to the client (1·4).
- The Client will appoint the Consultant Team (named in First Recital), name the Leader (3·2) and may appoint a Cost Consultant (3·5).
- The Client will appoint Trade Contractors, taking into account the views of the Consultant Team. Appointments will normally be made after interview, an analysis of the tenders, and a written report by the Construction Manager (Fourth Schedule Part A).
- Contract documents comprise the completed Recitals, Articles, Conditions, Schedules and Appendix to the Agreement (C/CM). Documents referred to include the Initial Brief, Preliminary Cost Plan, and developed Project Brief, Project drawings, Project Programme, Project Specification, and Project Cost Plan (Eighth Schedule Part D item 1·2).
- Further drawings, Specifications, details and Schedules will be provided as necessary to explain or amplify the Project information (3·8).

2 Time

- The agreement refers to the work as relating to a pre-construction period and a construction period.
- There is no start and completion date with this agreement as found with traditional forms, and the construction period runs from the date of commencement of work on site by the Trade Contractor first on the scene, and ends with the date of issue of the Interim Project Completion Certificate (1·3).
- There will be a Project Programme prepared by the Construction Manager after consultation with the Consultant Team. This will identify critical path, lead times, and key milestones (Fourth Schedule item 5·1). The Construction Manager will update and expand this programme in liaison with the Client and Consultant Team (Fourth Schedule item 5·4).
- The Construction Manager will, before Trade Contract tenders are invited, prepare a detailed week by week programme (Fourth Schedule item 5·2).

JCT C/CM

- During construction the Construction Manager will advise the Client on matters which may cause delay in completing the Project (Fourth Schedule item 9·8), and report on all matters related to progress after consulting the Consultant Team (Fourth Schedule item 9·11).
- The Construction Manager is not to be held responsible for delay, where this has been caused by members of the Consultant Team, but is required to use 'all reasonable efforts' to avoid or mitigate the effects (3·3).
- The Construction Manager, with agreement by the Consultant Team Leader, will certify practical completion in respect of each Trade Contract (2·2).
- After completion of the last Trade Contract, the Construction Manager with agreement by the Consultant Team Leader, will issue the Interim Project Completion Certificate and the Defects Liability Period (normally six months from the day named in the Interim Project Completion Certificate) will commence (2·2).
- When defects in work carried out under all Trade Contracts have been made good, the Construction Manager will issue a Certificate of Making Good defects in respect of the Project (2·3).
- When the Construction Manager advises the Client that all obligations under the Trade Contracts have been fulfilled, the Client will issue a Final Project Completion Certificate (2·4).

3 Control

- Names of the Construction Manager's personnel are to be entered in the Fifth Schedule and any changes require the consent of the Client (2·2).
- Neither party to the agreement may assign the agreement without written consent (4·1).
- The Construction Manager cannot sub-contract his obligations without the Client's written consent (4·2).
- The Client will appoint the Trade Contractors, after receiving recommendations from the Construction Manager and where relevant the Consultant Team Members (3·6·1).
- The Trade Contracts will be on the current JCT Trade Contract (TC/C) unamended, unless otherwise agreed with the Client (3·6·2).
- The Client may issue to the Construction Manager such instructions in writing as are reasonably necessary (3·7).
- The Construction Manager will manage and coordinate the work of Trade Contractors (Fourth Schedule item 9·2).

JCT C/CM

- The Construction Manager will hold regular meetings with Trade Contractors and provide monthly written reports for the Client and Consultant Team Leader (9·4).
- The Construction Manager will arrange and chair regular site progress meetings, to which the Client and the Consultant Team will be invited. He is also responsible for the minutes (9·5).

4 Money

- The Client undertakes to pay to the Construction Manager a Pre-Construction Period Management Fee as entered in Part 1 of the Seventh Schedule. This sum, exclusive of VAT, can be adjusted if circumstances change (5·8).
- Construction Manager Fees comprise of Reimbursable Cost and Construction Management fee (4·1); the amounts payable under this contract are exclusive of VAT.
- The Construction Manager shall submit interim accounts to the Employer at monthly intervals stated in Contract Particulars (4·2), and each interim account shall state the amount the Construction Manager considers due and the basis for the calculation. The due date for each payment shall be the later of the date of receipt of the account from the Contractor or the monthly date specified in the Contract particulars (4·3).
- The Employer is to issue a payment notice within five days of each due date, stating the amount due to the Construction Manager on the relevant due date and the basis for calculating the amount.
- The final date of payment is 17 days from the due date (4·3). Subject to a payless notice the Employer is to pay the sum stated on the Payment Notice on or before the final date of payment. Where the Employer has not issued a Payment Notice, the amount due for payment on the Final Payment Date will be the amount stated as due in the Interim Account (4·3·3).
- The Employer may not later than five days to the final date of payment issue a notice of his intention to pay less to the Construction Manager – stating the sum he considers due to the Construction Manager at the date of the notice and how it was calculated. When a Pay Less Notice is issued, the amount to be paid on the final date of payment shall be the amount stated therein (4·3·4).
- Any late payment shall attract interest on the amount owing (4·3·6) and the Contractor is entitled to suspend some or all of his obligations upon service of the requisite seven day notice. Reasonable expenses of such suspension will be paid by the Contractor (4·4).

5 Statutory obligations

- The CDM Regulations apply in full (Second Recital).

JCT C/CM

- Where the Construction Manager is the Principal Contractor he must ensure that the Health and Safety Plan complies with the Regulations (2·8).
- Where the Construction Manager is appointed Planning Supervisor he must ensure compliance with the CDM Regulations, and in particular Regulations 14 and 15 (2·9).
- The Construction Manager is to liaise with statutory authorities and statutory undertakers relating to site services (4·1).
- The Construction Manager is to advise the Client on orders to be placed with statutory bodies, and to manage implementation of their work (4·2).
- The Construction Manager will monitor Trade Contractors' compliance with statutory requirements and verify that all necessary approvals have been obtained (4·3).

6 Insurance

- Insurance and indemnities are dealt with in the Conditions by a very brief reference to the Second Schedule.
- The Construction Manager is to indemnify the Client against claims relating to personal injury and death, and against damage to property real or personal, other than the Project (Second Schedule item 13).
- The Construction Manager must take out insurance in respect of claims for personal injury or damage to property for the sum entered in the Appendix (Second Schedule item 17·2).
- The liability of the Construction Manager under this agreement is limited to the sum entered in the Appendix, provided that the Appendix states that clause 2·7 is to apply.
- The Construction Manager may be required to take out professional indemnity insurance for an amount entered in the Appendix (2·5).
- Insurance of the Project will be taken out by the client under a joint names policy for all risks cover, for the full reinstatement value of the Project and replacement value of site facilities, plus the amount entered in the Appendix for professional fees. Where the Project comprises work to existing structures, cover must include the contents owned by the Client, but this will be only in respect of Specified Perils (Second Schedule item 1).

7 Termination

- Termination relates to the Construction Manager's engagement.
- Termination may be by the Client in the event of the Construction Manager's insolvency, or failure to exercise the degree of skill, care and diligence required under the Agreement (7·2).

JCT C/CM

- The Client may also terminate the engagement of the Construction Manager at will (7·3).
- The Construction Manager may terminate his own engagement in the event of the client's insolvency; failure to pay amounts properly due; or if work is suspended for a continuous period of six months (7·4).
- The consequences of termination are set out in detail (7·6).

8 Miscellaneous

- Third party rights under the Contracts (Rights of Third Parties) Act 1999 are excluded (1·12).
- The Agreement is to be construed in accordance with the law of England (8·1).
- The Agreement is not for use under Scots law.

9 Disputes

- Article 5 confirms the right of either party to seek adjudication in the event of a difference or dispute (Article 5).
- Nominators for an adjudicator can be agreed and shown by appropriate deletions made in the Appendix (Tenth Schedule item A·2).
- The conduct of the adjudication and effects of adjudicator's decision are covered in the Tenth Schedule.
- Final determination will by the courts of England and Wales unless the Appendix shows that clause 8·3 (arbitration) is to apply.
- Where arbitration applies, appropriate deletions in the Appendix will indicate the appointors of an arbitrator. The conduct of the arbitration and effects of the award are covered in the Eleventh Schedule.
- A footnote to Section 8 of the Conditions is a reminder that disputes may also be resolved by the process of mediation.

JCT C/CM

This contract?

If considering using C/CM 2011 remember that:

It is intended for use with large projects where the Client wishes to enter into separate contracts with members of the Consultant Team who will be responsible for design, the Construction Manager who will provide services during both the pre-construction period and the construction period, and each of the Trade Contractors who will carry out and complete the Works. The Client assumes the central role, although a Client's Representative and a Cost Consultant may also be appointed. This is not a lump sum agreement (although the Trade Contracts may be), and the Client will pay the Construction Manager reimbursable costs and a management fee.

The form is not for use in Scotland, and the SBCC have decided not to publish a Scottish version.

The agreement is in one version only, and is the head contract in a standard construction management pack of documents. The Conditions apply to both the pre-construction and construction periods, and the operative details are entered in a single Appendix. The Conditions include for completion in phases and partial possession.

When completing the form decisions are required relating to preparing the Project Cost Plan; insurance cover including professional indemnity insurance; limitation of liability; any amendments to the standard Trade Contracts; reimbursable costs; and payments to the Construction Manager during the pre-construction period. The 10 Schedules are a particularly important part of the Agreement and should be checked for content and completeness of entries.

If acting as design consultant, remember that the Construction Manager may also advise the Client in preparing the Project Brief, make recommendations and review design and other drawings. A close working relationship with the Consultant Team is essential.

If acting as Client's Representative, then remember that this could involve carrying out all the functions ascribed to the Client, acting as agent unless the Agreement specifically states otherwise.

Clearly this is an arrangement which will appeal only to an experienced client probably with in-house services. It is relatively low risk for the Construction Manager. The Agreement has the merit of being logically structured, clearly laid out, and in taking just over 65 pages to cover a very sophisticated operation.

12 Management procurement: management forms

JCT C/CM

Related matters

Documents

Construction Management Agreement C/CM 2011
Trade Contract TC/C

Tender Document TC/T
Part 1: Invitation to Tender
Part 2: Tender by the Trade Contractor
Warranty TCWa/P&T (warranty to purchaser or tenant)
Warranty TCWa/F (warranty to funder)
Fluctuations Code

References

JCT Guide to Construction Management Documentation

Partnering arrangements 13

Partnering agreements

The Joint Contracts Tribunal Ltd
JCT Framework Agreement (FA)
JCT Framework Agreement Non-binding (FA/N)
JCT Partnering Charter (Non-binding) (PC/N)

The Institution of Civil Engineers (ICE)
NEC3 Partnering Option X12

The Association of Consultant Architects Ltd
ACA Standard Form of Contract for Project Partnering PPC2000 (amendments 2008 and 2011)

'Partnering is neither a particular procurement approach, nor is it a particular type of contract: it is about culture and the way in which the participants view and manage the project' (JCT Note on Partnering).

Partnering as an ethos which attempts to avoid adversarial conflict was the subject of a number of studies and publications in the 1990s, and endorsed in both the Latham and Egan Reports. Arrangements may take the form of project partnering applicable to a single project, or strategic partnering which may embrace a number of projects over time.

Project Team Partnering is about working together to achieve the client's objectives for a project by adopting a management approach in which efficient coordinated working is measured against performance indicators and targets. There must first be some formalised expression of agreement between the partners, and this is usually achieved by using either a free-standing non-binding charter for a single project; a binding agreement for single project or strategic partnering, perhaps through the incorporating of additional clauses in a standard contract; or by using a form of contract specially drafted for multi-party partnering.

Partnering remains a central focus for improving construction outcomes.

The recent movement towards Building Information Modelling (BIM) and integrated project teams underscore the importance of the concept of partnering to the future success of the construction industry.

The Joint Contracts Tribunal Ltd

JCT Framework Agreement (FA) JCT Framework Agreement Non-Binding (FA/N)

Background

In 2001 the JCT published a Non-binding Partnering Charter, its first publication to address the increased interest in partnering principles. This was a model charter, extremely simple and only three pages long, intended for use on a single project to supplement any of the main JCT standard forms.

In 2005 the JCT published two new Framework Agreements, in addition to the model charter, one binding and one non-binding, together with a guide on their use. These are longer and more sophisticated documents than the model charter. They take the same approach as the model charter in that they are intended for use alongside another contract. The model charter has been republished in a 2011 edition, downloadable from the JCT website. Together these offer flexible options for those wishing to introduce partnering principles into their contractual arrangements.

Nature

The non-binding version is 12 pages long. It is a formal document by which the Client and the Service Provider agree to work together in a collaborative and open manner, to achieve agreed objectives. It includes provisions regarding framework objectives, organisational structure and decision making, collaborative working, the supply chain, sharing of information, communication, confidentiality, risk assessment and allocation, health and safety, sustainable development, value engineering, change control procedures, early warning and team approach to problem solving, and performance indicators.

The binding version is a little longer at 18 pages, and has additional provisions relating to applicable law (8) and dispute resolution (23-28), and has a facility for executing the agreement under hand or as a deed. The clause covering the legal status of the framework agreement is different, but otherwise all clauses are identically worded.

Use

The Framework Agreements are intended to be used with either one or several underlying contracts, and are entered into for a term set out in the framework particulars at the back of the forms. They can be used alongside any other JCT contract, and standard forms produced by other publishing bodies. They are bilateral

JCT FA and FA/N

agreements between the Employer and the Service Provider (between for example client and contractor, or contractor and sub-contractor). The service provider must endeavour to see that the members of its supply chain adhere to the principles of collaborative working.

The Framework Agreements are intended to supplement and complement those of the underlying contracts. In the case of conflict, the underlying contract prevails (3·3). The Agreements state that 'the Framework Agreement shall not in any way have any legal or contractual effect or bearing upon the formation, interpretation or enforceability of any of the Underlying Contracts (6). The non-binding version in addition states that neither party shall become liable to the other for any breach of the Framework Agreement.

The Latham Report called for contract Conditions which included a specific duty for all parties to deal fairly, and that there should be firm duties of teamwork with a general presumption to achieve 'win-win' solutions to problems rather than apportion blame. Unlike some standard forms, most JCT contracts do not expressly call for parties to act with mutual cooperation and deal fairly, although this may well be implied.

But the climate is changing, and increasingly emphasis is placed on achieving improved, more efficient and more integrated team working through better management of the supply process.

Features (clause numbers refer to FA)

- Underlying contracts, start and end date, and performance indicators are to be set out in framework particulars. In the binding version the name of the adjudicator and arbitrator are also to be set out (note there is also provision for mediation).
- The framework objectives include 'greater predictability of out-turn costs and programme', 'improvements in environmental performance', 'right first time with zero defects' and the avoidance of disputes (5).
- Performance Indicators are to be identified in the Particulars, and the Guide usefully sets out the performance indicators published by the DTI Best Practice Programme.
- Transparency of management arrangements is emphasised – each party is to provide the other with an organisation and management diagram of its internal structure (9).
- Collaborative working (10), sharing of information and know-how (12) are all included.
- The Service Provider is to endeavour to ensure members of its supply chain 'embrace and adhere to' the principles of collaborative working set out in the Agreement, and where practicable, engage them on terms reflecting those principles (11).
- The Service Provider must consult the supply chain on essential aspects of the project, eg design development and early warning (11).

JCT FA and FA/N

- The parties must endeavour to agree a communications protocol (13).
- Identification of risks (15) – prior to entering into any underlying contract, the service provider must undertake a risk analysis with the other project participants. The employer then prepares a risk allocation schedule or matrix, to be periodically reviewed and updated.
- Value engineering (18) – service provider encouraged to suggest saving measures, and Employer and service provider to negotiate the provider's share of the benefits if implemented (there is no prior agreement as to share).
- The parties are to endeavour to agree cost etc of any changes before implementation (19).
- Both parties are required to promptly warn the other of any matter which may affect time quality cost (20), and to adopt a team approach to problem solving (21).
- Health and safety and sustainability (16 and 17) are important features of the Agreements, with further explanation included in the Guide.

Related matters

Documents

JCT Framework Agreement
JCT Framework Agreement Non-binding
JCT Framework Agreement Guide

X12

The Institution of Civil Engineers

NEC3 Partnering Option X12

Background

The Third Edition Engineering and Construction Contract requires the two parties, the Employer and the Contractor, to act as stated in the contract and in a spirit of mutual trust and cooperation. This main contract also provides for an early warning of matters likely to result in increased price, delayed completion or impaired performance of the Works in use.

This partnering option, which touches others beyond the main contracting parties, was published as a First Edition in June 2001. It can be used with any NEC contract except the Adjudicator's Contract. As the title implies, it is not a free-standing document, but is an option which may be incorporated into those NEC contracts for any Team Members involved with a Project, whether as Contractor, sub-contractors, consultants or sub-consultants. If the Option X12 is incorporated, then the parties to these contracts will have additional responsibilities in common.

Nature

The Option can be used for single project partnering or for strategic partnering over several projects. It can of course only be used with NEC contracts, and does not result in a multi-party contract.

The Option requires additional Contract Data, some of which will not change (eg Client's Objective and Partnering Information on agreed methods of operating), and a Schedule of Partners, and Schedule of Core Group Members, which might change during progress of the Works. The Schedule of Partners will include identity and contribution of the partners, joining and leaving dates, and details of Key Performance Indicators, targets, measurement arrangements and any incentive payments. The Schedule of Core Group Members will give identity of partners, and joining and leaving dates. Both Schedules will probably need revising from time to time.

Option X12 also includes 22 short clauses set out under four headings, and the document includes helpful guidance notes on these clauses.

Use

The Option is incorporated into the contracts of the partners by entering 'X12' in the first line of Contract Data Part One: Data provided by the Employer and by completing the 'Optional Statements' Option X12 entry, including identifying the document in which the Partnering Information has been set out. The information for this entry is

X12

suggested in the text of the NEC Partnering Option, and covers details of the Client, the Client's Objective, and Partnering Information.

Synopsis of clauses

- The Option does not create legal partnerships outside contracts.
- Each partner collaborates to achieve the Client's Objective, and the stated objectives of every other partner.
- Each partner nominates a representative with authority to act.
- The Client is a partner.
- Partners are to cooperate over providing information, and giving early warnings of matters likely to affect other partners. Partners may give advice, information and opinion and if so it must be given fully, openly and objectively.
- A Core Group is selected by the partners, with authority to act on behalf of partners. The Core Group is led by the Client's Representative (a position not specifically defined in the Option or the contract).
- The Core Group is responsible for preparing a timetable of partner's contributions, and is pivotal to the partnering operation.
- Partnering Information is defined as that contained in the documents referred to in Contract Data, or in an instruction under the contract.
- The partners work together as stated in the Partnering Information in a spirit of mutual trust and use common information systems as set out in that Information.
- Partners will be paid the amount stated in the Schedule of Partners if the target stated for a Key Performance Indicator is improved upon or achieved.

X12

This contract?

If considering using Option X12 remember that:

It is intended only for use with any NEC Contract (except the Adjudicator's Contract). It brings more than the two main contracting parties into a partnering relationship, but it does not create a multi-party contract.

The responsibilities for Team Members included under Option X12 will be in addition to the contractual responsibilities which they might have.

There will be additional Contract Data, and additional clauses incorporated.

The Option is a neat way of bringing about partnering relationships, and the partnering clauses set out the actions necessary to achieve this.

Related matters

Documents

NEC3 Partnering Option: Option X12
First Edition (June 2001)

References

Construction Industry Council, Guide to Project Team Partnering

PPC2000

The Association of Consultant Architects Ltd

ACA Standard Form of Contract for Project Partnering PPC2000 (with 2008 and 2011 amendments)

Background

Generally partnering as a concept denotes the intention of parties to work together to deliver a project or series of projects, with the objective of reducing disputes, avoiding confrontational/adversarial behaviour and refraining from self-seeking activities such as seeking commercial or legal advantage at the expense of the project/other project participation. It has been suggested that:

"The concept means that ideally all partners should benefit from the success of their collective efforts and conversely be prepared to share the consequences of failure." [Stanley Cox]

The PPC2000 was produced by the Association of Consultant Architects Ltd, and drafted by David Mosey of Trowers & Hamlins, Solicitors. As a partnering contract, it is a brave attempt to bring together partnering arrangements, consultant appointment terms and a building contract into one document covering the whole process of delivering the project. It is the first standard form of contract for project partnering, it is the first multi-party building contract, and it is an architect- led initiative. It is claimed that merging a partnering agreement and a building contract could benefit the partnering process.

Since it was launched by Sir John Egan in September 2000, it has received the recommendation of the Housing Forum, the Movement for Innovation, the Local Government Task Force, and the Construction Best Practice Programme. It has also been endorsed by the Construction Industry Council and the Housing Corporation. It was amended in 2008 to relax the timetable on objection to instructions by the Client Representative and the time for the Client Representative to respond to a Contractor's proposal, it also featured new concepts like the KPIs, Risk Register and Partnering Timetable, Project Bank accounts among others. The 2011 amendment was to bring the contract in compliance with new legislation and concentrates mainly on the payment clauses.

Nature

Between the glossy covers, there are 58 pages covering the Project Partnering Agreement, the Partnering Terms, and Appendices.

PPC2000

The Partnering Agreement is signed or most likely executed as a deed, by the Client, the Constructor, Client's Representative and each consultant or specialist member of the Partnering Team. The Agreement will carry details of the Project, the site, composition of the Partnering Team, Partnering Documents, and Core Group composition. The Design Team and Lead Designer are identified, and any amendments to the design development process as described in Section 8 of the Partnering Terms noted. Details are entered on other matters usually found in the Appendix or Contract Data with conventional contracts, but here also including matters such as incentives and insurance cover to be carried out by each member of the Partnering Team.

The Partnering Terms are set out under 28 headings. The language is plain English, but some terminology is peculiar to this contract and may be unfamiliar. Helpfully there is a full set of definitions. There are nine Appendices, the content of which may be summarised as follows:

Appendix 1: Definitions

Appendix 2: Form of Joining Agreement (with a Project of long duration inevitably there will be changes to the Partnering Team over time, and this is a mechanism for bringing in new joining parties who will be bound by the already established obligations)

Appendix 3:

- Part 1. Form of Pre-Construction Agreement (this is in essence an agreement to cover preliminary or enabling works to be undertaken by the Constructor)
- Part 2. Form of Commencement Agreement (confirmation by the Partnering Team that the Project is ready to proceed to commencement of work on site)

Appendix 4:

- Part 1. Insurance of Project and Site
- Part 2. Third Party Liability Insurance
- Part 3. Professional Indemnity or Public Liability Insurance
- Part 4. Insurance, General

Appendix 5:

- Part 1. Conciliation
- Part 2. Adjudication
- Part 3. Arbitration (if applicable)

Appendix 6:

Form Partnering Timetable (this sets out clearly the nature, sequence and duration of the activities to be undertaken by each Partnering Team member, including outlining pre-conditions to any of the activities. Issues to be covered under this Timetable include Design development and submission, Risk management Actions including any risk register, business case, Client approvals, among others.

PPC2000

Appendix 7:

Form of Risk Register (the risk register should outline the nature of each risk, likely impact on the project, the member of the team responsible for risk management actions, agreed risk management actions and the deadlines for the implementation of such actions).

Appendix 8 (this appendix allows the parties to indicate any Key Performance Indicators and the Target set for achieving them.

Appendix 9 (This allows the parties to include a Project Bank Account as part of their partnering agreement.

PCC2000 is unique and crosses traditional boundaries. It is a combination of project management principles, legal conditions and procedural rules. It is logically structured, with commendable cross-referencing. It holds out the prospect of an integrated team approach and seamless delivery of the Project, but it calls for a high degree of commitment on the part of all concerned.

Use

Reports indicate that PCC2000 has been successfully used for both private and public sector projects ranging in value from multi-million pounds down to £600,000.

Partnering depends on an effective management structure, attentive administration, and good communications. The Partnering Team is the key to this and it will be beneficial to set it up as soon as possible. PCC2000 accepts that the composition is likely to change during the progress of the project. Ideally there should be opportunity to bring consultants, key specialists, Constructor and some sub-contractors and suppliers together at pre-construction stages. The Partnering Team members' liabilities are proportional to their responsibilities, as are incentive payments.

A Core Group is to be established by the Partnering Team Members, with responsibility to meet regularly to review and stimulate progress of the Project. Partnering Team Members must comply with decisions reached by the Core Group.

The Client's Representative has considerable authority. He or she may call, organise, attend and minute meetings of the Core Group and Partnering Team, and may issue instructions to the Constructor as empowered by the Partnering Terms. He or she will also be responsible for organising partnering workshops for the Partnering Team. However, restrictions can be placed on his or her authority and these are to be entered in the Project Partnering Agreement.

The Partnering Adviser will be a person who brings enthusiasm and a knowledge of partnering, and preferably already has a good track record. He or she has a very wide remit which includes reviewing all contracts for consistency with the Partnering Documents; preparing any Partnering Charter; preparing any of the agreements listed

PPC2000

in Appendix 3; giving advice on the partnering process, partnering relationships, and partnering contracts; attending relevant meetings of the Core Group and Partnering Team; and assisting in the solving of problems and resolution of disputes. A tall order!

The Partnering Documents are listed as being:

- the commencement agreement;
- the Project Partnering Agreement;
- the Partnering Terms;
- the Partnering Timetable;
- Consultant's Services Schedules and payment terms;
- the Project Brief;
- the Project Proposals;
- the Price Framework;
- any Joining Agreements;
- any Pre-construction Agreement;
- any risk registers;
- the Key Performance Indicators;
- any other Partnering Documents.

Unless there is anything to the contrary, this is the hierarchy of documents which prevail in the event of discrepancy or dispute.

The ACA advises that at the time of signing the Project Partnering Agreement, the team should have agreed the following:

- Client's Project Brief and the Constructor's Project Proposals;
- an initial Price Framework;
- provisional Key Performance Indicators;
- Consultant's Services Schedules and payment terms for those appointed by the Client.

With so many separate arrangements, this agreement cannot be stated in terms of a lump sum contract. The Client is responsible for payment to the consultants of agreed amounts properly due under the Consultant Payment Terms, and for payment to the Constructor of agreed amounts properly due in respect of Pre-Construction Agreement activities, and an Agreed Maximum Price calculated by reference to the Price Framework and other relevant Partnering Documents.

Synopsis of clauses

(Despite the fact that this is a unique type of contract, for the purposes of comparisons the same headings are used as those applied to more conventional contract forms earlier in this book.)

PPC2000

1 Intentions

- Roles, expertise and responsibilities are described in the Project Brief and Consultant's Services Schedules (Partnering Agreement) and Team Members work in a spirit of trust, fairness and mutual cooperation for the benefit of the Project (1·3).
- Partnering Objectives which apply to each member of the Partnering Team including Client and Constructor, are set out under seven headings in clause 4·1 and cover design stages through to completion of the Project within the agreed time, price and quality. Also included are objectives such as innovation, improved efficiency, cost-effectiveness, lean production, reduction of waste, and measurable continuous improvement by reference to Key Performance Indicator targets and trust, fairness and mutual cooperation (4·1).
- Partnering Objectives are followed by Partnering Targets under 10 headings, and each member of the Partnering Team undertakes to pursue these for the benefit of the Project and for the mutual benefit of the Team Members (4·2).
- In all matters the Partnering Team Members shall act reasonably and without delay (1·7).
- The Partnering Documents govern the relationships between Partnering Team Members (2·1).
- The Partnering Documents comprise the Partnering Agreement, Partnering Terms, together with any of the documents listed in clause 2.2.
- Priority of documents in the event of discrepancy is in descending order as listed in clause 2·6.
- Partnering Team Members work to achieve transparent and cooperative exchange of information, and integrate activities as a collaborative team (3·1).
- Communications between Team Members are to be in writing except where otherwise agreed (3·2).
- Team Members are to establish a Core Group, membership as listed in the Project Partnering Agreement (3·3).
- Decisions of the Core Group are by consensus, and Partnering Team Members must comply with authorised decisions (3·6).
- Partnering Team Members operate an early warning system, and each member notifies others as soon as he or she is aware of matters adversely affecting the project (3·7).
- Meetings of the Partnering Team are convened by the Client's Representative as scheduled or requested, and will normally be chaired by the Client's Representative. Only matters on the agenda are dealt with, and decisions are by consensus (3·8).

PPC2000

- Partnering Team Members are to develop arrangements for secondments, office sharing arrangements, access to computer networks and databases etc as may benefit the Project (3·10).
- Partnering Team Members pursue together joint initiatives which might benefit the Project and such initiatives are considered by the Core Group (24·1).
- Partnering Team Members shall keep records as required by the Partnering Documents and permit inspection by other members of the Partnering Team (3·11).
- The Client's Representative is to act in accordance with the Partnering Terms and other Partnering Documents to facilitate an integrated design, supply, and construction process (5·1).
- The Client's Representative is authorised to represent the client in all matters, except membership of the Core Group, and always subject to any restrictions stated in the Project Partnering Agreement (5·2).
- The Client's Representative may issue empowered instructions to the Constructor (5·3).
- The Client's Representative is to call, organise, attend and minute meetings of the Core Group and Partnering Team Members as required or scheduled (5·1).
- The Client's Representative organises workshops for the Partnering Team Members, and organises and monitors contributions of Partnering Team Members to value engineering, value management and risk management (5·1).
- The Partnering Adviser as named in the Project Partnering Agreement may be replaced at any time by a decision of the Core Group (5·7).
- The Partnering Team Members may seek the advice and support of the Partnering Adviser on a range of matters, including those listed in clause 5·6.

2 Time

- The Partnering Timetable is a Partnering Document (2·6) and covers the activities of the Partnering Team Members during the pre-construction period.
- The Project Timetable covers the period of construction following the Commencement Agreement.
- Members of the Partnering Team are to proceed regularly and diligently in the stages and by the dates in the Partnering Timetable (6·1).
- The Project Timetable is to be annexed to the Form of Commencement Agreement, and entries will show the date of possession and date for completion (6·2). The Constructor will submit the proposed timetable to the Client's Representative for review by the Core Group and approval by the Client (6·2).
- Where the Project is to be completed by Sections, then completion dates will relate to each Section and the Project (6·3).

PPC2000

- Possession of the site by the Constructor may be exclusive or non-exclusive, and programming may take this and any arrangements for deferred possession and interrupted possession into account (6·4).
- The Client's Representative may instruct acceleration, postponement or resequencing of any date or period in the Project Timetable (6·6).
- The Constructor will update the Project Timetable regularly and circulate it to the other Partnering Team Members (6·7).
- The Constructor is to use best endeavours at all times to minimise any delay or increased costs in the Project (18·3).
- An appropriate extension of the date for completion may be given for any one of 16 reasons listed in detail, all due to matters beyond the Constructor's control and including some neutral causes (18·3).
- The Constructor must notify the Client's Representative as soon as he becomes aware of any of the events listed, and supply appropriate evidence and detailed proposals for overcoming the events or minimising their impact (18·4).
- The Client's Representative must respond within 20 working days of the notification and make a fair and reasonable extension of time. The Client or the Constructor has 20 working days from the date of the Client's Representative's notice to dispute the award (18·4).
- An extension of time which affects consultants, and is not caused by their default, will bring an equivalent extension of time for performance of Consultant's Services (18·7).
- The Constructor will give the Client's Representative five working days' notice when he considers that Project Completion has been achieved. The Client's Representative is invited to inspect and test as appropriate (21·1).
- The Client's Representative, together with other appropriate Partnering Team Members, shall inspect and test, and within two working days following completion of this, the Client's Representative shall issue a notice to the client and Constructor either confirming that Project Completion has been achieved, or indicating aspects of the Project which the Constructor must rectify (21·2).
- Following completion of the Project the Constructor must rectify any defects, excessive shrinkages or other faults in the Project, which are due to materials, goods, equipment or workmanship not in accordance with the Partnering Documents. The Defects Liability Period is to be entered in the Project Partnering Agreement (21·4).
- The Client's Representative shall issue a notice to the Client and the Constructor confirming that the defects have been rectified (21·5).

PPC2000

3 Control

- None of the rights or obligations of the Partnering Agreement may be assigned or sub-contracted without the prior consent of all the other Partnering Team Members (25·2).
- Specialists and Preferred Specialists may be included in the Partnering Team. The Constructor is responsible for the performance of the specialists, except for any appointed direct by the Client (10·12).
- Instructions to the Constructor are given by the Client's Representative, and in accordance with the methods of communication for the Partnering Team (3·2).
- Instructions may require opening up for inspection or testing of any part of the Project, and rectification at no cost to the Client of any designs, works, services, materials, goods or equipment that are defective or otherwise not in accordance with the Partnering Documents (5·3).
- The Constructor can raise objections to an instruction for specific reasons, within five working days of issue of the instruction (5·4).
- The Constructor must promptly carry out empowered instructions issued by the Client's Representative. If it fails to do so after five working days of a further notice from the Client, the Client may pay another party to carry out the instruction and the cost shall be borne by the Constructor (5·5).
- Any Partnering Team Member may propose a Change to the Client, and proposed Changes shall be considered by the Client and the Client's Representative, and if approved will be notified by the Client to the Constructor (17·1).
- The Constructor within 10 working days will then submit to the Client a Constructor's Change Submission setting out the likely effects in terms of cost and progress (17·2).
- Within five working days from the Constructor's Change Submission, the Client's Representative will either instruct the Constructor to proceed (subject to reservation of any aspects until later) or withdraw the Change (17·3).
- The Constructor and specialists are to use and supply materials, goods and equipment of the types and standards stated in the Partnering Documents (16·2).
- The Constructor is responsible for security of the Project and the site (15·3).
- Ownership of materials, goods and equipment pass to the Client when they are incorporated into the Project, or when the Constructor receives payment for them. Such unfixed materials must not be removed from the site, must be stored separately and clearly marked as owned by the Client (15·4).
- Partnering Team Members are to implement a Quality Management System as set out in the Project Brief, Project Proposals, and Consultant's Services Schedules (16·3).

PPC2000

- From the date of the Commencement Agreement until completion date, the Constructor is responsible for managing all risks associated with the Project and the site, unless otherwise agreed (18·2).

4 Money

- The Constructor is to be paid in accordance with the Partnering Terms and the Price Framework (Project Partnering Agreement). The amounts for pre-construction activities are as entered in the Form of Pre-Construction Agreement and the Client undertakes to pay these (12·2).
- The Agreed Maximum Price will be developed by reference to the Price Framework and other Partnering Documents and is to be as entered in the Form of Commencement Agreement. This is the sum payable by the Client to the Constructor, subject to increases or decreases in accordance with the Partnering Terms.
- Any fluctuation provisions must be set out in the Price Framework and Consultant Payment Terms (20·10).
- If the Partnering Documents link payment to performance targets stated in the Key Performance Indicators, then when the level of achievement of the Constructor or each consultant is demonstrable, the Client's Representative will determine the consequential additional or reduced payment (13·3).
- Where an extension of the completion date is awarded for certain events, the Constructor shall be entitled to additional payment in respect of site overheads and unavoidable additional work or expenditure (18·5 and 18·6).
- Applications for payment by the Constructor and by each consultant is made to the Client and Client's Representative, at the intervals stated in the Project Brief, or at the end of each calendar month. Payment can also be related to payment milestones, activity schedules, etc as set out in the Price Framework. Each application must state the sum the relevant consultant or constructor considers due to him on the said payment due date, as well as the basis for the calculation of the sum. The application shall be accompanied by details as stated in the Project Brief, and such further information as the Client's Representative may reasonably require (20·2).
- The due date for payment shall be the date the client receives the relevant application from the consultant or constructor (20·2).
- The Client's Representative will issue a payment notice within five days from receipt of the Constructor's application (or under other circumstances required by the terms of partnering), in accordance with clause 20.5 specifying the sum due the Constructor at the relevant due date and the basis for calculation of that sum. Unless a notice is issued in accordance with clause 20.7, the Client shall pay the Constructor the sum stated as due in the payment notice by the final date of payment. Except where revised dates are stated in the Price Framework, the final date for payment by

PPC2000

the Client shall be the later of 20 working days from the due date for payment or 15 working days from the receipt from the Client of any required VAT invoice (20·3).

- Within five days of the receipt by the Client of an application for payment by a consultant in accordance with clause 20.2, the Cclient shall issue a payment notice to each consultant, calculated according to relevant consultant payment terms taking account of any sums that may be due under clauses 20·10 and 20·17 and stating the sum the Client considers due on the payment due date and the basis on which this sum was calculated. Except for a notice under clause 20·7, the Client is to pay the amount stated in the payment certificate on the final date of payment which is the later of 30 days from the payment due date or 25 days from the receipt by the Client of the relevant VAT invoice from the Consultant (20·4).
- Where the Client or the Client's Representative fails to issue a payment notice as envisaged by this section, the relevant payment Application by the Consultant or Constructor shall be deemed a payment notice. Therefore the Client shall be liable to pay the sums stated in such notices by the final payment date (20·6).
- Not later than two days before the final date for payment of any sum due under this contract, the party liable to make payment may issue the other party a notice of their intention to pay a sum less than the amount stated in the payment notice. Such a Pay Less Notice will state the sum in the opinion of the payee that is due at the time of the service of the notice and basis for the calculation of this sum (20·7).
- Where a party liable to make a payment serves a Pay Less Notice under 20·7, the amount to be paid on the final date of payment is as stated in the Pay Less Notice.
- Delay in payment by the Client (or the party liable to make a payment) beyond the final date of payment will result in interest at the percentage specified in the Project Partnering Agreement (20·10) and may give rise to a right by a consultant or the Constructor to suspend some or all performance until payment is received in full, such suspension is prefaced by a seven day notice to the client requiring rectification of the default in payment and only proceeds if the Client fails to make payment within this period. In the event of such suspension, the constructor/consultant will be entitled to reasonable amounts arising from such suspension (20·17).
- Within 20 working days following Project Completion (or as stated in the Price Framework) the Client's Representative shall issue to the Client and the Constructor an account confirming the balance of the Agreed Maximum Price due, and the Client and Constructor shall seek to agree taking into account any adjustments, and subject to the amount stated as retention in the Price Framework (20·15).
- Within 20 working days following notice by the Client's Representative confirming that the Constructor has fulfilled all obligations in respect of rectifying defects, the Client's Representative shall issue to the Client and the Constructor a Final Account. When agreed this will be conclusive evidence as to the balance of the Agreed

PPC2000

Maximum Price due, and the Client's Representative shall then issue a Final Account valuation (20·16).

- The contract also makes detailed provisions for final payment akin to its provisions on interim payments (20·16).

5 Statutory obligations

- Partnering Team Members must comply with all laws and regulations currently in force in the country stated in the Partnering Agreement (ie the applicable law) and in the country in which the site is located, and with all statutory and other legal requirements (25·4).
- The Constructor will act as Principal Contractor for the purposes of the CDM Regulations, and the Planning Supervisor will be the person named in the Project Partnering Agreement (7·1)
- All Partnering Team Members must fulfil their obligations under the CDM Regulations including development of the Health and Safety Plan (7·1). Although not expressly stated, this will also of course relate to the Health and Safety File.
- Each Partnering Team Member shall use reasonable skill and care to ensure that all individuals for whom he is responsible adhere to the Partnering Contract, and each Member will be liable to the other Team Members for any loss, damage, injury or death caused by employees under their control (7·4).

6 Insurance

- Insurance of the Project and of the site, including structures on it, will be the responsibility of the Constructor or the Client as shown in the Commencement Agreement in the joint names of the parties and with waivers of subrogation (19·1). Where stated in the Commencement Agreement, the Constructor is to take out insurance in respect of damage to property other than the Project, not caused by default of the Constructor or specialist or consultant and which could not reasonably have been foreseen.
- The risks to be insured against are those set out in Appendix 4 Part 1.
- Each Partnering Team Member is to take out and maintain third party liability insurance for the amount stated in the Project Partnering Agreement and in accordance with Appendix 4 Part 2 (19·3).
- Professional indemnity or product liability insurance is to be taken out by Partnering Team Members named in the Project Partnering Agreement in accordance with Appendix 4 Part 3 (19·4).
- Further insurance as required by entries in the Commencement Agreement can include environmental risk insurance (19·5), latent defects insurance (19·6), and whole project insurance (19·7).

PPC2000

7 Termination

- The Client may terminate the appointments of all Partnering Team Members if he no longer wishes to proceed with the Project either because of failure to achieve the pre-conditions to a start on site as set out in clause 14.1 or for any other reason not foreseeable by the client prior to the date of the Commencement Agreement. Procedures for giving notice and the consequences are set out (26·1).
- The Client (or Constructor as appropriate) may terminate the appointment of a Partnering Team Member for material breach of the Partnering Contract (26·3).
- The appointment of a Partnering Team Member will automatically terminate in the event that the Member becomes bankrupt or insolvent (26·2).
- The Client may terminate the appointment of the Constructor for specified defaults or breaches of the Partnering Documents. Procedures for giving notice and the consequential actions are set out in the Partnering Terms (26·4).
- A Partnering Team Member may terminate his own appointment in the event of specified defaults or breaches of the Partnering Documents by the Client. Procedures for giving notice and the consequential actions are set out in the Partnering Terms (26·5).
- If after the date of possession it becomes impossible to proceed with or complete the Project due to specified reasons, the Constructor must give notice to the Client's Representative. A Core Group meeting must be convened to consider the position and possible solutions. If an acceptable solution cannot be found then the Client may suspend or abandon the Project (26·6).
- Termination of the appointment of any Partnering Team Member does not affect the mutual rights and obligations of that and the other Partnering Team Members (26·15).

8 Miscellaneous

- All Partnering Team Members are to use reasonable skill and care appropriate to their respective roles, expertise and responsibilities, and owe to each other such duty of care as stated in the Project Partnering Agreement (22·1).
- Each Partnering Team Member is to provide or obtain collateral warranties as listed in the Project Partnering Agreement (22·2).
- The Constructor is to obtain specialist warranties in favour of the Client (22·3).
- The Agreement can also include for a design obligation by the Constructor, and in this event the obligation under clause 22·1 can be amended in the Project Partnering Agreement whereby the Constructor accepts full responsibility to the Client for the design, supply, construction and completion of the Project including the selection and standards of all materials, goods, equipment and workmanship, and including any design undertaken before or after the date of the Commencement Agreement

PPC2000

by any other Partnering Team Member. The Constructor may also be required to warrant that the completed Project shall be fit for its intended purposes.

- Section 8 in the Partnering Terms otherwise states that design development is in the hands of the Lead Designer and other Design Team Members, who are to develop the design with the object of achieving best value for the Client (8·1).
- At pre-commencement stages the Lead Designer submits outline designs to the Client and Core Group, and following Client approval, developed design is submitted to the Client and Core Group with detail sufficient for a full planning application (8·3).
- Following Client approval, and after Core Group consultation, the Lead Designer applies for full planning permission, and with other Design Team Members brings the design to the level necessary for the selection of specialists, development of the Price Framework, and satisfying of planning conditions and other regulatory approvals (8·3).
- After commencement all further design work is prepared and submitted to the Client and other Partnering Team Members for approval or comment in accordance with periods stated in the Project Timetable (8·6).
- Each Partnering Team Member retains intellectual property rights in all designs and other documents that he prepares for the Project, but grants to the Client and other Partnering Team Members a licence to copy and use such designs relating to completion of the Project (9·2).
- Nothing in the Project Partnering Agreement or Partnering Terms confers any benefits or rights to third parties, unless expressly stated otherwise (22·4).
- Nothing in the Partnering Documents creates a partnership between Partnering Team Members (25·1).
- Any special terms to be imported into the contract must be identified as special terms by reference to this clause and must be set out in or attached to the Project Partnering Agreement or the Commencement Agreement (28).

9 Disputes

- In the event of any difference or dispute with other Partnering Team Members, a Member must give notice to the other Members and the Client's Representative (27·1).
- The Partnering Team Members involved are to apply the Problem-Solving Hierarchy shown in the Commencement Agreement, guided as necessary by the Partnering Adviser (27·2).
- Where use of the Hierarchy fails to provide an acceptable solution within a stated timetable, the Client's Representative will convene a meeting of the Core Group in an attempt to reach an agreed solution (27·3).

PPC2000

- If the dispute is still not resolved, the parties may chose to refer the matter to conciliation as described in Appendix 5 Part 1, or mediation, or any other form of alternative dispute resolution (27·4). The conciliator may be named in the Project Partnering Agreement.
- The parties involved may exercise the right to refer their difference to adjudication (27·5) in accordance with Appendix 5 Part 2. The adjudicator may be named in the Project Partnering Agreement.
- If the difference or dispute is not finally resolved by adjudication, the parties may refer the matter either to arbitration or to the courts (27·6). Arbitration is covered in Appendix 5 Part 3. The nominating body for an arbitrator may be named in the Project Partnering Agreement.

This contract?

If considering using PPC2000 remember that:

It is the only standard contract specifically drafted for project partnering.

The conditions are plainly worded and easy to read. However attractive the notion of a single contract bringing all important parties together in a binding relationship is, inevitably this calls for an open and receptive mind.

Contract administration and project management under this contract would require experience and expertise, it is encouraging that the contract has been used in practice with successful results.

If the ultimate in partnering arrangements is desired, then this form, which is the result of an architect-led initiative, has no competitors as yet.

Related matters

Documents

ACA Standard Form of Contract for Project Partnering PPC2000 (amendments 2008, and 2011)
ACA Standard Form of Specialist Contract for Project Partnering SPC2000

References

Introduction and Explanatory Notes (included with PPC2000)

Choice scenarios 14

There will be times when operations cannot be tidily covered by a single standard form of contract. For example, some work may be needed ahead of the main contract, or the need for some additional specialist work may become apparent only as the main contract works proceed. This may bring the need for enabling contracts, or separate contracts proceeding in sequence or in parallel, and a combination of otherwise unrelated standard agreements. Care is obviously needed in such circumstances to make sure that there is no conflict of responsibilities, and that the rights and obligations of contracting parties are clearly set out.

Standard forms currently published will adequately cover most situations, although this might necessitate the use of optional clauses or supplements or amendments as provided for in the particular contract form. There may be exceptional circumstances where only a bespoke agreement would be suitable or where there is the need to combine different aspects of numerous standard forms, where this is the case, it should be drafted by an experienced construction lawyer instructed directly by the client.

At all times the contract should try to take account of eventualities that can be foreseen, and to ensure that the intentions of the parties are expressed clearly, with certainty, and that the allocation of risks is as intended.

There is an increasing body of legalisation impacting on construction contracts as outlined in Chapter 1. The existence of these regulations will have a bearing on the choice of the contract:

Construction (Design and Management) Regulations 2007

This will apply to nearly all temporary and permanent works. The statutory duties for the Employer and contractor are usually made contractual obligations also.

Check whether: the contract terms take into account the role of the Employer in respect of appointments, and the obligations of the CDM Coordinator and Principal contractor in respect of the Health and Safety Plan and File.

Unfair Terms in Consumer Contracts Regulations 1994

This legislation applies to contracts for goods and services between a consumer and a supplier. The former will be a natural person acting in a personal way (eg a homeowner) and the latter a person acting in the course of business (eg a consultant or a builder). This is primarily a consumer protection measure, and applies to any term in a contract which has not been individually negotiated. It calls for fair terms, to be expressed in plain intelligible language. An unfair term will not be binding on the consumer. In assessing the requirement of good faith, the bargaining strength of the parties will be taken into account.

Check whether: one of the parties is a consumer, and if so care is needed to ensure that the contract complies with the requirements for fair terms and plain language. Most standard forms have not been individually negotiated. Hence the present attempts to publish building contracts which are 'consumer contracts' for smaller domestic works. Care is needed if drafting special clauses in building or consultant appointment agreements to make certain that the terms are understandable and understood by the consumer.

Housing Grants, Construction and Regeneration Act 1996, Part II Construction Contracts as amended.

This will apply to 'construction contracts' and this definition will include contracts for professional services, interior or exterior decoration, landscape and building contracts. It will not apply to contracts with a residential occupier, provided that the work is principally on a dwelling for owner occupation.

Check whether: the contract terms expressly include the right to refer disputes to adjudication, and whether payment procedures meet the requirements stipulated in the Act as amended. If the Act is applicable and yet not expressly included for, then the appropriate Scheme for Construction Contracts Regulations will automatically apply.

Party Wall, etc Act 1996

As with much legislation relating to development such as the Town and Country Planning Acts, Building Acts, etc, this will not usually feature in the contract Conditions, although where party wall agreements or awards are concerned this might bring significant implications for contract administration.

Check whether: it is likely that work will affect party walls, because if so notices might be issued or received during the course of the Works, and construction work might be affected due to a party wall award. Contract Conditions should provide for instructions to cover postponement, variations, extensions of time, disturbance costs, etc which might become relevant.

Contracts (Rights of Third Parties) Act 1999

It used to be held that at common law only the parties to a contract had obligations and benefits from it. The agreement touched only the parties, and third parties were outside the contract. Now this piece of legislation has brought the right of a third party to enforce contractual terms, always provided that the contract expressly provides for this or purports to confer a benefit, and that the third party is identified in the contract. The contract may expressly exclude or limit liability.

Check whether: it is intended that certain third party rights are to apply, and if so, whether the contract expressly includes this in the manner required by the Act. If uncertain on this matter, it might be advisable to obtain legal advice. The majority of published standard forms of building contract now expressly state that the rights of third parties under this legislation will not apply.

Scenarios on choice decisions

Preliminary or enabling works contracts

Scenario A

The tennis club in the affluent village of Fairview has a benefactor who has promised to donate a new prefabricated pavilion, produced by a subsidiary to the company he owns. This will be supplied and erected as a package. Internal decoration will be needed, which the members feel they can undertake themselves. External works will also be required, which must be completed prior to delivery. A local contractor will be needed to carry out this work which includes the access road, hard standing, bringing the site to proper levels, drainage, and the necessary concrete base for the pavilion.

Which contract?

According to the nature of the work for this preliminary contract, consider a lump sum contract. A minor works form such as JCT MW11 or the NEC Short Construction Contract might be appropriate if the work is relatively straightforward.

Comment

Difficulties can arise over phasing where there are sequential contracts, particularly when different contractors are involved. The contractor responsible for erection must be able to rely on getting unimpeded possession on the due date and the site being ready to the agreed state. Practical completion of the preliminary contract will need to be certified, and the respective liabilities for defects and damage clearly established at the beginning (for example, MW11 only refers to defects in work under that contract, being made good by the original contractor). A separate Health and Safety Plan and File contribution will probably be required.

Scenario B

Planning permission for the latest 'Homeforce' DIY Superstore contained a condition that the main facade of the 19th-century Boon Mills, which now occupies the site, should be retained. Site clearance is imminent and the selected part of the listed facade needs to be stabilised and protected in what could be a delicate operation. It is decided that this work should be entrusted only to an expert demolition contractor.

Which contract?

A separate contract is required for the demolition work. Consider a suitable minor works building contract or, better still, a specialist contract (eg the Standard Form of the National Federation of Demolition contractors). Make sure that the Specification and Conditions include relevant provisions for indemnity and insurance, and that the contract for the building works allows for another contractor to work on the site occupied by the main contractor.

Comment

The demolition contractor needs to be given clear information about respective obligations for the safety and protection of the site. If material is to be salvaged and stored, it should be clearly stated. (The Employer might expect to be credited if the contractor is allowed to acquire salvaged material.) Demolition work can be dealt with as a preliminary contract or as a sub-contract of the main contract. If the former, then a Health and Safety Plan specific to this work might be required or it might be contained in the Plan produced by the principal contractor.

Scenario C

Victoria Towers has been allowed to deteriorate ever since a disastrous fire last century. Now Country Heritage is prepared to fund substantial restoration and has commissioned a detailed survey and report on the condition of the fabric. A contractor will be needed to carry out clearance and opening-up to allow investigation work, the precise extent of which cannot be known at the outset.

Which contract?

Consider contacting a reliable builder, preferably one with experience of this kind of work who employs and personally supervises craftsmen with a knowledge of the relevant materials and methods. This is unlikely to be a lump sum contract, and a cost plus approach is the only practicable option. Use any of the standard building contracts for cost plus procurement. Alternatively (and possibly preferably) a bespoke contract may be entered into to suite the peculiar circumstance of the project.

Comment

Proper protection and safety measures are the contractor's responsibility, but check that these are not skimped. Such work needs close direction, and the contractor should appreciate when quoting rates that this might not be a single continuous operation. Returns to site for further investigation are a likely requirement.

Trades contracts for work of an intermittent nature

Scenario D

Champers is a popular cellar bar and restaurant in Westville. Success has brought more sophisticated patrons, a need for expansion, and a more chic ambience. Further vaults have recently become available, and these development ideas can now be realised. The restaurant's reputation is such that there must be no complete shutdown during building work, which may need to be carried out in a rather piecemeal fashion. What is equally important, patrons of Champers must at all times be able to enjoy their food and wine safe from any intrusion of dirt, dust, unsavoury smells and unwelcome noise resulting from the renovations.

It has been suggested that whilst builders' work and attendance can be provided by one reasonable building contractor, services installations and bar and kitchen work must be left to specialists. It is envisaged that the work will be carried out in a periodic or phased manner possibly over an extended period, and that integration and overall direction will be critical. The Architect agreed to act as project manager, but the situation now suggests that the role is developing more into management of separate trades contracts.

Which contract?

The situation calls for sound management, effective coordination, and firm control. Because of the intermittent nature of the work, a standard lump sum contract with the builder is thought to be unlikely to achieve the desired result. It is thought that this could best be carried out by a consultant operating as a management contractor. However, the capital costs involved are likely to be relatively small, and probably separate trades contracts entered into direct between the client and each specialist firm would be the most satisfactory answer. A short form (eg JCT MW11, or CIOB Small Works Contract 2011) might be an appropriate document to use for these, although there might also be a need to include additional conditions.

Comment

Any agreement, on whatever form, should include for matters such as the following:

- Time: state dates for commencement and completion. Consider problems of phasing and possession.
- Money: state basis for valuing work done. State when payments are to be made and the procedures involved. State the amount of retention.
- Control: state the need for architect's instruction before any deviation is made. Establish procedures to ensure integration and coordination of the various trades involved, who is to be responsible for setting up site access, welfare provisions and storage facilities etc
- Insurance: state who will be responsible for insuring the existing structure, contents and new work. Consider cover for any consequential losses arising from the carrying out of the work.
- Termination: if this is to be included, state whether it is an option open to either party and if so on what grounds. Trades contracts are almost certain to be construction contracts to which adjudication would be a statutory requirement.

It might also be worth considering whether there should be a provision which, in the event of key contractors falling behind, would allow the architect to take action (at no extra cost to the Employer) to bring the work back to time. This might be by bringing in an additional labour force, or even another firm.

An architect involved in such a management role would need an appropriate contract for professional services with the Employer, and should expect an appropriate fee.

Contracts with substantial specialist content

Scenario E

The catalytic degrader at Hotwells Heavy Water and Associated Products (1981) Ltd has become redundant, and is due to be replaced by the very latest installation from Superlink Fibreoptics. The new detached plant room will be a relatively simple structure, but the services installation it is to house is of mind-blowing complexity and far exceeds the capital cost of the actual building work.

Which contract?

If the entire operation is to be covered by one building contract, then consider a lump sum contract (JCT SBC11) which allows for the installation specialists to be nominated sub-contractors.

Alternatively, the specialist installation firm could be considered as the principal contractor with overall responsibility for carrying out the work. The builder would then be a sub-contractor responsible for carrying out work on the building envelope including necessary attendant builders' work. Consider either a lump sum building contract (eg SBC11) or an appropriate engineering contract as the main form (NEC3 ECC). Where appropriate, and if the work is conveniently self-contained, there could be separate parallel contracts for the building work and the engineering work.

Comment

Where parallel contracts are used, great care is needed to ensure effective coordination and to eliminate the risk of duplication. There might also be complications where consultants with differing functions and duties under different contracts of engagement are employed on the same project.

Contracts for landscape work

Scenario F

For the proposed Eventide Homes cluster development, specially designed with the needs of the over-60s in mind, it is thought that the external landscaping needs to provide a particularly tranquil setting. The architect-led design team includes a landscape architect, and although both soft and hard landscaping are to be carried out, it is thought best to treat this as a sub-contract to the main building contract. It is intended to use a particular landscape firm as sub-contractor.

Which contract?

The Landscape Works contract might prove useful, other alternatives include the JCT IC 2011.

Comment

The Specification or bills of quantities preambles should make specific reference to special provisions to cover such matters as plant failure and maintenance, and malicious damage or theft before practical completion. These items are in the Landscape contract.

Scenario G

Developers Rushe & Roulette have acquired a redundant office block in the City for the proverbial song, and promptly set about converting it to make apartments attractive to young executives. The site needs the attentions of an innovative landscape architect, and much of this will be hard landscape using non-traditional materials and specialist technology. It is therefore proposed that although this work will proceed at the same time as the building work it should be undertaken as a quite separate contract.

Which contract?

Consider a lump sum contract, ie JCLI Landscape Works contract, perhaps the IC 2011 is a suitable alternative. Alternatively, if the type of work suggests that remeasurement is more practicable (eg if there is a substantial amount of earth-moving, contouring and associated work of a civil engineering type), it may be more appropriate to consider the ICC Minor Works Version.

Comment

If this is a self-contained contract for landscape work, it is probably best administered by a landscape architect. Careful coordination will be needed if it is a contract in parallel with another building contract.

Scenario H

The new council offices under construction at Tan-y-groes have attracted a great deal of media interest. Work has not proceeded to programme and failure to complete by the contract completion date would be a matter of intense civic embarrassment, as arrangements are already in place for an opening ceremony by a distinguished person. To make sure that this will go ahead as planned, it has been decided to omit all the landscape work to the central sculpture court. The building can be occupied and the landscape work can proceed at a later date under a separate contract.

Which contract?

Consider the JCLI Form of Agreement for Landscape Works. This is closely modelled on the JCT MW11 contract, but includes additional provisions for dealing with situations such as plant failure, malicious damage or theft, after-care and maintenance. The latter will require a separate JCLI Agreement.

Comment

It is perfectly acceptable for the administrator of the JCLI landscape contract to be other than a landscape architect (eg an architect), but the duties presuppose a knowledge which an architect experienced only in building operations might not possess.

Contracts for fitting out

Scenario J

Ground floor shop units on the new Castle Gates Development are to be left as shells, to be fitted out by tenants. They will assume responsibility for fitting out the interiors and for providing shop fronts, under direct contracts quite separate from the developer's contract with the principal contractor.

Which contract?

Shop-fitting and interior work could be carried out under a lump sum contract in respect of each unit. At its simplest this could be by written acceptance of the specialist firm's offer. However, such quotations are often subject to each firm's own conditions, and these might not be acceptable. Architects acting for tenants might be wiser to suggest an appropriate standard form of contract (eg JCT MW11 or IC11, depending on the scale and nature of the work). Alternatively an agreement suitable for interior work is available from the Chartered Society of Designers (formerly the Society of Industrial Artists and Designers).

Comment

If the main contractor is still on site, care should be taken to establish respective site responsibilities and in particular proper insurance arrangements. The principal contractor might require other contractors to work in accordance with the Health and Safety Plan for the site, or if the tenant's work is carried out under separate unrelated contracts, then a Health and Safety Plan for these works might be necessary.

Joint venture contracts

Scenario K

The oil rich port of Fyl-yr-Up requires new state of the art terminal facilities. This is likely to be a large-scale and sophisticated construction operation calling for significant engineering installations which must be coordinated and integrated with great precision into a series of buildings which will operate as the necessary plant housings. The conventional arrangement of appointing a main contractor and various sub-contractors specialists is not likely to prove satisfactory. A tremendous amount of detailed planning and coordination will be required before the complex work starts on site, and there must be absolutely no risk of delays or disruption because of installation or integration problems.

Which contract?

Consider a joint venture approach, partnering or a management contract. If joint venturing, then the selected tendering companies must be willing to combine under one legally constituted partnership and accept joint and several liability. The use of a traditional lump sum form (eg JCT SBC11) would not necessarily be precluded, as the contractor would be a single entity, albeit a specially formed partnership or company. Other appropriate contracts would include CE11, ACA PPC2000 and the NEC3 ECC.

Comment

The partnership agreement should provide for joint and several liability and a performance bond would normally be required. This method of working can be particularly effective where design input is required, with elements of the design contributed by the various specialist partners, and all effectively coordinated within the larger organisation.

Completion contracts

Scenario L

The contractor for a new group practice veterinary surgery in Fairmeadow became insolvent after the seventh week of a 36-week contract. His employment was automatically determined under the terms of the contract, and it is accepted that reinstatement is out of the question.

Which contract?

Select a new contractor (ideally under the same contract Conditions as the original) to take the place of the first contractor. This might be achieved through negotiations with the second lowest tenderer on the original tender list, but if the work has been made more onerous by the efforts and departure of the failed contractor, there will certainly be an increase in the Contract Sum.

Comment

If the circumstances or climate for tendering has changed markedly since the original tenders, it might be necessary to amend the original documents and invite new competitive tenders. An insolvency practitioner acting on behalf of the original contractor should be consulted and must be kept fully informed of all developments. Employer's costs and expenses arising out of the determination might be part of the claim to be brought against the original contractor.

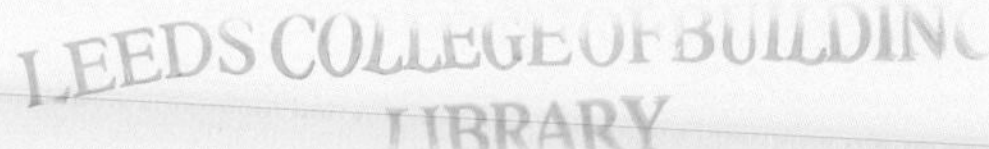

Scenario M

Work on the Limboland Fitness Centre was well over two-thirds complete before the contractor's performance became progressively slower and somewhat erratic. It was no great surprise when a letter arrived from a firm appointed to act as receiver. After discussions, it was generally agreed that the most satisfactory course of action is to have the contract completed by a substitute contractor.

Which contract?

The contract just might be completed by reinstatement and assignment. Here the substitute contractor accepts responsibility for completing under the terms of the original contract. A deed of assignment would be required as agreed between the Employer, receiver acting on behalf of original contractor, and the substitute contractor.

Alternatively, the contract might be completed by reinstatement and novation. In this case, although the substitute contractor might accept responsibility for completing the Works, all the terms of the original contract might not be acceptable. A deed of novation would be required as agreed between the employer, receiver acting on behalf of the original contractor, and the substitute contractor.

Comment

Where a substitute contractor is willing to complete the work, an adjustment of the completion date is almost inevitable. The contractor might also have reservations about accepting responsibility for work already carried out and perhaps covered up, and additional work might be inevitable. The risks of taking on work undertaken by a previous contractor can often be squared by an additional single fixed premium payable to the new contractor. A new Health and Safety Plan might be required.

Scenario N

The Dragon Housing Association refurbishment scheme was complete except for a few outstanding items. With great reluctance, the architect yielded to pressure and certified practical completion to allow unhappy decanted tenants to resume occupation. Unfortunately, all efforts to bring back the contractor to complete the outstanding work failed. By the expiry of the defects liability period the contractor had become insolvent. Some money was held back at practical completion, in addition to half the retention figure. The issue now is to have the work completed.

Which contract?

The outstanding work could be carried out on a lump sum or preferably a cost plus basis by another contractor. An exchange of letters might be considered sufficient, but this would probably still be a 'construction contract' to which the payment procedures and adjudication option would apply. Depending on the extent and nature of the outstanding work, it might be preferable to use a short form (eg JCT MW11 or ECC Short Contract).

Comment

A Specification or Schedule will be needed if competitive quotations are to be sought. The best course of action should first be discussed with the receiver or liquidator, who should be kept fully informed of developments.

Contracts for jobbing repairs or maintenance

Scenario O

When the date for judging this year's Best Kept Municipal Vista competition was announced, it was decided to undertake a clean-up and repainting of several High Street facades as a group operation. Rendering to the facades is in need of some renovation and some stonework requires attention. Woodwork and ironwork also needs repainting, and fascia boards relettered. This is mostly routine maintenance work, and well within the competence of the local builders.

Which contract?

For small-scale straightforward jobs, tenders might be sought on the basis of minimal drawn information, and a Specification or Schedule. This might result in just a lump sum, or if sufficiently itemised, the contractor's figures could give a useful breakdown. Standard forms of contract that could be used include MW 2011 and the ECC Short Contract).

Comment

If the entire work is to be treated as one contract, then the client would need to be identified, and would presumably have authority to appoint a contract administrator. Channels of communication would need to be clearly established to avoid the risk of individual property owners issuing instructions directly. If the individual property owners prefer to enter into separate contracts with a common contractor, then assuming that the same standard forms are used, and the same contract administrator is appointed under each, coordination might be more exacting.

Scenario P

The New Cambrian Bank, which has premises in major towns throughout the Principality, is about to embark on a programme of regular maintenance and repair. It is envisaged that parcels of work on a regional basis will be offered for tender, in some cases with the added proviso that appointed contractors must also make themselves available to tackle emergency repairs at short notice.

Which contract?

Consider a term contract. Contractors can be selected by competition on a Schedule of rates. There may also be a standard call-out charge for emergency visits. The contract might cover a specified number of properties and run for a fixed time period. Orders would be issued to authorise ad hoc work. It is usual to advise the contractor of the approximate total value of the work envisaged, but any firm guarantees should be avoided.

Comment

The JCT publishes the Standard Form of Measured Term Contract MTC11. Some bodies have their own model documents for such contracts. These contracts usually require the presence of a contract administrator appointed by the Employer.

Scenario Q

The Architect engaged by the Allday family has given them advice on what is needed to update the cottage they have just acquired. It amounts to a small amount of alteration work and some maintenance and repair work. It is agreed that this work can safely be entrusted to the excellent local builder.

Which contract?

Assuming that the architect's services are no longer required, and that this is a private residence for occupation by the Allday family, then a consumer contract (eg JCT Building Contract for a Home Owner/Occupier) would be a safe recommendation.

Comment

An exchange of letters, or a very basic formal agreement (eg JCT Contract for Home Repairs and Maintenance) could be considered as an alternative, but neither is likely to provide adequate contract Conditions. The fact that this is work to a private residence for owner occupation means that statutory requirements relating to adjudication and payment provisions under the Housing Grants, Construction and Regeneration Act 1996 as amended will not apply.

Index

Index

C

Index

D

Index

M

Index

M

Index

P

Index

S

Index

X